Fighting Japan's Cold War

Yasuhiro Nakasone, who served as prime minister for more than five years in the 1980s, was one of Japan's leading postwar politicians. This book is a biography of him, but by interweaving international politics and media appraisals of him, it also serves as an examination of Japan's postwar politics. Nakasone was an innovative conservative who actively criticized the conservative mainstream, and this book reveals from both domestic and foreign policy perspectives how the Liberal Democratic Party governed. The Nakasone government served not only as the final phase of the Cold War era of LDP factional politics but also as the starting point for the general mainstream faction system that followed. With the lengthy passage of time since the end of the Cold War and the collapse of Japan's 1955 party system, there is a need to reassess Nakasone, showing that there was much more to him than the popular picture of him as a far-right hawk who loudly advocated for Japan to engage in autonomous self-defense and as an opportunist leader of a small faction, and to place the era in which Nakasone lived its proper historical context.

Ryuji Hattori is a Professor in the Faculty of Policy Studies at Chuo University, Japan

Graham B. Leonard is an Independent Translator and Researcher based in Seattle, Washington, USA

Routledge Studies in the Modern History of Asia

Power and Politics at the Colonial Seaside
Leisure in British Hong Kong
Shuk-Wah Poon

British Engagement with Japan, 1854–1922
The Origins and Course of an Unlikely Alliance
Antony Best

India after the 1857 Revolt
Decolonising the Mind
M. Christhu Doss

Two-way Knowledge Transfer in Nineteenth Century China
The Scottish Missionary-Sinologist Alexander Wylie (1815–1887)
Ian Gow

Fighting Japan's Cold War
Prime Minister Yasuhiro Nakasone and His Times
Hattori Ryūji (Translated by Graham B. Leonard)

Women in Asia under the Japanese Empire
Tatsuya Kageki and Jiajia Yang

Reassessing Lee Kuan Yew's Strategic Thought
Ang Cheng Guan

Beer in East Asia
A Political Economy
Edited by Paul Chambers and Nithi Nuangjamnong

For a full list of available titles please visit: https://www.routledge.com/Routledge-Studies-in-the-Modern-History-of-Asia/book-series/MODHISTASIA

Fighting Japan's Cold War
Prime Minister Yasuhiro Nakasone and His Times

Ryuji Hattori

Translated by **Graham B. Leonard**

First Published in English 2023
by Routledge
4 Park Square, Milton Park, Abingdon, Oxon OX14 4RN

and by Routledge
605 Third Avenue, New York, NY 10158

*Routledge is an imprint of the Taylor & Francis Group,
an informa business*

© 2023 Ryuji Hattori

Translated by Graham B. Leonard

The right of Ryuji Hattori to be identified as author of this work has been asserted in accordance with sections 77 and 78 of the Copyright, Designs and Patents Act 1988.

First Published in Japanese in 2015 by Chuo Koron Shinsha Inc., Japan as NAKASONE YASUHIRO: "DAITŌRYŌTEKI SHUSHŌ" No KISEKI by Ryuji Hattori ©2015 by Ryuji Hattori.

All rights reserved. No part of this book may be reprinted or reproduced or utilised in any form or by any electronic, mechanical, or other means, now known or hereafter invented, including photocopying and recording, or in any information storage or retrieval system, without permission in writing from the publishers.

Trademark notice: Product or corporate names may be trademarks or registered trademarks, and are used only for identification and explanation without intent to infringe.

British Library Cataloguing-in-Publication Data
A catalogue record for this book is available from the British Library

Library of Congress Cataloging-in-Publication Data
Names: Hattori, Ryūji, 1968- author. | Leonard, Graham B., translator.
Title: Fighting Japan's Cold War : Prime Minister Yasuhiro Nakasone
    and his times / Ryuji Hattori ; translated by Graham B. Leonard
    Other titles: Nakasone Yasuhiro. English | Prime Minister
    Yasuhiro Nakasone and his times
Description: Abingdon, Oxon ; New York, NY : Routledge, 2023. |
    Series: Routledge studies in the modern history of Asia | "First
    Published in Japanese in 2015 by Chuo Koron Shinsha Inc., Japan
    as NAKASONE YASUHIRO: "DAITŌRYŌTEKI SHUSHŌ"
    No KISEKI by Ryuji Hattori ©2015 by Ryuji Hattori." | Includes
    bibliographical references and index. | Provided by publisher.
Identifiers: LCCN 2022044239 (print) | LCCN 2022044240 (ebook) |
    ISBN 9781032399096 (hardback) | ISBN 9781032399102 (paperback) |
    ISBN 9781003351931 (ebook)
Subjects: LCSH: Nakasone, Yasuhiro, 1918-2019. | Prime ministers--
    Japan--Biography. | Japan--Politics and government--1945- | Cold War.
Classification: LCC DS890.N35 H3813 2023 (print) |
    LCC DS890.N35 (ebook) | DDC 952.04/8092--dc23/eng/20230103
LC record available at https://lccn.loc.gov/2022044239
LC ebook record available at https://lccn.loc.gov/2022044240

ISBN: 978-1-032-39909-6 (hbk)
ISBN: 978-1-032-39910-2 (pbk)
ISBN: 978-1-003-35193-1 (ebk)

DOI: 10.4324/9781003351931

Typeset in Times New Roman
by KnowledgeWorks Global Ltd.

Contents

List of Tables	vii
List of Acronyms	viii
Usage Notes	ix

	Introduction	1
1	**Nakasone's Youth: From Lumber to the Home Ministry**	4
2	**Deployment and Defeat: A Lieutenant in the Navy**	13
3	**The "Young Officer": Nakasone's Time in the Opposition**	25
4	**The Conservative Merger and Nakasone's First Cabinet Position: Director-General of the Science and Technology Agency under Kishi**	50
5	**From "Killing Time" to Becoming a Faction Leader**	69
6	**"Autonomous Defense" and the Three Non-Nuclear Principles: Nakasone under Satō – Minister of Transportation and Director-General of the Defense Agency**	88
7	**"Neoliberalism" and the Oil Crisis: MITI Minister in the Tanaka Government**	107
8	**The "Sankaku Daifuku Chū" Era: LDP Secretary-General, General Council Chairman, and Director-General of the Administrative Management Agency**	124

vi   *Contents*

9 1,806 Days as Prime Minister: Seeking to Be a "Presidential Prime Minister"   152

    I. *Tanaka Kakuei's Shadow and the Results of Proactive Diplomacy: Nakasone's First Term 152*
    II. *"Pacific Cooperation" and Privatization: Nakasone's Second Term 180*
    III. *The Weight of 304 Seats: Nakasone's Third Term 198*

10 "Rain of Cicada Cries": The 32 Years after Being Prime Minister   227

Conclusion   253

Timeline   259
Index   264

Tables

3.1	Nakasone and Fukuda's Placement and Votes in Gunma 3rd District (1952–86)	36
9.1	Factional Breakdown of Nakasone's Cabinets	157
9.2	Nakasone's Private Advisory Councils (1983–1987)	160

Acronyms

Acronyms

AMA	Administrative Management Agency
CCP	Chinese Communist Party
DPJ	Democratic Party of Japan
EPA	Economic Planning Agency
GHQ	General Headquarters (Supreme Commander for the Allied Powers)
IIGP	International Institute for Global Peace
JAL	Japan Airlines
JNR	Japanese National Railways
JR	Japan Railways
LDP	Liberal Democratic Party
METI	Ministry of Economy, Trade and Industry
MITI	Ministry of International Trade and Industry
NPR	National Police Reserve
NTT	Nippon Telegraph and Telephone
PRC	Policy Research Council
SDF	Self-Defense Forces

Source Acronyms

MOFA	Diplomatic Archives of the Ministry of Foreign Affairs of Japan, Tokyo
NA	US National Archives, College Park
NDL	National Diet Library, Tokyo
SMH	Seiunjuku Memorial Hall, Tokyo
STM	Soho Tokutomi Museum, Ninomiya

Usage Notes

To reduce ambiguity, the Republic of China is generally referred to as "Taiwan," and the People's Republic of China as "China."

Chinese names are romanized using Hanyu Pinyin in a name in more common use such as Chiang Kai-shek.

Japanese names are listed family name first.

Introduction

Nakasone Yasuhiro was born in Takasaki, Gunma in 1918. He joined the Ministry of Home Affairs after his graduation from Tokyo Imperial University but was soon dispatched to the Pacific War as a twenty-three-year-old lieutenant in the Imperial Japanese Navy, where he served as a paymaster. He was in Takamatsu when Japan surrendered. In an imperial capital reduced to ruins, he decided to go into politics and was elected to the House of Representatives at the age of twenty-eight in the first general election held under the new postwar constitution. He was elected in the same year as Tanaka Kakuei, with whom he also shared a birth year, and the relationship between the two men would have important consequences during his political career.

The young Nakasone criticized Prime Minister Shigeru Yoshida's "secret bureaucratic diplomacy," and became known as the "young officer" for his calls for a more independent constitution. While Yoshida and his lineage of politicians became known as the "conservative mainstream," Nakasone called himself a "innovative conservative" and pushed for greater Japanese independence from the United States. After touring a research facility on atomic energy in the US, he also became a proponent of nuclear energy after his return home.

Nakasone's first cabinet position was as director-general of the Science and Technology Agency during the government of Nobusuke Kishi. During the 1960 revision of the US-Japan security treaty, he urged Kishi to cancel US President Eisenhower's planned visit to Japan.

After being admonished by elder statesman Ishii Mitsujirō to "kill time" during the government of Ikeda Hayato, he began using his time without a cabinet position to gather strength for the future. After becoming the youngest leader of an LDP faction following the death of Ichirō Kōno, Nakasone served as transportation minister and director-general of the Defense Agency in the Satō Eisaku government and called for "autonomous defense." He rode out the oil crisis as MITI minister under Tanaka Kakuei and then began serving in major LDP party positions such as secretary-general and General Council chairman from the Miki Takeo government on.

DOI: 10.4324/9781003351931-1

2 Introduction

This was the "Sankaku Daifuku Chū" era of factional conflict with the LDP, so-named due to the major factional leaders of the time: Miki, Tanaka, Ōhira Masayoshi, Fukuda Takeo, and Nakasone.

After finally reaching his long-sought position of prime minister at the age of sixty-four in 1982, Nakasone called for a "final settlement of postwar politics" and pushed for the privatization of Japan's major public corporations.

He made great use of brain trusts, establishing a number of private advisory councils on both domestic and foreign policy, and managed his government in a manner that he referred to as being a "presidential prime minister." Nakasone's approach to politics serves as the roots of contemporary prime ministerial leadership in Japan.

The LDP lost seats in the following general election after the verdict in the Lockheed corruption case was delivered in 1983 and Tanaka was found guilty, but he won a landslide victory in the 1986 joint elections. While he was unable to introduce a sales tax, he was able to calmly retire after naming Takeshita Noboru as his successor. While Nakasone's diplomacy elevated Japan's status on the global stage, his administration consistently suffered from economic frictions with the United States, the consequence of Japanese economic power being at its greatest. It was also Nakasone who made an official visit to Yasukuni Shrine, thereby producing an issue that continues to cause tensions between Japan and its Asian neighbors.

Nakasone served as prime minister for 1,806 days, making him the seventh longest serving prime minister after Abe Shinzō, Katsura Tarō, Satō Eisaku, Itō Hirobumi, Yoshida Shigeru, and Koizumi Jun'ichirō. He was forced to retire from the House of Representatives by Koizumi in 2003, but he did not close his office and continued to wield influence in the background as an elder statesman. With the death of Miyazawa Kiichi in 2007, Nakasone became the last prime minister to have experienced Japan's postwar history in its entirety.

This book is a critical biography of Nakasone. While it naturally analyzes the words and deeds of the man, I would also like to examine factional politics by weaving in discussion of "Sankaku Daifuku" and media appraisals of Nakasone. Nakasone was a reform conservative who criticized the conservative mainstream, as is symbolized as his beginning in politics opposed to Yoshida, and he is key to understanding the internal politics of the LDP. The Nakasone government was the final phase of the "Sankaku Daifuku Chū" era and the origins of the general leader system that followed.

Nakasone had two reputations as a politician. One as a far-right hawk who loudly advocated for Japan to engage in autonomous self-defense. And another as an opportunist leader of a small faction. It is undeniable that Nakasone's image has become so dominated by media reporting that it has become difficult to form a comprehensive picture of the man. But now, more than thirty years after he stepped down as prime minister, it has become possible to obtain primary documents through freedom of information requests and other means. Over twenty-nine interviews with Nakasone,

Introduction 3

I heard about his strategic ideas and personal relationships directly from him. I also conducted interviews with reporters and those affiliated with him like former secretaries.

Following the course of Nakasone's life also means tracing the course of Japan through its defeat in war to the zenith of its postwar accomplishments. The time has come for providing a true picture of the man.

1 Nakasone's Youth
From Lumber to the Home Ministry

Matsugorō and Yuku

Nakasone Yasuhiro was born on May 27, 1918, in Takasaki, Gunma, the second son of Nakasone Matsugorō, a lumber dealer, and his wife Yuku.[1] He was their third child, coming after Hatsuko and Kichitarō, and would later be followed by another brother, Ryōsuke. Matsugorō and Yuku would also have two other children, but both died prematurely.

When I asked Nakasone about his family's history, he explained: "I believe it likely that the ancestors of the Nakasone family were vassals of Takeda [Shingen]. After the Takeda army failed to conquer Kōzuke province, most of it withdrew but some chose to stay and return to farming. There's an area of Gunma District known as Kamiyama, and it seems that my ancestors were former Takeda soldiers who settled there and began farming."[2]

His father Matsugorō managed a lumber business named "Kokumatsu" after a large black pine that grew in the garden. He was a brusque man but passionate about his work. He was also public-minded and served as deputy chair of the local chamber of commerce and industry. Kokumatsu had about thirty craftsmen, many of whom lived on the business' premises. It also owned the rights to a mountain.

Nakasone was weak as a child, and Matsugorō would often feed him eel in the hope that it would make him stronger. Come summer, he would also take his family on trips to swim in the ocean in the belief that the sea air was good for the body.

Nakasone's mother Yuku had been born into the Nakamura family of Annaka, a neighboring town. The Nakamura family was wealthy, owning four rice warehouses and holding agricultural and commercial interests. His grandfather served as the local postmaster – a significant position at the time – and his mother's name came from the first and last consonants of the Japanese word for "post office," *yūbinkyoku*. Yuku attended Kyōai Girls School, a missionary school.

His mother taught Nakasone Christian hymns as she bathed him as a child, and he picked up the habit of humming these. He also read the Bible as a student at Shizuoka High School. While neither he nor Yuku was

DOI: 10.4324/9781003351931-2

Christian, his knowledge of the Bible would prove useful as he engaged with others as a politician on the global stage.

As Matsugorō was not a particularly sociable man, management of his business' craftsmen was left to Yuku. Nakasone later said of his parents that "I respected my mother more than my father. My mother's death hit me harder and left me in tears. I did not cry when my father died."[3]

Ordinary Primary School

Nakasone entered Takasaki Kita Ordinary Primary School on April 8, 1926. According to Nakasone, "Everything I wore – the hat I pulled over my eyes, the backpack on my shoulders, the sandals on my feet – was brand new and been prepared by my mother for that day. They had all been laid out at my bedside the night before, and my heart pounded with secret excitement." As his mother changed him into a new kimono, she looked down fondly at him and told him how impressive he looked.[4]

According to his sister Hatsuko, while Kichitarō was a terror as a child, Nakasone was obedient and patient, and her mother often remarked on how easy he was to raise. Nakasone was popular at school, and the Kokumatsu lumberyard became a playground for children.

Nakasone believed that he could do anything, an optimistic attitude that led his teacher Ochiai Tatsuji to tell him that he was "going to grow up to be another Saigō Takamori."[5]

Nakasone's strongest memories of primary school had to do with his mother. While serving as transportation minister in 1968, he submitted an article, "Thoughts of My Mother's Warmth Inspired by Windblown Snowflakes," to the women's magazine *Fujin Seikatsu* in which he described his mother as a "beautiful person":

> I hesitate to write this, as I am her son, but my mother was a beautiful person. While it is said that memories are purified by the passage of time, I still believe that to be the honest truth. I was proud that she was my mother. As a child, I secretly wished that she would never grow to become a wrinkly old woman.

While Yuku was a strict disciplinarian, Nakasone was an obedient child who loved to read. "I don't remember ever being beaten for having gotten myself into trouble."

Nakasone was especially good at writing essays at school. Whenever he received a perfect score on an essay, he would run home and read it aloud to his mother in the hopes of receiving her praise. She would always smile and tell him how well he had done.[6]

According to Nakasone, a local newspaper solicited essays while he was in primary school and a piece he wrote about building a sandcastle at the beach was chosen. While the essay itself was inconsequential, Yuku was

6 *Nakasone's Youth*

extremely pleased at the accomplishment and carried the newspaper clipping in her pocket so that she could proudly show it to visitors.

As Nakasone was completing his primary school studies, Japan was moving to a semi-war footing. Matsugorō spoke patriotically about the situation, but Yuku was upset by the possibility of war.[7]

Interest in Politics

Nakasone was five years old when the Great Kantō Earthquake struck. While damage to Takasaki was relatively light, rumors of violence by Koreans spread, and the young Nakasone was concerned that they were true as there were a few Korean students in his grade at school. "I was only in primary school, but I was conscious of other cultures, other ethnicities."[8]

As he entered the sixth grade, developments caused him to start to take an interest in politics. He began discussing things with Kaneko Hiroshi, a shy boy in his class. The Fifteenth Infantry Regiment, stationed in Takasaki, was redeployed to China. And he started reading the newspaper.

Nakasone entered Takasaki Middle School in April 1931. His interest in foreign affairs was sparked by the Manchurian Incident in September of that same year: "The largest factors in my becoming interested in foreign and diplomatic matters were the Manchurian Incident (1931), which happened when I was thirteen, and the announcement of Japan's withdrawal from the League of Nations (1933). Reading newspapers, I understood that Japan was becoming isolated and became concerned about the future, wondering 'What is going to become of Japan if it does these things?'"

He discussed these issues with his classmate Moteki Saburō. Moteki was captain of the swimming team, and Nakasone would later hire him as the manager of his campaign office after he went into politics.

Nakasone served as president of his class during every year that he was at Takasaki Middle School, and he had nearly perfect grades. The major exception was physical education; he was skilled at kendo but poor at gymnastics. His favorite subject was history, and he loved reading the works of Kunikida Doppo and Natsume Sōseki.

Nakasone's rival for the best grades in his class was Yamaguchi Takeo, the son of a girls school teacher. Middle school lasted for five years under the prewar educational system, but Nakasone and Yamaguchi decided to try to take the entrance exam for Shizuoka High School during their fourth year. Nakasone Shigeo (a member of the main branch of the Nakasone family) was attending the school and had strongly encouraged him to take the exam.

Nakasone was accepted into the school's Humanities C course, which meant that he would be majoring in French. This was an uncompetitive course; the best students at the school majored in German or English, and Nakasone himself had hoped to study one of these languages. He had the option of completing his fifth year of middle school and then applying for admission to the First Higher School in Tokyo, but he ultimately decided to attend Shizuoka High School. Yamaguchi entered the school's science department.[9]

Shizuoka High School

Nakasone entered Shizuoka High School's French course in April 1935 at the age of sixteen. While the course would not have been his first choice, he found that it suited him very well: "The French style of education tends to create interesting, somewhat dilettantish students rather than the stereotypical hard-studying ones." He would later remark that his decision to attend Shizuoka High School was "one of the most appropriate of my life."

The atmosphere at the school was thoroughly typical of the prewar high school system, and he lived in one of the school's dormitories with about 200 other students. There was a strong sense of solidarity among the student body, and Nakasone made close friends.

While the world was experiencing an era of totalitarianism, Nakasone was inspired by the school's ethos of freedom:

> There was no politician I admired in particular, not Roosevelt, Stalin, nor Hitler. We all looked down on Hitler. There was a lot of adoration for him [in Japan] at the time, but the old high schools were quite hostile towards the kind of totalitarianism he represented. Hitler's reputation at Shizuoka High School was absolutely zero. [...] The most notable characteristic of the high school was the liberalism that underlay its values.

Later, in 1938, he would spend summer vacation as a college student in Karuizawa with members of the Hitler Youth visiting Japan. There are no indications that this had any influence on his beliefs, however.

While in high school, Nakasone belonged to the track-and-field team and competed in the 400-meter dash, although he achieved no particular results of note. He was also put in charge of the dorm's kitchen, something he used as an excuse for spending time at the dormitory of a nearby girls school "conducting research for the menu." The dorm was named "Gyōshūryō," and Shizuoka High School alumni would later form a political support organization for him called the Gyōshūkai.

Nakasone's time at the school coincided with important political events. The February 26 Incident, an attempted coup against the government by young army officers, occurred in 1936, and Nakasone heard rumors (that would later turn out to be true) that the genrō Saionji Kinmochi had fled to the residence of the governor of Shizuoka. The Second Sino-Japanese War began in July 1937. While there were far-right groups among the students, most of the student body was liberal and uneasy about the rise of the militarists.

8 *Nakasone's Youth*

Nakasone received letters from his mother Yuku nearly every week in which she admonished him not to "go out at night with bad students" or to "take care not to catch a cold." "She sent me so many postcards and letters."[10]

In one letter dated October 3, Yuku wrote that "the war is all people talk about everyday. So many people are being killed." Nakasone could not help but feel that Japan was entering "an era of a dark setting sun."

According to his sister Hatsuko, "I believe it was as a high school student that Yasuhiro somehow decided that he would become a politician." Their mother told her around this time that "Yacchan is saying that he's going to be a politician, but I don't know. Maybe he could make it as far as governor or something."[11]

Tokyo Imperial University

Nakasone's grades at Shizuoka High School were good, particularly those in history. Hiratsuka Kinpei, his Western history teacher, told him that he should "go study under Imai Toshiki at Tokyo Imperial University's school of literature and aim to become a professor."

But Nakasone's interest in politics only increased, and when he entered the university in April 1938, he joined the school of law's political science department instead. No one was happier about this than Yuku, who would sometimes visit him in Tokyo, bringing chocolate or pots of flowers with which to decorate his lodgings. Nakasone and his friends would go to the bathhouse Kamenoyu in Dangozaka at night.[12]

While at Tokyo Imperial University, Nakasone studied European political history under Oka Yoshitake, the history of political science under Nabara Shigeru, and diplomatic history under Kamikawa Hiromatsu. He viewed all of these with great interest, but it was Yabe Teiji's politics courses that had the greatest impact on him.

According to Nakasone, "Yabe's take on political science reconciled Japan's traditional national character with modern political science." Yabe was well-versed in international affairs, having studied abroad in Europe and America, and made frequent trips to China. While Nakasone was unaware of this fact, he was also a close advisor to Prime Minister Konoe Fumimaro. He would meet Yabe again after becoming a politician.

During his time as a student, Rōyama Masamichi and some of the school's other professors began promoting the idea of the "East Asian Community" (a predecessor to the Greater East Asia Co-Prosperity Sphere concept), a rationale meant to provide support for Konoe's announcement that the Second Sino-Japanese War was intended to "construct a new order in East Asia."

Nakasone was skeptical of his professors' arguments: "Discussion at the time was dominated by right-wing ideologies, and I suspected that the 'East Asian Community' idea was merely a front for Japanese control. I harbored fundamental doubts about whether any such community would actually be created."[13]

To the Home Ministry

On the evening of March 9, 1940, as Nakasone furiously studied for his final exams, he received a phone call from his father: "Come home right away. Your mother's in critical condition."

He was shocked. "Why am I only learning this now?" When he arrived at Ueno Station, he found that the last train to Takasaki had already left. While he took the first available train in the morning, his mother had already passed away by the time he arrived.

Sitting at her bedside, he yelled at his father for the first time in his life. "I would have quit school had I known that it would mean missing her death!"

With tears in his eyes, Matsugorō said, "I wanted to let you know earlier. I honestly did. But this is what Yuku wanted."

Yuku had suddenly fallen ill on March 3 after seeing off soldiers at the train station as a member of the National Defense Women's Association. She had refused to rest, thinking it only a mild cold, but her condition grew worse and developed into pneumonia. She came down with a fever of more than 40 degrees.

When Matsugorō had told her that they should inform their children of her condition, Yuku had stopped him, saying, "They're taking exams. Please don't cause them any unnecessary worry" (Nakasone's younger brother Ryōsuke was studying at Otaru Commercial High School at the time).

Her high fever continued for nearly a week. On her final evening, she called Matsugorō to her bedside and asked him to visit eight shrines and temples in her stead to pray for their sons' success in their exams.

He departed immediately. When he returned and reported that he had done as she had asked, Yuku was extremely happy and then quietly breathed her last. "I began to cry as he told me this and was unable to stop."

Nakasone returned to Tokyo but found himself unable to study: "Images of my mother appeared before me, even in my books. I couldn't concentrate at all, no matter how hard I tried." His grades declined, and he passed his time listlessly.

One day, he snapped back to reality. "What did my mother die for ... her last thoughts were of us." "I felt like a cloud had come crashing down on my head."

> "I have undergone many harsh trials in my life since that point, and every time it has been my mother's love that has urged me to stay strong. I want to be able to offer her my happiness when I visit her grave. It has been with that hope in mind that I have never stopped working."

Nakasone resumed his studies, working hard to make up for lost time. He hoped to enter the Ministry of Home Affairs so as to become involved in national administration. While he felt alarmed by the rise of militarism at home, he also harbored doubts about the Anglo-American style of politics.

10 Nakasone's Youth

In October, Nakasone passed the administrative version of the Higher Civil Service Examination, coming in eighth. He then interviewed with the home ministry, receiving a provisional offer of acceptance. The home ministry was the largest bureaucratic body at the time, handling areas like regional governance, the police, and elections. Attracted by the sophisticated image given off by the navy, Nakasone also applied to and was accepted by the Naval Accounting School in December.

After graduating with a degree in political science, Nakasone entered the home ministry in April 1941. Machimura Kingo was serving as director of the ministry's personnel section when he took his oral exam, and this position was held by Furui Yoshimi at the time that he joined the ministry. Both would go on to become politicians belonging to the Liberal Democratic Party (LDP).[14]

Notes

1 For existing research on Nakasone and his government, see: Muramatsu Michio, "Nakasone Seiken no Seisaku to Seiji," *Revaiasan* No. 1 (1987), 11–30; Igarashi Jin, "Nakasone Moto-Shushō in okeru Rīdāshippu no Kenkyū," *Revaiasan* No. 5 (1989), 167–82; Iio Jun, *Min'eika no Seiji Katei – Rinchō-gata Kaikaku no Seika to Genkai* (Tokyo: University of Tokyo, 1993), 41–178; Ōtake Hideo, *Jiyūshugi-teki Kaikaku no Jidai – 1980 Nendai Zenhan no Nihon Seiji* (Tokyo: Chūō Kōron, 1994), 67–295; Kusano Atsushi, "Nakasone Yasuhiro – Daitōryō-teki Shushō no Menboku," in Watanabe Kazuo, ed., *Sengo Nihon no Saishō-tachi* (Tokyo: Chūkō Bunko, 2001), 405–48; Sadō Akihiro, *Sengo Nihon no Bōei to Seiji* (Tokyo: Yoshikawa Kōbunkan, 2003), 223–69; Takenaka Harukata, "Nakasone Yasuhiro," in Mikuriya Takashi, ed., *Rekidai Shushō Monogatari* (Tokyo: Shinshokan, 2003), 228–35; Soeya Yoshihide, *Nihon no "Midoru Pawā" Gaikō – Sengo Nihon no Sentaku to Kōsō* (Tokyo: Chikuma Shinsho, 2005), 133–65; Nakashima Takuma, "Sengo Nihon no 'Jishu Bōei' Ron – Nakasone Yasuhiro no Bōeiron o Chūshin to shite," *Hōgaku Kenkyū* 71:4 (2005), 505–35; Nakashima Takuma, "Nakasone Yasuhiro – Reisenki no Nihon Gaikō no Kiketsuten," in Sadō Akihiro, Komiya Kazuo, and Hattori Ryūji, eds., *Jinbutsu de Yomu Gendai Nihon Gaikōshi – Konoe Fumimaro kara Koizumi Jun'ichirō made* (Tokyo: Yoshikawa Kōbunkan, 2008), 269–82; Satake Tomohiko, "'Nakasone Kōsō' no Saikentō – Bōeichō Chōkan Jidai ni okeru Nakasone Yasuhiro no Bōei Kōsō ni tsuite," *Hōgaku Seijigaku Ronkyū* No. 86 (2006), 33–64; Segawa Takao, "Nakasone Seiken no Kaku Gunshuku Gaikō – Kyokutō no Chūkyori Kaku Senryoku (SS-20) Mondai o meguru Himitsu Kōshō," *Keizaigaku Kenkyū* 58:3 (2008), 167–81; Segawa Takao, "'Ron-Yasu' Jidai no Heiwa to Gunshuku – Shinreisen no Tenkanki ni okeru Nihon no Kadai Settei to Takakuteki Kōshō," *Nenpō Kōkyō Seisakugaku* No. 4 (2010), 91–109; Segawa Takao, "Reisen Makki no Nichibei Dōmei Kyōryoku to Kaku Gunshuku – INF Sakugen Kōshō ni Miru 'Ron-Yasu' Kankei no Kiketsuten," *Kokusai Seiji* No. 163 (2011), 81–95; Tanaka Akihiko and Tadokoro Masayuki, "Shin Jiyūshugi no Jidai – 1980 Nendai," in Iokibe Makoto, ed., *Nichibei Kankei-shi* (Tokyo: Yuhikaku, 2008), 266–79; Toyonaga Ikuko, *Shin-hoshushugi no Sayō – Nakasone/Burea/Busshu to Seiji no Hen'yō,* (Tokyo: Keisō Shobō, 2008), 3–36; Wakatsuki Hidekazu, *Taikoku Nihon no Seiji Shidō 1972–1989* (Tokyo: Yoshikawa Kōbunkan, 2012), 170–244; Kanda Yutaka, "1980 Nendai no Reisen to Nihon Gaikō ni okeru Futatsu no Chitsujokan – Nakasone Seiken

Nakasone's Youth 11

no Taichū Gaikō o Jiku to shite," *Ajia Taiheiyō Tōkyū* No. 19 (2013), 53–69; Tobe Ryōichi, *Kokka Keiei no Honshitsu* (Tokyo: Nihon Keizai Shimbun, 2014), 99–134; Satō Susumu, "'Keizai Taikoku' Nihon to Ajia – 1980 Nendai," in Miyagi Taizō, ed., *Sengo Nihon no Ajia Gaikō* (Tokyo: Minerva Shobō, 2015), 194–204, etc.

2 Nakasone Yasuhiro, *Nakasone Yasuhiro ga Kataru Sengo Nihon Gaikō*, eds. Nakashima Takuma, et al. (Tokyo: Shinchōsha, 2012), 29. Nakasone Yasuhiro, *Seiji to Jinsei – Nakasone Yasuhiro Kaikoroku* (Tokyo: Kōdansha, 1992), 12–15.

3 Nakasone, *Seiji to Jinsei*, 12–18. Nakasone, *Nakasone Yasuhiro ga Kataru*, 30–31.

4 Nakasone Yasuhiro, "Ochiai Sensei no Koto" (March 5, 1970), in Nakasone Yasuhiro, "Chichi o Kataru, Haha no Omokage, Ochiai Sensei nc Koto" (June 1, 1972), Author's collection, 27–28.

5 Nakasone Yasuhiro, *Rīdā no Jōken* (Tokyo: Fusō-sha, 197), 47–48, 59.

6 Nakasone Yasuhiro, "Fūka ni Omou Haha no Onjō," *Fujin Seikatsu* (February 1968), 164–65.

7 Nakasone, *Nakasone Yasuhiro ga Kataru*, 33. According to page 16 of Narai Shigeo's *Saishō Nakasone Yasuhiro* (Tokyo: Taishū Nihon-sha, 1986), "a local newspaper" ran an essay of Nakasone's when he was in his third year of primary school. I was unable to find such an essay in contemporary issues of the *Jōmō Shimbun*.

8 Nakasone Yasuhiro, Kim Young-sam, "Watashi no 'Nikkan,'" *Asahi Shimbun*, January 27, 2010.

9 Nakasone, *Seiji to Jinsei*, 18–24. Nakasone, *Nakasone Yasuhiro ga Kataru*, 36–37.

10 *Sankei Sports*, August 9, 1963. Nakasone Yasuhiro, "Bōgen Tasha (Onshi Gunzō)," in Shizuoka Kōtō Gakkō Dōsōkai, ed., *Seishun Kanazuneshi – Kanritsu Shizuoka Kōtō Gakkō 60 Shūnen Kinen Hensan* (Shizuoka: Kyūsei Shizuoka Kōtō Gakkō Dōsōkai, 1982), 634. Nakasone, *Seiji to Jinsei*, 24–34. Nakasone Yasuhiro, *Nakasone Yasuhiro Kushū 2008* (Tokyo: Hokumei-sha, 2008), 10, 15–19. Nakasone Yasuhiro, "Saigo no Nihon Ryōkasai ni Omou," *Bungei Shunjū* (January 2011), 77–78. Nakasone, *Nakasone Yasuhiro ga Kataru*, 32, 38–44. Hayano Tooru, *Seijika no Hondana* (Tokyo: Asahi Shimbun, 2002), 29–32. Iwakawa Takashi, *Nihon no Chika Jinmyaku – Sengo o Tsukutta Kage no Otoko-tachi* (Tokyo: Shōdensha Bunko, 2007), 27–33.

11 Nakasone, *Rīdā no Jōken*, 48–49, 164. Nakasone Yasuhiro, *Mirai no Otona e Kataru – Watashi ga Rīdāshippu ni tsuite Kataru nara* (Tokyo: Popura-sha, 2010), 89–93. Iwakawa, *Nihon no Chika Jinmyaku* 28, 33–40.

12 Kobayashi Kōsuke, "Hiratsuka Kinpei Sensei," in Shizuoka Kōtō Gakkō Dōsōkai, 619–20. Nakasone, *Seiji to Jinsei*, 30–32. Nakasone Yasuhiro, *Jiseiroku – Rekishi Hōtei no Hikoku to shite* (Tokyo: Shinchōsha, 2004), 21. Nakasone, *Mirai no Otona e Kataru*, 95.

13 "Tōkyō Teikoku Daigaku Hōgakubu Sotsugyō Kinen" (March 1941). Nakasone Yasuhiro, *Nihon no Furontia* (Tokyo: Tsunebunsha, 1966), 236–42. Nakasone, "Fūka ni Omou Haha no Onjō," 164–65. Nakasone, *Seiji to Jinsei*, 35–39. Nakasone, *Rīdā no Jōken*, 28–29. Nakasone, *Nakasone Yasuhiro ga Kataru*, 32, 45–47. Iwami Takao, *Seijika* (Tokyo: Mainichi Shimbun, 2010), 100.

14 Ibid.

References

Iwakawa Takashi. *Nihon no Chika Jinmyaku – Sengo o Tsukutta Kage no Otoko-tachi*. Tokyo: Shōdensha Bunko, 2007.

Iwami Takao. *Seijika*. Tokyo: Mainichi Shimbun, 2010.

Nakasone Yasuhiro. "Fūka ni Omou Haha no Onjō." *Fujin Seikatsu* (February 1968).

12 *Nakasone's Youth*

Nakasone Yasuhiro. *Jiseiroku – Rekishi Hōtei no Hikoku to shite*. Tokyo: Shinchōsha, 2004.

Nakasone Yasuhiro. *Mirai no Otona e Kataru – Watashi ga Rīdāshippu ni tsuite Kataru nara*. Tokyo: Popura-sha, 2010.

Nakasone Yasuhiro. *Nakasone Yasuhiro ga Kataru Sengo Nihon Gaikō*. Edited by Nakashima Takuma, Hattori Ryūji, Noboru Amiko, Wakatsuki Hidekazu, Michishita Narushige, Kusunoki Ayako, Segawa Takao. Tokyo: Shinchōsha, 2012.

Nakasone Yasuhiro. *Nakasone Yasuhiro Kushū 2008*. Tokyo: Hokumei-sha, 2008.

Nakasone Yasuhiro. *Nihon no Furontia*. Tokyo: Tsunebunsha, 1966.

Nakasone Yasuhiro. *Rīdā no Jōken*. Tokyo: Fusō-sha, 1997.

Nakasone Yasuhiro. "Saigo no Nihon Ryōkasai ni Omou." *Bungei Shunjū* (January 2011).

Nakasone Yasuhiro. *Seiji to Jinsei – Nakasone Yasuhiro Kaikoroku*. Tokyo: Kōdansha, 1992.

Nakasone Yasuhiro, Kim Young-sam. "Watashi no 'Nikkan.'" *The Asahi Shimbun*, January 27, 2010.

Shizuoka Kōtō Gakkō Dōsōkai, ed. *Seishun Kanazubeshi – Kanritsu Shizuoka Kōtō Gakkō 60 Shūnen Kinen Hensan*. Shizuoka: Kyūsei Shizuoka Kōtō Gakkō Dōsōkai, 1982.

2 Deployment and Defeat
A Lieutenant in the Navy

Naval Accounting School

On April 18, 1941, Nakasone entered the Naval Accounting School as part of its sixth class of supplementary students. As mentioned in the previous chapter, he had been accepted to the school at the same time that he had passed the Higher Civil Service Examination. He had already joined the home ministry, but it was possible at the time for government officials to briefly serve in the navy to gain experience.

The "supplementary student" (*hoshū gakusei*) program was an intensive training course for naval paymasters that was limited to university graduates and those who had passed the civil service exam. Students took on a two-year service commitment and were commissioned as lieutenants (junior grade) after just four months of training. One of Nakasone's classmates at the school was Hatoyama Iichirō, the eldest son of future prime minister Hatoyama Ichirō. Iichirō had been valedictorian of Tokyo Imperial University's law department and, like Nakasone, had immediately entered both the civil service and the accounting school upon graduation.

Nakasone said of his motives for volunteering for the navy that "while it's not the reason I joined, I was born on May 27, Navy Day. The navy was more refined than the army, and I had received the impression that it had a broader perspective as well." The Naval Accounting School was located in Tsukiji, near Kachidoki Bridge. Of Nakasone's class of 110, 22 would be killed in the war.[1]

Departure from Kure

After graduating from the Naval Accounting School in August 1941, Nakasone was immediately assigned to the heavy cruiser *Aoba* (part of the Combined Fleet's 6th Cruiser Division) as a lieutenant (junior grade) and participated in naval exercises in Tosa Bay off the coast of Shikoku.

Nakasone departed the ship in southern Kyushu in mid-November after receiving new orders and headed for the Kure Naval District. The navy had four administrative districts – headquartered in the military ports of Kure,

DOI: 10.4324/9781003351931-3

14   *Deployment and Defeat*

Yokosuka, Sasebo, and Maizuru – that exercised jurisdiction over units assigned to them.

On November 20, Nakasone was made chief paymaster of the Kure Naval District's 2nd Construction Party (*setsuei-han*). Unfamiliar with this term, he inquired about it upon reporting to the chief of staff. The chief of staff gravely answered that it was "a unit tasked with occupying enemy airfields and making them capable of carrying out operations using our aircraft." This just left Nakasone with more questions:

> "Where are we going?"

> "That's a closely guarded secret. You'll find out when we depart on the 29th."

> "Deploying a large unit is expensive. I need money for our workers' salaries and to make arrangements for military scrip with which to procure supplies locally. But I can't make the necessary preparations unless I know where we're going."

After emphasizing that "This is a military secret. Guard it with your life," the chief of staff grabbed a pen and wrote down, "Enough for three months in the Philippines and three months in the Dutch East Indies." After showing the paper to Nakasone, he burned it. Now sure that Japan would finally be going to war, Nakasone made the scrip and staffing arrangements.

Nakasone departed from Kure on the evening of November 29 aboard the *Taitō Maru* (a requisitioned civilian transport) as part of a flotilla of fourteen ships. The ship held naval technicians, doctors, and 1,162 drafted workers.

His thoughts as he departed for war were that "I have done everything I could as a Japanese naval officer to prepare for and carry out my duties. I have shown my loyalty to my country in a way that no one else could have." He brought a copy of the Bible and a recording of Schubert's *Winterreise* with him on the voyage.

He found himself unconsciously crying as he gave himself over to the rhythm of the engines. Watching the lights of his homeland fade away into the darkness of the late autumn night, he muttered to himself that "All that's left is the assault."[2]

The Philippines, Dutch East Indies, and Taiwan

Nakasone learned of the attack on Pearl Harbor on December 8, 1941, on Palau in the western Pacific. Palau was a trust territory of Japan, and the ships had stopped there to replenish their stores. He nervously thought to himself that "The war's begun. We're actually going to have to use that military scrip."

Taitō Maru landed at Davao on the island of Mindanao in the Philippines on December 10. According to Nakasone, "the enemy had wrecked and abandoned an airfield, and we had three days to get it back up and running so that our planes could use it. That's why we had brought 2,000 drafted workers with us."

Deployment and Defeat   15

He then participated in the invasion of the Dutch East Indies as part of the Japanese attempt to capture oil fields, landing at Takaran, Borneo, on January 10, 1942, and then at Balikpapan on the 24th.

The *Taitō Maru* was hit by enemy shells during the Battle of Balikpapan and caught fire. Nakasone lost many of his subordinates in the ensuing carnage. "It was sheer hell. Some had had their arms torn off, others had had their heads caved in. The air was filled with the stench of blood and smoke."

On March 10, Nakasone was ordered to Taiwan, so he flew to Takao (Kaohsiung) en route to Magong in the Penghu Islands off the west coast of Taiwan. He was attached to the local naval construction department (*kaisetsu-bu*) and was promoted to lieutenant in November. In April 1943, he was reassigned to the naval construction department in Takao. His job in Taiwan was preparing airfields against American attacks.

Gotōda Masaharu, a man who had entered the home ministry two years before Nakasone and would go on to serve as his chief cabinet secretary, was stationed in Taipei at the time. A captain in the army, he competed with Nakasone in procuring materials in Taiwan:

> Nakasone joined the home ministry two years after me, although he didn't really do any work there until after the war because he immediately joined the navy. [...] We would occasionally see each other [in Taiwan] at army-navy meetings and the like.
>
> There was a shortage of everything, so there was constant fighting between the army and navy over who got supplies. Nakasone was really good at his job. Major Sakawa of our materials section was always yelling, "I can't do it! That bastard has already grabbed them all!"

Nakasone's wartime experiences served as an opportunity for him to speculate about the relationships between nations, and between people and their nations:

> There is nothing as fierce as battle, and my harsh wartime experiences became a cornerstone for the way that I lived the rest of my life. They served me well when I returned to the Ministry of Home Affairs after the war. They influenced how I approached people, and how I felt about the general public.

Of all Japan's prime ministers, Nakasone is likely the only one to have come under close enemy fire and lost subordinates to it.[3]

The Defeat of Japan and Returning Home

On November 1, 1944, Nakasone was reassigned to the 3rd Section of the Ministry of the Navy Procurement Bureau, which was attached to the Yokosuka Naval District. This section would later be divided into the 2nd Section of the Procurement Bureau and the 3rd Section of the Naval Affairs Bureau.

16 *Deployment and Defeat*

He was named adjutant to Captain Hayashi Takayoshi of the 2nd Section of the Procurement Bureau and put in charge of administering Hainan Island off the southern coast of China and countering inflation in Shanghai.

The commander of the 3rd Section of the Naval Affairs Bureau was Captain Hamada Yūsei. Hamada's rise in the ranks had been delayed by poor health, but Nakasone respected him, describing him as "an intellectual humanist."

Nakasone married on February 11, 1945. His bride was Kobayashi Tsutako, daughter of Dr. Kobayashi Giichirō, a geologist, and the younger sister of one of his colleagues in the navy. He asked Ochiai Tatsuji, his former primary school teacher, to act as his go-between in arranging the match, and the wedding was held at Takasaki Shrine. Nakasone warned Tsutako that "my life will be a turbulent one, and I ask that you prepare yourself for that," to which she answered, "I understand."

On February 25, his younger brother Ryōsuke, a member of the navy's Kisarazu Air Group, was killed in the line of duty when the plane he was aboard went down in a blizzard in the Suzuka Mountains, killing all eleven passengers.

Nakasone was privately informed of the accident in early March by the naval ministry. Because the information was not public, however, he was not permitted to let the rest of his family know. Ryōsuke was later enshrined at Chidorigafuchi National Cemetery before being moved to Yasukuni Shrine. This was one of the reasons that Nakasone would be so insistent about making an official visit to Yasukuni as prime minister.

On June 20, Nakasone was transferred to the navy's Transportation Department and stationed in Takamatsu, where he was to oversee transportation and communications between the Kure Naval District and the kamikaze units being formed around Tosa Bay. His office was located in Kagawa Prefectural Girls High School.

Nakasone later stated that he saw smoke rising from the west of Takamatsu on the morning of August 6. He had heard of American efforts to develop an atomic bomb from his father-in-law, and he recalled thinking, as he watched the smoke rise, "So this is the power of an atomic bomb? This will bring an end to the war." However, given that Takamatsu and Hiroshima are more than 150 kilometers apart and the incident is not mentioned in any of his other accounts, it seems unlikely that he actually saw the Hiroshima mushroom cloud from Takamatsu.

The August 15 surrender broadcast was the first time he ever heard the Emperor's voice. While the reception on his radio was quite poor and filled with static, he understood that the war had been lost and started to cry.

According to Nakasone: "Losing the war was frustrating, but I felt that it couldn't be helped if the Japanese race was to survive. At the same time, I bitterly grieved the fact that our generation had left a large stain on Japanese history. It was that night, as I saw electric lights being used for the first time in years (the blackout restrictions having been lifted) that it hit me: 'The

Deployment and Defeat   17

war's over. My life is saved.'" He was promoted to lieutenant commander on September 5.[4]

Nakasone's wartime experiences provided the motivation for him to go into politics. He later wrote:

> I had been born and raised as just a member of the public, but my wartime experiences could be said to have lit a fire under me. The things I felt – Misfortune cannot be inflicted upon the people. The people cannot be betrayed. – later served as the great spiritual motivation for me to become a politician. I believe that they still serve, even now, as my bedrock as a politician. [...] I could not stand the idea that those who had spent the war warm and comfortable, looking out for their own safety, could be allowed to govern Japan.[5]

The Occupation

After being discharged from the navy, Nakasone returned to the home ministry, who assigned him to the Cabinet Research Office on October 22, 1945. His primary duty there was communicating with Eighth Army headquarters under Major General Eichelberger. His direct counterpart was Colonel Bullard, and these Occupation-era negotiations provided his first direct experience with the United States.

Bullard was a gentleman who attempted to treat Japanese officials like Nakasone as equals, despite them representing a defeated nation. "I admired every action taken by the American officers, NCOs, and soldiers under Colonel Bullard. Interacting with them made it painfully clear to me that Japan losing should have come as no surprise. Had we won, we would have flaunted our success and treated Asia with contempt."

On November 28, Nakasone invited Bullard to Nikkō. As he entertained the American officer with geisha at an inn on the shore of Lake Chūzenji, his first son Hirofumi was born. When Tsutako complained that "as I suffered in childbirth, you were having a grand old time with the occupying forces and geisha," Nakasone defended himself by saying that he had "only been doing the business of the nation." The couple would go on to have two more children, Michiko and Mieko, both daughters.

Nakasone also met Robert Fearey, who had been US Ambassador Grew's secretary at the time that the war began. Now an assistant to Political Advisor in Japan Atcheson, Fearey briefed GHQ on the Japanese political situation. Nakasone got along well with Fearey, and he developed a positive impression of Americans through his work as liaison. He said that they "treated me as another person" rather than looking down on Japan as a defeated nation.

But despite these positive impressions, seeds of resentment were also being planted. Around the time of Hirofumi's birth, GHQ dumped the cyclotron that Nishina Yoshio had developed at Riken into Tokyo Bay. A cyclotron

18 *Deployment and Defeat*

was a device used for the artificial destruction of atomic nuclei and similar tasks, and GHQ had destroyed it as part of the Occupation's ban on Japanese atomic research.

Nakasone wrote that "I was overwhelmed with anger at America [upon learning of the destruction]. Dr. Nishina had used the cyclotron to continue his research on peaceful uses [for the atom]. I felt like America intended to reduce Japan to a fourth-rate agricultural nation."[6]

The Youth Discussion Group

Spurred on by the Occupation, Nakasone formed a study group with colleagues at the home ministry like Takahashi Mikio and Hayakawa Takashi in January 1946. They called it the "Youth Discussion Group" (Seinen Konwakai), and Nakasone explained that the motivation behind the group was "gathering young comrades with the goal of rebuilding our homeland."

The group started holding meetings on the second floor of a soba restaurant in Shimbashi, and others gradually began to join, including Ozawa Tatsuo of the home ministry, Higaki Tokutarō of the agricultural ministry, Yoshikuni Jirō of the finance ministry, Nakagawa Yukitsugu of the Bank of Japan, and Akasawa Shōichi of the commerce ministry.

The group swelled to twenty members, many of whom, like Nakasone and Hayakawa, would go on to become members of the Diet. Higaki would work toward the privatization of NTT as postal minister in the Nakasone government. Takahashi went on to become commissioner general of the National Police Agency. Yoshikuni would serve as administrative vice-minister of finance, and Akasawa as chairman of the Japan External Trade Organization. Nakasone would also use Nakagawa as an economic advisor while prime minister.

There were also those from outside of the government, like Gotō Noboru of Tōkyū Railways and Minagawa Hiromune of Mitsubishi. Gotō would arrange food for the group from the black market, and they would all discuss the Occupation's policies until late in the night.

According to Gotō, the group continued its activities after Nakasone entered politics and served as the source for much of Nakasone's knowledge of economics (a subject he had struggled with):

> Even back then, Nakasone was an eloquent speaker. When he got drunk, he would make everyone laugh, putting on a headband and dancing along as he sang "Kikori no Uta," his specialty. [...]
>
> He continued attending meetings even after becoming a politician. He said that he wanted to "get better at economic issues," so Nakagawa would explain public finance, Minagawa Hiromune and I would go over current events in the business world, and Akasawa would explain economic policy. This might be the reason that, at some point, he came to be seen as the center the group.

Deployment and Defeat   19

After deciding to go into politics, Nakasone invited his former professor Yabe Teiji to one of the group's meetings. Yabe had become an advocate of the "returning home" movement *(kikyō undo)*, which called for young people to return to their hometowns and become a force for rebuilding Japan. This somewhat resembled Nakasone's later founding of the Seiunjuku in Takasaki to serve as a base for the revival of the country.

In February 1946, Nakasone became director of the Kagawa Prefecture Police Section. When the Shidehara Kijūrō government scheduled the first postwar election for the House of Representatives for April 10, Nakasone's home ministry colleague Hayakawa decided to run. In addition to writing him a recommendation, Nakasone also hurried to his district in Wakayama to support his campaign.

After Hayakawa was elected, becoming the youngest member of the Diet at the age of twenty-nine, Nakasone wrote his father on April 24. He explained that he wanted to run for national office and that "waiting until after things have settled down would mean having missed my opportunity." "I can't stand up to GHQ unless I'm a politician representing the people. There are limits to what I can do as a home ministry official."

Matsugorō opposed the idea, but with Yabe and Hayakawa's support behind him, Nakasone's determination remained firm. Hayakawa introduced him to his acquaintances, explaining, "This is my friend Nakasone Yasuhiro from Gunma. He's definitely going to be elected in the next election. I think you two should talk. He's a pretty sensible guy."[7]

The Ideals of Youth

Nakasone returned home to Takasaki in December 1946 to found a youth organization. When Matsugorō asked him what he would do if he was elected, Nakasone replied, "I will put Japan back on course."

While Matsugorō had initially been opposed to Nakasone running, he ultimately gave him his support, saying, "If you become a Diet member, act like Sakura Sōgorō." Sakura was a 17th-century village headman famous for illegally appealing directly to the shogun to have the heavy taxes placed on local farmers reduced, something that cost him his life. His father's words had a lasting impression on Nakasone. He also consulted with Yabe about running.[8]

On New Year's Day 1947, Gokoku Shrine in Takasaki was packed with worshippers. Nakasone stood before them and gave his first electoral speech, telling them that he was determined to stand for election one day to bring about the "rebuilding of Japan." He was a large man, standing 174 cm and weighing 74 kg, so he easily drew the crowd's attention. He tendered his resignation to the home ministry on January 15.

He also submitted an article to the *Jōmō Shimbun*, a local Gunma newspaper, in which he explained his theory of "young politicians." In it, he asserted that "history teaches us that it is always the young who are at the

20 *Deployment and Defeat*

forefront of revolutions and restorations" and that "we are living in another great revolutionary period, and people are crying out for the arrival of such young politicians."[9]

Nakasone expanded on these ideas in his book *The Ideals of Youth*, which was published on March 31. In it, he argued that – unless the young rose up – Japan would become an "old and impoverished nation":

> Japan must be a nation of the young. In every period of history, when it comes time for a state to grow, it is always the young who act. Look at the history of Japan. The Taika Reforms were carried out by Prince Naka-no-Ōe and Nakatomi no Kamatari, both young men in their twenties. [...] In the unlikely event that the youth fail to rise to action, this nation's great opportunity for rapid progress will be lost and Japan will be doomed to become an old and impoverished nation.

Youth was the force that would set Japan right, Nakasone argued, and that youth would come from farming villages. He described Japan as being "like a bean being held by chopsticks. The upper chopstick is the United States, and the other is the Soviet Union. And the force gripping the chopsticks is the Potsdam Declaration."

His language was stiff but fresh, and he sold 43,000 copies despite a paper shortage (although he purchased many of these himself).[10]

First Election

Oddly enough, *The Ideals of Youth* was published on the same day that Prime Minister Yoshida Shigeru dissolved the House of Representatives. Nakasone ran not on Yoshida's Liberal Party ticket, however, but for Ashida Hitoshi's Democrats. The Liberals were descended from the old pre-war Seiyūkai and the newly founded Democratic Party from the Minseitō.

Nakasone had been a supporter of the Minseitō before the war, and Kokumatsu had produced a prefectural assembly member for the party. "As I was ideologically opposed to the Seiyūkai, I ultimately decided to run for the Democratic Party rather than the Liberals."

Nakasone used his retirement allowance from the home ministry to purchase a bicycle which he painted white and used to campaign. He chose the color white after the Emperor's white horse and to represent his opposition to the Reds, noting that "it is the Whites who fight against the extremist Reds." Communist-affiliated labor unions were attempting to organize a general strike at the time, and Nakasone increased his notoriety by traveling around making speeches in opposition to their efforts. In addition to his bicycle, he also sometimes used a truck from Kokumatsu to travel.

Times were favorable for the communists and socialists, but Nakasone took a firmly anti-communist position. He had investigated communist

Deployment and Defeat 21

ideology while at the home ministry and come to the conclusion that it was irreconcilable with Japan's national character and social structure.

But while opposition to communism served as the foundation for Nakasone's positions, he was not a supporter of laissez-faire economics, either, instead calling for moderate, reformed capitalism: "Ever since running for the Diet, I have advocated for reformed capitalism, that is, the position that a sense of society must be added to 'laissez-faire et laissez-passer' and the old liberalism of the Liberal Party. I have deeply pondered the question of what our society would look like if reformed capitalism were applied to our social structure."

After Matsugorō provided him with a rental property to use as a campaign office, passionate supporters began to gather there. He was supported not only by old classmates but by large numbers of young, demobilized military personnel, something that would later lead him to create his Seiunjuku support organization. It was his clear opposition to communism and belief that "rejection of the emperor system is the ideology of a fallen nation" that garnered him so much support among the former military. He also enjoyed the backing of the police and firefighters, so there was little doubt going into the election that he would be elected.

In the April 25 general election, Nakasone came in first among the four candidates. He wrote that he would "never forget" 65,484, the number of votes he received. At twenty-eight years old, Nakasone was the youngest person elected in the country, and this marked the first of his twenty successful electoral campaigns.

This was also the second election in which women were allowed to vote, and Nakasone seems to have received considerable support from them. He was popular with women because, in addition to being a gifted speaker, he was tall and handsome. Believing that he would receive more votes if he appeared single, he did not have his wife make any public appearances.

After the election, Nakasone visited his mother's grave and made an offering of a certified copy of the election results and a haiku:

kono hana o	I wish to decorate
haha ni soetaki	my mother's grave with this flower
ayame kana	an iris, I believe

The Ayame-kai (Iris Association), a women's support organization for Nakasone, was formed by women who, upon learning of the poem, decided to "support Nakasone in his mother's place." This and the Seiunjuku would serve as his most important support organizations. He earned the ire of Occupation officials by having the Seiunjuku fly the Japanese flag.

Now that he had been elected, Nakasone's initial goal was overcoming the Occupation-era politics symbolized by the new constitution and Yoshida Shigeru and securing true independence for Japan. He departed Takasaki to attend a general meeting of the Democratic Party's Diet

22 *Deployment and Defeat*

members. The Democratic Party was only the third-largest party in the Diet, however, and proved unable to even decide upon a party president. Realizing that the party lacked the ability to gain support for itself, Nakasone would boldly go forward on his own, gaining the nickname of the "young officer" for himself. These efforts will be examined in the next chapter.[11]

Notes

1 Nakasone Yasuhiro, *Warera Taishōkko* (Tokyo: Tokuma Shoten, 1961), 14. Nakasone Yasuhiro, *Nakasone Yasuhiro ga Kataru Sengo Nihon Gaikō*, ed. Nakashima Takuma, et al. (Tokyo: Shinchōsha, 2012), 48.

2 Nakasone Yasuhiro, *Nihon no Furontia* (Tokyo: Tsunebunsha, 1966), 223. Nakasone Yasuhiro, *"Zoku" Kaigun Shukei Taii* (Tokyo: Tōyō Kōron-sha, 1978), 8–15. Nakasone Yasuhiro, "Watashi no Kaigun Gurafiti," in Uesugi Kimihito, ed., *Nakasone Yasuhiro Kaigun Gurafiti* (Tokyo: Chidō Shuppan, 1983), 15–34. Nakasone Yasuhiro, *Nakasone Yasuhiro Kushū* (Tokyo: Kadokawa Shoten, 1985), 191–95. Nakasone Yasuhiro, *Seiji to Jinsei – Nakasone Yasuhiro Kaikoroku* (Tokyo: Kōdansha, 1992), 43–54. Nakasone, *Nakasone Yasuhiro ga Kataru*, 49–50.

3 Nakasone, *Kaigun Shukei Taii*, 16–27. Nakasone, *Seiji to Jinsei*, 57–59. Nakasone, *Nakasone Yasuhiro ga Kataru*, 50–52. Gotōda Masaharu, *Sasaeru Ugokasu Watashi no Rirekisho* (Tokyo: Nihon Keizai Shimbun, 1991), 47, 150–52. Kishi Nobusuke, et al., *Watashi no Rirekisho: Hoshuseiken no Ninaite* (Tokyo: Nihon Keizai Shimbun, 2007), 491.

4 Nakasone Yasuhiro, "Hamada Gakkō no Ki," *Ekonomisuto* (March 14, 1967), 58–59. Nakasone Yasuhiro, "Hamada Gakkō no Ki – Senjō de Kiita Fuyu no Tabi," in Ibatake Kenji, Noma Hiroshi, eds., *Kaigun Shukeika Shikan Monogatari – Ninen Gen'eki Hoshū Gakusei Sōran* (Tokyo: Yokuon Shuppankai, 1968), 157–64. Nakasone, *Seiji to Jinsei*, 70–88. Nakasone, *Nakasone Yasuhiro ga Kataru*, 53–57. Ōta Katsutaku, Ōta Chieko, eds., "Nakasone Yasuhiro Daigishi Shiryōshū (Sono 16) Nakasone Ryōsuke Kaigun Chūi Kankei Shiryōshū: Ji Shōwa 2-nen 8-gatsu shi Shōwa 58-nen 2-gatsu" (1983), NDL. Nakasone Tsutako, Suzuki Sachi, Kamisaka Fuyuko, "Tsuma-tachi no 'Unmei Kyōdōtai' Ron," *Bungei Shunjū* (May 1983), 132. On page 42 of *Jiseiroku*, Nakasone wrote that "Hiroshima is more than 150 kilometers away from Takamatsu. I don't know if it's related or not, but I definitely saw a large, white cloud." But according to the July 17, 2011 issue of the *Asahi Shimbun*, Nakasone never made any other references to having seen the Hiroshima mushroom cloud from Takamatsu.

5 Nakasone, *Warera Taishōkko*, 27–28.

6 References from this section are combined with those of the following endnotes.

7 Takahashi Mikio, *Keisatsu Saijiki* (Tokyo: Chūō Senkō, 1976), 4, 23, 180, 182, 301. *Nihon Keizai Shimbun,* January 5, 1983. Tachibana Shōhei, ed., *Hayakawa Takashi – Sono Shōgai to Gyōseki* (Tokyo: Daiippōki, 1988), 24, 27–28, 30–33, 37–39, 45–49, 54, 90, 92, 104, 109, 134, 146, 242, 299, 440. Nakasone, *Seiji to Jinsei*, 88–103. Nakasone Yasuhiro, *Nihon no Sōri-gaku* (Tokyo: PHP Shinsho, 2004), 19–20. Nakasone Yasuhiro, "Genshiryoku no Shinwa Jidai," *Nihon Genshiryoku Gakkaishi* 49:2 (2007), 38. Nakasone, *Nakasone Yasuhiro ga Kataru*, 44, 57–62. Yoshikuni Jirō, *Zeikin Kobore Hanashi – Waga Kuni no Sozei Hensen Taikenki* (Tokyo: Zaikei Shohō-sha, 1996), 1, 76–77. Nakasone Yasuhiro, Itō Takashi, Satō Seiburō, *Tenchi Ujō – Gojū Nen no Sengo Seiji o Kataru* (Tokyo:

Deployment and Defeat 23

Bungei Shunjū, 1996), 97–100. Higaki Tokutarō, Terayama Yoshio, *Nōgyō-Nōson ni Mirai wa Aru ka – Higaki Bushi Kaisō to Tenbō* (Tokyo: Chikyū-sha, 1998), 11, 147, 149, 160, 165–71. Niigata Nippō Jigyō-sha, *Aikyō Mugen Ozawa Tatsuo to Sono Jidai* (Niigata: Niigata Nippō, 2001), 38. National Graduate Institute for Policy Studies COE Oral Policy Research Project, *Yamashita Hideaki Ōraru Hisutorī* (Tokyo: GRIPS, 2005), 299. Iwakawa Takashi, *Nihon no Chika Jinmyaku – Sengo o Tsukutta Kage no Otoko-tachi* (Tokyo: Shōdensha Bunko, 2007), 67–73. National Graduate Institute for Policy Studies COE Oral Policy Research Project, *Yamashita Hideaki Ōraru Hisutorī (Zoku)* (Tokyo: GRIPS, 2007), 21–22. Murakami Masakuni, *Seijika no "Arubeki Yō wa" – Nihon o Sentaku Itashi Sōrō* (Tokyo: Bungei-sha, 2012), 44–45. The Youth Discussion Group continued its activities for decades.

8 Nakasone Yasuhiro, "Chichi no Omoide" (October 10, 1969), author's collection, 13. Yabe Teiji, *Yabe Teiji Nikki Keyaki no Maki*, ed. Nikki Kankōkai (Tokyo: Yomiuri Shimbun, 1974), 59, 113–14, 119–22, 136, 138–39, 144, 148, 155, 234, 279, 282, 293, 302–03, 306, 308, 310, 326, 329, 360, 377, 384, 386, 392–93, 397–98, 463, 481, 496, 503, 521, 612, 664, 722, 774, 777, 782, 789, 795–96, 802, 811, 818, 827, 830, 833, 889, 892. Nakasone, *Tenchi Ujō*, 84–90.

9 Nakasone Yasuhiro, "Seinen Seijika-ron," *Jōmō Shimbun* (January 23, 1947). Nakasone Yasuhiro, *Seinen no Risō* (Tokyo: Ichiyō-sha, 1947), 47–50. Nakasone Yasuhiro, *Sengo Seiji* (Tokyo: Yomiuri Shimbun, 2005), 5–7. Nakasone Yasuhiro, *Mirai no Otona e Kataru – Watashi ga Rīdāshippu ni tsuite Kataru nara* (Tokyo: Popura-sha, 2010), 167–82. Hyakunenshi Shiryōshū Henshū Iinkai, ed., *Takushoku Daigaku Hyakunenshi Kokuji-hen* (Tokyo: Takushoku University, 2005), 243.

10 Nakasone, *Seinen no Risō*, 17–18, 43–44. Nakasone, *Nihon no Sōri-gaku*, 20. Nakasone, *Sengo Seiji,* 6–7. Nakasone, *Tenchi Ujō*, 90–91.

11 Nakasone, *Seiji to Jinsei*, 103–07, 116–21. Nakasone, *Nakasone Yasuhiro Kushū*, 181. Nakasone Yasuhiro, *Nakasone Yasuhiro Kushū 2008* (Tokyo: Hokumei-sha, 2008), 33. Nakasone, *Nakasone Yasuhiro ga Kataru*, 63–67. Nakasone, *Tenchi Ujō*, 91–95, 100–08. Iwakawa 75–76.

References

Gotōda Masaharu. *Sasaeru Ugokasu Watashi no Rirekisho*. Tokyo: Nihon Keizai Shimbun, 1991.

Hatoyama Ichirō, and Hatoyama Kaoru. *Hatoyama Ichirō/Kaoru Nikki*. Edited by Itō Takashi, Suetake Yoshiya. Tokyo: Chūō Kōron Shinsha, 1999.

Higaki Tokutarō, and Terayama Yoshio. *Nōgyō-Nōson ni Mirai wa Aru ka – Higaki Bushi Kaisō to Tenbō*. Tokyo: Chikyū-sha, 1998.

Hyakunenshi Shiryōshū Henshū Iinkai, ed. *Takushoku Daigaku Hyakunenshi Kokuji-hen*. Tokyo: Takushoku University, 2005.

Iwakawa Takashi. *Nihon no Chika Jinmyaku – Sengo o Tsukutta Kage no Otoko-tachi*. Tokyo: Shōdensha Bunko, 2007.

Kishi Nobusuke, Kōno Ichirō, Fukuda Takeo, Gotōda Masaharu, Tanaka Kakuei, and Nakasone Yasuhiro. *Watashi no Rirekisho: Hoshuseiken no Ninaite*. Tokyo: Nihon Keizai Shimbun, 2007.

Murakami Masakuni. *Seijika no "Arubeki Yō wa" – Nihon o Sentaku Itashi Sōrō*. Tokyo: Bungei-sha, 2012.

Nakasone Tsutako, Suzuki Sachi, and Kamisaka Fuyuko. "Tsuma-tachi no 'Unmei Kyōdōtai' Ron." *Bungei Shunjū* (May 1983).

24 Deployment and Defeat

Nakasone Yasuhiro. "Genshiryoku no Shinwa Jidai." *Nihon Genshiryoku Gakkaishi* 49:2 (2007), 38–42.

Nakasone Yasuhiro. "Hamada Gakkō no Ki." *Ekonomisuto* (March 14, 1967).

Nakasone Yasuhiro. "Hamada Gakkō no Ki – Senjō de Kiita Fuyu no Tabi." Ibatake Kenji, Noma Hiroshi, eds. *Kaigun Shukeika Shikan Monogatari – Ninen Gen'eki Hoshū Gakusei Sōran.* Tokyo: Yokuon Shuppankai, 1968.

Nakasone Yasuhiro. *Mirai no Otona e Kataru – Watashi ga Rīdāshippu ni tsuite Kataru nara.* Tokyo: Popura-sha, 2010.

Nakasone Yasuhiro. *Nakasone Yasuhiro ga Kataru Sengo Nihon Gaikō.* Edited by Nakashima Takuma, Hattori Ryūji, Noboru Amiko, Wakatsuki Hidekazu, Michishita Narushige, Kusunoki Ayako, and Segawa Takao. Tokyo: Shinchōsha, 2012.

Nakasone Yasuhiro. *Nakasone Yasuhiro Kushū.* Tokyo: Kadokawa Shoten, 1985.

Nakasone Yasuhiro. *Nakasone Yasuhiro Kushū 2008.* Tokyo: Hokumei-sha, 2008.

Nakasone Yasuhiro. *Nihon no Furontia.* Tokyo: Tsunebunsha, 1966.

Nakasone Yasuhiro. *Nihon no Sōri-gaku.* Tokyo: PHP Shinsho, 2004.

Nakasone Yasuhiro. *Seiji to Jinsei – Nakasone Yasuhiro Kaikoroku.* Tokyo: Kōdansha, 1992.

Nakasone Yasuhiro. *Seinen no Risō.* Tokyo: Ichiyō-sha, 1947.

Nakasone Yasuhiro. "Seinen Seijika-ron." *Jōmō Shimbun* (January 23, 1947).

Nakasone Yasuhiro. *Sengo Seiji.* Tokyo: Yomiuri Shimbun, 2005.

Nakasone Yasuhiro. *Warera Taishōkko.* Tokyo: Tokuma Shoten, 1961.

Nakasone Yasuhiro. "Watashi no Kaigun Gurafiti." Uesugi Kimihito, ed. *Nakasone Yasuhiro Kaigun Gurafiti.* Tokyo: Chidō Shuppan, 1983.

Nakasone Yasuhiro. *"Zoku" Kaigun Shukei Taii.* Tokyo: Tōyō Kōron-sha, 1978.

Nakasone Yasuhiro, Itō Takashi, and Satō Seiburō. *Tenchi Ujō – Gojū Nen no Sengo Seiji o Kataru.* Tokyo: Bungei Shunjū, 1996.

National Graduate Institute for Policy Studies COE Oral Policy Research Project. *Yamashita Hideaki Ōraru Hisutorī.* Tokyo: GRIPS, 2005.

National Graduate Institute for Policy Studies COE Oral Policy Research Project. *Yamashita Hideaki Ōraru Hisutorī (Zoku).* Tokyo: GRIPS, 2007.

Niigata Nippō Jigyō-sha. *Aikyō Mugen Ozawa Tatsuo to Sono Jidai.* Niigata: Niigata Nippō, 2001.

Tachibana Shōhei, ed. *Hayakawa Takashi – Sono Shōgai to Gyōseki.* Tokyo: Daiippōki, 1988.

Takahashi Mikio. *Keisatsu Saijiki.* Tokyo: Chūō Senkō, 1976.

Yabe Teiji. *Yabe Teiji Nikki Keyaki no Maki.* Edited by Nikki Kankōkai. Tokyo: Yomiuri Shimbun, 1974.

Yoshikuni Jirō. *Zeikin Kobore Hanashi – Waga Kuni no Sozei Hensen Taikenki.* Tokyo: Zaikei Shohō-sha, 1996.

3 The "Young Officer"
Nakasone's Time in the Opposition

Chaos in the Democratic Party

The Democratic Party, the party under whose banner Nakasone was elected for the first time in the April 25, 1947 general election, was in chaos. The Socialist Party had made great strides in the election, becoming the largest party in the Diet. Meanwhile, Yoshida Shigeru's Liberals occupied the second spot, leaving the Democratic Party in third. Among the Socialist Diet members elected for the first time in this election was future LDP president and prime minister Suzuki Zenkō.

In the House of Representatives, the Socialists now had 143 seats, the Liberals 131, the Democrats 124, the National Cooperative Party 31, and the Communist Party 4. As there were 466 seats total, no party could secure a majority even if they managed to convince independent Diet members to join them.

The Democratic Party had been formed on March 31 through a merger of Shidehara Kijūro's Japan Progressive Party and Ashida Hitoshi's faction of the Liberal Party. It had been the largest party in the Diet at the time of its formation but had gone into the general election without a party president and had now fallen to third place.

If the party were going to enter into a coalition, it would have to choose between the Liberals and the Socialists. The choice was dependent on the views of Yoshida, the Liberal's president. This was another point upon which the party – still unable to even choose a president – was divided.

The "Young Officer"

Nakasone departed Takasaki to attend the Democratic Party's general meeting of its Diet members in Tokyo on May 5. At the meeting, he hit it off with Sakurauchi Yoshio and Sonoda Sunao, both of whom had also just been elected for the first time. Sakurauchi's father, Yukio, had been an important prewar politician, having served as secretary-general of the Minseitō and finance minister. Sonoda was a former army officer.

DOI: 10.4324/9781003351931-4

26 The "Young Officer"

Nakasone would frequently interact with Sakurauchi for the rest of his life. He was six years younger than Sakurauchi and five years younger than Sonoda.

Another newly elected Democratic Party member present was Tanaka Kakuei, who – like Nakasone – was twenty-eight years old. Tanaka had been born on May 4, 1918, three weeks earlier than Nakasone. The two men's ways of thinking were opposed from the very start.

First, the two men differed on the candidate they supported for the party president. Tanaka had high regard for Shidehara, who was internationally well-known and a former prime minister, but Nakasone saw the "intellectual and young" Ashida as the more suitable candidate. While the fifty-nine-year-old Ashida was significantly younger than the seventy-four-year-old Shidehara, he had actually had a longer career as a politician.

Because Shidehara had been a prominent diplomat before the war, he seemed bureaucratic to Nakasone, another Yoshida. He believed that Ashida, with his rich experience as a party politician, to be more suitable for the position of party president. Nakasone wanted to be rid of the conservatism of prewar politics.

Their age was not the only significant difference between Shidehara and Ashida. The critical difference between the two men at this point was who they envisioned as being the best coalition partner. Shidehara had a close relationship with the Liberal Party, and Yoshida had served as foreign minister in his government. Ashida, however, had split off from the Liberals and disliked Yoshida. He believed that a coalition with Katayama Tetsu's Socialists was possible. Tanaka, who backed Shidehara, was largely comfortable with Yoshida, while Nakasone had strong anti-Yoshida leanings. The party was having difficulty selecting its president.

In an attempt to break the deadlock, Nakasone, Sakurauchi, Sonoda, and other young Diet members burst into a meeting of the party leadership and pressured elder statesmen like Hitotsumatsu Sadayoshi and Nagao Tatsuo to make Ashida president. This act was partly motivated by the feeling that it was the politicians remaining from before the war who were responsible for the situation. According to Sakurauchi, their demands were sternly rebuffed – they were told that "the young should keep quiet" – leading to a ferocious back and forth.

He wrote that Nakasone was "gallant and brilliant, skilled with both the tongue and the pen, and he immediately became a star of those of a more theoretical bent."

Nakasone and the others became known as the "young officers" (after the young military officers involved in political violence in the 1930s) for their unrestrained conduct and their willingness to disrupt the hierarchy between young and old. When the Democratic Party general congress was held on May 18, 1947, Nakasone got his wish, and Ashida was chosen as president.[1]

"Rivalry" with Tanaka Kakuei

From his first Diet appearance, Nakasone always wore a black tie during the Occupation under the premise that "Japan is in mourning so long as it is occupied." The Yoshida government resigned en masse on May 20, and a new coalition government led by Socialist Chairman Katayama Tetsu was formed on June 1. Ashida held the position of foreign minister in the new government.

The Katayama government worked to get inflation under control and one of its acts was to pass the National Management of the Coal Industry Act. The Democratic Party was divided in its opinion of this law. While Ashida and Nakasone were in favor, Shidehara and Tanaka opposed it and left the party, ultimately merging with Yoshida's Liberals.

There were increasingly strong divisions within the Socialist Party as well, which ultimately led to the government's resignation and the formation of the Ashida government on March 10, 1948. This would also prove to be short-lived, however, as its members were soon implicated in a corruption scandal involving the chemical company Shōwa Denkō. This was Nakasone's first, albeit brief, experience of belonging to the government party.

When later asked whether he had had a rival, Nakasone suggested Tanaka Kakuei: "It would probably be Tanaka Kakuei since we were first elected to the House of Representatives at the same time. I think that we were both aware that we were following different paths when it came to politics, policies, and ideals. I took up atomic energy; Kaku chose highways. We were both proud men, but we never had any big arguments."

Not only did Nakasone and Tanaka share the same birth month and electoral history, but they also had their offices in the same building for many years: the Subō Kaikan in Hirakawa-chō. Nakasone's office was on the fourth floor, Tanaka's on the third.

It is debatable whether Tanaka considered Nakasone a worthy opponent, however. Tanaka was the first of the two to hold a cabinet position, the first to serve as LDP secretary-general, and the first to be prime minister. While Nakasone may have become a faction leader before Tanaka, Tanaka's faction was the largest in the party, twice the size of the Nakasone faction.

Probably the only area in which the two could truly be considered equals was in their oratory skills. In a 1981 survey of Diet members, Nakasone came in second in the ranking of politicians who gave the best speeches. The top five spots went to Kaifu Toshiki, Nakasone, Miki Takeo, Tanaka, and Kasuga Ikkō (a former chairman of the Democratic Socialist Party).[2]

Nakasone's Starting Point in Politics: Opposition to Yoshida

When Yoshida returned to the position of prime minister on October 15, 1948, Tanaka – now a member of the Liberal Party – was appointed parliamentary vice-minister of justice despite his lack of seniority. The Yoshida

28 *The "Young Officer"*

government would prove to be long-lived, remaining in place until December 10, 1954. For Nakasone, this meant spending six years and two months in the opposition.

Nakasone was critical of the Liberal Party. He believed that "Yoshida is content to merely follow GHQ's instructions and puts forth no uniquely Japanese ideas." He said that, while "I didn't go as far socialism in standing against Yoshida-style liberalism and capitalism, I did highlight reform capitalism and social solidarity." This was a moderate position (in the sense that it was between Yoshida and the Socialists) and one that he had also advocated for in his first electoral campaign.

Nakasone attempted to differentiate his foreign policy from the Liberals by calling for "autonomous defense and independence from America." He would repeat this call for "autonomous defense" after becoming director-general of the Defense Agency more than a decade later. Nakasone's starting point as a politician was defined by opposition to Yoshida, and he saw himself as a reform conservative standing in contrast to the conservative mainstream represented by Yoshida, Ikeda Hayato, and Satō Eisaku. His particular opposition to the US-Japan security treaty supported by Yoshida will be discussed later.[3]

He was also dissatisfied with the Tokyo Trials. He believed that "crimes against peace and civilization are something that have been created ex post facto and in violation of legal principles" and refused to accept "MacArthur's historical view of the Tokyo Trials."

Nakasone believed that "the great majority of our countrymen drafted into the war fought for the defense of their homeland, and some fought for anti-colonialism and to liberate Asia." But he did also acknowledge that "while against Britain, America, France, and the Netherlands it had been a normal war, it had an aggressive nature when it came to Asia."[4]

Tokutomi Sōho

As the Tokyo Trials neared their conclusion in the fall of 1948, Nakasone paid several visits to the prominent journalist Tokutomi Sōho. Tokutomi was a relative of Nakasone's and had been purged by GHQ. Eighty-five years old, he lived in Izusan in Atami, southwest of Tokyo. He had been a proponent of the war, and Nakasone wanted to learn how he was taking Japan's defeat and what he believed the future held.

Wearing traditional Japanese clothing, Tokutomi spoke broadly of the state of the world from his study overlooking Sagami Bay:

> "China will never become a vassal of the Soviet Union. All the Soviets should expect is betrayal. Mao Zedong may even surpass Tito." "Join forces with America for the time being. You must remember that Japan is a vulnerability for them right now, one they can't get rid of no matter what difficulty it causes them."

The "Young Officer" 29

Nakasone found Tokutomi's worldview appealing, and he was surprised by his mental flexibility and ability to come up with new ideas. According to Tokutomi, "Katsu Kaishū once said to 'follow heaven's course.' A politician is not an officer of the Salvation Army. You have no obligation to hold steadfast to ideology or established concepts."

Nakasone would later call this the "advice of the weathervane":

> A saying that has given me a lot of courage is "it's alright to make major compromises so long as you don't lose sight of the big picture." Put another way, this could perhaps be called the "advice of the weathervane." No other words have had a greater impact on how I viewed life. After learning them, I came to view the work of compromise and consensus-building as vital.

Nakasone's interactions with Tokutomi led to him becoming a firm admirer of Katsu Kaishū, a 19th-century statesman and naval officer. He spent his time in the opposition expanding his circle of contacts, visiting, for example, the purged politician Hatoyama Ichirō at his villa in Karuizawa.[5]

The National Democratic Party and the "Kitamura School"

Inukai Takeru succeeded Ashida as Democratic Party president and began exploring the possibility of a coalition government with Yoshida. These efforts resulted in the party splitting into "coalition" and "opposition" factions in March 1950. Prominent members of the coalition faction (in addition to Inukai) included Hori Shigeru and Kosaka Zentarō. Tomabechi Gizō, Kitamura Tokutarō, Ashida, Nakasone, Sakurauchi, and Inaba Osamu were among those who belonged to the opposition faction.

Nakasone and the rest of the opposition faction joined with Miki Takeo's National Cooperative Party to form the National Democratic Party in April. Tomabechi became the new party's chairman, and Nakasone was appointed deputy chairman of the Policy Research Council (PRC).

Nakasone greatly admired PRC Chairman Kitamura, who was an experienced politician. An upright Christian, he had served as transportation minister in the Katayama government and finance minister in the Ashida government. He was an early advocate for normalizing relations with China (something he shared with Nakasone) and was considered on the far-left side of conservatism.

Nakasone, Kawasaki Hideji, Sakurauchi, Sonoda, and Inaba gathered around Kitamura. This was not a large enough group to be considered a Kitamura "faction" and instead served as more a "Kitamura school" for younger members of the party. According to Inaba, Kitamura acted "like the manager of the young officers group."

The National Democratic Party was reorganized into the Reform Party in February 1952 under Shigemitsu Mamoru, but the Kitamura school

30 The "Young Officer"

continued its activities. Kōmoto Toshio, Tamura Hajime, and Yamanaka Sadanori would also sometimes join the group.

While Nakasone's time in the opposition was a lengthy one, he did not become discouraged. He later wrote that "when I look back on the time I spent in the opposition, what I realize is that it was the decisions I made then that would determine my later political life."[6]

Pursuing Rearmament

Nakasone remained active, attending the MRA World Congress in Caux, Switzerland, in June 1950. MRA – which stood for "Moral Re-Armament" – was a non-ideological and non-religious peace movement based on the idea of the brotherhood of humanity. Nakasone attended the event in the company of Kitamura.

It was while receiving a haircut in Switzerland that Nakasone learned of the outbreak of the Korean War over the radio. He visited West Germany, France, Britain, and America after leaving Switzerland.

Germany was divided under the Cold War, and Nakasone paid a courtesy call on Chancellor Adenauer in the West German capital of Bonn. When they met, he said, "I bring greetings from the youth of Japan to the youth of Germany. Do you have any words for the youth of Japan?"

Adenauer replied that he would "convey your respects to the youth of Germany" and asked, "How old are you?" When Nakasone answered, "thirty-two," Adenauer shook his hand and said, "The rebuilding of Japan and Germany will depend on the power of the young. May we do it together."

Nakasone returned to Japan on August 15. During his absence, MacArthur had established the National Police Reserve (NPR) in a letter to Yoshida. While the NPR would have an initial size of 75,000 personnel and was the first step toward Japanese rearmament, Nakasone felt that it was insufficient.

It was Ashida who Nakasone would partner with in his fight for rearmament. He visited Kyoto in late October to campaign for the former prime minister. Nakasone was thirty-one years his junior, and it was unusual for a young Diet member to campaign for a former prime minister, but Ashida had been arrested in connection with the Shōwa Denkō scandal. He had been released on bail, but his case was still pending.

As they traveled by car from Kyoto to Ayabe, Nakasone brought up the topic of rearmament:

> Having recently traveled around the world and seen how serious things have become, it has become very clear to me that no independent state can remain unarmed and neutral. Once the Korean War broke out, General MacArthur, who had once told Japan to become the "Switzerland of the Pacific," frantically moved to create the NPR.

The "Young Officer" 31

But a nation must willingly exercise its own defense. Even if we enter into an alliance with the United States, Japanese must still undergo an appropriate level of rearmament so that as many American forces leave as possible and American bases are reduced as much as possible. Should we fail to do that, Japan will be forever under occupation by a foreign army and must satisfy itself with being a vassal. Don't you think so?

Ashida agreed. "You're absolutely right. And since you feel the same way that I do, we should undertake this effort together."

For Ashida, backing rearmament was also part of a gamble for returning to the premiership. The two men's rearmament plan would later be incorporated into the Reform Party's platform as an endorsement of the creation of a "democratic self-defense military" (*minshuteki jieigun*). Ashida's not guilty verdict would not come until February 11, 1958, however, and he would pass away the following year.

Nakasone wrote a lengthy petition to MacArthur on January 23, 1951, arguing that "we have reached a stage where domestic politics and national defense should be carried out on the basis of the responsibility and honor of the Japanese people." That same day, he argued in favor of rearmament at a rally hosted by the National Democratic Party.

He met Dulles on February 2 and sought to have Japan granted permission to construct civil aircraft and investigate the peaceful uses of atomic energy. Dulles was in Japan as a special advisor to President Truman and was consulting with Yoshida on national security and a peace treaty.[7]

Working with Former Naval Personnel

A distinctive characteristic of Nakasone's promotion of rearmament was his contact with former naval personnel. Around the same time that Dulles came to Japan, he was carrying out "research on the establishment of a defense force" with former Vice Admiral Hoshina Zenshirō, former director of the Bureau of Naval Affairs, and former Captain Ōi Atsushi.

He also invited Nomura Kichisaburō, an old hand with the navy and former foreign minister and ambassador to the United States, and Fukudome Shigeru, former chief of staff of the Combined Fleet, to join the study group.

Most of the participants in the group were former naval officers; Nakasone was the only Diet member. He explained that he "didn't approach other legislators because I knew that national defense and defense issues were touchy issues. [Participating] would have hurt their reelection chances."

Nakasone's primary interest was "correcting the shortcomings of Article 9" of the new constitution. With that point in mind, he gathered young Diet members from both government and opposition parties and held the first meeting of the Independent Defense Study Group on March 1. Thirteen of those invited participated, including Ishida Hirohide, Kawasaki,

32 The "Young Officer"

Sakurauchi, Sonoda, and Inaba, and the men discussed the basic requirements for a peace treaty in a non-partisan fashion.

Nakasone would continue to discuss defense issues with Hoshina and Fukudome even after the San Francisco Peace Treaty was signed.[8]

Clashing with Yoshida

Yoshida concluded peace and security treaties with the United States in San Francisco, and these were passed by the House of Representatives on October 26, 1951. Nakasone voted in favor of the peace treaty but abstained on the security treaty as objected to the lack of an expiration date and the granting of the right to intervene in domestic disturbances to the US under the terms of the treaty. He was also dissatisfied with the fact that Japan had no right to try American military personnel under the US-Japan administrative agreement.

According to one newspaper reporter, Nakasone took a strong stand against the treaty at the Democratic Party's congress, going so far as to say that "[The Democratic Party] cannot share responsibility for such a disgraceful treaty. The United States caused untold damage to the Japanese people through its indiscriminate bombing, and we should demand reparations."

Nakasone's criticism of Yoshida reached its peak at the January 31, 1952 meeting of the House of Representatives' Budget Committee. During the meeting, he criticized a letter that Yoshida had sent Dulles (in which he said that Japan would establish relations with Taiwan rather than China) as "bureaucratic secret diplomacy" and raised doubts about the constitutionality of the NPR. Nakasone had carried out an inspection of the NPR in preparation for the meeting.

Yoshida did not respond to Nakasone's accusations directly, however, leaving most of the testimony to State Minister Okazaki Katsuo and Finance Minister Ikeda Hayato.

Growing irritated, Nakasone yelled at Yoshida: "Don't you have the confidence to testify for yourself? You should resign from the cabinet."

The exchange seemed to be going in Nakasone's favor. That would rapidly change after he referenced the Emperor's abdication, however.

After discussing the Emperor's possible "human distress" over the war and the "external restraints" placed on that distress by his position, he noted that "I believe that it may be necessary to tell the Emperor that, should he have the desire [to abdicate], that we would do away with his distress" and then asked Yoshida for the government's position.

Yoshida's cheeks quivered as he turned to answer.

> "For His Majesty to abdicate would harm the stability of the nation. I would regard anyone who desired such a thing as a traitor."

Nakasone's intention had been for the matter to be left for the Emperor to freely decide, but Yoshida had misunderstood him as promoting abdication. This time it was Yoshida's response which drew applause from the room.[9]

Formation of the Reform Party and the Reformist Faction

On February 8, 1952, Nakasone participated in the formation of the Reform Party, the successor to the National Democratic Party. This effort involved a number of formerly purged figures who had now been permitted to return to politics, such as Shigemitsu Mamoru, Matsumura Kenzō, Ōasa Tadao, Nakajima Yadanji, and Miyazawa Taneo. Former foreign minister Shigemitsu was chosen as the party's first president, and Matsumura became secretary-general.

As a member of the preparatory committee for the party's formation, Nakasone (along with others like Kawasaki Hideji) was involved in drafting the party platform. Looking at that platform, there are two clauses that stand out: those concerning "independent defense" (*dokuritsu jiei*) and "corporatism" (*kyōdōshugi*):

- "Our party will accomplish the independent defense of the Japanese people in anticipation of the realization of world peace and the revival of Asia."
- "Based on the ideal of corporatism, our party will correct capitalism and promote the welfare of the general Japanese public."

In terms of specific policies, the platform called for the creation of a "democratic self-defense force" and the reexamination of the constitution and existing laws. Its goal was the rectification of Yoshida's Occupation-era policies.

The Reform Party consisted of four factions: the "presidential faction" including men like Matsumura and Ōasa, the "reform faction" with Miki Takeo, Kitamura, Kawasaki, and Nakasone, the "moderate faction" with Furui Yoshimi and Machimura Kingo, and the Ashida faction with Ashida and Araki Masuo. The reform faction drew from former members of the National Cooperative Party like Miki and younger members of the former Democratic Party like Nakasone.

While Nakasone belonged to the reform faction, he greatly admired Matsumura of the presidential faction. He was impressed by his character and good judgment, and he assumed the role of his pupil. "Matsumura had served as welfare minister in Prince Higashikuni's cabinet that was formed immediately after the end of the war. He was very much our senior, but he still took great care to foster the careers of young politicians. I felt an obligation towards him."

He was particularly inspired by Matsumura's views on China. According to Nakasone, "Matsumura wanted relations restored with China quickly, and he was ready to sacrifice himself for Sino-Japanese friendship. [...] His views on the importance of China were largely the same as my own."

Matsumura also saw great things in Nakasone's future, and when Nakasone formed his own faction, later on, he asked Diet Member Tagawa Seiichi to "please assist Nakasone."[10]

34　*The "Young Officer"*

An "Explosive Question"

Now a member of the Reform Party, Nakasone demanded answers from Transportation Minister Ishii Mitsujirō and State Minister Ōno Banboku on the ongoing shipbuilding scandal at the February 22, 1954 session of the House of Representatives' Budget Committee. Prefacing his words by saying that "my words are based on indisputable sources, and I will take political responsibility if they are incorrect," he accused Ishii and Ōno of having received one million yen from Namura Shipbuilding and called for the entire Yoshida government to resign.

Deputy Prime Minister Ogata Taketora denied this, saying that no cabinet minister was involved in the scandal. Nakasone's "explosive question" damaged the perception of innocence of not only Ishii and Ōno but that of Finance Minister Ikeda and Liberal Party Secretary-General Satō Eisaku as well. His actions here would be an indirect cause of the lengthy wait Nakasone would have to endure before he was finally able to join the cabinet during the Satō government.[11]

The Reform Party leadership also took a dim view of Nakasone's grandstanding. Secretary-General Matsumura had attempted to dissuade him from making his attack on the government only to be brushed off, and President Shigemitsu criticized the actions in his journal:

> Secretary-General Matsumura's attempt to stop him had no effect, and Diet Member Nakasone exposed corruption (and the involvement of cabinet members therein) at the Budget Committee. His arguments were not convincing, and his statements will bring misfortune. We need to avoid excessively antagonizing the Liberal Party.
>
> Those like Nakasone act as if the point of Diet testimony is to come up with something, anything, that can be used as fodder for the newspapers. No matter how many years pass, he will make no progress as a Diet member. Truly regrettable.

Nakasone would continue to have a reputation for grandstanding when serving as director-general of the Defense Agency and prime minister as well. As can be seen from Shigemitsu's words, these criticisms were being made from early on in his career, even by those within the same party.[12]

The "Jōshū War" with Fukuda Takeo

Nakasone steadily built up his political career during this period, winning reelection in the January 23, 1949 and October 1, 1952 general elections.

In the 1952 election, Fukuda Takeo, former director of the finance ministry's Budget Bureau, ran as a candidate in the same district as Nakasone (Gunma 3rd) and came in second. Ōhira Masayoshi, another former finance ministry official who had served as Ikeda's secretary while he was finance

The "Young Officer" 35

minister, was also elected for the first time in this election, albeit in Kagawa 2nd district.

Both Fukuda and Ōhira would go on to become faction leaders in the LDP, but Nakasone needed to be particularly aware of Fukuda as they served the same district. Fukuda had been born in 1905, so he was thirteen years older than Nakasone. Like Nakasone, he was a graduate of both Takasaki Middle School and Tokyo Imperial University. His expertise in economic policy led to him frequently referred to as "Economic Fukuda."

Nakasone had already seen himself as having a rival in Tanaka, but he now faced a strong opponent in his electoral district as well. The electoral battles between Nakasone and Fukuda were intense and became commonly known as the "Jōshū War" (after an old name for Gunma). Fukuda would inherit Kishi Nobusuke's faction in 1962, and Nakasone would later describe his relationship with Fukuda as having been part of his opposition to the "prewar bureaucrats":

> There was antagonism between the prewar bureaucrats and the young politicians who had gone into politics after experiencing the war. Fukuda received most of his support from businessmen and those involved in the economy. But I received my support from young housewives and those that could in a sense be considered intellectuals. I was very aware of the generational divisions that existed without the prefecture's population. [...]
>
> In making his appeals to the people of Gunma and the nation, Fukuda generally concentrated on economics and fiscal policy. I focused on more fundamental national issues like education, administrative reform, and constitutional revision.

The issues that Nakasone devoted himself to like direct election of the prime minister, foreign policy, national security, and atomic energy, were things that were relevant nationally more than they were specific to Gunma.[13]

Gunma 3rd

How did the people of Gunma view the relationship between Nakasone and Fukuda? I would like to take a look at a special feature run by the *Jōmō Shimbun* on January 1, 1966 to provide some insight on this question. The newspaper had arranged a conversation between the two men, choosing economic topics such as the state of the economy, public finance, regional finance, and prices. Fukuda was the finance minister at the time, while Nakasone did not hold a cabinet position.

Asked about that year's likely economic growth, Fukuda began a long-winded, detailed explanation, noting that "I would like to aim for 7% in real terms. And public finance will have an extremely important role to play in making that happen. In compiling the budget for the coming financial year,

36 The "Young Officer"

my approach was to use public finance to overcome the downturn in capital investment."

Nakasone, however, had little to say, commenting only that "there are rumors that the recent increases in the stock market [...] are due to capital entering the country from Southeast Asia."

Fukuda immediately rebutted him, saying, "I don't think there is any trend of [increased] outside investment. If there was, it would be visible in the balance of payments."

Fukuda overwhelmed Nakasone in the discussion. While Fukuda brought up specific facts and figures regarding exports and economic growth, Nakasone's responses were fragmentary, and he likely came across as lifeless to readers. He had to have known going into the discussion that he had no chance of going up against Fukuda on the economy. That the discussion topics revolved around the economy was disadvantageous to Nakasone, although the newspaper doubtless chose them based on local interest.[14]

Belonging to the same multimember district meant that Nakasone and Fukuda would compete in fourteen general elections from 1952 to 1986. Nakasone only received more votes than Fukuda four times. Notably, Fukuda took the lead in six consecutive elections from 1972 to 1986, meaning that Nakasone came in second even in the two elections held while he was prime minister (see Table 3.1).

Gunma 3rd was a very conservative district, and it would also send future prime minister Obuchi Keizō to the Diet for the first time in 1963 at the age of twenty-six. Obuchi described "being squeezed between Fukuda and Nakasone" as comparable to being "a ramen place located between two high-rises."

Table 3.1 Nakasone and Fukuda's Placement and Votes in Gunma 3rd District (1952–86)

General election	Nakasone	Fukuda
25th (October 1, 1952)	71,697 (1st)	46,531 (2nd)
26th (April 19, 1953)	65,878 (1st)	52,665 (4th)
27th (February 27, 1955)	83,399 (1st)	61,090 (2nd)
28th (May 22, 1958)	70,852 (2nd)	88,027 (1st)
29th (November 20, 1960)	75,274 (2nd)	92,099 (1st)
30th (November 21, 1963)	84,504 (2nd)	95,378 (1st)
31st (January 29, 1967)	72,731 (2nd)	100,573 (1st)
32nd (December 27, 1969)	106,823 (1st)	99,465 (2nd)
33rd (December 10, 1972)	93,879 (2nd)	178,281 (1st)
34th (December 5, 1976)	56,454 (4th)	148,736 (1st)
35th (October 7, 1979)	95,961 (2nd)	122,542 (1st)
36th (June 22, 1980)	96,930 (2nd)	128,542 (1st)
37th (December 18, 1983)	117,970 (2nd)	129,100 (1st)
38th (July 6, 1986)	115,381 (2nd)	120,500 (1st)

Sources: *Asahi Shimbun*, etc.

The "Young Officer" 37

Nakasone came in fourth (of four positions) in the 1976 election that followed the Lockheed scandal, managing to be surpassed by not only Fukuda and Obuchi but the Socialist candidate, Yamaguchi Tsuruo, as well. [5]

From around 1975, the LDP members of the Gunma prefectural assembly also became divided into pro-Nakasone and pro-Fukuda camps. The Nakasone faction was known as the Kenseijuku, and the Seisaku Dōshikai was the Fukuda-aligned group. As both men sought to become prime minister, they became involved not only in the prefectural assembly but in gubernatorial and mayoral races as well as they sought to expand their local support base. It was only in 2006, eleven years after Fukuda's death, that the two factions would be dissolved.[16]

Accepting the US-Japan Security Framework

At the time that Nakasone was reelected for the second time in October 1952, there was a collective security concept known as the "Pacific alliance format" (Taiheiyō dōmei hōshiki) or the "Pacific pact concept" (Taiheiyō kyōtei kōsō) under consideration. This idea – proposed by the United States – would have established a Pacific equivalent to NATO that included countries like Australia and the Philippines in addition to the US and Japan.

While such an organization never materialized, the idea was close to Nakasone's own thoughts. One of the reasons that he was critical of the US-Japan security treaty signed by Yoshida was that he envisioned a collective security plan for the Pacific.

By 1953, however, his views had changed. In the February 14 meeting of the Budget Committee, he argued that Japan should "be extremely wary and careful when it comes to the Pacific alliance format," showing that he had become skeptical of that particular form of collective defense.

Asked about this, Nakasone recalled that "the idea of Asian solidarity was unrealistic, as could be seen from the poor relations between Japan and South Korea. And there were difficult issues [that would have needed to be addressed], like the standoff between China and Taiwan, and the division of the Korean Peninsula. Ultimately, I had a change of heart and decided that there was no viable means of approaching security other than concluding a treaty with the United States."[17]

While he believed that alterations were needed, Nakasone had come to broadly accept the US-Japan security framework and shifted his focus to atomic energy. His July visit to America would serve as an opportunity for this.

Seminar at Harvard

Nakasone participated in Harvard University's Summer International Seminar from July 6 to August 30, 1953. The seminar brought together forty-five people from twenty-two countries in Europe and Asia from a broad variety of fields, including politicians, newspaper editorialists, radio

38 *The "Young Officer"*

broadcasters, university professors, diplomats, civil servants, writers, commentators, and lawyers.

On July 30, Nakasone spoke for fifty minutes in English on "various issues relating to Japanese democracy." His central argument was that "Japan needs to adopt direct election of the prime minister to avoid giving rise to the defects of Weimar Germany that produced Hitler, namely, political chaos and instability."

The general belief at the time was that indirect elections were less likely to give rise to a dictatorship, but Nakasone argued otherwise. "Hitler became dictator under the Weimar constitution by abusing the course of parliamentary politics, taking advantage of political instability and the struggles between smaller parties. Direct election of the prime minister is the way for Japan to avoid this path." He argued that adopting a system under which the prime minister was elected in a national vote would lead to the formation of a two-party system and the entrenchment of democracy.

The lecture was well received by the representatives of the United States, Germany, India, and Pakistan.

The seminar was overseen by then-Professor Henry Kissinger, who would later serve as a presidential advisor during the Nixon administration. Due to Kissinger's strong German accent, Nakasone was only able to understand about a third of what he said. Even so, the seminar marked the beginning of several decades of contact between the two men.[18]

Conversation with Reischauer

On August 11, Nakasone visited the home of Professor Edwin Reischauer, a well-known scholar of Japanese history. Entering Reischauer's parlor, he felt a bit like he was back home, as it was decorated with a Sesshū painting and an ikebana pot.

Because Reischauer had worked for the State Department during the Pacific War, Nakasone was curious about his views on the use of the atomic bombs:

N: What do you think of the decision to use the atomic bombs even though Japan was undertaking peace efforts through Russia?

R: It was unavoidable. There were too many among the leadership of the Japanese military who wanted to continue to fight.

N: You don't think there's something unreasonable about instantly wiping out 200,000 lives in the name of ending a war?

R: Such is the nature of war.

N: Were the atomic bombs used in the way that they were to promote peace? Or was it to confirm their power?

R: While it is psychologically plausible that the people who made the bombs wanted to test them, officially, it was, of course, done to bring about peace.

N: India has said that the decision to drop the bombs on Japan but not on Germany was due to racism.

The "Young Officer" 39

R: Had the war gone on longer, they would certainly have also been used on Germany. There was no racism involved.

N: If American was going to use such a weapon, I think they should have dropped it on a small uninhabited island nearby as a demonstration for the Japanese people.

R: I agree that that would have been better. But dropping it on a small island would have minimized the impact and may have reduced its ability to end the war.

N: What are your views on the emperor system issue?

R: I was working for the State Department at the time, and I strongly argued for maintaining the emperor system.

N: There are those who argue that the Emperor should have abdicated and passed the throne to the crown prince.

R: I don't think the crown prince becoming emperor would have made any difference, as the former emperor would still be behind him.

The roughly two months that Nakasone spent at Harvard provided him with an excellent opportunity to view Japan from the perspective of the United States.[19]

The Peaceful Use of Atomic Energy

From Harvard, Nakasone headed for Washington, where he met with Vice President Nixon and Assistant Secretary of State Robertson in September. During these meetings, he argued for the creation of a self-defense force, revision of the US-Japan security treaty, and the gradual withdrawal of American forces from Japan. In October, he toured the US Naval Academy and West Point and visited Berkeley's UC Radiation Laboratory (today's Lawrence Berkeley National Laboratory) to learn about atomic energy.

The most significant event during this time was likely his meeting with Sagane Ryōkichi, a University of Tokyo professor on sabbatical at the UC Radiation Laboratory. Sagane convinced Nakasone that the Japanese laws on atomic energy needed to be clarified and that the same was true for its funding. Nakasone became convinced that "the peaceful use of atomic energy is a national matter, and as such decisions concerning it must be made by politicians."

Nakasone spent almost four months in America, returning home on October 30. He brought home a large number of recordings of political speeches. His wife Tsutako complained to her friends that "whenever he goes to America, he never buys any classical records, just speeches."[20]

"Mister Atom" – Securing the Budget for Atomic Energy

Back home, Nakasone devoted himself to studying atomic matters in the belief that "failing to establish a national framework for atomic energy would prove a fatal loss for Japan's future." With support from Kawasaki

40   The "Young Officer"

Hideji and others, he was able to put together a 235-million-yen budget for atomic energy research on March 2, 1954.

Why was Nakasone able to participate in budgetary planning despite belonging to the opposition? Because while the Liberal Party had control of the budget under the 5th Yoshida government, it was a minority government that needed the support of the Reform Party to pass a budget.

The amendment that Nakasone pushed through the Budget Committee would serve as the catalyst for full-scale research into the peaceful uses of atomic energy. As there were those in the media who pushed back against his efforts due to the Japanese nuclear allergy, Nakasone submitted articles to newspapers arguing for the necessity of atomic energy development and organized round-table discussions on the topic.

The March 2 inclusion of the budget on atomic research immediately preceded the Fukuryū Maru Incident becoming known. This incident involved a Japanese tuna ship, the eponymous *Fukuryū Maru* No. 5, which was exposed to radiation by the American hydrogen bomb testing at Bikini Atoll. After the ship returned to its home port of Yaizu on March 14, its twenty-three crewmen were all confirmed to be suffering from radiation sickness.

This incident did nothing to shake Nakasone's resolve, however, and he participated in the UN International Conference on the Peaceful Uses of Atomic Energy in Geneva from August 8 to 20, 1955 with Maeda Masao of the Liberal Party.

Nakasone wrote a letter to EPA Director-General Takasaki Tatsunosuke on August 20 in which he wrote that "We, representatives of four parties, pledge to cooperate in a completely non-partisan manner on the development of atomic energy and vow to bring about such cooperation in our parties." By "representatives of four parties," he was referring to himself (Democratic Party), Maeda (Liberal Party), Matsumae Shigeyoshi (Right Socialists), and Shimura Shigeharu (Left Socialists).

He left to tour nuclear facilities in France, Britain, Canada, and the US in late August, returning to Japan on September 15. Once home, he was appointed chairman of the Joint Committee on Atomic Energy. This was a non-partisan committee composed of members of both houses of the Diet. The Basic Law on Atomic Energy was passed as a member's bill on December 19. Nakasone's efforts in this area caused him to receive the nickname "Mister Atom."[21]

Approaching the Anti-Yoshida Faction and the Creation of the Defense Agency

While Nakasone worked on atomic energy on a non-partisan basis, he was also exploring cooperation with the Liberal Party's anti-Yoshida faction. He visited Ishibashi Tanzan on February 25, 1954. Ishibashi wrote in his diary that "Diet Member Nakasone of the Reform Party visited at around 11 by appointment and proposed a reform movement be formed to bring down

The "Young Officer" 41

the Yoshida government." While Ishibashi was a member of the Liberal Party, he was strongly opposed to Yoshida and was becoming involved in Kishi Nobusuke's efforts to found a new conservative party. Nakasone also wanted to be involved in this movement.

Nakasone and Ishibashi remained in contact. Ishibashi wrote in his diary on November 7 that "I invited Nakasone, Kawasaki, Sakurauchi [Yoshio], and Inaba [Osamu] of the Reform Party over and we talked." Just as he had once been known as a "young officer" of the Democratic Party, Nakasone was now regarded as being at the center of the group of young Reform Party politicians calling for opposition to Yoshida.[22]

The laws establishing the Defense Agency and Self-Defense Forces (SDF) were passed on June 9 of that same year. As the 5th Yoshida government was a minority government, the Liberal Party had no choice but to work with Miki Bukichi and Kōno Ichirō's Japan Liberal Party and the Reform Party to pass these laws. Nakasone worked with Nishimura Naomi of the Liberal Party and Nakamura Umekichi of the Japan Liberal Party in the formulation of both laws, keeping the need for civilian control in mind as he did so.

According to Nakasone, "Yoshida didn't really make any clear statements when it came to gradually increasing Japan's defense capabilities. Which is to say, he had no interest in defense issues and didn't feel the need to speak on them. [...] The Reform Party was united in the belief that it was up to us to fill in the holes in his policies." The self-confidence evident in this statement can be linked to his later decision to volunteer to serve as director-general of the Defense Agency.[23]

Observing the Communist Bloc

Excluding his wartime experiences, Nakasone had hitherto only spent time abroad in Western Europe and North America. He had never visited the communist bloc, something that he considered necessary for considering foreign policy during the Cold War. Thus, from June 21 to August 10, 1954, Nakasone visited the Soviet Union and China as part of a nonpartisan observation tour by Diet members. Among those in the group were Nishimura Naomi, Kuroda Hisao, Sakurauchi Yoshio, Sonoda Sunao, and Matsumae Shigeyoshi.

Before departing, Nakasone visited Shigemitsu in his office as Reform Party president on May 18 to receive permission to go. Shigemitsu was opposed to the trip, telling him that "This would be a great deviation. I advise you, as a friend, not to go. I need you to become one of the leaders of the Japanese political world, and this will do great damage to your political career. You should absolutely drop this."

Nakasone was undeterred, replying, "I thank you for the advice, but – particularly now – there is a need for a conservative politician to see the Soviet Union and Communist China firsthand and consider what our national policies towards them should be."

42   The "Young Officer"

Shigemitsu wrote in his diary that "Nakasone brought up Russia. I tried to discourage him. The man will do anything for newspaper coverage. He will accomplish nothing unless he improves himself." As always, he had a low opinion of Nakasone and considered his desire to visit the communist bloc as just another publicity stunt.[24]

His assessment may not have been correct, however. It was rare for a conservative politician to visit a communist country during this period, and there was value to doing so beyond any publicity that the act would bring.

While Nakasone was not concerned about being criticized as a publicity hound, he *was* worried that his visit to the communist bloc could lead America to see him as pro-communist. He wrote a joint letter with the other members of the group to US Ambassador Allison in which they stated that, while they would be visiting the USSR and China, they had absolutely no desire to "destroy the bonds of friendship and trust between Japan and the United States, nor those between our peoples."

Nakasone's visit to the communist bloc could be considered to infringe the United States' anti-communist Immigration and Nationality Act of 1952, and he wanted to avoid being denied entry to the United States in the future.[25]

After arriving in Moscow via Scandinavia, he found his hotel's lights dim and everything there – from the towels to the toilet paper – to be of poor quality. He toured a factory but considered it to be a far cry from the advanced facilities shown in Soviet propaganda.

The Japanese group brought up the issues of territorial waters and fishing rights to Acting Foreign Minister Vyshinsky and visited former Kwantung Army Commander Yamada Otozō, imprisoned in Siberia for war crimes. He wrote that "The Soviet Union of that period befitted its nickname of the 'gulag archipelago.' The eyes of the secret police were always watching from the shadows. It felt just like being in a detainment camp."

Nakasone then flew to Beijing via Mongolia. Upon arriving and seeing the fruit for sale and the expressions on people's faces, he felt like he had "returned to human society."

He met with Vice-Premier Guo Moruo and President of the Chinese Red Cross Li Dequan. Guo took an extremely anti-Japanese stance in their discussion, criticizing "Japanese imperialism." Despite Sino-Soviet solidarity still being strong at the time, Nakasone argued for the broad expansion of Japanese commercial and cultural ties with China. He remembered Tokutomi Sōho's words that "Mao Zedong will inevitably become like Yugoslavia's Tito."

Nakasone also met with Liao Chengzhi, Sun Pinghua, Xiao Xiangqian, and Liu Deyou, men involved with Chinese relations with Japan. According to Liu, "Nakasone was a gifted speaker. There was something in his extemporaneous speeches that rallied the hearts of those listening." Liao arranged for a banquet for him, and Nakasone sang *Kōjō no Tsuki*. Nakasone did his best to understand the socialist reforms that China was implementing and visited various facilities including a blanket factory in Tianjin.

The "Young Officer" 43

His final destination on the trip was Hong Kong. When Sonoda announced at dinner there that he would "handle the China issue in the future," Sakurauchi responded that he would "take on the Soviet issue." Nakasone then "volunteered to handle the Americans" at which time the men toasted. Having experienced the communist bloc, Nakasone decided to strive to become the foremost authority on relations with the US.

From this point on, Nakasone would make repeated trips to the United States, Southeast Asia, Latin America, South Korea, and Europe. His extensive experience with foreign countries would be a major asset for him as a politician, one that he would make particularly good use of as prime minister.[26]

Notes

1 References from this section are combined with those of the following endnote.
2 *Asahi Shimbun*, May 6, 1947. *Mainichi Shimbun,* May 19, 1947. *Yomiuri Shimbun,* February 24, 1954. Nakasone Yasuhiro, *Nihon no Furontia* (Tokyo: Tsunebunsha, 1966), 164. Nakasone Yasuhiro, *Seiji to Jinsei – Nakasone Yasuhiro Kaikoroku* (Tokyo: Kōdansha, 1992), 108–11, 208–11. Nakasone Yasuhiro, *Seizan Jōunpo – Nakasone Yasuhiro Taidan-shū* (Tokyo: Mainichi Shimbun, 2012), 41. Nakasone Yasuhiro, *Nakasone Yasuhiro ga Kataru Sengo Nihon Gaikō* (Tokyo: Shinchōsha, 2012), 69–70. Hori Shigeru, *Sengo Seiji no Oboegaki* (Tokyo: Mainichi Shimbun, 1975), 33. Ashida Hitoshi, *Ashida Hitoshi Nikki*, ed. Shindō Eiichi (Tokyo: Iwanami Shoten, 1986), 2:44, 62, 80, 212, 221, 281, 290. Inaba Osamu, *Inaba Osamu Kaisōroku* (Niigata: Niigata Nippō Jigyō-sha Shuppan-bu, 1989), 36. Sakurauchi Yoshio, "Watashi no Rirekisho 15," *Nihon Keizai Shimbun* (January 16, 1994). Yamasaki Taku, *2010-Nen Nihon Genjitsu* (Tokyo: Daiyamondo-sha, 1999), 245. Hattori Ryūji, *Shidehara Kijūrō to 20 Seiki no Nihon – Gaikō to Minshushugi* (Tokyo: Yuhikaku, 2006), 234. Iwami Takao, *Enzetsuryoku* (Tokyo: Hara Shobō, 2009), 66–67, 113–14, 233–34. On Shidehara, see also: Hattori Ryūji, *Japan at War and Peace: Shidehara Kijūrō and the Making of Modern Diplomacy* (Canberra: Australian National University Press, 2021).
3 Nakasone Yasuhiro, *Shūsei Shihonshugi to Shakai Rentei Shugi* (Tokyo: Ichiyō-sha, 1947). Nakasone Yasuhiro, *Rīdā no Jōken* (Tokyo: Fusō-sha, 1997), 69–70. Nakasone Yasuhiro, *Hoshu no Yuigon* (Tokyo: Kadowa one Tēma 21, 2010), 52–53. Nakasone, *Nakasone Yasuhiro ga Kataru*, 65–68, 96–97, 569–72. Nakasone Yasuhiro, Itō Takashi and Satō Seiburō, *Tenchi Ujō – Gojū Nen no Sengo Seiji o Kataru* (Tokyo: Bungei Shunjū, 1996), 105–06.
4 Nakasone, *Rīdā no Jōken*, 242–44. Nakasone Yasuhiro, *Jiseiroku – Rekishi Hōtei no Hikoku to shite* (Tokyo: Shinchōsha, 2004), 32. Nakasone, *Nakasone Yasuhiro ga Kataru*, 79–80.
5 Letters from Nakasone Yasuhiro to Tokutomi Sōho (February 1, 1954; May 8, 15, 1957), STM. Nakasone, *Nihon no Furontia*, 170. Nakasone, *Seiji to Jinsei*, 112–15. Nakasone, *Jiseiroku*, 32–36. Nakasone Yasuhiro, *Nihon no Sōri-gaku* (Tokyo: PHP Shinsho, 2004), 26–28. Nakasone, *Tenchi Ujō*, 110–13. Hatoyama Ichirō, *Hatoyama Ichirō/Kaoru Nikki, Vol. 1*, eds. Itō Takashi and Suetake Yoshiya (Tokyo: Chūō Kōron Shinsha, 1999), 680. Nakasone argued in his article "Gendai Nihonjin no Kekkan," *Jōmō Shimbun,* October 28, 1948, that "unless we secure friendly relations with our neighbor China, it will be impossible – both politically and economically – for us to become independent."

44 The "Young Officer"

6 Inaba Osamu, *Kōsei Osoru Beshi* (Tokyo: Tokyo Shimbun, 1988), 63–65, 83–84. Nakasone, *Seiji to Jinsei*, 111. Nakasone, *Hoshu no Yuigon*, 51–54. Komiya Hitoshi, *Jiyū Minshu-tō no Tanjō – Sōsai Kōsen to Soshiki Seitō-ron* (Tokyo: Bokutaku-sha, 2010), 155, 176.

7 Letter from Nakasone Yasuhiro to Nakasone Tsutako (June 28, 1950), in Ōta Katsurō and Ōta Chieko, eds., *Nakasone Yasuhiro Daigishi Shiryōshū (Sono 22) Takuetsu shita Gaikō Shuwan no Gensen Dai Ikkan – Dai Ikkai – Dai Gokai ni Wataru Gaiyū no Kiseki*, 80, NDL. Nakasone Yasuhiro, "Ōbei Tayori," *Jōmō Shimbun*, June 25–26; July 14–16, 18–20, 23; August 2–3, 6–7, 9, 11, 13, 1950. Nakasone Yasuhiro, "Sōri Daijin no Tsumori" (1950), SMH. Nakasone Yasuhiro, "Jieiryoku no Seijiteki Mondaiten to Zaiseiteki Genkaiten" (February 8, 1951), in Ōta Katsurō and Ōta Chieko, eds., *Nakasone Yasuhiro Daigishi Shiryōshū (Sono 54) Denki Kankei Shiryōshuū*, 37–38, NDL. Nakasone Yasuhiro, *Nihon no Shuchō* (Tokyo: Keizai Ōrai-sha, 1954), 277–330. Nakasone, *Nihon no Furontia*, 165–67. Nakasone, *Seiji to Jinsei*, 126–35, 351–71. Nakasone Yasuhiro, *Sengo Seiji* (Tokyo: Yomiuri Shimbun, 2005). Nakasone, *Nihon no Sōri-gaku*, 28–34. Nakasone, *Sengo Seiji*, 15. Nakasone, *Nakasone Yasuhiro ga Kataru*, 71–74, 78, 101. Nakasone, *Tenchi Ujō*, 66–75, 97, 105, 117–18, 128, 138–43, 184. Kitamura Tokutarō, *Kitamura Tokutarō Zuisōshū* (Tokyo: Gendai-sha, 1959), 39. Ashida 3:186, 284, 375–77, 382, 413, 415, 418, 443–44, 457, 481, 506, 513, 568. Nishiyama Sen, "Omomi Motsu 'Taiwa no Rekishi,'" *Nikkei Bijinesu* (August 1, 1994), 5. Nishizumi Tetsu, ed., *Kitamura Tokutarō Danron-hen* (Nagasaki: Shinwa Ginkō Furusato Shinkō Kikin, 2002), 36–39, 325–41.

8 Letter from Nakasone to Ashida (January 30, 1951), "Ashida Hitoshi Kankei Bunsho," Shokan no Bu 92, NDL. Photograph of Hoshina Kishirō, Ōi Atsushi, Nomura Kichisaburō, and Fukudome Shigeru (from around the time of Dulles's arrival in Japan), SMH. Letter from Hoshina to Nakasone (August 24, 1953), SMH. Letter from Fukudome to Nakasone (March 20, 1960), SMH. Nakasone, *Nihon no Furontia*, 167. Nakasone, *Nakasone Yasuhiro ga Kataru*, 75–78, 110–11. James E. Auer, *Yomigaeru Nihon Kaigun*, trans. Sen'o Sadao (Tokyo: Jiji Tsūshin-sha, 1972), 2:54. Ashida 7:417–18. Nakajima Shingo, *Sengo Nihon no Bōei Seisaku – "Yoshida Rosen" o Meguru Seiji/Gaikō/Gunji* (Tokyo: Keio University, 2006), 61. Todaka Kazushige, ed., *Shōgenroku Kaigun Hanseikai* (Tokyo: PHP Kenkyūjo, 2009), 382. Shibayama Futoshi, *Nihon Saigunbi e no Michi – 1945-1954-Nen* (Tokyo: Minerva Shobō, 2010), 387, 481, 692. Yajima Akira, "Sengo Nihon ni Okeru Saigunbiron no Rinen to Sono Kigen – 'Shin Gaikō' Ronsha Ashida Hitoshi no Senzen/Senchū/Sengo" (Osaka University doctoral dissertation, 2013), 120, 124.

9 "Budget Committee Minutes" (January 31, 1952). Nakasone, *Nihon no Furontia*, 169–70. Asahi Shimbun Shuzai-han, *Sensō Sekinin to Tsuitō* (Tokyo: Asahi Shimbun, 2006), 126–28. Itō Yukio, *Shōwa Tennō-den* (Tokyo: Bunshun Bunko, 2014), 17–21, 523–24, 528–29, 555–56.

10 *Asahi Shimbun*, November 24, 1952. Nakasone, *Nihon no Furontia*, 173–74. Nakasone, *Seiji to Jinsei*, 137-39. Nakasone, *Nakasone Yasuhiro ga Kataru*, 92-96. Tagawa Seiichi, *Matsumura Kenzō to Chūgoku* (Tokyo: Yomiuri Shimbun, 1972), 12, 82–83, 126, 129–31. Matsumura Kenzō, *Kakō Getsuen – Matsumura Kenzō Bunshō*, ed. Matsumura Masanao (Tokyo: Seirin Shoin Shinsha, 1977), 291. Nakasone, *Tenchi Ujō*, 147–49. Takeda Tomoki, *Shigemitsu Mamoru to Sengo Seiji* (Tokyo: Yoshikawa Kōbunkan, 2002), 198–200. Nishizumi 337–38.

11 *Asahi Shimbun*, February 22–23, 1954 evening editions. Miyazaki Yoshimasa, *Seikai 25 Nen* (Tokyo: Yomiuri Shimbun, 1970), 141. Miyazaki Yoshimasa, *Seikai 18000 Nichi Miyazaki Nikki* (Tokyo: Gyōken Shuppankyoku, 1989), 1:330, 336. Satō Eisaku, *Satō Eisaku Nikki*, ed. Itō Takashi (Tokyo: Asahi Shimbun, 1998), 1:117, 120–21, 129, 134.

The "Young Officer" 45

12 Shigemitsu Mamoru, *Zoku Shigemitsu Mamoru Shuki*, ed. Itō Takashi, Watanabe Yukio (Tokyo: Chūō Kōron-sha, 1988), 549, 573, 618.

13 Nakasone Yasuhiro, "Gunma no Seiji Fūdoki," *Heiwaken Dayori* No. 171 (December 2007), 2, 5.

14 Fukuda Takeo, Nakasone Yasuhiro, "Senpai/Kōhai," *Jōmō Shimbun* (January 1, 1966).

15 *Asahi Shimbun*, October 3, 1952; April 21, 1953; March 1, 1955; May 24, 1958; November 22, 1960; November 23, 1963; January 31, 1967; December 29, 1969; December 12, 1972; December 7, 1976; October 9, 1979; June 24, 1980; December 20, 1983; July 8, 1986; June 9, 1998.

16 *Asahi Shimbun*, March 8, 2006.

17 National Diet Records Search System, http://kokkai.ndl.go.jp/ (Accessed on September 17, 2014). Nakasone, *Nakasone Yasuhiro ga Kataru*, 101.

18 References from this section are combined in endnote 21.

19 References from this section are combined in endnote 21.

20 References from this section are combined in endnote 21.

21 Nakasone Yasuhiro, "Jieigun Sōsetsu Yōkō-an" (May 27, 1952), in Ōta. *Nakasone Yasuhiro Daigishi Shiryōshū (Sono 54)*, 55–56. Nakasone Yasuhiro, "Gantan Sanshi," *Kaishin Shinbun* (January 1, 1954), 84. Nakasone, *Nihon no Shuchō*, 3–273, 331–65. Nakasone Yasuhiro, "Nōshuku Uran Kyōtei ni tsuite," *Yomiuri Shimbun* (June 3, 1955). Nakasone Yasuhiro, "'Aoi Hi' Kisou Orinppiku – Genshiryoku Kokusai Kaigi Shusseki ni Sai shite," *Yomiuri Shimbun* (August 6, 1955). Nakasone Yasuhiro, "Nihon ni Okeru Genshiryoku Seisaku," *Kokusai Seiji* No. 2 (1957), 145–52. Nakasone Yasuhiro, "Genshiryoku Kaihatsu e no Junbi," in Genshiryoku Kaihatsu Jūnen-shi Hensan Iinkai, ed., *Genshiryoku Kaihatsu Jūnen-shi* (Tokyo: Nihon Genshiryoku Sangyō Kaigi, 1965), 26–27. Nakasone, *Nihon no Furontia*, 175–76. Nakasone, *Seiji to Jinsei*, 142–46, 164–75, 183–88. Nakasone, *Rīdā no* Jōken, 65–67. Nakasone. *Jiseiroku*, 42–46. Nakasone, *Hoshu no Yuigon*, 59–61. Nakasone, *Nakasone Yasuhiro ga Kataru*, 102–09, 238, 591–604, 644–45. Letter from Henry A. Kissinger to Yasuhiro Nakasone (May 20, 1953) in Ōta, *Nakasone Yasuhiro Daigishi Shiryōshū (Sono 22)*, 1:102. Nakasone Yasuhiro, "The Problems of Japanese Democracy: Text of a Speech at the International Seminar Forum," Harvard University (July 30, 1953), "Yabe Teiji Kankei Bunsho," 1–177, National Graduate Institute for Policy Studies Library. Memorandum of Conversation between Robertson, Nakasone, Shuji Maki, Franklin Hawley (September 25, 1953), Lot File 55d388, Box 6, RG59, NA. Letter from Ashida Hitoshi to Nakasone (September 3, 1953), SMH. Letter from Nakasone to Tokutomi (August 6, 1955), SMH. Nakasone Yasuhiro, "Ze ka Hi ka 'Nichibei Genshiryoku Kyōtei,'" *Asahi Shimbun*, April 16, 1955. Matsumae Shigeyoshi and Shirai Hisaya, *Matsumae Shigeyoshi Waga Shōwa-shi* (Tokyo: Asahi Shimbun, 1987), 224–27. Shimamura Takehisa, "Genshiryoku Gōdō Iinkai Yonnin no Samurai," in "Matsumae Shigeyoshi Sono Seiji Katsudō" Hensan Iinkai, ed., *Matsumae Shigeyoshi Sono Seiji Katsudō Dai Nikan Furoku* (Tokyo: Tokai University, 1989), 6. Miyazaki, *Seikai 18000 Nichi*, 1:293–94, 299, 301, 487. Nagaike Masanao, *Bunkyō no Hata o Agete – Sakata Michita-sho* (Tokyo: Nishi Nihon Shimbun, 1992), 28. Nakasone, *Tenchi Ujō*, 150–52, 166–72. Haruna Mikio, *Himitsu no Fairu – CIA no Tainichi Kōsaku* (Tokyo: Shinchō Bunko, 2003), 2:432–41. Ikeda Shintarō, *Nichibei Dōmei no Seiji-shi – Arison Chūnichi Taishi to '1955-Nen Seidō' no Seiritsu* (Tokyo: Kokusai Shoin, 2004), 76. Arima Tetsuo, *Genpatsu-Shōriki-CIA – Himitsu Bunsho de Yomu Shōwa Rimen-shi* (Tokyo: Shinchō Shinsho, 2008), 44–46. Tsuchiya Yūka, "Kōhō Bunka Gaikō to shite no Genshiryoku Heiwa Riyō Kyanpēn to 1950 Nendai no Nichibei Kankei," in Takeuchi Toshitaka, ed., *Nichibei Dōmei-ron – Rekishi-Kinō-Shūhen Shokoku no Shiten* (Tokyo: Minerva Shobō, 2011), 180–209.

46   *The "Young Officer"*

Tomotsugu Shinsuke, "'Ajia Genshiryoku Sentā' Kōsō to Sono Zasetsu – Aizenhawā Seiken to Tai-Ajia Gaikō no Ichidanmen," *Kokusai Seiji* No. 163 (2011), 21. Yamazaki Masakatsu, *Nihon no Kaku Kaihatsu 1939–1955 Genbaku kara Genshiryoku e* (Tokyo: Sekibundō, 2011), 147, 153–54, 232, 234–35, 253–57, 261, 263–67. Yoshioka Hitoshi, *Shinpan Genshiryoku no Shakai-shi – Sono Nihon-teki Tenkai* (Tokyo: Asahi Shimbun, 2011), 30–31, 63, 70–73, 80, 83–84, 91, 102, 107, 196. Katō Tetsurō, "Nihon ni Okeru 'Genshiryoku no Heiwa Riyō' no Shuppatsu – Genpatsu Dōnyū-ki ni Okeru Nakasone Yasuhiro no Seiryaku to Yakuwari," in Katō Tetsurō and Ikawa Mitsuo, eds., *Genshiryoku to Reisen – Nihon to Ajia no Genpatsu Dōnyū* (Tokyo: Kaden-sha, 2013), 15–53. Chūnichi Shimbun Shakai-bu, ed., *Nichibei Dōmei to Genpatsu – Kakusareta Kaku no Sengo-shi* (Nagoya: Chūnichi Shimbun, 2013), 50–51, 66–68, 85–86, 101–30, 137, 174–75. Lee Hyeon-ung, *Genshiryoku o Meguru "Nichibei Kyōryoku" no Keisei to Teichaku 1953-1958* (Tokyo: Ryūkei Shosha, 2013), 19, 96, 120–22. Ōta Masakatsu, *Nichibei "Kaku" Dōmei – Genbaku, Kaku no Kasa, Fukushima* (Tokyo: Iwanami Shinsho, 2014), 14, 134, 138–39, 218. Kurosaki Akira, "Beikoku no 'Heiwa no tame no Genshiryoku' Seisaku e no Nihon no Butsurigakusha no Taiō, 1952–1955-Nen – Reisen to Genshiryoku o Meguru Nichibei Kankei to Genshiryoku o Meguru Nichibei Kankei no Keisei ni Kan suru Ikkōsatsu," *Dōjidai Shigakkai* No. 7 (2014), 63–64, 70. For more on Nakasone's interactions with Kissinger, see: Ishii Osamu, Gabe Masaaki, and Miyazato Seigen, eds. *Amerika Gasshūkoku Tainichi Seisaku Bunsho Shūsei* (Tokyo: Kashiwa Shobō, 2003), 13:3, 29, 24:3 133–47.

22 Masuda Hiroshi, *Ishibashi Tanzan* (Tokyo: Chūkō Shinsho, 1995), 191–92. Ishibashi Tanzan, *Ishibashi Tanzan Nikki – Shōwa 20-31 Nen*, ed. Ishibashi Tan'ichi, Itō Takashi (Tokyo: Misuzu Shobō, 2001), 2:646, 704.

23 Letter from Kimura Tokutarō (August 14, 1953), SMH. Letter from Sakurauchi Yoshio to Nakasone (September 24, 1953), SMH. Nakasone, *Sengo Seiji*, 20–21. Nakasone, *Nakasone Yasuhiro ga Kataru*, 96–101, 112–13. Nakasone, *Tenchi Ujō*, 129–30.

24 Shigemitsu, 644, 670–71.

25 The letter was dated April 24, 1954. Ōta Katsurō and Ōta Chieko, eds., *Nakasone Yasuhiro Daigishi Shiryōshū (Sono 25) Takuetsu shita Gaikō Shuwan no Gensen – Dai Nikkan – Dai Rokkai – Dai Jūkai ni Wataru Gaiyū no Kiseki*, NDL.

26 Nakasone, *Seiji to Jinsei*, 156–61. Nakasone, *Nakasone Yasuhiro ga Kataru*, 94–95, 115–18. Nakasone, *Tenchi Ujō*, 114–18, 130–33. Sun Pinghua, *Nihon to no 30 Nen – Nicchū Yūkō Zuisōroku*, trans. Andō Hikotarō (Tokyo: Kōdansha, 1987), 42. Xiao Xiangqian, *Eien no Rinkoku to shite*, trans. Takeuchi Minoru (Tokyo: Saimaru Shuppankai, 1997), 35–36. Liu Deyou, *Toki wa Nagarete – Nicchū Kankei Hishi 50 Nen*, trans. Wang Yadan (Tokyo: Fujiwara Shoten, 2002), 1:90, 2:629–30.

References

Arima Tetsuo. *Genpatsu-Shōriki-CIA – Himitsu Bunsho de Yomu Shōwa Rimen-shi.* Tokyo: Shinchō Shinsho, 2008.

Asahi Shimbun Shuzai-han. *Sensō Sekinin to Tsuitō.* Tokyo: Asahi Shimbun, 2006.

Ashida Hitoshi. *Ashida Hitoshi Nikki.* Edited by Shindō Eiichi. Tokyo: Iwanami Shoten, 1986.

Auer James E. *Yomigaeru Nihon Kaigun.* Translated by Sen'o Sadao. Tokyo: Jiji Tsūshin-sha, 1972.

The *"Young Officer"* 47

Chūnichi Shinbun Shakai-bu, ed. *Nichibei Dōmei to Genpatsu – Kakusareta Kaku no Sengo-shi*. Tokyo: Chūnichi Shimbun, 2013.

Fukuda Takeo and Nakasone Yasuhiro. "Senpai/Kōhai." *Jōmō Shimbun* (January 1, 1966).

Haruna Mikio. *Himitsu no Fairu – CIA no Tainichi Kōsaku*. Tokyo: Shinchō Bunko, 2003.

Hatoyama Ichirō and Hatoyama Kaoru, *Hatoyama Ichirō/Kaoru Nikki*. Edited by Itō Takashi, Suetake Yoshiya. Tokyo: Chūō Kōron Shinsha, 1999.

Hattori Ryūji. *Shidehara Kijūrō to 20 Seiki no Nihon – Gaikō to Minshushugi*. Tokyo: Yuhikaku, 2006.

Hori Shigeru. *Sengo Seiji no Oboegaki*. Tokyo: Mainichi Shimbun, 1975.

Ikeda Shintarō. *Nichibei Dōmei no Seiji-shi – Arison Chūnichi Taishi to "1955-Nen Seidō" no Seiritsu*. Tokyo: Kokusai Shoin, 2004.

Inaba Osamu. *Inaba Osamu Kaisōroku*. Niigata: Niigata Nippō Jigyō-sha Shuppan-bu, 1989.

Inaba Osamu. *Kōsei Osoru Beshi*. Tokyo: Tokyo Shimbun, 1988.

Ishibashi Tanzan. *Ishibashi Tanzan Nikki – Shōwa 20-31 Nen*. Edited by Ishibashi Tan'ichi and Itō Takashi. Tokyo: Misuzu Shobō, 2001.

Itō Yukio. *Shōwa Tennō-den*. Tokyo: Bunshun Bunko, 2014.

Iwami Takao. *Enzetsuryoku*. Tokyo: Hara Shobō, 2009.

Katō Tetsurō. "Nihon ni Okeru 'Genshiryoku no Heiwa Riyō' no Shuppatsu – Genpatsu Dōnyū-ki ni Okeru Nakasone Yasuhiro no Seiryaku to Yakuwari." In Katō Tetsurō and Ikawa Mitsuo, eds., *Genshiryoku to Reisen – Nihon to Ajia no Genpatsu Dōnyū*. Tokyo: Kaden-sha, 2013.

Kitamura Tokutarō. *Kitamura Tokutarō Zuisōshū*. Tokyo: Gendai-sha, 1959.

Komiya Hitoshi. *Jiyū Minshu-tō no Tanjō – Sōsai Kōsen to Soshiki Seitō-ron*. Tokyo: Bokutaku-sha, 2010.

Kurosaki Akira. "Beikoku no 'Heiwa no tame no Genshiryoku' Seisaku e no Nihon no Butsurigakusha no Taiō, 1952-1955-Nen – Reisen to Genshiryoku o Meguru Nichibei Kankei to Genshiryoku o Meguru Nichibei Kankei no Keisei ni Kan suru Ikkōsatsu." *Dōjidai Shigakkai* No. 7 (2014).

Lee Hyeon-ung. *Genshiryoku o Meguru "Nichibei Kyōryoku" no Keisei to Teichaku 1953–1958*. Tokyo: Ryūkei Shosha, 2013.

Liu Deyou. *Toki wa Nagarete – Nicchū Kankei Hishi 50 Nen*. Translated by Wang Yadan. Tokyo: Fujiwara Shoten, 2002.

Masuda Hiroshi. *Ishibashi Tanzan*. Tokyo: Chūkō Shinsho, 1995.

Matsumae Shigeyoshi, Shirai Hisaya. *Matsumae Shigeyoshi Waga Shōwa-shi*. Tokyo: Asahi Shimbun, 1987.

Matsumura Kenzō. *Kakō Getsuen – Matsumura Kenzō Bunshō*. Edited by Matsumura Masanao. Tokyo: Seirin Shoin Shinsha, 1977.

Miyazaki Yoshimasa. *Seikai 25 Nen*. Tokyo: Yomiuri Shimbun, 1970.

Miyazaki Yoshimasa. *Seikai 18000 Nichi Miyazaki Nikki*. Tokyo: Gyōken Shuppankyoku, 1989.

Nagaike Masanao. *Bunkyō no Hata o Agete – Sakata Michita-sho*. Tokyo: Nishi Nihon Shimbun, 1992.

Nakajima Shingo. *Sengo Nihon no Bōei Seisaku – "Yoshida Rosen" o Meguru Seiji/Gaikō/Gunji*. Tokyo: Keio University, 2006.

Nakasone Yasuhiro. "'Aoi Hi' Kisou Orinppiku – Genshiryoku Kokusai Kaigi Shusseki ni Sai shite." *Yomiuri Shimbun* (August 6, 1955).

48   *The "Young Officer"*

Nakasone Yasuhiro. "Genshiryoku Kaihatsu e no Junbi." In Genshiryoku Kaihatsu Jūnen-shi Hensan Iinkai, ed., *Genshiryoku Kaihatsu Jūnen-shi.* Tokyo: Nihon Genshiryoku Sangyō Kaigi, 1965.

Nakasone Yasuhiro. "Gunma no Seiji Fūdoki." *Heiwaken Dayori* No. 171 (December 2007).

Nakasone Yasuhiro. *Hoshu no Yuigon.* Tokyo: Kadokawa one Tēma 21, 2010.

Nakasone Yasuhiro. *Jiseiroku – Rekishi Hōtei no Hikoku to shite.* Tokyo: Shinchōsha, 2004.

Nakasone Yasuhiro. *Nakasone Yasuhiro ga Kataru Sengo Nihon Gaikō.* Edited by Nakashima Takuma, Hattori Ryūji, Noboru Amiko, Wakatsuki Hidekazu, Michishita Narushige, Kusunoki Ayako, and Segawa Takao. Tokyo: Shinchōsha, 2012.

Nakasone Yasuhiro. "Nihon ni Okeru Genshiryoku Seisaku." *Kokusai Seiji* No. 2 (1957).

Nakasone Yasuhiro. *Nihon no Furontia.* Tokyo: Tsunebunsha, 1966.

Nakasone Yasuhiro. *Nihon no Shuchō.* Tokyo: Keizai Ōrai-sha, 1954.

Nakasone Yasuhiro. *Nihon no Sōri-gaku.* Tokyo: PHP Shinsho, 2004.

Nakasone Yasuhiro. "Nōshuku Uran Kyōtei ni tsuite." *Yomiuri Shimbun* (June 3, 1955).

Nakasone Yasuhiro. "Ōbei Tayori." *Jōmō Shimbun* (June 25–26; July 14–16, 18–20, 23; August 2–3, 6–7, 9, 11, 13, 1950).

Nakasone Yasuhiro. *Rīdā no Jōken.* Tokyo: Fusō-sha, 1997.

Nakasone Yasuhiro. *Seiji to Jinsei – Nakasone Yasuhiro Kaikoroku.* Tokyo: Kōdansha, 1992.

Nakasone Yasuhiro. *Seizan Jōunpo – Nakasone Yasuhiro Taidan-shū.* Tokyo: Mainichi Shimbun, 2012.

Nakasone Yasuhiro. *Sengo Seiji.* Tokyo: Yomiuri Shimbun, 2005.

Nakasone Yasuhiro. *Shūsei Shihonshugi to Shakai Rentei Shugi.* Tokyo: Ichiyō-sha, 1947.

Nakasone Yasuhiro, Itō Takashi, and Satō Seiburō. *Tenchi Ujō – Gojū Nen no Sengo Seiji o Kataru.* Tokyo: Bungei Shunjū, 1996.

Nishiyama Sen. "Omomi Motsu 'Taiwa no Rekishi.'" *Nikkei Bijinesu* (August 1, 1994).

Nishizumi Tetsu, ed. *Kitamura Tokutarō Danron-hen.* Nagasaki: Shinwa Ginkō Furusato Shinkō Kikin, 2002.

Ōta Masakatsu. *Nichibei "Kaku" Dōmei – Genbaku, Kaku no Kasa, Fukushima.* Tokyo: Iwanami Shinsho, 2014.

Sakurauchi Yoshio. "Watashi no Rirekisho 15." *Nihon Keizai Shimbun* (January 16, 1994).

Satō Eisaku. *Satō Eisaku Nikki.* Edited by Itō Takashi. Tokyo: Asahi Shimbun, 1997.

Shibayama Futoshi. *Nihon Saigunbi e no Michi – 1945-1954-Nen.* Tokyo: Minerva Shobō, 2010.

Shigemitsu Mamoru. *Zoku Shigemitsu Mamoru Shuki.* Edited by Itō Takashi and Watanabe Yukio. Tokyo: Chūō Kōron-sha, 1988.

Shimamura Takehisa. "Genshiryoku Gōdō Iinkai Yonnin no Samurai." In Matsumae Shigeyoshi Sono Seiji Katsudō and Hensan Iinkai, eds., *Matsumae Shigeyoshi Sono Seiji Katsudō Dai Nikan Furoku.* Tokyo: Tokai University, 1989.

Sun Pinghua. *Nihon to no 30 Nen – Nicchū Yūkō Zuisōroku.* Translated by Andō Hikotarō. Tokyo: Kōdansha, 1987.

Tagawa Seiichi. *Matsumura Kenzō to Chūgoku.* Tokyo: Yomiuri Shimbun, 1972.

The *"Young Officer"* 49

Takeda Tomoki. *Shigemitsu Mamoru to Sengo Seiji*. Tokyo: Yoshikawa Kōbunkan, 2002.

Todaka Kazushige, ed. *Shōgenroku Kaigun Hanseikai*. Tokyo: PHP Kenkyūjo, 2009.

Tomotsugu Shinsuke. "'Ajia Genshiryoku Sentā' Kōsō to Sono Zasetsu – Aizenhawā Seiken to Tai-Ajia Gaikō no Ichidanmen." *Kokusai Seiji* No. 163 (2011).

Tsuchiya Yūka. "Kōhō Bunka Gaikō to shite no Genshiryoku Heiwa Riyō Kyanpēn to 1950 Nendai no Nichibei Kankei." In Takeuchi Toshitaka, ed., *Nichibei Dōmeiron – Rekishi-Kinō-Shūhen Shokoku no Shiten*. Tokyo: Minerva Shobō, 2011.

Xiao Xiangqian. *Eien no Rinkoku to shite*. Translated by Takeuchi Minoru. Tokyo: Saimaru Shuppankai, 1997.

Yajima Akira. "Sengo Nihon ni Okeru Saigunbiron no Rinen to Sono Kigen – 'Shin Gaikō' Ronsha Ashida Hitoshi no Senzen/Senchū/Sengo." Osaka University doctoral dissertation, 2013.

Yamasaki Taku. *2010-Nen Nihon Genjitsu*. Tokyo: Daiyamondo-sha, 1999.

Yamazaki Masakatsu. *Nihon no Kaku Kaihatsu 1939–1955 Genbaku kara Genshiryoku e*. Tokyo: Sekibundō, 2011.

Yoshioka Hitoshi. *Shinpan Genshiryoku no Shakai-shi – Sono Nihon-teki Tenkai*. Tokyo: Asahi Shimbun, 2011.

4 The Conservative Merger and Nakasone's First Cabinet Position

Director-General of the Science and Technology Agency under Kishi

From the Japan Democratic Party to the Liberal Democratic Party

After Nakasone's return from Hong Kong on August 10, 1954, efforts began within the Reform Party to create a new party through a merger with elements of the Liberal Party, including Hatoyama Ichirō's faction. Nakasone remained steadfast in his opposition to Yoshida and tried to have members of the Liberal Party mainstream, like Ikeda Hayato and Satō Eisaku, excluded from the merger.

As this was going on, Ashida Hitoshi contacted Ikeda and sought to have him look after Araki Masuo, Kojima Tetsuzō, and Arita Kiichi, members of his faction in the Reform Party. Nakasone and Kawasaki Hideji attacked him at the November 13 meeting of the Reform Party's central committee after learning of this.

According to Ashida's diary, "I had lunch with my comrades Araki, Kojima, and Arita, and they warned me that the reform faction was boasting about how they were going to denounce me at today's central committee meeting. They asked me not to get angry. I then attended the meeting from 2 at the Diet. [...] Kawasaki Hideji said that I had violated party policy and asked me three or four questions. Then Nakasone and Yoshida [Sei] from Yokohama piled on."

Nakasone may have forcefully pushed for making Ashida president at the time of the formation of the Democratic Party, and the two men may have agreed on rearmament, but they were now estranged.

Nakasone sought to lay the groundwork for a government that could take the place of Yoshida, with Hatoyama in mind as president of the new party. He wrote years later that he had "worked hard with the factions of Hatoyama Ichirō, Miki Bukichi, Kōno Ichirō, and Kishi Nobusuke on the creation of a new party through a merger with the Reform Party."

But while he listed Hatoyama, Miki, Kōno, and Kishi as partners in this effort, Kishi's goal was different from his. Kishi had his eye set on a total merger of all the conservatives into a new conservative party and the dissolution of both the Liberal and Reform parties.

DOI: 10.4324/9781003351931-5

The Conservative Merger and Nakasone's First Cabinet Position   51

According to Kishi, "The Reform Party was divided between a group including Matsumura Kenzō, Miki Takeo, and Nakasone Yasuhiro and one including Ashida Hitoshi and Chiba Saburō. The thinking of the latter group was closer to my own. While the first group put on reformist airs, referring to themselves as the 'faction in favor of saving the nation through the creation of a new party,' they were fundamentally proponents of having two conservative parties. Their basic goal was carrying out a struggle for leadership between the Liberal and Reform parties, toppling Yoshida, and gaining control of the government. This is why they were noncommittal when the opportunity provided by the new party movement arrived."

As shown by Kishi's description of Nakasone as being a "proponent of having two conservative parties," the key difference between the two men was that Nakasone opposed any merger with Yoshida's Liberal Party into a single party.[1]

The Formation of the Hatoyama Government

The new conservative party under Hatoyama that Nakasone had envisioned arrived on November 24, 1954: the Japan Democratic Party. The major party posts went to Shigemitsu Mamoru (vice-president), Kishi (secretary-general), Miki Bukichi (General Council chairman), and Matsumura Kenzō (PRC chairman). Ishibashi, Ashida, and Ōasa Tadao were named senior councilors. Kōno Ichirō also joined the new party, meaning that Hatoyama, Nakasone, and Kōno were together in the same party for the first time.

The Yoshida government, backed into a corner by this development, resigned en masse, leading to the formation of the Hatoyama government on December 10. After six years and two months in the opposition, Nakasone now once again belonged to the government party. He was named head of the new party's Party Organization Bureau. His main role in this position was organizing the party's electoral strategy.

After the Japan Democratic Party came in first in the February 27, 1955 general election, Nakasone became deputy secretary-general. Hatoyama's confidante Miki Bukichi called for the party to merge with the Liberal Party, but Nakasone remained opposed under the rationale that the option for a conservative coalition should be left open. But after the left and right Socialists merged on October 13 to form a unified Socialist Party, the conservatives followed suit. The Liberal Democratic Party (LDP) was born on November 15.

For Nakasone, the conservative merger meant joining with politicians like Ikeda, Ōhira, and Miyazawa Kiichi. It also meant that he once again belonged to the same party as Tanaka Kakuei. Satō did not immediately join the LDP, although he would do so immediately before the formation of the Kishi government. Given his opposition to Yoshida, it is not difficult to

52 *The Conservative Merger and Nakasone's First Cabinet Position*

imagine Nakasone's discomfort with Ikeda and Satō, the "honor students of the Yoshida school."

According to Nakasone, he "couldn't believe that, just as we had finally created the Hatoyama Democratic Party with which to stand against the Yoshida Liberal Party, the parties merged." But at the same time, he accepted that, with the Socialist merger, "we wouldn't have been able to compete unless the conservatives also united."[2]

Forming His Theory for an Autonomous Constitutional System

In September 1955, shortly before the conservative merger, Nakasone had the Constitutional Research Group (Kenpō Chōsa-kai) release a pamphlet entitled "The Fundamental Nature of an Autonomous Constitution: Piercing the Errors of the Defenders of the Current Constitution."

The Constitutional Research Group was an organization that Nakasone had created with Yabe Teiji, Inaba Osamu, Utsunomiya Tokuma, Akagi Munenori, Sugihara Arata, Kōyama Iwao, and others. Yabe had become president of Takushoku University; Inaba, Utsunomiya, and Akagi were members of the House of Representatives; Sugihara was in the House of Councillors; and Kōyama was a professor at Kanagawa University. The group's office was located in Ginza.

Nakasone quoted from sources like Ashida's diary in the pamphlet and wrote that "This constitution was not created by Japanese. The draft was written by GHQ with even the smallest amendments by the Diet requiring GHQ approval; no major amendments were permitted. We had to swallow our tears and adopt it under threat of foreign abolition of the emperor system."

Nakasone tied the continued American military presence in Japan to the constitution, asserting that "So long as a foreign military continues to be stationed here, the autonomy of the Japanese government will be limited, foreign nations will have a strong voice in our defense, and the possibility of Japan being dragged into unforeseen matters will remain. [...] It will be quite difficult for a spirited defense to be mustered under any constitution that is vague when it comes to the national defense, as the current one is." He also argued that constitutional provisions "containing proactive ideas for the promotion of the public welfare should be expanded."[3]

One of Nakasone's supporters at this time was Tokutomi Sōho, who he viewed as a mentor. In a letter to Nakasone, Tokutomi cheered him on, writing that "constitutional revision is the most important matter for the future of Japan." Nakasone responded that "the constitution should be written by the youth of today, those who will live in the next era," and that "I am ashamed that our efforts are insufficient."[4]

On April 13, 1956, Nakasone unveiled the "Constitutional Revision Song" at the Takarazuka Theater in Tokyo. The song's lyrics had been written by him, and he had had the musician Akemoto Kyōsei put them to music:

The Conservative Merger and Nakasone's First Cabinet Position   53

Before a packed crowd, the singer Anzai Aiko passionately sang:

Ah, defeated in war
the enemy's armies stationed here
an occupation constitution enforced
in the name of peaceful democracy
the dissolution of our homeland planned
this was six months after the end of the war

Ordered by the occupation forces
the Emperor's status not guaranteed
unless this constitution was adopted
swallowing their tears, the people
lamenting their nation's future
accepted Mac's constitution

Ten long years
freedom still far away
we should put forth a constitution
establish the country's foundation
fulfill our duty to history
our bosoms bursting with determination

The song was released as a single by Victor, and Nakasone had a copy sent to Hatoyama. He is said to have earned 3,000 yen in royalties for the song. It received little coverage in major newspapers, however, and does not seem to have had any major impact. While one reader did submit a letter to the *Asahi Shimbun* regarding the song, it was critical: "it is hard for me to understand on what grounds the writer of these lyrics wrote them, what his feelings were as he did so, and what kind of complaints he had."[5]

Restoration of Relations with the Soviet Union – Nakasone's Disruptive Speech

The Hatoyama government had made restoring relations with the Soviet Union the primary task on its agenda, and Hatoyama signed the Soviet-Japanese Joint Declaration in Moscow on October 19, 1956, which legally ended the state of war between the two countries. Hatoyama returned home via Hawaii. As Kōno believed that Hatoyama should now retire, he ordered Nakasone to go meet Hatoyama in Hawaii and convince him to do so.

Kōno believed that Kishi would be Hatoyama's successor as prime minister. According to what Nakasone learned from Kōno, he had made an agreement with Kishi prior to the formation of the LDP under which Kishi would support Hatoyama as party president in exchange for Kōno's support as Hatoyama's successor.

Nakasone thus traveled to Hawaii and met with Hatoyama accompanied by Deputy Chief Cabinet Secretary Tanaka Eiichi. Nakasone was normally

54 *The Conservative Merger and Nakasone's First Cabinet Position*

fearless, but this one occasion proved to be different. He was thirty-five years younger than Hatoyama.

He kept looking for a proper occasion in which to broach the subject to Hatoyama but could not bring himself to speak the words "retirement." Finally, at breakfast, he was able to make himself say, "Hatoyama-sensei, you've secured a major accomplishment. So maybe, moving forward, you should focus on taking care of your health ..."

Despite the indirectness, Hatoyama immediately grasped the intent behind the words. According to Nakasone, Hatoyama remained completely silent but "made a face that showed how very disagreeable he found the idea."[6]

How did Nakasone see things playing out for Japan in the wake of the joint declaration? His views can be seen in an article – "Remove the San Francisco Plaster" – that he published in the Seiunjuku's magazine *Seiun* after his return to Japan. In it, he brought up the US-Japan security treaty and territorial issues:

> During this time of healing of the causes of the second great global war, this time of moves to correct the ugly compromises made by the United States and the Soviet Union, we, the Japanese people, also naturally find ourselves in a position where we must act to rectify the evils spawned by the ending of the Second World War: the security treaty and the territorial issues. To put things another way, while we wear the San Francisco plaster, the Japanese body is immobilized. We need to remove it immediately, return ourselves to a free and healthy state, and then embark upon cooperation with the United States on new, equal terms.[7]

On November 17, Nakasone addressed the restoration of relations with the Soviet Union on the floor of the House of Representatives. The speech began by noting that the idea that a comprehensive peace should have been reached at the San Francisco peace conference had never enjoyed the support of the Japanese people, and he criticized the Soviet Union's failure to return the Northern Territories (four Soviet-occupied islands near Hokkaido) to Japan as "truly regrettable."

The "comprehensive peace" (*zenmen kōwa*) argument mentioned here, which had largely been supported by the Left, had held that Japan should only agree to a peace treaty if it was supported by all of the warring parties, including the USSR and China. The Japanese government under Yoshida had instead followed a "separate peace" (*tandoku kōwa*) policy under which Japan signed the Treaty of San Francisco and then pursued separate peace treaties with any remaining parties.

At one point in the speech, Nakasone likened communism to a germ, causing members of the Socialist and Communist parties – those who had called for a comprehensive peace – to stand and jeer. Members of the opposition surrounded his podium, and the scene became so chaotic that he could no longer be heard. Holding the microphone close to his face, Nakasone

The Conservative Merger and Nakasone's First Cabinet Position   55

shouted into it. His face was dripping with sweat when the speech – fifty minutes long – finally came to an end.

Incensed, the opposition demanded that the speech be stricken from the Diet record on the grounds that it had slandered the Soviet Union and, by criticizing a comprehensive peace, had been dismissive of their position. Nakasone opposed having his speech stricken, but the LDP leadership, concerned that the matter might delay ratification of the joint declaration, agreed to the measure.

Afterwards, Nakasone contacted Shōriki Matsutarō, president of the Yomiuri Shimbun, and arranged for the paper to print his speech in full. While it had been erased from the Diet record, it thus became more well-known among the public than it likely would have otherwise.[8]

San'enshugi

The Hatoyama made Japanese admission to the United Nations its last hurrah, resigning en masse on December 20, 1956. It is likely that Hatoyama had already had resignation on his mind when Nakasone had been dispatched to talk to him, and no persuasion had been necessary.

It was around this time that Nakasone adopted the practice of writing three words in his notebook at the beginning of each year: *ketsuen, son'en,* and *zuien*. These were the three components of *san'enshugi,* a term that Nakasone coined himself that could be loosely translated as "the three principles of connections":

    ketsuen: make connections with others
    son'en: always respect those connections
    zuien: act in accordance with those connections

He referred to this as "my lifelong motto" and explained:

> Of all the people you know – including relatives, former classmates, work colleagues, people in your neighborhood, etc. – there will only be maybe sixty or seventy at the most with whom you have a close relationship. As we interact with them, our life rushes past. I believe that, at least for the brief time we're here, we should be on good terms with them, so that when it comes time to say our "final goodbye," we can do so with fond thoughts. Because we respected the connections we had.

Nakasone had become fond of Zen Buddhism shortly after graduating from college. But although he showed a deep interest in Buddhism and Christianity, this never reached the level of believing in any particular religion. He later recalled, "I seem to be lacking in the opportunity and cultivation needed to believe in any particular existing religion. I arrogantly hold to reason and lack in piety."[9]

56   *The Conservative Merger and Nakasone's First Cabinet Position*

The Kōno Faction's Shunjūkai

After the formation of the LDP, Nakasone joined the faction of Kōno Ichirō, formally known as the Shunjūkai. The Kōno, Ōno, Ishibashi, and Miki/Matsumura factions were known as the LDP's "party politician" factions because they contained a large number of prewar politicians. In contrast, the Kishi, Ikeda, and Satō factions were known as the "bureaucratic" factions because of their large number of former bureaucrats. Ishii Mitsujirō's faction existed in the neutral ground between the two factional camps.

In addition to those coming from the former Reform Party like Nakasone, Kitamura Tokutarō, Sakurauchi Yoshio, Sonoda Sunao, and Inaba Osamu, the Kōno faction also included members like Nakamura Umekichi of the Japan Liberal Party, former businessman Takasaki Tatsunosuke, and Matsumoto Shun'ichi, former ambassador to the UK.

The Kōno faction was part of the LDP mainstream (factions supporting the government), with Kōno and Takasaki belonging to the Hatoyama government as agricultural minister and director-general of the EPA, respectively.

The Shunjūkai was notable for its diversity. Watanabe Tsuneo of the Yomiuri Shimbun explained, "Their unifying characteristic is that they had all reputations as the fighting men of the political world, people ready to comment on anything and everything. To put it in a positive way, they were thinkers who were ready to take action. It was a wonder that such a disparate group was able to come together so well into a single group."

Kōno was a dominating presence, even among the Shunjūkai's large number of colorful characters. Nakasone said that he was one of the few politicians to ever intimidate him: "There were only two men who I would feel intimidated by if I saw them coming the other way as I walked down the halls of the Diet. One was Yoshida Shigeru, and the other was Kōno Ichirō. […] It is a well-known fact that those two men did not get along, and I feel that it is extremely unfortunate for the nation of Japan that that was the case."

When Yabe Teiji asked him why he had chosen to join the Kōno faction, Nakasone reportedly replied that "It's not because I respect Kōno Ichirō as a politician. But you need power in politics, and I'm using his power."[10]

Kōno had high expectations for Nakasone and often took him with him on the campaign trail along with Nakamura Umekichi, one of his former comrades from the Japan Liberal Party. Nakasone would serve as the opening act at events, followed by Nakamura and, finally, Kōno. Nakasone was a gifted speaker and would draw in listeners. Kōno had a low voice and his speeches would frequently come across as lifeless even when well-written.

It was Nakasone who came away from these events with increased popularity, to the extent that Nakamura asked him (through his secretary) to tone things down a little when appearing with Kōno.

Nakasone was a naturally gift speaker, but his success was not entirely due to talent. He would also buy collections of speeches by figures like

The Conservative Merger and Nakasone's First Cabinet Position   57

Nakano Seigō and Nagai Ryūtarō (famous orators of the prewar period) and study them.[11]

From Ishibashi to Kishi

The Kōno faction decided to throw its support behind Kishi Nobusuke in the December 14, 1956 LDP presidential election, but Nakasone cast his vote for Ishibashi Tanzan, the ultimate winner. He later explained his rationale for going against his faction: "I had served in the Great East Asian War and lost many subordinates to it. My younger brother had died in the war. For those reasons, I thought it still premature to make Kishi prime minister. I felt it was more reasonable to vote for Ishibashi Tanzan, who had fought against the military. So, I did so. [My decision here] would do a great deal to slow my later advancement [in the party]."

Kishi had supported the declaration of war on the United States as minister of commerce and industry in the Tōjō Hideki government, and he had been held on suspicion of class A war crimes during the Occupation (although he was ultimately released without being charged).

The Ishibashi government was formed on December 23 but would last only a mere sixty-five days before Ishibashi had to step down due to poor health. It was the second-shortest lived government in Japanese history, following Prince Higashikuni's fifty-four days in office.

Ishibashi was replaced by Kishi, who established his government on February 25, 1957. According to Nakasone, his decision to vote for Ishibashi over Kishi in the previous election led to him "not being treated well at the beginning of the Kishi government." By comparison, after Kishi reorganized his cabinet on July 10, Tanaka Kakuei would enter the cabinet for the first time as postal minister at the young age of thirty-nine.[12]

Visits to Asia and Africa

Nakasone was appointed LDP deputy secretary-general and to the cabinet's Constitutional Research Committee. While Kishi would become known for his efforts revising the US-Japan security treaty, he decided to begin his government by solidifying his position in Asia. He thus chose to make Southeast and South Asia the destination for his first foreign trip, beginning with Burma. Nakasone accompanied him as part of a Diet delegation.

Nakasone would visit Burma, India, Pakistan, Iran, Iraq, Lebanon, Syria, Egypt, Austria, Yugoslavia, Hungary, Turkey, Britain, Greece, Israel, Ceylon, Singapore, Indonesia, Hong Kong, and Taiwan from May 20 to July 13, 1957, a lengthy trip of two months that would be unthinkable for a politician today.

Nakasone and the other Diet members accompanied Kishi as he met with Nehru at the Indian prime minister's office on May 23. After Kishi finished his greeting, Nakasone told Nehru that "the youth of Japan would greatly welcome a visit to Japan by Prime Minister Nehru. They would

58 *The Conservative Merger and Nakasone's First Cabinet Position*

also like to interact with the youth of India." After Nehru nodded, he joked that "you're more famous in Japan than the prime minister is." Nehru commented that he had "been deeply impressed by the rapid rebuilding of Japan since the war."

Nakasone and Kishi went their separate ways in Pakistan, with Nakasone continuing his travels in the company of former Diet member Nakatani Takeyo and Shimonaka Yasaburō, president of the Heibonsha publishing house. Nakasone viewed the situation in Egypt under President Nasser as being of particular importance given that it "occupies a pivotal position for world policy given its strategic location in the Middle East and possession of the Suez Canal."

He met with Nasser on June 6. Both men were thirty-nine years old, but Nasser had a significant number of grey hairs. He said of his experience shaking Nasser's hand that "it was an extremely solid, soft, and warm hand" and that the feeling "resembled that of Kōno Ichirō."

Nakasone made a proposal to Nasser: "The Japanese people support the nationalization of the Suez Canal. [...] But they do not think highly of the idea of the Aswan High Dam being built by the white people of the West. Isn't it something that should be done by our hands, the people of Asia and Africa? I ask that you have Japanese technology take on this task." President Nasser replied that it was a "very good idea."

After the meeting ended, Nakasone immediately called former EPA director-general Takasaki Tatsunosuke and told him what Nasser had said about the dam. The top three Egyptian officials involved with the dam later visited Japan, but the order would ultimately be placed with the Soviets.

Later in his travels, Nakasone visited a nuclear power plant in Britain. And in Taiwan, Chiang Kai-shek's calls for retaking mainland China made a big impression on him.

After his return home, he submitted a piece to the *Yomiuri Shimbun* in which he called for the formation of "something that could perhaps be called an Asian Internationalism League" as a means of countering the "pro-Soviet bloc." He also argued that Japan could dispel the misconceptions that accompanied Japanese economic expansion overseas by creating "joint historical research centers" in those countries. While neither of these proposals would come to pass, Nakasone's lengthy travels abroad did serve as an opportunity for him to formulate a vision for the future of Asia.[13]

Visiting Okinawa

Nakasone next turned his eyes to Okinawa, then under American administration. The Kishi government's policy was to promote assistance for Okinawan economic development, and Nakasone and Sakurauchi (who was now chairman of the House of Representatives' Foreign Relations Committee) discussed developmental and financial assistance for Okinawa with Kishi and Foreign Minister Fujiyama Aiichirō.

The Conservative Merger and Nakasone's First Cabinet Position 59

The two also visited Okinawa from July 24 to 26, 1958. While there, they discussed assistance with Deputy Chief Executive of the Government of the Ryukyu Islands Ōta Seisaku and met with Civil Administrator Burger. They also toured American military facilities.

After returning to Tokyo, Nakasone told reporters that "this was already apparent from the recent changes in the [American] leadership on Okinawa, such as the appointment of Consul General Deming, but they were friendly during our meetings and clearly stated that they would listen to the desires of the Okinawan people as they governed. So, I believe that a path [for assistance] can be opened up so long as we act reasonably."

There was no hope for a return of Okinawa to Japanese administration at the time, and as such Nakasone's visit was made in line with the Kishi government's policy of increasing assistance to and cooperation with the islands.[14]

In in his position on the Constitutional Research Committee, Nakasone repeatedly argued in favor of implementing direct election of the prime minister. He also asked former foreign minister Okazaki Katsuo and Nishimura Kumao, former director of the foreign ministry's treaty bureau, about the process through which Article 9 of the constitution and the US-Japan security treaty were drawn up.[15]

Joining the Cabinet – Director-General of the Science and Technology Agency

After Kishi reshuffled his cabinet on June 18, 1959, Nakasone was appointed director-general of the Science and Technology Agency. He was forty-one and this was his first ministerial position. He was also named chairman of the Prime Minister's Office's committee on atomic energy at this time.

According to Nakasone, "ever since the end of the war, I had consistently worked towards the development of atomic power and for the promotion of science and technology policy. Receiving this position made me feel like I was back in [the center of things]."[16] He had been elected to the Diet six times at this point, and he was conscious of the fact that Tanaka Kakuei had entered the cabinet two years earlier at the age of thirty-nine.

Nakasone had desperately wanted to be appointed to the cabinet, but the relationship between Kōno and Kishi had seriously deteriorated. Kishi had refused to appoint Kōno as LDP secretary-general, and the Kōno faction had left the party mainstream. For this reason, when it came time to reorganize his cabinet, Kishi decided to leave the decision of who to appoint from the Kōno faction to LDP Vice President Ōno Banboku.

Ōno was a major player in the party and the leader of one of the party politician factions. Unfortunately for Nakasone, he had attacked Ōno during the shipbuilding scandal while serving in the Reform Party. Ōno detested him.

But there was no way that Nakasone would be able to enter the cabinet without Ōno's support, so he reached out to him through Watanabe Tsuneo of the Yomiuri Shimbun during the runup to the cabinet reshuffle. Watanabe

60 *The Conservative Merger and Nakasone's First Cabinet Position*

was assigned to cover Ōno and thus knew both men. He agreed to help and invited Ōno to Kinryū, a restaurant in Akasaka.

Nakasone arrived and awaited Ōno beside Watanabe. When Ōno entered, he roared at Nakasone:

> Hey, Nakasone! Don't think I've forgiven you for how you attacked me in the budget committee back during the shipbuilding scandal! You said you'd stake your career on my having taken bribes.

Putting both hands on the floor in front of him, Nakasone said, "I have no excuse. I was carried away by the rashness of youth. Please forgive me."

Watanabe quickly followed up by saying that "Nakasone was in the Reform Party, part of the opposition, at the time of the shipbuilding scandal. It wouldn't be like you to hold something that someone said while they were in the opposition against them now."

Ōno's mood improved and nodded, "Yeah, you're right. Okay, I understand."

After Ōno sat down across from Nakasone, Watanabe explained that "Nakasone is in trouble. As a member of the Kōno faction, he doesn't have anyone to speak for him during the formation of the cabinet. But you are able to give a recommendation on which member of the Kōno faction should serve [in the government], right? Is there any way that you could recommend him for the cabinet?" Nakasone bowed his head.

Unsurprised by the request, Ōno readily accepted the idea, in stark contrast to his earlier attitude. "Alright, I'll put you in the cabinet." Over the course of the three men's conversation, he seemed to come to accept Nakasone. At the end, he even said, "Nakasone, you have the looks of a prime minister. You'll be prime minister in the future."

Nakasone and Watanabe were surprised by the speed at which Ōno had changed his attitude, but this kind of mental flexibility was a necessary skill for a politician. Days later, Nakasone showed Watanabe copies of prosecutorial documents related to the shipbuilding scandal, saying, "Nabe, I want you to know the truth."[17]

Science, Technology, and Space

As the Kishi government worked on revising the US-Japan security treaty, it also called for eliminating the three vices of violence, corruption, and poverty. This call for eliminating poverty can be connected to the income-doubling plan of the following Ikeda government, but – significantly for Nakasone – it also involved promoting science and technology. This connection can be seen in a round-table discussion published in the September 1959 issue of *Seisaku Geppō*, an LDP magazine.

The participants in the discussion were Nakasone, LDP Science and Technology Special Committee Chairman Kosaka Zentarō, and Kaya Seiji, president of the University of Tokyo and a member of the Science

The Conservative Merger and Nakasone's First Cabinet Position   61

and Technology Council (an advisory body to the Prime Minister's Office formed in February).

Kosaka opened the discussion by explaining how the law creating the Science and Technology Council had come about and spoke on modernizing the equipment of national research organizations. He then turned things over to Nakasone by noting that "Science and Technology Agency Director-General Nakasone has, since becoming director-general, put forward new topics related to a space program and shown special interest in the development of electronics."

Nakasone followed-up by saying that "the government is working on an important concept: a national economic plan that sets a target of doubling incomes over the next ten years. Innovation in science and technology will be a major driving force behind that effort, and the promotion of those fields thus occupies a central place in the plan. I want our policies to conform with that plan as we move forward."

It was the promising field of space development that Nakasone put the most effort into. This was an era in which US-Soviet competition had reached space, and both countries were launching probes one after another. Shortly after assuming his new position, Nakasone enthusiastically decided that "Japan will also embark on the development of artificial satellites and a space program."

Nakasone created the Preparatory Committee on the Promotion of Space Science and Technology as an advisory body to the director-general on July 10, 1959, and had it put together the Space Science and Technology Development Plan on February 4, 1960. The committee had fifteen members and included figures like Fukui Shinji, director of the University of Tokyo's Aeronautical Research Laboratory, and Meteorological Agency Director-General Wadachi Kiyoo.

Nakasone announced the space development plan with the words, "One day, a satellite bearing the Hinomaru flag will be launched." But the Science and Technology Agency's space program's focus on rocket research led to criticism from the *Asahi Shimbun* and a Science Council of Japan symposium. There were concerns that this research would also be used by the Defense Agency for the development of ballistic missiles.

Nevertheless, Nakasone continued to try to lay the groundwork for a Japanese space program, establishing the Space Development Council on May 16 under the Prime Minister's Office. While he had previously focused on atomic energy, he now put all his energy into space. He also sought assistance from the United States, but the contemporary low level of Japanese technology meant that the Americans were cold to the idea.

A major typhoon struck Japan in late September 1959, causing 5,000 dead and missing, primarily near Ise Bay. In the wake of the disaster, Nakasone formed a committee on "scientific countermeasures to typhoons" to conduct scientific research on typhoons.

Another notable act taken by Nakasone as director-general was the publication of *Steps to the Twenty-First Century*, a compilation of predictions by

62 The Conservative Merger and Nakasone's First Cabinet Position

scientists and engineers regarding how far global technology would advance by the end of the century. The book covers a wide-ranging variety of topics, including atomic energy, control of typhoons and earthquakes, sleep control, biotechnology, and space development.

The book was intended to be an introductory work that would foster an interest in science among young people. It was printed in two parts that were released on June 30 and August 5, 1960.[18]

Criticism of Kishi and the Revision of the Security Treaty

The highest priority of the Kishi government was revising the US-Japan security treaty, which it accomplished when Kishi signed a new treaty in Washington on January 19, 1960. Under the terms of the new treaty, America's obligation to protect Japan was made explicit and the prior consultation system – a process through which the US would consult with the Japanese government prior to making significant changes to its military deployments in Japan – was introduced.

The Socialist Party had attacked the prior consultation system and the treaty's definition of the "Far East" in the Diet beginning in February, but the Kishi government forced the treaty through the House of Representatives in the early hours of May 20. Eisenhower was scheduled to visit Japan on June 19 – the first visit to Japan by an American president – and Kishi wanted the treaty ratified by that date. His strong-arm tactics alarmed much of the public, and 100,000 protestors descended upon the Diet.

While Nakasone felt that "the content of the new treaty made sense and, compared to the old one, restored Japan's independence and equality in accordance with our wishes," he also believed that Eisenhower's visit would cause disorder and should be postponed.

He thus argued at the May 25 cabinet meeting that "stabilizing the political situation is the most important thing right now. The new security treaty will automatically be ratified on June 19, and it's not a good idea to have President Eisenhower visiting on that day. We cannot chase two rabbits at the same time. We should postpone the visit while we have the chance."

Looking at MITI Minister Ikeda and Finance Minister Satō, he continued: "We cannot definitively guarantee the safety of the American president and His Majesty the Emperor. If something were to happen, it would cause a major incident between the United States and Japan. We cannot allow the Emperor to become embroiled in this kind of political dispute. He must remain transcendent as a symbol."

Kishi only said that he would give "serious consideration to the matter," however. He had poured his life's blood into the treaty revision and wanted Eisenhower's visit to serve as the finishing touch. He was not inclined to look favorably on Nakasone's proposal.

Even so, Nakasone repeated his call for a delay at the May 31 cabinet meeting, noting that "the security authorities are not confident [in their

The Conservative Merger and Nakasone's First Cabinet Position 63

ability to handle the situation]" and that "if there are casualties and blood is shed, we'll be sending the message that we're willing to allow the youth of Japan to bleed for the sake of the Americans. Continuing with this is foolish. And is the US president really going to be pleased speaking in a Diet session boycotted by the Socialists?"

Kishi continued to hold firm, however, saying that "It's already been decided, so we'll move forward with the existing plan and ensure that everything goes smoothly. I want to overwhelm [the Americans] with an enthusiastic welcome."

Thus, presidential press secretary Hagerty arrived in Japan on June 10 as part of Eisenhower's advance party. His car was swarmed by protestors at Haneda Airport and he needed to be evacuated with a US military helicopter. The protests continued to escalate, with protestors breaking into the Diet compound on June 15, an incident that left a student dead. Ikeda and Satō continued to call for a hardline response at cabinet meetings despite the deteriorating situation, however.

Nakasone met with Kōno on June 16 and received permission to submit his resignation from the cabinet if the Eisenhower visit went through as scheduled. This proved unnecessary, however, as Kishi called an emergency cabinet meeting that evening and postponed the visit. The new treaty was automatically ratified on June 19 and Kishi announced his resignation following the exchange of the ratifying documents on June 23.

Kishi himself later acknowledged that Nakasone had been critical of him: "Nakasone gave me advice concerning security and other issues involving Ike's visit. I don't remember the exact dates, but I believe that he told me that […] he suspected that something was going to happen if adequate public security measures weren't taken."

Had Nakasone actually submitted his resignation, it might have dramatically worsened his relations with members of the mainstream factions like Ikeda and Satō.[19]

With the election of Ikeda to the presidency on July 14, Nakasone's first time in cabinet came to a close after thirteen months. The Kōno faction would remain outside of the mainstream during the Ikeda government, and this would mark the beginning of a period that Nakasone spent in obscurity, building his strength.

Notes

1   Kōno Ichirō, *Kōno Ichirō Jiden*, ed. Denki Kankō Iinkai (Tokyo: Tokuma Shoten, 1965), 229. Kishi Nobusuke, *Kishi Nobusuke Kaikoroku – Hoshu Gōdō to Anpo Kaitei* (Tokyo: Kōsaidō Shuppan, 1983), 120–22. Ashida Hitoshi, *Ashida Hitoshi Nikki*, ed. Shindō Eiichi (Tokyo: Iwanami Shoten, 1986), 5:300, 305–06. Inaba Osamu, *Kōsei Osoru Beshi* (Tokyo: Tokyo Shimbun, 1988), 99. Nakasone Yasuhiro, *Seiji to Jinsei – Nakasone Yasuhiro Kaikoroku* (Tokyo: Kōdansha, 1992), 181–82. Nakasone Yasuhiro, *Nakasone Yasuhiro ga Kataru Sengo Nihon Gaikō*, eds. Nakashima, et al. (Tokyo: Shinchōsha, 2012), 119–20. Nakasone Yasuhiro,

64 *The Conservative Merger and Nakasone's First Cabinet Position*

Itō Takashi, and Satō Seiburō, *Tenchi Ujō – Gojū Nen no Sengo Seiji o Kataru* (Tokyo: Bungei Shunjū, 1996), 172–75, 185–87. Hiwatari Yumi, *Sengo Seiji to Nichibei Kankei* (Tokyo: University of Tokyo, 1990), 87–88, 101. Hara Yoshihisa, *Kishi Nobusuke* (Tokyo: Iwanami Shinsho, 1995), 164. Masuda Hiroshi, *Ishibashi Tanzan* (Tokyo: Chūkō Shinsho, 1995), 193. Takeda Tomoki, *Shigemitsu Mamoru to Sengo Seiji* (Tokyo: Yoshikawa Kōbunkan, 2002), 227–28.

2 Ibid.

3 Nakasone Yasuhiro, *Jishu Kenpō no Kihonteki Seikaku – Kenpō Yōgo-ron no Ayamari o Tsuku* (Tokyo: Kenpō Chōsakai, 1955), 1–6, 74–76, 83–84, 94, 105, appendix 53. Nakasone, *Nakasone Yasuhiro ga Kataru*, 107–08. Yabe Teiji, *Yabe Teiji Nikki Keyaki no Maki*, ed. Nikki Kankōkai (Tokyo: Yomiuri Shimbun, 1974), 795. Yabe Teiji, *Yabe Teiji Nikki Momiji no Maki*, ed. Nikki Kankōkai (Tokyo: Yomiuri Shimbun, 1975), 57, 92, 134, 214, 242, 267, 460, 496.

4 Letters from Nakasone to Tokutomi (January 1954, June 5, 1954, October 1955, January 28, 1956), STM. Letter from Tokutomi to Nakasone (January 26, 1956), SMH.

5 Letter from Nakasone to Tokutomi (February 27, 1956), STM. *Asahi Shimbun*, April 6, 1956. Jishu Kenpō Kisei Giin Dōmei, "Kenpō Kaisei no Uta Minzoku Dokuritsu no Uta Happyōkai" (April 13, 1956) in Ōta Katsurō and Ōta Chieko, eds., *Nakasone Yasuhiro Daigishi Shiryōshū (Sono 54) Denki Kankei Shiryōshū*, NDL, 167–69. Miyazaki Yoshimasa, *Seikai 18000 Nichi Miyazaki Nikki* (Tokyo: Gyōken Shuppankyoku, 1989), 1:514. Nakasone, *Seiji to Jinsei*, 212–13. Nakasone Yasuhiro, *Rīdā no Jōken* (Tokyo: Kōdansha, 1992), 156–57. Nakasone Yasuhiro, *Nihon no Sōri-gaku* (Tokyo: PHP Shinsho, 2004), 74. Hatoyama Ichirō, Hatoyama Kaoru, *Hatoyama Ichirō/Kaoru Nikki, Vol. 2* (Tokyo: Chūō Kōron Shinsha, 1999), 241, 247, 265.

6 Hosokawa Ryūgen, *Otoko Degozaru Ryū no Kan* (Tokyo: Yamanote Shobō, 1981), 160–61. Ōta Katsurō and Ōta Chieko, eds., *Nakasone Yasuhiro Daigishi Shiryōshū (Sono 25) Takuetsu shita Gaikō Shuwan no Gensen Dai Nikan*, NDL, 185–201. Nakasone, *Tenchi Ujō*, 190–92. Hatoyama, 320. Murase Shin'ichi, *Shushō ni Narenakatta Otoko-tachi – Inoue Kaoru/Tokonami Takejirō/Kōno Ichirō* (Tokyo: Yoshikawa Kōbunkan, 2014), 311–12.

7 Nakasone Yasuhiro, "San Furanshisuko no Gipusu o Hazuse," *Seiun* (November 25, 1956).

8 *Yomiuri Shimbun,* November 29, 1956. Nakasone Yasuhiro, *Nihon no Furontia* (Tokyo: Tsunebunsha, 1966), 144–59. Nakasone, *Seiji to Jinsei*, 161–64. Nakasone Yasuhiro, *Sengo Seiji* (Tokyo: Yomiuri Shimbun, 2005), 25–26. Nakasone, *Nakasone Yasuhiro ga Kataru*, 125–27. Okada Haruo, *Kokkai Bakudan Otoko Okapparu Ichidaiki* (Tokyo: Gyōken Shuppankyoku, 1987), 55–59. Miyazaki, 565–66. Nakasone, *Tenchi Ujō*, 175–82. Ishibashi Masashi, *Ishibashi Masashi Kaisōroku – "55 Nen Taisei" Uchigawa kara no Shōgen* (Tokyo: Shōdensha Bunko, 2007), 89–90. Ishibashi, *Ishibashi Tanzan Nikki*, 2:834. Hatoyama, 335. Watanabe Tsuneo, *Watanabe Tsuneo Kaikoroku*, ed. Mikuriya Takashi, Itō Takashi, and Iio Jun (Tokyo: Chūō Bunko, 2007), 169–74.

9 Nakasone, *Nihon no Furontia*, 179, 264. Nakasone, *Seiji to Jinsei,* 342. Nakasone Yasuhiro, *Nihonjin ni Itte Okitai Koto – 21 Seiki o Ikiru Kimi-tachi e* (Tokyo: PHP Kenkyūjo, 1998), 25–26. Nakasone Yasuhiro, *Jiseiroku – Rekishi Hōtei no Hikoku to shite* (Tokyo: Shinchōsha, 2004), 239–47. Nakasone, *Nakasone Yasuhiro ga Kataru*, 149.

10 Nakasone, *Nihon no Furontia*, 251. Inaba Osamu, *Kōsei Osoru Beshi* (Tokyo; Tokyo Shimbun, 1988), 103. Nakasone, *Tenchi Ujō*, 192-93. Iwakawa Takashi, *Nihon no Chika Jinmyaku – Sengo o Tsukutta Kage no Otoko-tachi* (Tokyo: Shōdensha Bunko, 2007), 73. Koeda Yoshita and Kōno Yōhei, eds., *Tōjin Kōno*

The Conservative Merger and Nakasone's First Cabinet Position 65

Ichirō – Saigo no Jūnen (Tokyo: Shunpū-sha, 2010), 67, 70. Murase 243, 250, 252–54, 282, 296, 302, 306, 311, 316–17, 322, 334, 358–60, 364–65. Watanabe Tsuneo, *Habatsu – Hoshutō no Kaibō* (Tokyo: Kōbundō, 2014), 121, 148–50.

11 Nakasone, *Rīdā no Jōken*, 164–65. Nakasone Yasuhiro, *Seizan Jōunpo – Nakasone Yasuhiro Taidan-shū* (Tokyo: Mainichi Shimbun, 2012), 42–43. For examples of Nakasone's speeches, see: "Nihon Minshutō Daienzetsukai ni okeru Nakasone Yasuhiro Enzetsu, Shōwa 30-nen 1-gatsu 31-nichi (Getsu) Gogo Ichiji O Tōkyō Hibiya Kōkaidō," CD, SMH, and "Nakasone Yasuhiro Seijika no Kiseki," DVD, SMH.

12 Nakasone, *Rīdā no Jōken*, 280–81. Nakasone, *Jiseiroku*, 59.

13 Ministry of Foreign Affairs Asian Affairs Bureau, "Kishi Sōri Daijin to Purasado Indo Daitōryō oyobi Radakuryunan Indo Fukudaitōryō to no Kaidanroku" (May 1957), "Kishi Sōri Dai Ichiji Tōnan Ajia Hōmon Kankei Ikken (1957/6) Kaidanroku" A'.1.5.1.3-5, MOFA. Ministry of Foreign Affairs Asian Affairs Bureau, "Kishi Sōri Daijin to Nēru Indo Shushō to no Dai Ichiji Kaidanroku" (May 1957), "Kishi Sōri Dai Ichiji Tōnan Ajia Hōmon Kankei Ikken (1957/6) Kaidanroku" A'.1.5.1.3-5, MOFA. Postcard from Nakasone to Tokutomi (June 20, 1957), STM. Ministry of Foreign Affairs, "Waga Gaikō no Kinkyō Tokushū Ichi Kishi Sōri no Dai Ichiji Tōnan Ajia Shokoku Hōmon" (September 1957), 1. Nakasone Yasuhiro, "Nihon mo Kazantai no Ikkan," *Seiun* (February 25, 1957). Nakasone Yasuhiro, "Tōnan Ajia Dayori," *Seiun* (May 25, 1957). Nakasone Yasuhiro, "Kenmin narabi ni Dōshi no Mina-san e," *Seiun* (June 25, 1957). Nakasone Yasuhiro, "'Kokuminshugi Rengō' o Teishō – Ajia Seisaku no Shuppatsuten ni Tatte," *Yomiuri Shimbun* (July 24, 1957). Nakasone Yasuhiro, "Kichō Aisatsu," *Seiun* (July 25, 1957). Nakasone Yasuhiro, "Naseru Daitōryō to Chūkintō Jōsei," *Minzoku to Seiji* (July 1957), 15–17. Nakasone Yasuhiro, "Ki ni Kakaru Nēru no Kotoba," *Keizai Tenbō* 29:12 (1957), 24–29. Nakasone Yasuhiro, "Hentai no Sekai to Atarashii Seiji," *Keizai Tenbō* 30:4 (1958), 37–39. Nakasone, *Nihon no Furontia*, 256–63. Nakasone, *Seiji to Jinsei*, 175–79. Nakasone, *Rīdā no Jōken*, 192–93. Nakasone, *Nihon no Sōri-gaku*, 105–06. Nakasone, *Nakasone Yasuhiro ga Kataru*, 79, 129–32, 577–78. Nakasone Yasuhiro and Nakatani Takeyo, "Naseru Daitōryō no Omoide," *Minzoku to Seiji* (November 1970), 28–35. Shimonaka Yasaburō, Nakasone Yasuhiro, and Nakatani Takeyo, "Asuwan Hai Damu no Kensetsu to Arabu Rengō Kyōwakoku no Seiritsu ni Tsuite," in Nakatani Takeyo, *Arabu to Nihon – Nihon Arabu Kōryū-shi* (Tokyo: Hara Shobō, 1983), 108–28. Tamura Hideji, *Arabu Gaikō 55 Nen* (Tokyo: Keisō Shobo, 1983), 1:211–14. Nakasone, *Tenchi Ujō*, 61, 197–200. Hatoyama, 432. Yongseok Kwon, *Kishi Seikenki no "Ajia Gaikō" – "Taibei Jishu" to "Ajiashugi" no Gyakusetsu* (Tokyo: Kokusai Shoin, 2008), 178–83.

14 *Asahi Shimbun,* July 26, 1958. *Yomiuri Shimbun,* July 27, 1958. Nakasone, *Nakasone Yasuhiro ga Kataru*, 134.

15 "Kenpō Chōsakai Dai Sanjūkai Sōkai Gijiroku" (May 6, 1959), "Nihon Koku Kenpō Kankei Ikken Kenpō Chōsakai Kankei Chōsho Shiryō" Vol. 4, A'.3.0.0.3-3-1, MOFA. Nakasone, *Seiji to Jinsei*, 213–17, 371–73. Nakasone Yasuhiro, *21 Seiki Nihon no Kokka Senryaku* (Tokyo: PHP Kenkyūjo, 2000), 50, 160–62. Nakasone, *Tenchi Ujō*, 217–24. The records of the Constitutional Research Committee are also available from the National Archive of Japan's Digital Archives (http://www.digital.archives.go.jp/).

16 Nakasone, *Seiji to Jinsei*, 220.

17 Watanabe Tsuneo, *Ten'un Tenshoku: Sengo Seiji no Rimenshi, Hansei, Kyojin-gun o Akasu* (Tokyo: Kōbunsha, 1999), 136–37. Watanabe, *Kaikoroku*, 190–92. Murase, 315–17.

66   *The Conservative Merger and Nakasone's First Cabinet Position*

18 Nakasone Yasuhiro, "Kagaku Gijutsu Shinkō no Kadai," *Seisaku Geppō* No. 44 (1959), 81. *Asahi Shimbun,* October 3, 1959, February 4, 1960 evening, March 13, April 19, 1960 evening edition. Nakasone Yasuhiro and Suzue Yasuhira, "Kaihō Keizai to Kagaku Gijutsu no Shinkō," *Seisaku Geppō* No. 101 (1964), 76–86. Kaya Seiji and Nakasone Yasuhiro, "Kagaku Gijutsu no Shinkō o Kataru," *Seisaku Geppō* No. 117 (1965), 60–74. Nakasone, *Seiji to Jinsei*, 220–24. Nakasone, *Rīdā no Jōken*, 67. Nakasone, *Nakasone Yasuhiro ga Kataru*, 135–36. Nakasone, *Tenchi Ujō*, 196–97, 212–14. Kurosaki Akira, *Kaku Heiki to Nichibei Kankei – Amerika no Kaku Fukakusan Gaikō to Nihon no Sentaku 1960–1976* (Tokyo: Yūshisha, 2006), 112–13. Science and Technology Agency, ed., *21 Seiki e no Kaidan Dai Ichibu (Fukkokuban)* (Tokyo: Kōbundō, 2013). Science and Technology Agency, ed., *21 Seiki e no Kaidan Dai Nibu (Fukkokuban)* (Tokyo: Kōbundō, 2013).
19 Nakasone, *Seiji to Jinsei*, 224–31. Nakasone, *Jiseiroku*, 67–70. Nakasone Yasuhiro, "Watashi wa Aizenhawā Hōnichi Enki o Shingen shita," *Bungei Shunjū* (December 2010), 302–04. Nakasone, *Nakasone Yasuhiro ga Kataru*, 136–41. Nakasone, *Tenchi Ujō*, 200–09. Hara Yoshihisa, ed., *Kishi Nobusuke Shōgen-roku* (Tokyo: Chūō Bunko, 2014), 355–56.

References

Ashida Hitoshi. *Ashida Hitoshi Nikki.* Edited by Shindō Eiichi. Tokyo: Iwanami Shoten, 1986.

Hara Yoshihisa. *Kishi Nobusuke.* Tokyo: Iwanami Shinsho, 1995.

Hara Yoshihisa, ed. *Kishi Nobusuke Shōgenroku.* Tokyo: Chūō Bunko, 2014.

Hatoyama Ichirō and Hatoyama Kaoru, *Hatoyama Ichirō/Kaoru Nikki.* Edited by Itō Takashi and Suetake Yoshiya. Tokyo: Chūō Kōron Shinsha, 1999.

Hiwatari Yumi. *Sengo Seiji to Nichibei Kankei.* Tokyo: University of Tokyo, 1990.

Hosokawa Ryūgen. *Otoko Degozaru Ryū no Kan.* Tokyo: Yamanote Shobō, 1981.

Inaba Osamu. *Kōsei Osoru Beshi.* Tokyo: Tokyo Shimbun, 1988.

Ishibashi Masashi. *Ishibashi Masashi Kaisōroku – "55 Nen Taisei" Uchigawa kara no Shōgen.* Tokyo: Tabata Shoten, 1999.

Iwakawa Takashi. *Nihon no Chika Jinmyaku – Sengo o Tsukutta Kage no Otoko-tachi.* Tokyo: Shōdensha Bunko, 2007.

Kishi Nobusuke. *Kishi Nobusuke Kaikoroku – Hoshu Gōdō to Anpo Kaitei.* Tokyo: Kōsaidō Shuppan, 1983.

Koeda Yoshita, Kōno Yōhei, ed. *Tōjin Kōno Ichirō – Saigo no Jūnen.* Tokyo: Shunpū-sha, 2010.

Kōno Ichirō. *Kōno Ichirō Jiden.* Edited by Denki Kankō Iinkai. Tokyo: Tokuma Shoten, 1965.

Kurosaki Akira. *Kaku Heiki to Nichibei Kankei – Amerika no Kaku Fukakusan Gaikō to Nihon no Sentaku 1960–1976.* Tokyo: Yūshisha, 2006.

Kwon, Yongseok. *Kishi Seikenki no "Ajia Gaikō" – "Taibei Jishu" to "Ajiashugi" no Gyakusetsu.* Tokyo: Kokusai Shoin, 2008.

Masuda Hiroshi. *Ishibashi Tanzan.* Tokyo: Chūkō Shinsho, 1995.

Miyazaki Yoshimasa. *Seikai 18000 Nichi Miyazaki Nikki.* Tokyo: Gyōken Shuppankyoku, 1989.

Murase Shin'ichi. *Shushō ni Narenakatta Otoko-tachi – Inoue Kaoru/Tokonami Takejirō/Kōno Ichirō.* Tokyo: Yoshikawa Kōbunkan, 2014.

Nakasone Yasuhiro. *21 Seiki Nihon no Kokka Senryaku.* Tokyo: PHP Kenkyūjo, 2000.

The Conservative Merger and Nakasone's First Cabinet Position 67

Nakasone Yasuhiro. "Hentai no Sekai to Atarashii Seiji." *Keizai Tenbō* 30:4 (1958), 36–39.

Nakasone Yasuhiro. *Jiseiroku – Rekishi Hōtei no Hikoku to shite*. Tokyo: Shinchōsha, 2004.

Nakasone Yasuhiro. *Jishu Kenpō no Kihonteki Seikaku – Kenpō Yōgo-ron no Ayamari o Tsuku*. Tokyo: Kenpō Chōsakai, 1955.

Nakasone Yasuhiro. "Kagaku Gijutsu no Shinkō o Kataru." *Seisaku Geppō* No. 117 (1965).

Nakasone Yasuhiro. "Kagaku Gijutsu Shinkō no Kadai." *Seisaku Geppō* No. 44 (1959).

Nakasone Yasuhiro. "Kenmin narabi ni Dōshi no Mina-san e." *Seiun* (June 25, 1957).

Nakasone Yasuhiro. "Ki ni Kakaru Nēru no Kotoba." *Keizai Tenbō* 29:12 (1957), 24–29.

Nakasone Yasuhiro. "Kichō Aisatsu." *Seiun* (July 25, 1957).

Nakasone Yasuhiro. "'Kokuminshugi Rengō' o Teishō – Ajia Seisaku no Shuppatsuten ni Tatte." *Yomiuri Shimbun* (July 24, 1957).

Nakasone Yasuhiro. *Nakasone Yasuhiro ga Kataru Sengo Nihon Gaikō*. Edited by Nakashima Takuma, Hattori Ryūji, Noboru Amiko, Wakatsuki Hidekazu, Michishita Narushige, Kusunoki Ayako, and Segawa Takao. Tokyo: Shinchōsha, 2012.

Nakasone Yasuhiro. "Naseru Daitōryō to Chūkintō Jōsei." *Minzoku to Seiji* (July 1957).

Nakasone Yasuhiro. "Nihon mo Kazantai no Ikkan." *Seiun* (February 25, 1957).

Nakasone Yasuhiro. *Nihon no Furontia*. Tokyo: Tsunebunsha, 1966.

Nakasone Yasuhiro. *Nihon no Sōri-gaku*. Tokyo: PHP Shinsho, 2004.

Nakasone Yasuhiro. *Nihonjin ni Itte Okitai Koto – 21 Seiki o Ikiru Kimi-tachi e*. Tokyo: PHP Kenkyūjo, 1998.

Nakasone Yasuhiro. *Rīdā no Jōken*. Tokyo: Fusō-sha, 1997.

Nakasone Yasuhiro. "San Furanshisuko no Gipusu o Hazuse." *Seiun* (November 25, 1956).

Nakasone Yasuhiro. *Seiji to Jinsei – Nakasone Yasuhiro Kaikoroku*. Tokyo: Kōdansha, 1992.

Nakasone Yasuhiro. *Seizan Jōunpo – Nakasone Yasuhiro Taidan-shū*. Tokyo: Mainichi Shimbun, 2012.

Nakasone Yasuhiro. *Sengo Seiji*. Tokyo: Yomiuri Shimbun, 2005.

Nakasone Yasuhiro. "Tōnan Ajia Dayori." *Seiun* (May 25, 1957).

Nakasone Yasuhiro. "Watashi wa Aizenhawā Hōnichi Enki o Shingen shita." *Bungei Shunjū* (December 2010).

Nakasone Yasuhiro, Itō Takashi, and Satō Seiburō. *Tenchi Ujō – Gojū Nen no Sengo Seiji o Kataru*. Tokyo: Bungei Shunjū, 1996.

Nakasone Yasuhiro, Nakatani Takeyo. "Naseru Daitōryō no Omoide." *Minzoku to Seiji* (November 1970).

Nakasone Yasuhiro and Suzue Yasuhira. "Kaihō Keizai to Kagaku Gijutsu no Shinkō." *Seisaku Geppō* No. 101 (1964).

Nakatani Takeyo. *Arabu to Nihon – Nihon Arabu Kōryū-shi*. Tokyo: Hara Shobō, 1983.

Okada Haruo. *Kokkai Bakudan Otoko Okapparu Ichidaiki*. Tokyo: Gyōken Shuppankyoku, 1987.

Science and Technology Agency, ed. *21 Seiki e no Kaidan (Fukkokuban)*. Tokyo: Kōbundō, 2013.

68 The Conservative Merger and Nakasone's First Cabinet Position

Takeda Tomoki. *Shigemitsu Mamoru to Sengo Seiji.* Tokyo: Yoshikawa Kōbunkan, 2002.

Tamura Hideji. *Arabu Gaikō 55 Nen.* Tokyo: Keisō Shobo, 1983.

Watanabe Tsuneo. *Habatsu – Hoshutō no Kaibō.* Tokyo: Kōbundō, 2014.

Watanabe Tsuneo. *Ten'un Tenshoku: Sengo Seiji no Rimenshi, Hansei, Kyojingun o Akasu.* Tokyo: Kōbunsha, 1999.

Watanabe Tsuneo. *Watanabe Tsuneo Kaikoroku.* Edited by Mikuriya Takashi, Itō Takashi, and Iio Jun. Tokyo: Chūō Bunko, 2007.

Yabe Teiji. *Yabe Teiji Nikki Keyaki no Maki.* Edited by Nikki Kankōkai. Tokyo: Yomiuri Shimbun, 1974.

Yabe Teiji. *Yabe Teiji Nikki Momiji no Maki.* Edited by Nikki Kankōkai. Tokyo: Yomiuri Shimbun, 1975.

5 From "Killing Time" to Becoming a Faction Leader

Outside the Mainstream under Ikeda

Ikeda Hayato defeated Ishii Mitsujirō and Fujiyama Aiichirō in the July 14, 1960 LDP presidential election. Kōno Ichirō had backed Ishii in the election alongside the party's other party politician factions, but it had not been enough. When the Ikeda government was formed on July 19, neither Nakasone nor Kōno received positions in the cabinet.

The mainstream factions during the Ikeda government remained the same as at the end of the Kishi government, the Ikeda, Kishi, and Satō factions. But while the bureaucratic factions occupied the mainstream, the defeated Ishii was also appointed as MITI minister.

While the Kōno faction, in general, was receiving cool treatment from the Ikeda government, Nakasone and Ikeda also had a history. As a member of the Reform Party, Nakasone had severely criticized Ikeda in an October 20, 1953 *Sangyō Keizai Shimbun* article, "Special Envoy Ikeda in Distress." Ikeda was in the US at the time, acting as a special envoy for Prime Minister Yoshida in talks with Assistant Secretary of State Walter Robertson on increasing Japan's defense capabilities.

Nakasone was also in Washington during the talks, and he criticized Ikeda's performance using an exaggerated comparison: "Special Envoy Ikeda's party finds itself in a very tough spot. They're like the Japanese fleet at Midway. Wait, no. That fleet was composed of the best of the best. This time, we've sent only a handful of training ships. They're not even going to be able to put up a fight." Nakasone also attacked Miyazawa Kiichi, then a member of the Diet, writing that "the members of Mr. Ikeda's party are completely useless."

Ikeda did not respond to the article at the time, but given that Nakasone also indirectly disparaged him during his attack on the Yoshida cabinet during the shipbuilding scandal a few months later, it is not difficult to imagine that Ikeda did not have a particularly favorable view of him. Nakasone had had no idea at the time that the conservative merger would mean that he would soon be sharing a party with Ikeda and Satō.

This was not the only development that Nakasone would fail to predict. After becoming prime minister, Ikeda had his government adopt the slogan

DOI: 10.4324/9781003351931-6

70   *From "Killing Time" to Becoming a Faction Leader*

of "tolerance and forbearance" (*kan'yō to nintai*), assuming a low profile. Ikeda was infamous for his arrogance and, just eleven months earlier, had pushed for the demonstrators outside of the Diet to be dealt with harshly. Nakasone found himself wondering, "can a man really change so much, even as part of a strategy?"[1]

Estrangement from Kōno and "Killing Time"

In addition to having a poor relationship with Ikeda, a rift had also formed between Nakasone and Kōno. According to Nakasone, "Kōno was popular among professionals, while I was popular among amateurs and students. It is the way of the world that the person in the number one spot doesn't rejoice at seeing their number two rise. I could feel a slight sense of rivalry from those in the faction who had joined at the same time that I did or earlier."

He believed that Kōno had become jealous of him.

Additionally, as Kōno continued to remain outside of the party mainstream, he became disaffected with the LDP and began working on forming a new party. The relationship between Nakasone and Kōno would worsen even further after Nakasone advised against this.

One day in August, Nakasone was called to a room at the Imperial Hotel by Nagata Masichi, president of Daiei Film. Well-known for producing movies such as *Rashōmon*, Nagata lived in the hotel and was also one of Kōno's major backers. He was known for talking big, something that had earned him the nickname "Trumpet Nagata."

Awaiting Nakasone in the room were not only Nagata and Kōno but also Mori Kiyoshi and Shigemasa Seishi (leaders of the Kōno faction), Hagiwara Kichitarō (president of Hokkaido Colliery & Steamship), and Kodama Yoshio (a political fixer).

Upon Nakasone's entrance, Kōno entered into a passionate argument for the formation of a new party, emphasizing that "there are twenty-five [Diet members] who will definitely join us." Nakasone curtly replied that "You have maybe ten. And most of those will only go along with it because they feel like they have no choice." Kōno's face darkened and he demanded that Nakasone leave the room.

Kōno ultimately decided to remain in the LDP, choosing to improve his relationship with Ikeda instead.

Inaba Osamu, a fellow member of the Kōno faction, noticed how delicate the relationship between Ikeda and Kōno had become and told Nakasone that "a tree cannot grow large while in the shade of another. You should take things easy for a while." This was a warning to stay out of the limelight for a while and work on Kōno's behalf.

MITI Minister Ishii Mitsujirō (who was also LDP vice president) also told Nakasone, "You should kill time for a while." Nakasone took these words to heart and began regarding his time outside of the cabinet more positively as a time to gather strength.[2]

The Kennedy Brothers and Showing Off

One day, Nakasone found himself sharing a train car with Miura Saneji, a reporter for the *Asahi Shimbun*. Miura was known as a shrewd political reporter with an acid tongue for powerful politicians like Kōno.

Miura approached him with the question, "Hey, Nakasone. You want to be prime minister?" When Nakasone answered, "Yeah, I do," Miura said, "If you're aiming to be prime minister, don't serve in the cabinet and don't hold any party positions for the next ten years. The only thing on your mind should be giving speeches for your comrades and finding new talent and getting them elected."

Which is to say, Miura was telling him to prepare to form his own faction.

Nakasone did not need Miura to tell him that he needed to become a faction leader to have a hope of becoming prime minister. While Nakasone had focused on keeping himself in the public eye, he had also decided to yield government and party positions to others for the time being, expand his network of personal connections, and gain experience.

He attended President Kennedy's inauguration in Washington with Diet Member Takasaki Tatsunosuke on January 20, 1961. He commented years later that "even now, the image of President Kennedy placing his left hand on the Bible and raising his right to take the oath is vivid in my mind."

After the inauguration, Nakasone traveled to Mexico, Peru, Chile, Argentina, Uruguay, Brazil, Venezuela, and Cuba as a member of the Constitutional Research Committee with his mentor Yabe Teiji.

Of particular note, he met Prime Minister Castro in post-revolutionary Cuba. When he asked, "You're risking war with America. Are you sure you can win if that happens?" Castro confidently replied, "They will come, but we are fully prepared."

After Nakasone returned to Washington on March 5, he met with Attorney General Robert F. Kennedy, the president's brother. Kennedy earnestly questioned him about the situation in Cuba, and Nakasone advised that "there's no guarantee that the US will win if it attempts to land [on Cuba]. Any halfhearted effort will likely fail. Prime Minister Castro already has a substantial number of troops deployed along the coast."

Nakasone got along well with Kennedy and invited him to come to Japan, which he did. After arriving on February 6, 1962, Kennedy gave a performance that could rival Nakasone. He visited a skating rink with his wife, went out drinking with labor leaders, and jumped out of his car to shake hands with people lining the side of the street cheering for him.

Kennedy was clearly aware of the media and limited his official function as much as possible. The performance made a strong impression on Nakasone, a man who also liked to be bold. As he watched Kennedy, "I became painfully aware that a time would come when it would be necessary for [Japanese politicians to] act this way as well."[3]

72   From "Killing Time" to Becoming a Faction Leader

Putting Together the "Nakasone Machine"

Seeing the Kennedy brothers stirred Nakasone into action, and he poured over journalist Thomas White's *The Making of the President 1960* to find out what made them so formidable. This account of the 1960 American presidential election would go on to win the Pulitzer Prize.[4]

What he learned from the book was that President Kennedy had built a brain trust known as the "Kennedy machine," consisting of advisors with detailed policy knowledge, businessmen, public opinion analysts, media analysts, etc.

Determined to make use of such a system himself for developing policy and raising funds, he established the "Scientific Policy Study Group" with Watanabe Tsuneo and Ujiie Seiichirō of the Yomiuri Shimbun and Waseda University constitutional scholar Kobayashi Shōzō among its members.

Nakasone wanted to expand his circle of contacts and create a "Nakasone machine." This would incorporate businessmen like Gotō Noboru, Tsutsumi Seiji, and Ibuka Masaru, artists like Asari Keita and Ozawa Seiji, scientists like Mukaibō Takashi and Itogawa Hideo, entertainers like Minami Haruo and Misora Hibari, athletes like Kawakami Tetsuji, Nagashima Shigeo, and Taihō Kōki, and actors like Morishige Hisaya and Mifune Toshirō.

He also devoted a great deal of time to reading. He mainly read works on politics, religion, history, and science, but he also enjoyed reading the historical novels of Shiba Ryōtarō. While he engaged in swimming, golf, and Zen meditation, he disliked mahjong, feeling that "if you're going to spend time inside enjoying yourself, you should go study instead."[5]

The Movement for the Popular Election of the Prime Minister

On June 9, 1961, Nakasone gathered fifty interested LDP lawmakers at the Tokyo Kaikan for a ceremony marking the launch of the Research Group on a System for the Popular Election of the Prime Minister. The group had seven advisors, including Ishibashi Tanzan, Shōriki Matsutarō, and Takasaki Tatsunosuke. Nakasone served as the group's organizer. 169 Diet members from both houses agreed to be founders of the group.

The group intended to first research a system for popular election and only pursue basic constitutional revision at some later time. Future prime minister Kaifu Toshiki was one of those involved in the movement. Unsurprisingly, Prime Minister Ikeda and MITI Minister Satō were cool toward the idea of revising the constitution, and the movement did not make any inroads into the mainstream factions.

Matsumura Kenzō, a man who Nakasone considered a mentor alongside Kōno and Tokutomi, was also critical of constitutional revision: "Nakasone, if we were to implement what you propose, everything would become like it is in America. We would no longer have British-style dissolutions [of the Diet]. This is also a significant problem in America, but even

From "Killing Time" to Becoming a Faction Leader   73

as things are now, the Diet grows lazy after about two years. If we were to have a legislature here that had to continue for four years no matter what, wouldn't it just become completely lazy?"[6]

Travels Abroad

Nakasone also traveled to many foreign countries during this period. Stepping down as director-general of the Science and Technology Agency did nothing to reduce his interest in science, and he visited Antarctica in November 1962, raising the Japanese flag at the South Pole alongside a "flag for the direct election of the prime minister."

When Nakasone asked the captain of a US Navy icebreaker the secret to sailing in the South Pole, he immediately smiled and answered, "Patience, patience, patience." Nakasone found this enlightening: "If you find yourself enclosed in ice, don't try to force your way through. Just remain as you are and wait for the ice to move and a passage to open. I realized that this is also the key to politics: waiting, waiting, and more waiting."

Nakasone also visited the Philippines and Hong Kong in January 1963.

As Nakasone traveled, Kōno stubbornly curried favor with Ikeda. These efforts were successful, and he was appointed agricultural minister and then construction minister. According to Nakasone, "Ikeda and Kōno were quite similar in constitution; both were decisive 'men of passion.' They had never really had many opportunities to interact previously, but once they did, they recognized each other's talents and became [quite close]."

Some within the political world began to see Kōno as Ikeda's likely successor, and as that expectation spread to the general public, Kōno himself also came to believe that Ikeda would yield the premiership to him. He had doubtless realized, just as Nakasone had advised, that forming a new political party would have been a mistake. As Kōno's situation improved, he also began to repair his relationship with Nakasone.

With no invitation to join the cabinet forthcoming, Nakasone visited Korea in April 1964. He believed that relations with South Korea should be restored soon. When he called on Kōno and proposed making the trip "to find out what their true intentions are," Kōno readily agreed to it.

South Korea was under military dictatorship at the time, and Nakasone met with President Park Chung-hee and his confidante Kim Jong-pil. The Koreans were enthusiastic about restoring ties with Japan but made economic assistance a requirement. Nakasone introduced Kim's brother Kim Jong-lak to Kōno.

Nakasone's days "killing time" continued. He spent time on the Constitutional Research Committee investigating the process through which the constitution had been put in place and polished his personal plans for the direct election of the prime minister. It was also during this time that he purchased his Hinode Sansō in Tokyo's Nishitama District, where he would later host US President Reagan.[7]

74 *From "Killing Time" to Becoming a Faction Leader*

Launch of the Satō Government

In the fall of 1964, the center of political interest was the LDP presidential election that would determine Ikeda's successor. Ikeda had developed throat cancer and checked into the National Cancer Center in Tsukiji. He was there when the Tokyo Olympics began on October 10, and it was from there that he named his successor as president on November 9.

Ikeda chose Satō rather than Kōno, and the Satō government was launched that same day.

This development shocked Kōno. He had maintained a friendly relationship with Ikeda and had never doubted that he would abdicate in his favor. While tough-looking in appearance, Kōno was naïve in one way: once he had convinced himself of something, he believed it to the very end. He was absolutely crestfallen at being passed over, telling others that he just could not understand why it had happened.

Nakasone, now a leader of the Kōno faction, had predicted Ikeda's choice. In a meeting with Kosaka Tokusaburō, president of Shin-Etsu Chemical, he had said that "I suspect [Ikeda] might go with Satō. Choosing Kōno could cause a negative reaction from the business community."

Nakasone had a reputation for being blunt, but even so, this was a bold statement for a leader of the Kōno faction to make. The conversation was reported on in the *Ekonomisuto* magazine and shows that Nakasone had distanced himself from Kōno to some extent.[8]

Nakasone remained outside of the cabinet following the formation of the Satō government. As he ruminated over the twenty years that had passed since the end of the war, he continued to "kill time." He quoted *The Analects of Confucius* to himself: "Do not be desirous of having things done quickly."[9]

Meanwhile, Tanaka Kakuei (a member of the Satō faction) became finance minister in the Satō government and would later become LDP secretary-general under him. Tanaka enjoyed Satō's trust and would serve as secretary-general five times for a total of four years and two months, a record that would remain unbroken until 2020. Fukuda would also serve as secretary-general under Satō for two years and five months.

Nakasone was not appointed to any of the top three party positions. It would only be at the end of the Satō government that he would become General Council chairman.

10th Anniversary of the Afro-Asian Conference

In February 1965, Nakasone became deputy chairman of the LDP Research Commission on Foreign Affairs, and in March, he was made chairman of that committee's Afro-Asian Subcommittee. He visited Indonesia, Malaysia, Thailand, and South Vietnam from April 13 to 29.

The primary purpose of his trip was attending a ceremony commemorating the tenth anniversary of the Afro-Asian Conference (the Bandung

Conference). Representatives of thirty-seven countries attended the event, including Indonesian President Sukarno, Chinese Premier Zhou Enlai, North Korean Premier Kim Il-sung, and LDP Vice President Kawashima Shōjirō.

Nakasone wrote an article in the *Mainichi Shimbun* on the event in which he said that "what made the strongest impression on me was the way that President Sukarno boldly laid out his outline for the Conference of the New Emerging Forces with the firm support of Chinese Premier Zhou Enlai." He sent a postcard to Yabe Teiji in which he wrote, "I was made painfully aware of the fact that Japan is in need of a major politician capable of standing shoulder-to-shoulder with Sukarno and Zhou."[10]

Nakasone then visited Malaysia, Thailand, and South Vietnam. Just before returning home, he observed the Vietnam War, which America had begun to be directly involved in. He took the stance that "it's our ally the United States and we should stand by them, particularly in their time of difficulty." Privately, however, he disagreed with America's domino theory.[11]

China and America

The question of China's representation started to become a significant point of contention in the United Nations. The Satō government supported Taiwan alongside the US, but Nakasone argued at the New Year's meeting of the Seiunjuku in January 1966 that "we should seriously reconsider [Japan's] position":

> One of the most serious issues for the international community this year will be the question of Chinese admission [to the UN], which will be coming before the General Assembly this autumn. While the US was successful in its effort to have the matter deemed "an important question" last year, the General Assembly was evenly divided on the resolution on admitting China. Handling this issue will be one of the most important matters for Japanese foreign policy this year. This will be greatly influenced by China's international posture. If China continues to take a hard line, any significant change is unthinkable. But should it adopt a more humble attitude, we should seriously reconsider our position.[12]

The Vietnam War and Japanese policy toward China both involved US-Japan relations, and Nakasone visited America from March 14, 1966. At the Council on Foreign Relations and elsewhere, he argued for the US bombing of North Vietnam to be minimized and for its anti-Chinese policies to be re-examined.

He also called for the creation of a Pacific economic and cultural sphere, which he gave the acronym PEACE (the Pacific Economic and Culture

76 From "Killing Time" to Becoming a Faction Leader

Enclave). Nakasone asserted that the ultimate goal of the concept was the achievement of peace through the creation of regional bodies in Asia. He recognized the wariness remaining from Japan's wartime calls for the creation of a Greater East Asian Co-Prosperity Sphere and emphasized that "I am not making this call lightly."

At an April 5 press conference held upon his arrival at Haneda Airport, Nakasone said that "Japan should also hold ambassadorial-level talks with the Beijing government at a suitable venue." He told US embassy personnel that Japan could serve as a go-between between China and the US. Given the Satō government's determination to continue to recognize Taiwan rather than Beijing, it seems unlikely that Satō would have viewed Nakasone's actions favorably.[13]

Kōno's Death

Between his travels, Nakasone unexpectedly had to bid farewell to Kōno, with whom he had continued to have a complicated relationship. Kōno had retired to his home after complaining of severe stomach pain and suddenly died on July 8, 1965 of a stomach aneurysm. His final words were, "As if I could let something like this kill me."

He had met and dined with Nakasone, Inaba, Sakurauchi, and Yamanaka just two days earlier. He told them, "don't just go along with the party's direction"; "a politician doesn't act based on what's in his own personal interest"; and "you should work from the perspective of the entire nation." He also let slip that "it is unlikely that I will die a natural death." Nakasone wrote that "he had had an amazing hard-fought political career."[14]

In late August, following Kōno's death, he submitted a three-piece article to the *Jōmō Shimbun* on "Reform of the Liberal Democratic Party and the Party's Future." In it, he invoked Kōno:

> We will break new ground as a modern policy group, full of youthful energy, that will carry on into the next era of the LDP. We will follow the example of Kōno and act as politicians with a sense of mission. We will actively put policy first and continually research new, original policies. We will pioneer a new way of being a "faction" and light the fuse for the modernization of the LDP.[15]

Even when the previous faction leader is still alive, succession in political factions is frequently accompanied by conflict and often results in the faction splitting. In this case, Kōno had been only sixty-seven, and his death had been completely unforeseen; he had made no efforts to designate a successor, and it was expected that conflict would erupt over who would be the next chairman. Becoming a faction leader was an absolutely essential step for anyone wanting to become prime minister. A crucial moment for Nakasone was fast approaching.

Forming the Nakasone Faction

It was Mori Kiyoshi, not Nakasone, who became the new chairman of the Shunjūkai. Mori, who had been elected to the Diet six times, was part of the Kōno faction leadership and had been endorsed by other leaders like Shigemasa Seishi (a close confidante of Kōno's). He was also a former member of the Liberal Party. Despite being three years younger, Nakasone had been elected eight times by this point. He was not pleased by the selection of Mori.

This was the time of decision for Nakasone. He broke off from Mori, Shigemasa, and Sonoda Sunao, splitting the Kōno faction. He established his own faction (formally known as the Shinsei Dōshikai) on December 13. It had twenty-four members compared to the eighteen that had remained with the Shunjūkai.

According to Nakasone, "it was largely those who had been closest to Kōno who supported [Mori and] Shigemasa. The ones who supported me believed that there was no faction without me, not in terms of policy focus, popularity, or charismatic speeches. The faction's elder statesmen like Nakamura Umekichi and Noda Takeo, and my comrades like Sakurauchi Yoshio, Yamanaka Sadanori, and Inaba Osamu decided to stand with me, creating the Shinsei Dōshikai: the Nakasone faction."

In the inaugural issue of *Shinsei*, the factional magazine, twenty-four people were listed as belonging to the faction. Most were younger Diet members:

Advisor	Nakamura Umekichi (elected 10 times)
Representative	Nakasone Yasuhiro (9)
Chairman	Noda Takeo (7)
Organizers	Inaba Osamu (8), Ōishi Buichi (8), Sakurauchi Yoshio (8), Yamanaka Sadanori (6)
Managers	Kurauchi Shūji (4), Kuranari Tadashi (4), Yagi Tetsuo (4)
Members	Amano Kōsei (3), Tagawa Seiichi (3), Ōishi Hachiji (2), Ōtake Tarō (2), Kibe Yoshiaki (2), Sakamura Yoshimasa (2), Satō Takayuki (2), Shinomiya Hisakichi (2), Sunada Shigetami (2), Minato Tetsurō (2), Watanabe Michio (2), Kōno Yōhei (1), Nakao Eiichi (1), Mutō Kabun (1)

Nakasone also wrote an article – "A Vision for the LDP" – in the same issue in which he argued that the LDP "will continue to reach its wing out to the left. It will continue until it encompasses the Democratic Socialists, the Kōmeitō, and part of the Socialists. That is the LDP of tomorrow."

Later, looking back on the great victory he oversaw as prime minister in the 1986 joint elections, he would remark that "we have reached our wing out to the left."[16]

The Youngest Faction Leader

Nakasone's creation of the Shinsei Dōshikai came after the December 1, 1966 LDP presidential election. The only opponent Satō faced in the

78   *From "Killing Time" to Becoming a Faction Leader*

election was Fujiyama Aiichirō, and he received 289 votes, more than three times Fujiyama's 89. Among those supporting Satō was Secretary-General Tanaka.

While Mori, Shigemasa, and Sonoda had supported Satō in the hopes of entering the party mainstream, Nakasone and Sakurauchi had felt that the faction should back Fujiyama "in accordance with Kōno's final wishes that we oppose Satō."

Nakasone, who had long been focused on becoming prime minister, was now the party's youngest faction leader at the age of forty-eight. He recalled that "I began to think I might be able to do it." While his was only a small faction, he had managed to become a faction leader before his rival Tanaka.[17]

The freshman Diet members in the Nakasone faction were Mutō Kabun, Nakao Eiichi, and Kōno Yōhei, Kōno's son. Kōno Yōhei had tried to convince Nakasone and Mori to reunite the old Kōno faction and restore it to its place as a cornerstone of the party politician factions but had little success. He had ultimately decided to join the Nakasone faction after his cousin Tagawa Seiichi (who belonged to the Nakasone faction) criticized him for his indecisiveness.

Years later, Yōhei said of this decision that "while my father truly trusted Mori and his partner Shigemasa, they lacked Nakasone's charisma." Even so, it would not be long before he used the Lockheed scandal as a reason to leave the party entirely.[18]

The Nakasone Faction and the Business Community

What were the characteristics of the Nakasone faction? The Shinsei Dōshikai, a descendant of the party politician factions, was filled with distinctive personalities like Nakamura, who had been purged during the Occupation and served as construction minister, and Inaba, a former Chuo University professor. While Nakasone was known for being a skilled public speaker, there were many others in the party who would not be satisfied until they had also had an opportunity to say their piece at every meeting.[19]

It was also diverse ideologically. Indeed, the failure of its members to coalesce around any particular set of ideas could be considered another aspect of the faction's uniqueness. While it had pro-China Noda Takeo and liberal members like Tagawa Seiichi and Kōno Yōhei, it also had many who would go on to join the Seirankai.

The Seirankai was a right-wing group within the LDP that would be formed in 1973. Of the thirty-one founding members of the group, nine would come from the Nakasone faction, making it the second largest contributor after the Fukuda faction's ten. Not a single member would come from the Tanaka or Ōhira factions, despite them being the largest factions in the party.[20] Nakasone did not join himself and, despite being widely seen as a hawk, argued for the rapid normalization of relations with China, something that the Seirankai opposed.

From "Killing Time" to Becoming a Faction Leader   79

How was Nakasone able to hold such a disparate group together? Karasawa Shunjirō, a member, elected to the House of Representatives for the first time in December 1969, compared Nakasone's management style to cormorant fishing: "Nakasone's handling of people was just like cormorant fishing. The fisherman holds twelve cords attached to the cormorants. Everyone felt like *they* were his number one subordinate and did all they could for him. There were more than twelve of us, of course. And he made use of all of us rather than leaving everything to anyone in particular."[21]

The faction's weakness was that it had difficulty raising money, particularly because it was consistently outside of the mainstream during the long-lived Satō government. Nakasone went to great lengths to raise funds for managing the faction, creating the Kōkikai and Sannō Keizai Kenkyūkai as business community support groups for the faction. He also formed the Matsubarakai, a group that provided him with opportunities to meet with and exchange views with members of the media.

The Kōkikai was made up of leading members of the business community, while the Sannō Keizai Kenkyūkai consisted of leaders of second-tier companies. Journalists participating in the Matsubarakai included Watanabe Tsuneo, Miura Kineji, Miyazaki Yoshimasa, and Togawa Isamu.

It had been Nakao Eiichi who had suggested that the Nakasone faction form these support groups and gone around the business community. While Nakasone still lacked the power to be able to personally secure budget items the way that Kōno Ichirō had, the faction was slowly building its strength.

Even so, as the faction entered the 1970s, it remained the fourth largest in the party after the Tanaka, Fukuda, and Ōhira factions. It was half the size of the Tanaka faction, and there were times when it even fell below the Miki faction in size.

As for the Shunjūkai, Sonoda became chairman after Mori's sudden death on June 9, 1968. It then slowly tapered off in size until being absorbed into the Fukuda faction on July 12, 1972.

Fujinami Takao and Mukaiyama Kazuto departed the former Sonoda faction for the Nakasone faction at the time of the merger. Nakasone would come to trust Fujinami greatly, and he would serve as chief cabinet secretary in the second Nakasone government. Later, when the Miki government attempted to eliminate factions in the LDP, Nakasone would rename the Shinsei Dōshikai to the Seisaku Kagaku Kenkyūjo.[22]

Ashihama Nuclear Power Plant

During the period in which Nakasone was becoming a faction leader, the policy that he was most focused on was the plan to construct a nuclear power plant in Ashihama, Mie Prefecture. He toured the planned location for the plant with three Socialist Diet members on September 19, 1966, in his capacity as a director of the House of Representatives' Special Committee for Measures to Promote Science and Technology.

80   *From "Killing Time" to Becoming a Faction Leader*

According to the *Asahi Shimbun*, during this visit, the patrol boat they were riding in was surrounded by three hundred fishing boats protesting the building of the plant. The fishermen climbed onto the boat and shouted at the occupants. Nakasone ordered the captain of the boat to get it moving, but the fishing boats did all they could to prevent this. He ultimately had to abort the inspection, and about thirty fishermen were arrested for interfering with an official in the performance of their duties.

After Nakasone's return to Tokyo, the Mie Prefecture Fishing Cooperative Association petitioned for the release of the fisherman. He reportedly responded, "Accept the nuclear power plant. If you do that, I'll have them released immediately." Ultimately, the men were not released and twenty-five were found guilty. While Nakasone continued to give the plan his support, it would later be withdrawn.[23]

President of Takushoku University

The finishing touch to Nakasone's lengthy period of "killing time" that stretched all the way back to the beginning of the Ikeda government was his appointment as president of Takushoku University. On September 13, 1967, he became the university's twelfth president, taking over for former Diet member and director of the foreign ministry's treaties bureau Andō Yoshirō. He did not nominate himself for the position; it was the decision of a committee established by the university.

Nakasone was not the first active politician to simultaneously serve as a university president. LDP Vice President Kawashima Shōjirō, who served as president and chairman of Senshu University, is a previous example.

Nakasone's mentor Yabe Teiji had served as president of Takushoku for nine years, stepping down only three years earlier. It had been this connection that had led to Nakasone's name coming up for consideration. Another candidate had been Kajima Morinosuke, president of Kajima Construction and a member of the House of Representatives. After the committee recommended Nakasone, the decision was approved by the university's board of trustees in a majority vote.

Nakasone accepted the appointment, but he felt a little hesitant about serving as both a university president and a faction leader. The university had an important characteristic that influenced his decision, however. It had been founded by Katsura Tarō, and its list of past presidents included many powerful politicians like Gotō Shinpei, Nagata Hidejirō, Ugaki Kazushige, Shimomura Hiroshi, and Hatta Yoshiaki.

As symbolized by the lyrics of the school's anthem – "we hold to no discrimination or boundaries of skin, color, and land" – the university had a tradition of fostering talent in areas like Asia and South America. That tradition suited Nakasone's ideas well.

Following Nakasone's appointment, he gathered the students in the school's Myōkatani Hall and told them, "We must remember that Takushoku

From "Killing Time" to Becoming a Faction Leader 81

is the only ethnic international university that we, the Japanese people, have."
Continuing, he said that "Keio has Fukuzawa and its spirit of 'independence.'
Waseda has Marquis Ōkuma and its spirit of 'liberty.' This school has Prince
Katsura and its spirit of 'pioneering.' [...] To put it plainly, I want to develop
Takushoku University into an academic center for foreign policy, particularly
Asian policy. When Professor Yabe created the Institute of World Studies, he
did it with this in mind. And I want to carry on in that spirit."

Given that he was an amateur in the field, Nakasone was not directly
involved in education at the university. But he did gather the student body
for presidential speeches twenty-two times during his tenure. He also established a Korean language program at the school with an eye on future
Japan-Korean relations, a quite forward-thinking act for the time.

Nakasone established a liberal arts department and invited Inayama
Yoshihiro, president of Nippon Steel, and Watanabe Tsuneo, deputy head
of the Yomiuri Shimbun's political desk, to act as special lecturers. He also
created a doctoral program at the school's graduate school.

In June 1970, during his third year as president, an unfortunate incident
occurred at the university. A student belonging to the karate club died while
being hazed by an older student. Nakasone visited the student's parents in
Utsunomiya to apologize and handwrote a lengthy letter of apology, which
he sent to all students and their parents.

During his time as president, Nakasone also became concerned about
the state of university education. He saw a lack of individuality among the
students, and laziness and a desire to avoid trouble by some of the professors. In general, he believed that things had become too routine. He continued on as president for four years, until September 1971, and this served as
a good opportunity to deepen his thinking on education and contacts with
Asia. His budding interest in education reform, in particular, would lead
to the creation of the Provisional Council on Education after he became
prime minister.[24]

Notes

1 Nakasone Yasuhiro, Itō Takashi, and Satō Seiburō, *Tenchi Ujō – Gojū Nen no
   Sengo Seiji o Kataru* (Tokyo: Bungei Shunjū, 1996), 209–12. Nakasone Yasu-
   hiro, *Jiseiroku – Rekishi Hōtei no Hikoku to shite* (Tokyo: Shinchōsha, 2004),
   69–70. Hiwatari Yumi, *Sengo Seiji to Nichibei Kankei* (Tokyo: University of
   Tokyo, 1990), 254.
2 Nakamura Umekichi, *Watashi no Rirekisho* (Tokyo: Sachi Insatsu, 1984),
   92–94. Nakasone Yasuhiro, *Seiji to Jinsei – Nakasone Yasuhiro Kaikoroku*
   (Tokyo: Kōdansha, 1992), 190–92. Nakasone, *Jiseiroku*, 72–74. Nakasone
   Yasuhiro, *Nihon no Sōri-gaku* (Tokyo: PHP Shinsho, 2004), 34–35. Nakasone,
   Sengo Seiji, 29. Nakasone Yasuhiro, *Nakasone Yasuhiro ga Kataru Sengo
   Nihon Gaikō* (Tokyo: Shinchōsha, 2012), 143–44, 150. Nihon Keizai Shimbun,
   ed., *Watashi no Rirekisho Shōwa no Keieisha Gunzō 3* (Tokyo: Nihon Keizai
   Shimbun, 1992), 143–84. Koeda Yoshita, Kōno Yōhei, ed, *Tōjin Kōno Ichirō –
   Saigo no Jūnen* (Tokyo: Shunpū-sha, 2010), 80.

82 *From "Killing Time" to Becoming a Faction Leader*

3 Constitutional Research Committee Chairman Takayanagi Kenzō to Foreign Minister Kosaka Zentarō (January 12, 1961), Nihon Kenpō Kankei Ikken Kenpō Chōsakai Kankei Yabe Fukukaichō Nado Kaigai Shucchō Kankei, A'.3.0.0.3-3-3, MOFA. Memorandum of Conversation Between Nakasone and J. Graham Parsons (March 7, 1961), Assistant Secretary for Far Eastern Affairs Files, 1960–1963, Box 5, RG59, NA. Nakasone Yasuhiro, "Kyūba Kakumei no Chōryū," *Asahi Shimbun* (March 10, 1961) evening edition. Nakasone Yasuhiro, "Kokusai Seiji ni okeru Nihon no Hōkō – Atarashii Amerika o Hōmon shite," *Gaikō Jippō* (May 1961), 14–17, 23. Nakasone Yasuhiro, *Atarashii Hoshu no Riron* (Tokyo: Kōdansha, 1978), 211–13. Nakasone, *Seiji to Jinsei*, 253–55. Nakasone Yasuhiro, *Rīdā no Jōken* (Tokyo: Fusō-sha, 1997), 78–80. Nakasone, *Jiseiroku*, 74–77. Nakasone Yasuhiro, *Sengo Seiji* (Tokyo: Yomiuri Shimbun, 2005), 29–31. Nakasone, *Nakasone Yasuhiro ga Kataru*, 144–47, 150–52. Takasaki Tatsunosuke Shū Kankō Iinkai, ed., *Takasaki Tatsunosuke Shū* (Tokyo: Tōyō Seikan, 1965), 2:169. Yabe Teiji, *Yabe Teiji Nikki Tsutsuji no Maki*, ed. Nikki Kankōkai (Tokyo: Yomiuri Shimbun, 1975), 3, 10–42, 54–55, 77, 192. Ōta Katsurō, Ōta Chieko, ed., *Nakasone Yasuhiro Daigishi Shiryōshū (Sono 3) Robāto Kenedi Bei Shihōchōkan Rainichi Kankei Shiryōshū Shōwa 36-nen 12-gatsu 23-nichi – Shōwa 43-nen 6-gatsu 10-ka* (May 1987), NDL. Nakasone, *Tenchi Ujō*, 199, 214–15, 223–26. Watanabe Tsuneo, *Watanabe Tsuneo Kaikoroku*, eds. Mikuriya Takashi, Itō Takashi, and Iio Jun (Tokyo: Chūō Bunko, 2007), 233. George R. Packard, *Raishawā no Shōwa-shi*, trans. Moriyama Naomi (Tokyo: Kōdansha, 2009), 334–35. Yoshitsugu Kōsuke, *Ikeda Seiken-ki no Nihon Gaikō to Reisen – Sengo Nihon Gaikō no Zahyōjiku 1960–1964* (Tokyo: Iwanami Shoten, 2009), 48–50. Makimura Kentarō, *Nicchū o Hiraita Otoko Takasaki Tatsunosuke* (Tokyo: Asahi Shimbun, 2013), 160–63.
4 Theodore H. White, *The Making of the President 1960* (New York: Atheneum House, 1961).
5 Nakasone, *Tenchi Ujō*, 79–80. Nakasone, *Rīdā no Jōken*, 64–65, 206–10. Nakasone Yasuhiro, *Nihonjin ni Itte Okitai Koto – 21 Seiki o Ikiru Kimi-tachi e* (Tokyo: PHP Kenkyūjo, 1998), 290–96. Nakasone Yasuhiro, *Hoshu no Yuigon* (Tokyo: Kadowa one Tēma 21, 2010), 190–95.
6 *Asahi Shimbun,* June 10, 1961. Nakasone, *Seiji to Jinsei*, 214–16. Satō Eisaku, *Satō Eisaku Nikki*, ed. Itō Takashi (Tokyo: Asahi Shimbun, 1997) 2:53. Kimura Tokio, ed., *Matsumura Kenzō Shiryōshū* (Tokyo: Sakuradakai, 1999), 268.
7 *Asahi Shimbun,* December 7, 1962. Nakasone Yasuhiro, "Nankyoku no Otoko-gokoro," *Bungei Shunjū* (February 1963), 220–25. Nakasone Yasuhiro, "Kokumin no Sōi ni motozuku Minzoku Kenpō no Seitei o," *Keizai Jidai* 29:8 (1964), 19–21. Nakasone Yasuhiro, *Nankyoku – Ningen to Kagaku* (Tokyo: Kōbundō, 1965), 39. Nakasone, *Nihon no Furontia*, 113–28, 202. Nakasone Yasuhiro, "Kōno Ichirō," in Jiyū Minshutō Kōhō Iinkai Shuppan-kyoku, ed., *Hiroku Sengo Seiji no Jitsuzō* (Tokyo: Jiyū Minshutō Kōhō Iinkai Shuppan-kyoku, 1976), 566. Nakasone, *Seiji to Jinsei*, 214–24, 257–59. Nakasone, *Rīdā no Jōken*, 193–94, 258–60. Nakasone, *Nihonjin ni Itte Okitai Koto*, 213–26. Nakasone Yasuhiro, *21 Seiki Nihon no Kokka Senryaku* (Tokyo: PHP Kenkyūjo, 2000), 172–79. Nakasone Yasuhiro, "Shushō Kōsen-ron no Tesshō," in Kōbundō Henshūbu, ed., *Ima "Shushō Kōsen" o Kangaeru* (Tokyo: Kōbundō, 2001), 3–54. Nakasone, *Jiseiroku*, 77–80, 249–50. Nakasone, *Nihon no Sōrigaku*, 85. Nakasone, *Nakasone Yasuhiro ga Kataru*, 147–48, 158–61. "Kenpō Chōsakai Dai Nijūgo-kai Sōkai Gijiroku" (March 25, 1964), National Archives of Japan Digital Archives, http://www.digital.archives.go.jp/ (Accessed September 23, 2014). Hasegawa Takashi, *Bakushin no 25 Nen – Hasegawa Takashi no Kōseki* (Tokyo: Rihōsha, 1981), 96. Nakasone, *Tenchi Ujō*, 215–23.

From "Killing Time" to Becoming a Faction Leader   83

8   Nakasone Yasuhiro, Kosaka Tokusaburō, "Hoshutō wa Shisei o Tadase," *Ekonomisuto* (December 31, 1963/January 7, 1964), 68. Nakasone, *Seiji to Jinsei*, 192–93.
9   Kanaya Osamu, ed., *Rongo* (Tokyo: Iwanami Bunko, 1999), 259–60. Nakasone Yasuhiro, "Watashi ga 'Rongo' ni Mananda Koto," *Diamond Harvard Business Review* (October 2009), 70. On Satō, see also: Hattori Ryūji, *Eisaku Satō, Japanese Prime Minister, 1964–72: Okinawa, Foreign Relations, Domestic Politics and the Nobel Prize*, trans. Graham B. Leonard (London: Routledge, 2021).
10 Postcard from Nakasone to Yabe Teiji (April 1965), Yabe Teiji Kankei Bunsho 54-280. *Asahi Shimbun*, April 17, 1965. *Asahi Shimbun*, April 18, 1965. Kawashima Shōjirō and Ōno Katsumi, "Dai Ikkai AA Kaigi 10 Shūnen Kiken Shikiten Shusseki Hōkoku" (April 26, 1965), Ajia-Afurika Kaigi 2013-719, MOFA. Nakasone Yasuhiro, "AA Kaigi ni Nozonde," *Jōmō Shimbun* (April 15, 1965). Nakasone Yasuhiro, "Gijidō no Arashi no Naka kara – Jūsū-satsu ni oyobu Memo ni miru Sengoshi," *Bungei Shunjū* (April 1965), 126–33. Nakasone Yasuhiro, "'Kōdo no Yakuwari' Ninshiki no Kaname – AA Gaikō ni okeru Nihon no Tachiba Jakaruta-Saigon o Mawatte," *Mainichi Shimbun* (May 1, 1965). Nakasone, *Nakasone Yasuhiro ga Kataru*, 165–67. Nakasone Yasuhiro and Nakatani Takeyo, "Dai Nikai AA Kaidan ni Nozomu Kihonteki Taido," *Minzoku to Seiji* (June 1965), 37–44.
    Ōta Katsurō, Ōta Chieko, ed., *Nakasone Yasuhiro Daigishi Shiryōshū (Sono 25) Takuetsu shita Gaikō Shuwan no Gensen – Dai Nikkan – Dai Rokkai – Dai Jūkai ni Wataru Gaiyū no Kiseki*, NDL, 135.
11 Sakamoto Yoshikazu, Nakasone Yasuhiro, "Vetonamu Mondai to Nihon no Susumubeki Michi," *Bungei Shunjū* (September 1965), 57–58, 66, 80–81, 89, 96. Nakasone, *Tenchi Ujō*, 228.
12 Seiunjuku, "Seiunjuku Dai Jūkyūkai Nentō Taikai" (January 1966), Yabe Teiji Kankei Bunsho, 1-194. Nakasone, *Nakasone Yasuhiro ga Kataru*, 164.
13 *Asahi Shimbun*, April 6, 1966. Nakasone Yasuhiro, "Nihon ga Beichū no Kakebashi ni," *Ekonomisuto* (April 26, 1966). Memorandum of Conversation between Nakasone and Thomas W. Ainsworth (September 15, 1966), Bureau of East Asian and Pacific Affairs, Office of Japanese Affairs, Subject Files, 1960–1975, Box 1, NA. Satō 2:394. Ikeda Naotaka, *Nichibei Kankei to "Futatsu no Chūgoku" – Ikeda, Satō, Tanaka Naikaku-ki* (Tokyo: Bokutaku-sha, 2004), 187.
14 Kōno Ichirō Denki Kankō Iinkai, ed, *Kōno-sensei o Shinobu* (Tokyo: Shunjūkai, 1966), 7–10. Nakasone Yasuhiro, "Jiyūminken no Kikotsu (Ko Kōno Ichirō Shichi Kaiki Aisatsu)" (July 8, 1971), in Ōta Katsurō and Ōta Chieko, eds., *Nakasone Yasuhiro Daigishi Shiryōshū (Sono 56) Denki Kankei Shiryōshū – Hoi-hen III Ji Shōwa 45-nen 1-gatsu 22-nichi shi Shōwa 63-nen 8-gatsu 21-nichi* (May 2002), NDL, 324. Nakasone, "Kōno Ichirō," 566–67. Watabe Ryōjirō, *Sonoda Sunao Zenjinzō* (Tokyo: Gyōsei Mondai Kenkyujō Shuppan-kyoku, 1981), 314. Inaba Osamu, *Inaba Osamu Kaisōroku* (Niigata: Niigata Nippō Jigyō-sha Shuppan-bu, 1989), 98–100. Nakasone, *Seiji to Jinsei*, 203–04.
15 Nakasone Yasuhiro, "Jimintō no Kaikaku to sono Shinrō" (Parts 1 to 3), *Jōmō Shimbun* (August 27–29, 1965).
16 Nakasone Yasuhiro, "Jimintō no Bijon," *Shinsei* No. 1 (August 1967), 13. Nakasone, *Seiji to Jinsei*, 268. Nakasone, *Sengo Seiji*, 31. Ōishi Buichi, *Oze made no Michi – Midori to Gunshuku o Motomete* (Tokyo: Sankei Shuppan, 1982), 37. On pages of 22 to 25 of "Hoshutō Tatenaoshi no Bijon to Jissen," *Keizai Tenbō* 39:2 (1967), Nakasone argued:

> It is being reported that Prime Minister Satō's popularity has fallen to 25%. As a member of the LDP, this is a truly regrettable number. But

84   From "Killing Time" to Becoming a Faction Leader

there is something even more regrettable. Namely that, while Prime Minister Satō's popularity numbers are poor, Socialist Party Chairman Sasaki's are even worse. [...]

There is no way for Japan to break out of its shell and reform without the LDP doing the same. And for that to happen, we must first make sure that our feet are planted correctly and firmly. It is with those thoughts that we have dissolved the "Shunjūkai" and shed the clothes of the Kōno era, forming the new "Shinsei Dōshikai" and advancing towards a new horizon.

17 Nakasone, *Seiji to Jinsei*, 268–71. Nakasone, *Rīdā no Jōken*, 192, 195–96. Nakasone, *Jiseiroku*, 82–84. Nakasone, *Nihon no Sōri-gaku*, 36. Sakurauchi Yoshio, "Watashi no Rirekisho 21," *Nihon Keizai Shimbun* (January 22, 1994). Karasawa Shunjirō, *Karasawa Shunjirō Ōraru Hisutorī Sorosoro Zenbu Hanashimashō* (Tokyo: Bungei Shunjū Kikaku Shuppan-bu, 2009), 120. Prior to Kōno's death, Nakasone said the following on factions to Ishida Hirohide and others:

> While I don't think that the current factions are okay as they are, they do fulfill the functions of factions somewhat. That is, they prevent a dictatorship of the head of the party as spoken of by Mr. Utsunomiya. The Yoshida Liberal Party suffered greatly from that vice. In that sense, the way things are now is better than how they were then. Ishida Hirohide, Utsunomiya Tokuma, Nakasone Yasuhiro, and Hayakawa Takashi, "Shinhoshushugi no Mezasu mono," *Asahi Jānaru* (January 27, 1963), 19.

18 Gifu Shimbun, ed., *Shisei Ikkan – Mutō Kabun Hanseiki* (Gifu: Gifu Shimbun, 2008), 84–86, 95, 102–07, 125–26, 136–38, 142–62. Kōno Yōhei, "Jidai no Shōgensha 8 San'in Kaikaku Tsuranuita Oji," *Yomiuri Shimbun* (September 26, 2012). Despite coming into conflict with Nakasone, Mutō returned to the Nakasone faction.

19 Sakurauchi, "Watashi no Rirekisho 21."

20 Nakagawa Ichirō, *Seirankai – Keppan to Yūkoku no Ronri* (Tokyo: Rōman, 1973), 209–19.

21 Karasawa, 171.

22 Watabe 239, 317. Iseri Hirofumi, *Habatsu Saihensei* (Tokyo: Chūkō Shinsho, 1983), 89. Nakasone, *Tenchi Ujō*, 238–41. Tominomori Eiji, *Sengo Hoshutō-shi* (Tokyo: Iwanami Gendai Bunko, 2006), 266.

23 Nakasone Yasuhiro and Ōno Hisao, "Genshiryoku Hatsuden to Ashihama," Parts 1 to 6, *Ise Shimbun* (October 26–31, 1966). Nakasone, *Tenchi Ujō*, 289. Japanese Modern Historical Manuscripts Association, "Mori Kazuhisa Ōraru Hisutorī" (Tokyo: Japanese Modern Historical Manuscripts Association, 2008), 23, 29, 42, 44–45, 76–77, 110, 118. *Asahi Shimbun,* July 19, 2011.

24 Nakasone Yasuhiro, "Gakusei Shokun ni Tsugeru – Nakasone Sōchō Shūnin no Kotoba" (Tokyo: Takushoku University, 1967), 4–5. Nakasone Yasuhiro, "Hajime ni," in Yabe Teiji, *Yabe Teiji Nikki Ichō no Maki*, ed. Nikki Kankōkai (Tokyo: Yomiuri Shimbun, 1975). Nakasone, *Seiji to Jinsei*, 274–77. *Yomiuri Shimbun,* June 16, 1970 evening edition. *Asahi Shimbun,* June 18, 1970. Kusano Fumio, ed., *Takushoku Daigaku 80-Nenshi* (Tokyo: Takushoku Daigaku Sōritsu 80 Shūnen Kinen Jigyō Jimukyoku, 1980), 494–558. Nakasone, *Tenchi Ujō*, 232–33. Hyakunenshi Shiryōshū Henshū Iinkai, ed., *Takushoku Daigaku Hyakunenshi Kokuji-hen* (Tokyo: Takushoku University, 2005), 238–72. Hyakunenshi Shiryōshū Henshū Iinkai, ed., *Takushoku Daigaku Hyakunenshi Shiryōhen 6* (Tokyo: Takushoku University, 2008), 26–30. Nakajima Shingo, *Sengo Nihon no Bōei Seisaku – "Yoshida Rosen" o Meguru Seiji/Gaikō/Gunji* (Tokyo: Keio University, 2006), 265–66.

From "Killing Time" to Becoming a Faction Leader   85

References

Gifu Shimbun, ed. *Shisei Ikkan – Mutō Kabun Hanseiki*. Gifu: Gifu Shimbun, 2008.

Hasegawa Takashi. *Bakushin no 25 Nen – Hasegawa Takashi no Kōseki*. Tokyo: Rihōsha, 1981.

Hiwatari Yumi. *Sengo Seiji to Nichibei Kankei*. Tokyo: University of Tokyo, 1990.

Hyakunenshi Shiryōshū Henshū Iinkai, ed. *Takushoku Daigaku Hyakunenshi Kokuji-hen*. Tokyo: Takushoku University, 2005.

Hyakunenshi Shiryōshū Henshū Iinkai, ed. *Takushoku Daigaku Hyakunenshi Shiryōhen 6*. Tokyo: Takushoku University, 2008.

Ikeda Naotaka. *Nichibei Kankei to "Futatsu no Chūgoku" – Ikeda, Satō, Tanaka Naikaku-ki*. Tokyo: Bokutakusha, 2004.

Inaba Osamu. *Inaba Osamu Kaisōroku*. Niigata: Niigata Nippō Jigyō-sha Shuppan-bu, 1989.

Iseri Hirofumi. *Habatsu Saihensei*. Tokyo: Chūkō Shinsho, 1983.

Jiyū Minshutō Kōhō Iinkai Shuppan-kyoku, ed. *Hiroku Sengo Seiji no Jitsuzō*. Tokyo: Jiyū Minshutō Kōhō Iinkai Shuppan-kyoku, 1976.

Kanaya Osamu, ed. *Rongo*. Tokyo: Iwanami Bunko, 1999.

Karasawa Shunjirō. *Karasawa Shunjirō Ōraru Hisutorī Sorosoro Zenbu Hanashimashō*. Tokyo: Bungei Shunjū Kikaku Shuppan-bu, 2009.

Kimura Tokio, ed. *Matsumura Kenzō Shiryōshū*. Tokyo: Sakuradakai, 1999.

Kōbundō Henshūbu, ed. *Ima "Shushō Kōsen" o Kangaeru*. Tokyo: Kōbundō, 2001.

Koeda Yoshita, Kōno Yōhei, ed. *Tōjin Kōno Ichirō – Saigo no Jūnen*. Tokyo: Shunpū-sha, 2010.

Kōno Ichirō Denki Kankō Iinkai, ed. *Kōno-sensei o Shinobu*. Tokyo: Shunjūkai, 1966.

Kōno Yōhei. "Jidai no Shōgensha 8 San'in Kaikaku Tsuranuita Oji." *Yomiuri Shimbun* (September 26, 2012).

Kusano Fumio, ed. *Takushoku Daigaku 80-Nenshi*. Tokyo: Takushoku Daigaku Sōritsu 80 Shūnen Kinen Jigyō Jimukyoku, 1980.

Makimura Kentarō. *Nicchū o Hiraita Otoko Takasaki Tatsunosuke*. Tokyo: Asahi Shimbun, 2013.

Nakagawa Ichirō. *Seirankai – Keppan to Yūkoku no Ronri*. Tokyo: Rōman, 1973.

Nakajima Shingo. *Sengo Nihon no Bōei Seisaku – "Yoshida Rosen" o Meguru Seiji/ Gaikō/Gunji*. Tokyo: Keio University, 2006.

Nakamura Umekichi. *Watashi no Rirekisho*. Tokyo: Sachi Insatsu, 1984.

Nakasone Yasuhiro. *21 Seiki Nihon no Kokka Senryaku*. Tokyo: PHP Kenkyūjo, 2000.

Nakasone Yasuhiro. "AA Kaigi ni Nozonde." *Jōmō Shimbun* (April 15, 1965).

Nakasone Yasuhiro. *Atarashii Hoshu no Riron*. Tokyo: Kōdansha, 1978.

Nakasone Yasuhiro. *Gakusei Shokun ni Tsugeru – Nakasone Sōchō Shūnin no Kotoba*. Tokyo: Takushoku University, 1967.

Nakasone Yasuhiro. "Gijidō no Arashi no Naka kara – Jūsū-satsu ni oyobu Memo ni miru Sengoshi." *Bungei Shunjū* (April 1965).

Nakasone Yasuhiro. *Hoshu no Yuigon*. Tokyo: Kadokawa one Tēma 21, 2010.

Nakasone Yasuhiro. "Jimintō no Bijon." *Shinsei*, No. 1 (August 1967).

Nakasone Yasuhiro. "Jimintō no Kaikaku to sono Shinrō," Parts 1 to 3. *Jōmō Shimbun* (August 27–29, 1965).

Nakasone Yasuhiro. *Jiseiroku – Rekishi Hōtei no Hikoku to shite*. Tokyo: Shinchōsha, 2004.

86 From "Killing Time" to Becoming a Faction Leader

Nakasone Yasuhiro. "'Kōdo no Yakuwari' Ninshiki no Kaname – AA Gaikō ni okeru Nihon no Tachiba Jakaruta-Saigon o Mawatte." *Mainichi Shimbun* (May 1, 1965).

Nakasone Yasuhiro. "Kokumin no Sōi ni motozuku Minzoku Kenpō no Seitei o." *Keizai Jidai* 29:8 (1964), 19–21.

Nakasone Yasuhiro. "Kokusai Seiji ni okeru Nihon no Hōkō – Atarashii Amerika o Hōmon shite." *Gaikō Jippō* (May 1961).

Nakasone Yasuhiro. "Kyūba Kakumei no Chōryū." *Asahi Shimbun* (March 10, 1961) evening edition.

Nakasone Yasuhiro. *Nakasone Yasuhiro ga Kataru Sengo Nihon Gaikō.* Edited by Nakashima Takuma, Hattori Ryūji, Noboru Amiko, Wakatsuki Hidekazu, Michishita Narushige, Kusunoki Ayako, and Segawa Takao. Tokyo: Shinchōsha, 2012.

Nakasone Yasuhiro. *Nankyoku – Ningen to Kagaku.* Tokyo: Kōbundō, 1965.

Nakasone Yasuhiro. "Nankyoku no Otoko-gokoro." *Bungei Shunjū* (February 1963).

Nakasone Yasuhiro. "Nihon ga Beichū no Kakebashi ni." *Ekonomisuto* (April 26, 1966).

Nakasone Yasuhiro. *Nihon no Sōri-gaku.* Tokyo: PHP Shinsho, 2004.

Nakasone Yasuhiro. *Nihonjin ni Itte Okitai Koto – 21 Seiki o Ikiru Kimi-tachi e.* Tokyo: PHP Kenkyūjo, 1998.

Nakasone Yasuhiro. *Rīdā no Jōken.* Tokyo: Fusō-sha, 1997.

Nakasone Yasuhiro. *Seiji to Jinsei – Nakasone Yasuhiro Kaikoroku.* Tokyo: Kōdansha, 1992.

Nakasone Yasuhiro. *Sengo Seiji.* Tokyo: Yomiuri Shimbun, 2005.

Nakasone Yasuhiro. "Watashi ga 'Rongo' ni Mananda Koto." *Diamond Harvard Business Review* (October 2009).

Nakasone Yasuhiro, Itō Takashi, and Satō Seiburō. *Tenchi Ujō – Gojū Nen no Sengo Seiji o Kataru.* Tokyo: Bungei Shunjū, 1996.

Nakasone Yasuhiro, Kosaka Tokusaburō. "Hoshutō wa Shisei o Tadase." *Ekonomisuto* (December 31, 1963/January 7, 1964).

Nakasone Yasuhiro and Nakatani Takeyo. "Dai Nikai AA Kaidan ni Nozomu Kihonteki Taido." *Minzoku to Seiji* (June 1965).

Nakasone Yasuhiro and Ōno Hisao. "Genshiryoku Hatsuden to Ashihama," Parts 1 to 6. *Ise Shimbun* (October 26–31, 1966).

Nihon Keizai Shimbun, ed. *Watashi no Rirekisho Shōwa no Keieisha Gunzō 3.* Tokyo: Nihon Keizai Shimbun, 1992.

Ōishi Buichi. *Oze made no Michi – Midori to Gunshuku o Motomete.* Tokyo: Sankei Shuppan, 1982.

Packard, George R. *Raishawā no Shōwa-shi.* Translated by Moriyama Naomi. Tokyo: Kōdansha, 2009.

Sakamoto Yoshikazu, Nakasone Yasuhiro. "Vetonamu Mondai to Nihon no Susumubeki Michi." *Bungei Shunjū* (September 1965).

Sakurauchi Yoshio. "Watashi no Rirekisho 21." *Nihon Keizai Shimbun* (January 22, 1994).

Satō Eisaku. *Satō Eisaku Nikki.* Edited by Itō Takashi. Tokyo: Asahi Shimbun, 1997.

Takasaki Tatsunosuke Shū Kankō Iinkai, ed. *Takasaki Tatsunosuke Shū.* Tokyo: Tōyō Seikan, 1965.

Tominomori Eiji. *Sengo Hoshutō-shi.* Tokyo: Iwanami Gendai Bunko, 2006.

Watabe Ryōjirō. *Sonoda Sunao Zenjinzō.* Tokyo: Gyōsei Mondai Kenkyujō Shuppan-kyoku, 1981.

Watanabe Tsuneo. *Watanabe Tsuneo Kaikoroku*. Edited by Mikuriya Takashi, Itō Takashi, and Iio Jun. Tokyo: Chūō Bunko, 2007.

White, Theodore H. *The Making of the President 1960*. New York: Atheneum House, 1961.

Yabe Teiji. *Yabe Teiji Nikki Ichō no Maki*. Edited by Nikki Kankōkai. Tokyo: Yomiuri Shimbun, 1975.

Yabe Teiji. *Yabe Teiji Nikki Tsutsuji no Maki*. Edited by Nikki Kankōkai. Tokyo: Yomiuri Shimbun, 1975.

Yoshitsugu Kōsuke. *Ikeda Seiken-ki no Nihon Gaikō to Reisen – Sengo Nihon Gaikō no Zahyōjiku 1960–1964*. Tokyo: Iwanami Shoten, 2009.

6 "Autonomous Defense" and the Three Non-Nuclear Principles

Nakasone under Satō – Minister of Transportation and Director-General of the Defense Agency

A Letter to Satō

Satō's control over the government would prove to be long-lived, and, as always, Nakasone belonged to the LDP anti-mainstream. But despite being publicly antagonistic toward Satō, Nakasone did not bear him any personal ill will. This can be seen in a letter from Nakasone to Satō dated May 13, 1966, concerning the reversion of Okinawa, a matter close to Satō's heart. Nakasone had met with US Ambassador Reischauer earlier that day, and he was writing to inform Satō of what he had learned of the American position on Okinawa.

Reischauer had told Nakasone that a complete reversion of Okinawa to Japanese control would be possible if special arrangements could be reached on certain matters such as prior consultation and nuclear weapons, and he advised that the Japanese take the initiative in these areas. He also expressed agreement with Nakasone's concept for a Pacific economic and cultural sphere. The tone of the letter was informative rather than advisory; while Nakasone outlined what he had been told by Reischauer, he did not make any personal suggestions to Satō as to how he should respond.

Nakasone and Satō also owned villas near each other in Karuizawa, and Nakasone had once met with Satō following a gold tournament there. During this period, Nakasone was keeping an eye out for opportunities to become closer to Satō, and it seems likely that Satō had an inkling of this fact.[1]

Europe under the European Community

On October 2, 1967, two days before taking a trip to Western Europe and the USSR, Nakasone visited Satō at the prime minister's office to pay his respects. During the visit, he returned a farewell gift (*senbetsu*) from Satō that had been entrusted to his wife Tsutako. He seems to have believed that, given his public opposition to Satō, it would be inappropriate to accept the gift.

Satō was not impressed by the gesture, writing in his diary that "Nakasone told me that he would be departing for the Soviet Union, so we discussed the news from Southeast Asia. But he returned a gift that Hiroko [Satō's wife]

DOI: 10.4324/9781003351931-7

had passed on to his wife. I accepted it without comment. What a rude man. Is he an idiot?"

Satō had visited Southeast Asia a month earlier, so it is likely that "news from Southeast Asia" refers to any major points of interest he had picked up during his meetings there.[2]

Nakasone visited Britain, France, West Germany, and the Soviet Union from the 4th to the 26th. His visit came only a few months after six European nations – including France and West Germany – had signed the Treaty of Brussels, forming the European Community (EC), and a major purpose of his visit was to get a rough sense of what things were like in each nation in particular and between Europe and Japan in general. As he departed from Haneda Airport, he was seen off by a large number of students from Takushoku University.

Nakasone wrote a series of articles on his trip for the *Jōmō Shimbun*, a local Gunma newspaper, and one of these concerned the reports he had received from local Japanese after his arrival in London about the high esteem with which Japanese products had come to be regarded in Britain: "The great progress that Japan has made over the past twenty years is remarkable. There were many Japanese in the terminal. [...] Japan stands second in the world in the field of electronics, alongside the United States [...] and we greatly surpass Britain and Germany."

Nakasone's confidence in Japan is readily apparent in his words: "Europeans refer to the Japanese as 'economic animals,' but this is an expression of jealousy towards Japan's surprising economic growth. There is no need for Japan to pay any heed to any comments along these lines from Europeans."

French membership in the EC had resulted in the lowering of tariffs, and Nakasone's visit came shortly after a series of riots by French farmers.

West Germany came next, and Nakasone noted after seeing the Berlin Wall that "There are some things that make you wonder how your fellow humans could be so foolish, that are unbearable to see. There were wreaths laid on the ground here and there to mark where those who had failed to escape had been shot. I couldn't bear to look at them."

After visiting East Berlin, he observed that "it was more cheerful than I had expected. Setting aside the question of the freedom of the people living there, it is gradually catching up to West Berlin, at least economically."

Nakasone took an interest in the ongoing West German debate over the imminent ratification of the Nuclear Non-Proliferation Treaty. After returning to Japan via the Soviet Union, he told the press that "Germany's stance towards the non-proliferation treaty is an extremely firm one; they are determined to see the positions of the non-nuclear nations reflected on issues such as peaceful use and the treaty's duration."

He felt that Japan, like West Germany, should use nuclear technology solely for the purpose of power generation. He continued to be interested in the field of nuclear energy and told the reporters that "further development

90 *"Autonomous Defense" and the Three Non-Nuclear Principles*

in the production of enriched uranium – solely for peaceful uses – is indispensable for our nation as an industrialized state. I therefore believe that an agreement between the political parties should be reached that enables us to embark on the production of enriched uranium."[3]

Minister of Transportation

Nakasone's return home coincided with Satō reshuffling his cabinet. He was appointed minister of transportation on November 25, 1967, returning to the cabinet after an absence of seven years. While Nakasone had once criticized the Satō government for being an "unbalanced conservative government" (due to its lack of members from the anti-mainstream factions), he had adopted a more conciliatory stance toward Satō prior to his appointment and said that he wanted to "reduce [his] distance from the mainstream factions."

Nakasone attributed his rapid shift from opposition to Satō to joining his government to wanting to support his efforts to bring about the return of Okinawa. According to Nakasone, one night shortly before the formation of the new government, he was summoned to Satō's home, where Satō welcomed him in a formal *haori hakama* and they had the following exchange:

S: I'm taking on the return of Okinawa. I'm going to put everything on the line, and I want your help. I don't care whether it means I'll have to resign as prime minister, just so long as I can manage to get this done.
N: You're really going to go for it?
S: That's why I called you here for this meeting.
N: This is a matter of national importance. You will have my cooperation whether I'm in the government or not.

This conversation almost seems to have served as a "ceremony" marking the change in Nakasone's attitude toward Satō.

Nakasone also linked his shift with Okinawa in an interview, explaining, "We couldn't have the conservative party divided on the issue of Okinawa. There would be no force behind our demands to America unless we came together and had a united front. [...] Satō's intention was to avoid conservative disunity and to use that to bring about the return of Okinawa. And that decision resonated with me."

But while he primarily attributed his sudden rapprochement with Satō to the Okinawa issue, Satō had set his sights on the return of Okinawa much earlier and his intentions were widely known.

More than two years earlier, on August 19, 1965, Satō had given a speech at Naha Airport in which he had said that he was "well aware that, so long as the return of Okinawa to the homeland has not been accomplished, the postwar era will not have ended for our nation." Satō's determination to have Okinawa returned had thus been made clear by 1965 at the latest, and Nakasone's attribution of his joining Satō's cabinet to the Okinawa issue seems at least somewhat contrived.

"Autonomous Defense" and the Three Non-Nuclear Principles 91

Nakasone's behavior was a marked change from his traditional opposition to Satō, and he tried to justify it to those around him at the time by explaining that "No one cares about the barking of a distant dog. You need to get close if you want the tip of your sword to reach." As could be expected, Nakasone was criticized as an opportunist and turncoat by both his fellow conservatives and members of the Left after accepting the position of transportation minister.

Having foreseen this reaction, Nakasone acted indifferent to the criticism, saying that "a man must be a hero to understand a hero." His decision to accept a position in the cabinet was at least partially motivated by factional strategy and was made in the belief that it would help him one day become prime minister. Entering the mainstream enabled him to have numerous members of his faction appointed to positions such as parliamentary vice-minister, deputy secretary general, and deputy chair of the PRC.

Now that his period of "killing time" had come to an end, Nakasone used his new position to take on Japan's "urban issue" – the rapid increase in the size of the commuting population that had accompanied high-speed economic growth. He called for "traffic measures to achieve a breakthrough on the urban issue" and, through his use of the Colloquium on Transportation and the Economy, sought to have the status of the Ministry of Transportation upgraded from an "authorization" ministry (*kyoninka kanchō*) to a "policy" ministry (*seisaku kanchō*).

He put forward a general unified transportation policy covering land, sea, and air transport and sought to reform the money-losing Japan National Railways. This effort was stymied by the railway workers' union, however; carrying out railway reform was something that would have to wait until Nakasone became prime minister.[4]

The Three Non-Nuclear Principles

As the Satō government pressed forward on the return of Okinawa, it could not avoid running into the issue of nuclear weapons, and members of the cabinet found themselves being questioned in the Diet on the issue of what was going to happen to the large number of American nuclear weapons currently deployed there.

Satō decided to address the issue by having the cabinet adopt a set of principles on nuclear weapons. He was scheduled to make a policy speech to the Diet on January 27, 1968, and brought up these principles at the cabinet meeting held a day earlier. Satō suggested at the meeting that the Japanese government should adopt a policy of "neither producing nor possessing nuclear weapons," but Nakasone suggested the addition of a third principle, that the government would also not "permit their introduction into Japan."

He argued forcefully for this additional principle by saying that "These will remain for future generations and have worldwide influence. They will be the principles of Prime Minister Satō. For that reason – and particularly

92 "Autonomous Defense" and the Three Non-Nuclear Principles

because they are going to be stated before the Diet in a policy speech – the better move would be to be bold and push forward with these three principles rather than adopt half-measures."[5]

Nakasone's steadfast advocacy for the peaceful use of nuclear energy gave his words particular weight, and Satō accepted the addition of this third principle.

In his January 27 policy speech, Satō said, "We pray for the total elimination of nuclear weapons, and we are determined to neither possess them nor permit their introduction into Japan."

As these discussions were going on, Satō was engaged in negotiations with Nixon over the reversion of Okinawa, using Kyoto Sangyo University professor Wakaizumi Kei as a secret envoy.

According to a document prepared by North American Affairs Bureau Director Tōgō Fumihiko in October of the following year, Satō came to regret his words here, saying that "the inclusion of 'nor permit their introduction' in the three non-nuclear principles has been a mistake." Satō viewed the deterrence offered by having nuclear weapons present as having a certain role to play.[6]

The "Non-Introduction" Principle as a "Political Gesture"

It had been Nakasone's words that had led Satō to adopt a prohibition on the introduction of nuclear weapons into Japan. And Nakasone had not only been referring to the deployment of land-based nuclear weapons; but he had also meant prohibiting naval vessels carrying nuclear weapons from entering Japanese ports. That meant that the proposed principle was in conflict with reality, however, as it was difficult to imagine that American warships removed their nuclear weapons before visiting Japan.

Nakasone only acknowledged this contradiction after his retirement from the Diet. He explained that the three non-nuclear principles had only been a "political gesture" meant for public consumption:

> The Japanese are always boldly talking about the three non-nuclear principles, but that's done for public consumption. Explicitly invoking the Satō government's doctrine lets the Japanese people and the world know of Japan's peaceful intentions.
>
> But if you're going to talk about how things really are, it seems quite unlikely that America offloads its nuclear weapons somewhere in the Pacific just so that its ships can visit Japan. That means that pretending America is acting in accordance with Japan's principles and not voicing any objections is the realistic course of action. And I think that's fine.
>
> Picture cases where [American warships] enter ports or pass through our territorial waters – through the Tsugaru Straits, for example. It would be unthinkable, as a matter of international etiquette, for us to

board those ships and carry out inspections. Publicly declaring the principles to the Japanese people is an effective political gesture. And a necessary one.

Nakasone was thus well aware that the three non-nuclear principles did not conform to reality. And much of the public was also aware that, in actual practice, nuclear weapons *were* being brought into Japan and that the principles were only word, not fact. There are no indications that Nakasone ever sought out the kind of breakthrough that could be used to help bridge this gap between the government and the people over nuclear weapons.

Nakasone stands in marked contrast with Ōhira Masayoshi, who was tormented by the fact that Japan's secret agreements on nuclear weapons with the US would become public one day and hoped to take proactive action on the problem. But Ōhira is the exceptional one here; most of Japan's prime ministers were like Nakasone: satisfied with merely making gestures for public consumption.[7]

Narita Airport and the Japan-Soviet Aviation Negotiations

Japanese air policy faced two long-standing issues at the time of Nakasone's appointment as transportation minister: the purchase of land for construction of New Tokyo International Airport (Narita Airport) and reaching a new aviation agreement with the Soviet Union.

The Satō government had approved a cabinet resolution for the construction of Narita Airport on July 4, 1966, but the purchase of the necessary land had been delayed by protests by local residents opposed to noise pollution and giving up their land and by leftist groups motivated for political reasons. Nakasone repeatedly negotiated with Chiba and Narita officials in an attempt to resolve the issue.

Talks with representatives of local farmers were carried out in secret through the mediation of Diet Member Yamamura Shinjirō of Chiba's 2nd District (which included Narita) and Nemoto Shinsuke (a member of the New Tokyo International Airport Authority and a confidante of Chiba Governor Tomonō Taketo). These representatives would be key to the process. With Tomonō and Nakasone looking on, a land agreement was signed between the New Tokyo International Airport Authority and the "four conditional agreement factions" at the Ministry of Transportation on April 6, 1968 (the "four conditional agreement factions" were groups of farmers who had agreed – under certain conditions – to sell their land).

The land was purchased at the high price of 140 million yen per hectare, a result of Nakasone seeking out the assistance of Finance Minister Mizuta Mikio. Despite the agreement, however, construction of the airport would continue to be delayed by demonstrations by the three-faction Zengakuren alliance in support of those farmers who continued to oppose the airport.[8]

94 *"Autonomous Defense" and the Three Non-Nuclear Principles*

The other unresolved aviation issue was revising the Japan-Soviet Aviation Agreement. The only flights between Japan and the USSR at the time were carried out by Aeroflot, the Soviet flag carrier, and Nakasone sought to have JAL be permitted to carry out independent operations in Moscow. He met with Premier Kosygin and Minister of Civil Aviation Loginov in Moscow from October 24 to 28 to pursue the issue.

During the talks, Nakasone implied that – should JAL not be permitted to carry out independent flights – access to Tokyo by Soviet flights might be cut off, saying that "I do not believe that [you] intend to draw out the resolution of this issue, but should the present situation continue, the Japanese people may come to feel that they have been deceived by the Soviet Union, which would make the situation difficult for the government."

He wanted an explicit statement as to when independent flight operations could begin, but the Soviet balked at this, as they had implemented special measures due to the Vietnam War. Nakasone predicted that they would concede to the Japanese request in the end, however, as the Aeroflot route to Tokyo was an important source of income for them and losing it would be a significant blow.

Nakasone eventually unilaterally declared the negotiations over and departed for the airport, prompting the Soviets to rush after him. A memorandum in which the Soviets agreed to the basic points of Japan's demands was signed in a guest room at the airport. The actual new aviation agreement would be concluded by Harada Ken, Nakasone's successor at the ministry.[9]

Back to the Wilderness

At the November 27, 1968 LDP party congress, Satō was elected to a third term as president. He had held office for four years at this point and faced opposition from Miki Takeo and Maeo Shigesaburō but was still able to secure a majority on the first ballot.

Fukuda Takeo, serving as party secretary-general for the second time, had announced his support for a third Satō term even before his candidacy had been declared. It was Tanaka Kakuei, chairman of the party's research commission on urban policy (and soon to be Fukuda's successor as secretary-general), who nominated Satō for his third term.

When Ōhira contacted Nakasone and asked him to throw his support behind Maeo, Nakasone avoided giving a clear answer as to whether he would be voting for Maeo or Miki, saying only that he would do his "best to ensure that everyone took an anti-Satō position."

After struggling with what to do, Nakasone ultimately endorsed the call for "a renewal of public support" (*jinshin isshin*). This phrase served as a slogan for Miki and Maeo. The Nakasone faction cast its votes for Miki, who he had worked alongside since his time in the opposition.

Having learned of Nakasone's plans prior to the vote, an irritated Satō wrote in his diary on November 20 that "the Nakasone faction is still in flux.

"Autonomous Defense" and the Three Non-Nuclear Principles 95

Can't make up its mind. Kodama [Yoshio] is showing up more and more. Nakasone isn't any good, either. If you're going to oppose me, you should come out and say so clearly."

He showed a little more compassion two days later, writing in the diary that "the Nakasone faction still hasn't chosen which way to go. I feel great pity for them." Nakasone naturally did not receive a post when Satō formed his new cabinet on November 30. He had temporarily moved closer to Satō, but it had now been two years since he had formed his faction and his focus had shifted to the post-Satō political landscape.[10]

Between the United States and China

Despite being the leader of only a small faction, Nakasone had his eyes set on becoming prime minister. And as was to be expected of this golden age of factional conflict in the LDP, that meant changing positions at a dizzying pace. What held fast throughout it all, however, was his interest in the constitution, nuclear power, and foreign affairs.

What was Nakasone's perception of Japan's international relations at this time? Nixon became US president on January 20, 1969. When the US-Japan Parliamentary Exchange Conference was held three weeks later on February 9, the LDP's Diet membership were represented by Nakasone, Maeo, Fujiyama Aiichirō, and Funada Naka.

The primary topic of conversation at the conference was the status of the American nuclear weapons deployed on Okinawa following the prefecture's return to Japan. The members of Congress present were nearly unanimous in believing that an American military presence in Okinawa would be meaningless unless their bases possessed nuclear weapons.

Nakasone rejected this, asserting that "it is only natural that [Okinawa] will have the same status as the rest of Japan following its return." He also touched on American policy toward China, saying, "I believe that sooner or later the Nixon administration will embark on peace with China. And if that's the case, it's best that it does so decisively and as quickly as possible."

He told the American legislators that he believed "that the greatest diplomatic task facing Japan in the 1970s will be the issue of how to normalize relations with China. [...] The path leading to normalization will be a gradual one, and I feel that the time has come for us to make a great first step upon it."

Rapid Sino-Japanese normalization was a pet issue of Nakasone's, something he had supported for decades. While Maeo and Fujiyama also argued for China's return to the international community, Funada asserted that "in the absence of any guarantee that China will be a state that abides by the UN Charter, we cannot afford to think emotionally about this issue."[11]

Whenever Nakasone exited the cabinet, he would travel overseas to deepen his understanding of the international situation. This time, he chose to leave

96 *"Autonomous Defense" and the Three Non-Nuclear Principles*

for Europe on June 12, spending a week attending the Paris Air Show at the invitation of the French government and visiting Italy and Spain.[12]

Searching for a Defense Policy

Nakasone's father Matsugorō had been suffering from cerebral softening, and on June 25, shortly after Nakasone's return from Europe, he passed away at Takasaki National Hospital. Despite his illness, it was a sudden and unexpected farewell.

Matsugorō had visited Tokyo just a month earlier, and Nakasone had proposed that they travel together, telling him that "Once the Diet term ends, let's go to Hawaii. I'll act as interpreter." His father had smiled, innocent as a child, at the idea. It was the last time the two men ever spoke.[13]

Satō visited America in November for a summit with Nixon that culminated in the announcement that the leaders had agreed that Okinawa would be returned to Japan in 1972. Renewal of the security treaty was scheduled for 1970 and Nakasone (who had already had a serious interest in defense policy) made multiple statements on the subject.

Alongside Sino-Japanese normalization, the idea of "autonomous defense" was a long-standing aspect of Nakasone's foreign policy beliefs and something that he spoke about at his faction's meetings and elsewhere. He said that "Ultimately, we should engage in autonomous defense alongside the protection we receive from the American nuclear umbrella and the 7th Fleet. Or we should consider the matter flexibly and exit the security treaty around 1975 as circumstances permit."

Which is to say that when Nakasone spoke of "autonomous defense," he did not envision it as an entirely independent capability. It took the protection offered by the American nuclear umbrella and the 7th Fleet as a given. And as he was making these statements, he was making moves to become director-general of the Defense Agency.[14]

The Five Principles of Autonomous Defense –
Director-General of the Defense Agency

Nakasone was appointed director-general of the Defense Agency on January 14, 1970 at the beginning of the third Satō government. Planning to seek an almost unprecedented fourth term as party president that autumn, Satō was taking steps to ensure support from the party's various factions; Nakasone's return to the cabinet had thus been widely expected.

Nakasone was commonly seen as a hawk, and his philosophy of "autonomous defense" was well-known. Asked by an *Asahi Shimbun* reporter shortly after his appointment whether autonomous defense was "incompatible with the idea of steadfastly relying on the US-Japan security treaty," Nakasone answered that "the basic idea behind my thinking on this issue is that you should protect your own country with your own hands. But you

"Autonomous Defense" and the Three Non-Nuclear Principles 97

should shore up any areas in which you're lacking by coordinating with countries with which you share common goals."[15]

Nakasone called himself the "volunteer director-general"; prior to his appointment, he had communicated to Satō through his friend Yotsumoto Yoshitaka that director-general of the Defense Agency was his desired cabinet position.

The rationale behind his desire for the position was that "security is the cornerstone of the US-Japan relationship. There are many frictions between us, and I want to learn just how far that relationship goes, the innermost depths that aren't apparent from the surface." Yotsumoto would continue to serve as a confidante to Nakasone throughout his time as prime minister.

Nakasone frequently remarked that "it will be the Japanese SDF who protect the skies above Tokyo," and he pushed for the return of some American military bases and joint US-Japanese control over others. Lt. General Graham, commander of the US forces in Japan, responded by telling Nakasone that there would be a large-scale reduction in the size of the American forces stationed in Japan.

Nakasone's primary objective as director-general was a revision of the "Basic Policy for National Defense." This policy, which had been enacted during the Kishi government, provided the framework for the gradual strengthening of Japan's defensive capabilities and its cooperation with foreign forces. Section 4 of the policy stated that "until the United Nations becomes able to effectively exercise its function of preventing overseas aggression, Japan will base its response to such on its security framework with the United States."

Nakasone saw this passage as "overemphasizing [Japanese] reliance on the UN and America. It contains no sense that the Japanese people intend to defend their own country themselves." He felt that this should be revised to state that "any foreign aggression will be repulsed by responding with the gathered strength of the entire nation. Cooperation with the United States will be undertaken as necessary in carrying this out."

What exactly did Nakasone mean when he spoke of "autonomous defense?" Questioned on this by Socialist Diet Member Hanyū Sanshichi at the March 23 meeting of the House of Councillors' Budget Committee, he laid out what he saw as the "five principles" behind the concept:

> Having considered this question to the best of my ability, I have come up with a sort of "five principles" for autonomous defense. First, devotion to the defense of Japanese territory and adherence to the Japanese constitution. Second, unity with foreign policy and harmony with the nation's other policies. Third, thorough civilian control. Fourth, continued adherence to the three non-nuclear principles. And fifth, the strengthening of the US-Japan security framework. I believe that we should gradually and steadily expand our defensive capabilities in accordance with these five principles.

98 *"Autonomous Defense" and the Three Non-Nuclear Principles*

Given Nakasone's long history of calling for constitutional revision, his mention of "adherence to the Japanese constitution" in the first of these principles can be seen as him backtracking on the issue. And his deep involvement in the three non-nuclear principles mentioned in the fourth principle has already been discussed.

It was the fifth of these principles – "strengthening the US-Japan security framework" – that was the most significant. In another piece of testimony before the Budget Committee, Nakasone spoke of "doing away with our unprincipled reliance [upon the American military] and making clear which responsibilities fall to Japan and which fall to the United States. Once we have done that, we can move forward, each carrying out the functions that should properly belong to us."

Nakasone continually showed enthusiasm for revising the Basic Policy at meetings, but the other important members of the cabinet – most notably Satō – had little interest in such a controversial effort, especially with the return of Okinawa happening in the near future.[16]

"We Should Defer Any Decision on the Introduction of Nuclear Weapons"

While Nakasone had spoken of the three non-nuclear principles and strengthening the US-Japan security framework while testifying before the Diet, he showed a different side in his interactions with the United States. He visited America from September 8 to 20, 1970, meeting with Defense Secretary Laird, Secretary of State Rogers, Under Secretary of State Johnson, National Security Advisor Kissinger, Senator Mansfield, and others. I would like to draw particular attention to his discussions with Secretary Laird.

According to recently declassified Japanese documents, Nakasone revealed his intention to revise the Basic Policy on National Defense to Laird, saying that Japan "should make clear that we will defend against a foreign invasion through our own efforts, making effective use of the US-Japan security treaty." But he also said that his "personal view is that it would be better – to avoid foreign misunderstandings and maintain domestic consensus – to write in that we will not possess nuclear weapons. I also believe that we should defer any decision on the introduction of American nuclear weapons."

This last sentence is the most significant part of the statement as it clearly contradicts the third non-nuclear principle. Laird's agreement that "the location of nuclear weapons is an important issue for nuclear deterrence and shouldn't be discussed lightly" also carried the implication that nuclear weapons might be reintroduced in the future.

The American record of the meeting similarly states that Nakasone said, "In order to avoid any misunderstandings from other countries and to respect our national consensus, I believe that we should make clear that we will not possess nuclear arms. However, I believe that we should defer any

"*Autonomous Defense*" *and the Three Non-Nuclear Principles* 99

decision on the (re)introduction of American nuclear weapons. That would be a matter for prior consultation and the wise course would be to leave that open as a possible choice."

In other words, while Nakasone told the Americans that he intended to revise the Basic Policy, he also went so far as to make references to the introduction of American nuclear weapons into Japan.

His intention in doing so was to leave open the possibility of American nuclear weapons being introduced into Japan as an emergency measure following consultations with the Japanese government. But while leaving this option open provided flexibility, it clearly contradicted the non-nuclear principles that he himself had advocated for.

While Nakasone sought to revise the Basic Plan on National Defense, he did not seek to escape Japan's dependence on the American military's nuclear weapons, and he did not emphasize Japanese autonomy in his discussions with the US to the same degree that he had domestically. Taken alongside his stepping back from constitutional revision, it could perhaps be said that Nakasone was embarking on a more realistic course of action. But these positions were unlike him. This moderation of his views was likely related to Nakasone contemplating becoming a candidate for the LDP presidency in the near future.

Rather than these views, however, what would make him stand out as a director-general would be his promotion of the "Nakasone Concept" and his well-publicized rides in fighter aircraft.[17]

The "Nakasone Concept" and Japan as a "Non-Nuclear Mid-Tier State"

On October 7, 1970, Nakasone became the first serving director-general of the Defense Agency to visit Okinawa. While the visit came at the invitation of the American military, it was also motivated by his desire to gain a sense of what local conditions were like prior to the Self-Defense Forces' (SDFs) post-reversion deployment to the prefecture. His arrival at Naha Airport was marked by minor skirmishes between progressive groups opposed to his visit and conservative groups welcoming him.

He traveled directly to Zukeran in the middle of the island in a US military helicopter after arriving at Naha Airport and was welcomed by High Commissioner Lampert (the highest-ranking American official in Okinawa). He was also given a tour of Kadena Air Force Base.

Meeting with Chief Executive of the Government of the Ryukyu Islands Yara Chōbyō, he spoke about the Defense Agency's plans for the deployment of the SDF (although he prefaced his statement with the caveat that "as we adequately ascertain the intentions of the residents of Okinawa, they will be reflected in our defense policy").

Upon his return to Tokyo, Nakasone oversaw the launch of "Defense of Japan," an annual defense white paper, on October 20. In marking

100 *"Autonomous Defense" and the Three Non-Nuclear Principles*

the occasion, he referred to Japan as a "non-nuclear mid-tier state" and explained that it was an "economic power that would not become a military power":

> [The SDF] is devoted to the defense of our national territory and communities, and it exists under the leadership of a government that desires world peace. It does not possess offensive weaponry that poses a threat to those overseas. Nor does it send troops abroad or engage in conscription. And the government maintains the three non-nuclear principles as national policy.
>
> Based on these facts, I have advocated for Japan to have a defense concept suitable for a "non-nuclear mid-tier state." Under the Western European thinking that has been dominant up until this point, there has been a preconception that an economic power must also become a military power. We have challenged this way of thinking. We assert that the Japanese will be the great people who develop a culture of world peace, a spiritual order for the new era; an economic power that will not become a military power.

While Nakasone was seen as an advocate for military expansionism and increased the size of the defense budget, here he asserted that Japan's economic strength did not necessarily mean that it had to also become a military power.

On October 21, the day after the white paper's publication, Nakasone provided an outline of the "New Defense Program" (Shin Bōeiryoku Seibi Keikaku) which would cover the 1972 to 1976 fiscal years. This would normally have been called the Fourth Defense Program, but Nakasone adopted the new name to emphasize its uniqueness.

The new program's main distinguishing points were its emphasis on the domestic manufacture of defense equipment and its increase in the size of the SDF (particularly the MSDF and ASDF). The ASDF budget was increased to 2.8 times of its contemporary size. The defense budget under the plan was projected to raise Japan to roughly seventh in the world in terms of defense spending, an 18% increase, which caused it to come under fire from the opposition parties.

As mentioned earlier, Nakasone had referenced the introduction of nuclear weapons during his conversation with Secretary Laird. But this had not meant that he had forsaken the "autonomous defense" concept that he had advocated for ever since the Occupation. Increasing the defense budget and emphasizing domestic production were part of his vision for a future where the United States would only station forces in Japan in an emergency.

This vision of Japan's defense has been called the "Nakasone Concept" and would never come to fruition as it faced opposition from within the Defense Agency itself as well as from other quarters. Then-US Ambassador to Japan Meyer felt that the concept was "utterly foolhardy."

"Autonomous Defense" and the Three Non-Nuclear Principles   101

And while Nakasone called for Japan being a "non-nuclear mid-tier nation" in public, this was not the direction he was moving in with the Defense Agency, as he had directed the agency's technicians to examine the feasibility of Japan possessing nuclear weapons. Their findings were that they were confident that Japan could develop them within five years at the cost of two hundred billion yen.

One difficulty facing Japan in this respect was the absence of a suitable area within the country for nuclear testing. Nakasone judged that "There is nothing wrong, given the horrific damage suffered by Hiroshima and Nagasaki, with expressing anti-nuclear sentiment. But it is to Japan's benefit internationally to show that it chooses not to develop nuclear weapons despite being fully capable of doing so."[18]

Nakasone's "Stunts"

One of the unique characteristics of Nakasone as director-general was the manner in which he displayed his affection toward the SDF and its members. He rode in fighter aircraft, visiting units all across the country in an effort to raise the morale of SDF personnel.

Administrative Vice-Minister of Defense Obata Hisao and other members of the Defense Agency leadership opposed these visits, fearing a crash, but Nakasone brushed off these concerns, arguing that, with frontline pilots being asked to scramble every day, "it was obvious that their leader should be willing to shoulder the same risks."

Various medical tests were required before personnel were allowed to ride in jet fighters, and Nakasone was cleared by the ASDF's aeromedical laboratory in Tachikawa on January 20, 1970. He then flew to Hokkaido from Iruma Base in Saitama in a T-33 jet trainer. There, he stayed in snow-covered barracks and shared the communal baths with the members of the base. In Kyushu, he flew in anti-submarine reconnaissance planes and an F-104 fighter.

He was aware that these efforts were likely to be dismissed as being merely performative. But according to Nakasone, "the public of the time did not necessarily view the SDF in a positive light. I felt it important to become the comrade of those young service members and to help ease their minds."

Nakasone's words and actions were viewed with suspicion, not only by some members of the media and the public but by figures within the Defense Agency and SDF as well (notably Vice-Minister Obata).

Nakamura Teiji, head of the MSDF Staff Office's Defense Department at the time and a future MSDF chief of staff, recalled that "Those performances – going around to units and flying in fighter aircraft [...] they were the kind of thing suitable for a small unit commander, not for the director-general. I saw them as something that he was doing to boost his popularity and did not look upon them favorably."

102 *"Autonomous Defense" and the Three Non-Nuclear Principles*

Nakasone formed the "Committee to Examine Japan's Defense, the Defense Agency, and the Self-Defense Forces," a group of various civilian experts, to help further the public's understanding of defense issues. He was also the one who convinced Kyoto University professor Inoki Masamichi, an authority on international politics, to serve as president of the National Defense Academy.

While Nakasone would continue to show affection for the SDF, his time as director-general was short-lived. When Satō again reshuffled his cabinet on July 5, 1971, Nakasone was appointed LDP General Council chairman. His departure from the Defense Agency meant that his plans for revising the Basic Plan for National Defense fell by the wayside. A House of Councillors election had been scheduled for June, and Satō had told Nakasone that he was opposed to any revisions being made in the lead up the election and that he should "treat the matter carefully."[19]

Notes

1 Letter from Nakasone to Satō Eisaku (May 13, 1966). Satō Eisaku, *Satō Eisaku Nikki*, ed. Itō Takashi (Tokyo: Asahi Shimbun, 1997), 2:77, 432, 488, 3:313. Satō Hiroko, *Satō Hiroko no Saishō Fujin Hiroku* (Tokyo: Asahi Bunko, 1985), 174–76. Yamada Eizō, *Seiden Satō Eisaku* (Tokyo: Shinchō-sha, 1988), 2:162. Nakashima Takuma, *Okinawa Henkan to Nichibei Anpo Taisei* (Tokyo: Yuhikaku, 2012), 44. On page 176 of Ishida Hirohide, Ōhira Masayoshi, and Nakasone Yasuhiro, "Henbō suru Shakai ni Taiō dekiru ka," *Chūō Kōron* (August 1967), Nakasone argued that "the Kōno and Ikeda factions are sensible, but the Kishi and Satō factions have a lot of outdated thinking."
2 Satō Eisaku 3:145.
3 Nakasone Yasuhiro, "Yōroppa Dayori," *Jōmō Shimbun,* October 13, 16, 24, 25, 27, 1967.
4 *Asahi Shimbun,* November 21, 29, December 6, 1967; March 14, July 6, 1968. Miyazaki Yoshimasa, *Seikai 25 Nen* (Tokyo: Yomiuri Shimbun, 1970), 301. Nakasone Yasuhiro, *Seiji to Jinsei – Nakasone Yasuhiro Kaikoroku* (Tokyo: Kōdansha, 1992), 272–73. Nakasone Yasuhiro, *Rīdā no Jōken* (Tokyo: Fusō-sha, 1997), 68. Nakasone Yasuhiro, *Jiseiroku – Rekishi Hōtei no Hikoku to shite* (Tokyo: Shinchōsha, 2004), 84–87. Nakasone Yasuhiro, *Sengo Seiji* (Tokyo: Yomiuri Shimbun, 2005), 32. Nakasone Yasuhiro, *Nakasone Yasuhiro ga Kataru Sengo Nihon Gaikō* (Tokyo: Shinchōsha, 2012), 188. Nakasone Yasuhiro, *Tenchi Ujō – Gojū Nen no Sengo Seiji o Kataru* (Tokyo: Bungei Shunjū, 1996), 236–37, 244, 247–48. Satō Eisaku 3:47, 124, 182, 214, 221, 270. Watanabe Tsuneo, *Watanabe Tsuneo Kaikoroku*, eds. Mikuriya Takashi, Itō Takashi, and Iio Jun (Tokyo: Chūō Bunko, 2007), 272–73. Nakashima Takuma, *Kōdo Seichō to Okinawa Henkan 1960–1972* (Yoshikawa Kobunkan, 2012), 147.
5 Satō Eisaku 3:223. Kusuda Minoru, *Kusuda Minoru Nikki – Satō Eisaku Sōri Shuseki Hishokan no 2000 Nichi*, eds. Wada Jun and Iokibe Makoto (Tokyo: Chūō Kōron Shinsha, 2001), 159. Ōta Masakatsu, *Nichibei "Kaku Mitsuyaku" no Zenbō* (Tokyo: Chikuma Shobō, 2011), 236. Nakasone, *Nakasone Yasuhiro ga Kataru,* 179.
6 Ministry of Foreign Affairs North American Bureau Director Tōgō Fumihiko, "Shushō ni tai suru Hōkoku (Okinawa Kankei)" (October 7, 1969), http://www.mofa.go.jp/mofaj/gaiko/mitsuyaku/pdfs/k_1972kaku2.pdf (accessed

"Autonomous Defense" and the Three Non-Nuclear Principles 103

September 24, 2014). Prime Minister's Secretariat, ed., *Satō Naikaku Sōri Daijin Enzetsu-shū* (Tokyo: Prime Minister's Secretariat, 1970), 192. *Asahi Shimbun,* March 10, 2010. Nakashima, *Okinawa Henkan to Nichibei Anpo Taisei,* 237–38. Ōta, 100.

7   Nakasone Yasuhiro, *Nihon no Sōri-gaku* (Tokyo: PHP Shinsho, 2004), 131. Nakasone Yasuhiro, *Seizan Jōunpo – Nakasone Yasuhiro Taidan-shū* (Tokyo: Mainichi Shimbun, 2012), 29–31. Nakasone, *Nakasone Yasuhiro ga Kataru,* 180–83. Hattori Ryūji, *Ōhira Masayoshi Rinen to Gaikō* (Tokyo: Iwanami Shoten, 2014), 62–63, 112, 119–20, 145–49, 172–74, 188–89, 211.

8   *Asahi Shimbun,* April 6, 1968 evening edition. Nakasone, *Seiji to Jinsei,* 233–34. Nakasone, *Tenchi Ujō,* 245. Satō Eisaku 3:250–52, 262.

9   "Nihon-koku Unyu Daijin to Sovieto Shakai Shugi Kyōwakoku Renpō Minkan Kōkū Daijin to no Aida no Kōshō ni kan suru Oboegaki" (October 28, 1968), MOFA 2014-191. Ministry of Foreign Affairs Eurasian Affairs Bureau Eastern European Section, "Nakasone Unyu Daijin-Roginofu Soren Minkan Kōkū Daijin Kaidan Yōroku" (November 15, 1968), MOFA 2014-191. Eastern European Section, "Nakasone Unyu Daijin-Kosuigin Shushō Kaidanroku" (November 15, 1968), MOFA 2014-191. *Asahi Shimbun,* October 29, 1968. Letter from Premier Kosygin to Prime Minister Satō (February 3, 1969), "Kokusho oyobi Shinsho Kankei – Satō, Tanaka Sōri Shinsho Kankei" Vol. 6, N'1.8.0.1-1, MOFA. Nakasone, *Seiji to Jinsei,* 234–36. Nakasone, *Rīdā no Jōken,* 109–12. Nakasone, *Nakasone Yasuhiro ga Kataru,* 173–75. Nakasone, *Tenchi Ujō,* 245–47. Satō Eisaku 3:307.

10 *Asahi Shimbun,* November 3, 23, 25, 1968, November 26, 1968 evening edition. Satō Eisaku 3:338, 342, 345–46, 348–55.

11 Nakasone Yasuhiro, "Atarashii Nichibei Kankei no Kensetsu" (February 9, 1969), author's collection, 10–12. *Asahi Shimbun,* February 10, 1969.

12 Nakasone, *Nakasone Yasuhiro ga Kataru,* 634.

13 *Asahi Shimbun,* June 26, 1969. Nakasone Yasuhiro, "Chichi no Omoide" (June 26, 1969), author's collection, 15.

14 *Asahi Shimbun,* August 31, September 26, October 15, 1969.

15 *Asahi Shimbun,* January 13, 1970, evening edition, January 15, 18, 1970. Prior research includes: Nakashima Takuma, "Nakasone Yasuhiro Bōei Chōkan no Anzen Hoshō Kōsō – Jishu Bōei to Nichibei Anzen Hoshō Taisei no Kankei o Chūshin ni," *Kyūdai Hōgaku* No. 84 (2002), 107–60. Nakashima Takuma, "Sengo Nihon no 'Jishu Bōei' Ron – Nakasone Yasuhiro no Bōei Ron o Chūshin ni," *Hōsei Kenkyū* 71:4 (2005), 514–27. Nakashima, *Kōdo Seichō to Okinawa Henkan,* 244–47, 252–53, 264, 278–79. Ōta Masakatsu, *Meiyaku no Yami – "Kaku no Kasa" to Nichibei Dōmei* (Tokyo: Nihon Hyōron-sha, 2004), 254–64. Ōta, *Nichibei "Kaku Mitsuyaku" no Zenbō,* 246–47. Kotani Tetsuo, "Kūbo 'Middowei' no Yokosuka Bokōka o Meguru Nichibei Kankei," *Dōshisha Amerika Kenkyū* No. 41 (2005), 95–96, 105. Segawa Takao, "Nichibei Bōei Kyōroku no Rekishiteki Haikei – Nikuson Seikenki no Tainichi Seisaku o Chūshin ni," *Nenpō Kōkyō Seisaku Gaku* No. 1 (2007), 101–04. Toyoda Yukiko, *"Kyōhan" no Dōmei-shi – Nichibei Mitsuyaku to Jimintō Seiken* (Tokyo: Iwanami Shoten, 2009), 242–48. Ishii Osamu, *Zero kara Wakaru Kaku Mitsuyaku* (Tokyo: Kashiwa Shobō, 2010), 47. Lee Dong-jun, *Mikan no Heiwa – Beichū Wakai to Chōsen Mondai no Hen'yō 1969–1975 Nen* (Tokyo: Hosei University, 2010), 142, 185. Yoshida Shingo, *Nichibei Dōmei no Seidoka* (Nagoya: Nagoya University, 2012), 134, 142, 151–52, 156, 164–71. Nakajima Shingo, "Satō Seikenki ni okeru Anzen Hoshō Seisaku no Tenkai – 1964-72 Nen," in Hatano Sumio, ed., *Reisen Hen'yō-ki no Nihon Gaikō – "Hiyowana Taikoku" no Kiki to Mosaku* (Tokyo: Minerva Shobō, 2013), 168–71. Itō

104 *"Autonomous Defense" and the Three Non-Nuclear Principles*

Takashi, "Shiryō to Watashi no Kindai-shi – Daijūsankai Kaihara Osamu, Watanabe Tsuneo, Takaragi Fumihiko Ōraru Hisutorī 2," *Chūō Kōron* (June 2014), 163–64.

16 See endnote 19.
17 See endnote 19.
18 See endnote 19.
19 Nakasone Yasuhiro, "Kore kara no Nihon no Bōei – Daiyonji Bōeiryoku Seibi Keikaku Sakutei no Zentei ni tsuite" (March 19, 1970), in Sadō Akihiro, Taira Yoshitoshi, and Kimishima Yūichirō, eds., *Dōba Bunsho* (Tokyo: Maruzen DVD, 2013), Documents 2047, 2081. Nakasone Yasuhiro, "Jieitai Kōkyū Kanbu Kaidō ni okeru Bōeichō Chōkan Kunji (Yōshi)" (March 29, 1970), in Sadō, Document 2062. Nakasone Yasuhiro, "'Nihon no Bōei' no Hakkan ni Atatte," *Seisaku Geppō* No. 178 (1970), 50. Nakasone, *Seiji to Jinsei*, 52, 237–45, 343. Nakasone Yasuhiro. *21 Seiki Nihon no Kokka Senryaku* (Tokyo: PHP Kenkyūjo, 2000), 153–60. Nakasone, *Jiseiroku*, 224–25. Nakasone, *Nihon no Sōri-gaku*, 37. Nakasone, *Nakasone Yasuhiro ga Kataru*, 77, 194–222. Nakasone Yasuhiro, "Bōei Hakusho Kankō 40-kai ni Yosete," in *Bōei Hakusho* (2014). *Asahi Shimbun,* February 13–14, October 8, October 8 evening, October 9, October 9 evening, October 22, 1970, July 21, 2011. *Yomiuri Shimbun,* July 1, 10, October 22, 1970. "Nakasone-Reādo Kaidan Kiroku" (September 9, 1970). "Secretary's Meeting with Nakasone" (September 12, 1970), Digital National Security Archive, http://nsarchive.chadwyck.com (accessed January 28, 2012). Ambassador to the US Ushiba Nobuhiko to Foreign Minister Aichi Kiichi (September 10, 1970), "Nichibei Kankei (Okinawa Henkan) 37/1970-Nen SOFA no Tekiyō (Kichi no Seiri-Tōgō)," MOFA 2014-4126. "'Nihon no Bōei to Bōeichō-Jieitai o Shindan suru Kai' ni your Shindan ni tsuite," *Kokubō* 19:9 (1970), 93–98. Diet Proceedings Search System, http://kokkai.ndl.go.jp/ (accessed August 9, 2014). Armin H. Meyer, *Tokyo Kaisō*, trans. Asano Michiko, (Asahi Shimbun, 1976), 85, 90. Ushiba Nobuhiko, *Gaikō no Shunkan – Watashi no Rirekisho* (Tokyo: Nihon Keizai Shimbun, 1984), 122. Mainichi Shimbun Seiji-bu, *Anpo* (Tokyo: Kadokawa Bunko, 1987), 254–55. Nakasone, *Tenchi Ujō*, 50–51, 249–59, 544. Satō Eisaku 4:185, 292, 312–13, 366, 368. National Graduate Institute for Policy Studies COE Oral Policy Research Project, *Kaihara Osamu Ōraru Hisutorī* (Tokyo: GRIPS, 2000), 2:281–89. National Graduate Institute for Policy Studies COE Oral Policy Research Project, *Itō Kei Ōraru Hisutorī* (Tokyo: GRIPS, 2003), 1:184–89, 200–01, 222–29, 234–35, 2:15–20, 26–29. National Graduate Institute for Policy Studies COE Oral Policy Research Project, *Yoshino Bunroku Ōraru Hisutorī* (Tokyo: GRIPS, 2003), 113. National Graduate Institute for Policy Studies COE Oral Policy Research Project, *Hōshayama Noboru Ōraru Hisutorī* (Tokyo: GRIPS, 2005), 1:97–100. Bōeishō Bōei Kenkyūjo Senshi-bu, ed., *Utsumi Hitoshi Ōraru Hisutorī* (Tokyo: Bōeisho Bōei Kenkyūjo, 2008), 65, 92. Bōeishō Bōei Kenkyūjo Senshi-bu, ed., *Nakamura Ryūhei Ōraru Hisutorī* (Tokyo: Bōeisho Bōei Kenkyūjo, 2008), 275–77. Nakamura Teiji, *Shōgai Kaigun Shikan – Sengo Nihon to Kaijō Jieitai* (Tokyo: Chūō Kōron Shinsha, 2009), 225–41, 249–51, 254, 274. Bōeishō Bōei Kenkyūjo Senshi-bu, ed., *Yamada Ryōichi Ōraru Hisutorī* (Tokyo: Bōeisho Bōei Kenkyūjo, 2009), 208–12. NHK Shuzai-han, *Kichi wa Naze Okinawa ni Shūchū shite iru no ka* (Tokyo: NHK, 2011), 83. Bōeishō Bōei Kenkyūjo Senshi-bu, ed., *Suzuki Akio Ōraru Hisutorī* (Tokyo: Bōeisho Bōei Kenkyūjo, 2011), 140–44. Nakashima, *Okinawa Henkan to Nichibei Anpo Taisei*, 295, 297, 302–03, 305, 312, 317. Pan Liang, "Kyōryoku e no Michinori – Keizai Taikoku Nihon no Tōjō to 1970 Nendai Shoki no Nichigō Kankei no Keisei," in Hatano Sumio, 86. Kaihara Osamu, head of the Cabinet National Defense Council's Executive Bureau, wrote the following on pages 59–60 of his book *Nihon Bōei Taisei no Uchimaku* (Tokyo: Jiji Tsūshin-sha, 1997):

"Autonomous Defense" and the Three Non-Nuclear Principles 105

The Fourth Defense Plan, which was spectacularly advertised as the "Nakasone Concept," was released as the "New Defense Program (Defense Agency Draft) 46-4-26" without making advance arrangements with the relevant offices and ministries. Because a number of problematic parts were identified over the course of the National Defense Council's Executive Bureau's study of the plan, things did not proceed in the way that the Defense Agency had expected.

Defense of Japan was not published after from Nakasone's departure as director-general until June 1976. Sakata Michita, *Chiisakutemo Ookina Yakuwari* (Tokyo: Asagumo Shimbun, 1997), 39–43.

References

Bōeishō Bōei Kenkyūjo Senshi-bu, ed. *Nakamura Ryūhei Ōraru Hisutorī*. Tokyo: Bōeisho Bōei Kenkyūjo, 2008.
Bōeishō Bōei Kenkyūjo Senshi-bu, ed. *Suzuki Akio Ōraru Hisutorī*. Tokyo: Bōeisho Bōei Kenkyūjo, 2011.
Bōeishō Bōei Kenkyūjo Senshi-bu, ed. *Yamada Ryōichi Ōraru Hisutorī*. Tokyo: Bōeisho Bōei Kenkyūjo, 2009.
Hatano Sumio, ed. *Reisen Hen'yō-ki no Nihon Gaikō – "Hiyowana Taikoku" no Kiki to Mosaku*. Tokyo: Minerva Shobō, 2013.
Hattori Ryūji. *Ōhira Masayoshi Rinen to Gaikō*. Tokyo: Iwanami Shoten, 2014.
Kusuda Minoru. *Kusuda Minoru Nikki – Satō Eisaku Sōri Shuseki Hishokan no 2000 Nichi*. Edited by Wada Jun, Iokibe Makoto. Tokyo: Chūō Kōron Shinsha, 2001.
Mainichi Shimbun Seijibu. *Anpo*. Tokyo: Kadokawa Bunko, 1987.
Meyer, Armin H. *Tokyo Kaisō*. Translated by Asano Michiko. Tokyo: Asahi Shimbun, 1976.
Miyazaki Yoshimasa. *Seikai 25 Nen*. Tokyo: Yomiuri Shimbun, 1970.
Nakamura Teiji. *Shōgai Kaigun Shikan – Sengo Nihon to Kaijō Jieitai*. Tokyo: Chūō Kōron Shinsha, 2009.
Nakashima Takuma. *Kōdo Seichō to Okinawa Henkan 1960–1972*. Tokyo: Yoshikawa Kobunkan, 2012.
Nakashima Takuma. *Okinawa Henkan to Nichibei Anpo Taisei*. Tokyo: Yuhikaku, 2012.
Nakasone Yasuhiro. *21 Seiki Nihon no Kokka Senryaku*. Tokyo: PHP Kenkyūjo, 2000.
Nakasone Yasuhiro. "Bōei Hakusho Kankō 40-kai ni Yosete." In *Ministry of Defense, Bōei Hakusho*. Tokyo: Nikkei Insatsu, 2014.
Nakasone Yasuhiro. *Jiseiroku – Rekishi Hōtei no Hikoku to shite*. Tokyo: Shinchōsha, 2004.
Nakasone Yasuhiro. *Nakasone Yasuhiro ga Kataru Sengo Nihon Gaikō*. Edited by Nakashima Takuma, Hattori Ryūji, Noboru Amiko, Wakatsuki Hidekazu, Michishita Narushige, Kusunoki Ayako, and Segawa Takao. Tokyo: Shinchōsha, 2012.
Nakasone Yasuhiro. "'Nihon no Bōei' no Hakkan ni Atatte." *Seisaku Geppō* No. 178 (1970).
Nakasone Yasuhiro. *Nihon no Sōri-gaku*. Tokyo: PHP Shinsho, 2004.
Nakasone Yasuhiro. *Rīdā no Jōken*. Tokyo: Fusō-sha, 1997.
Nakasone Yasuhiro. *Seiji to Jinsei – Nakasone Yasuhiro Kaikoroku*. Tokyo: Kōdansha, 1992.
Nakasone Yasuhiro. *Seizan Jōunpo – Nakasone Yasuhiro Taidan-shū*. Tokyo: Mainichi Shimbun, 2012.

106 *"Autonomous Defense" and the Three Non-Nuclear Principles*

Nakasone Yasuhiro. *Sengo Seiji*. Tokyo: Yomiuri Shimbun, 2005.

Nakasone Yasuhiro. "Yōroppa Dayori." *Jōmō Shimbun*, October 13, 16, 24, 25, 27, 1967.

Nakasone Yasuhiro, Itō Takashi, Satō Seiburō. *Tenchi Ujō – Gojū Nen no Sengo Seiji o Kataru*. Tokyo: Bungei Shunjū, 1996.

National Graduate Institute for Policy Studies COE Oral Policy Research Project. *Hōshayama Noboru Ōraru Hisutorī*. Tokyo: GRIPS, 2005.

National Graduate Institute for Policy Studies COE Oral Policy Research Project. *Itō Kei Ōraru Hisutorī*. Tokyo: GRIPS, 2003.

National Graduate Institute for Policy Studies COE Oral Policy Research Project. *Kaihara Osamu Ōraru Hisutorī*. Tokyo: GRIPS, 2000.

National Graduate Institute for Policy Studies COE Oral Policy Research Project. *Utsumi Hitoshi Ōraru Hisutorī*. Tokyo: GRIPS, 2008.

National Graduate Institute for Policy Studies COE Oral Policy Research Project. *Yoshino Bunroku Ōraru Hisutorī*. Tokyo: GRIPS, 2003.

NHK Shuzai-han. *Kichi wa Naze Okinawa ni Shūchū shite iru no ka*. Tokyo: NHK, 2011.

"'Nihon no Bōei to Bōeichō-Jieitai o Shindan suru Kai' ni yoru Shindan ni tsuite." *Kokubō* 19:9 (1970), 93–98.

Ōta Masakatsu. *Nichibei "Kaku Mitsuyaku" no Zenbō*. Tokyo: Chikuma Shobō, 2011.

Prime Minister's Secretariat, ed. *Satō Naikaku Sōri Daijin Enzetsu-shū*. Tokyo: Prime Minister's Secretariat, 1970.

Sadō Akihiro, Taira Yoshitoshi, and Kimishima Yūichirō, eds. *Dōba Bunsho*. Tokyo: Maruzen DVD, 2013.

Satō Eisaku. *Satō Eisaku Nikki*. Edited by Itō Takashi. Tokyo: Asahi Shimbun, 1997.

Satō Hiroko. *Satō Hiroko no Saishō Fujin Hiroku*. Tokyo: Asahi Bunko, 1985.

Ushiba Nobuhiko. *Gaikō no Shunkan – Watashi no Rirekisho*. Tokyo: Nihon Keizai Shimbun, 1984.

Watanabe Tsuneo. *Watanabe Tsuneo Kaikoroku*. Edited by Mikuriya Takashi, Itō Takashi, and Iio Jun. Tokyo: Chūō Bunko, 2007.

Yamada Eizō. *Seiden Satō Eisaku*. Tokyo: Shinchō-sha, 1988.

7 "Neoliberalism" and the Oil Crisis

MITI Minister in the Tanaka Government

LDP General Council Chairman

When the Satō cabinet was reorganized on July 5, 1971, for the final time, Fukuda Takeo and Tanaka Kakuei were appointed foreign and MITI ministers, respectively. Satō had been prime minister for nearly seven years at this point, and these appointments meant that Fukuda and Tanaka would be competing to be his successor. The position of chief cabinet secretary went to Takeshita Noboru, who had been elected five times.

Ōhira Masayoshi and Miki Takeo did not receive any positions in the cabinet, but Nakasone was named LDP General Council chairman. The General Council deliberated on and made decisions regarding important matters involving the management of the party and the Diet. It was composed of thirty members: fifteen from the House of Representatives. seven from the House of Councillors, and eight named by the party president. The chair had the power to summon the council and oversee its meetings.[1]

General Council chair, along with secretary-general and PRC chair, was considered one of the top three positions in the party. At the time of Nakasone's appointment, Hori Shigeru was serving as secretary-general, and Kosaka Zentarō was PRC chairman. While neither was a faction leader, both were powerful men in the party. Nakasone's term as chairman was for one year.

Electoral Maneuvering Over Nakasone

This was the first time that Nakasone had been appointed to one of the top three party posts. He wrote that "It was during the Satō government that I felt like I had finally gotten close to the prime minister's chair. During the nearly eight years that he was prime minister, I served as transportation minister, director-general of the Defense Agency, and LDP General Council chairman. I felt like my stock was finally listed in the First Section [of the Tokyo Stock Exchange]."[2]

While Nakasone may have felt that he was getting closer to reaching his goal of becoming prime minister, Fukuda's interpretation of the situation was significantly different. According to Fukuda, Satō had told him that

DOI: 10.4324/9781003351931-8

108 *"Neoliberalism" and the Oil Crisis*

he was arranging things so that the position of prime minister would "naturally" fall to Fukuda, "and his maneuvers towards Nakasone were one of the pillars of that effort."

Put another way, Satō's decision to appoint Nakasone as General Council chairman was an attempt to tame the frequently anti-Satō Nakasone and solidify Fukuda's position as the next party president. He told Fukuda that "[Nakasone's appointment] is a strategic move."

It is unclear from Satō's diary whether he actually had this kind of plan. But it is clear that he intended for Fukuda to be his successor, not Nakasone. He expected Nakasone to support Fukuda (who was from the same electoral district, after all), and Fukuda himself was confident that he would be the next president.

Instead of acting in accordance with the two men's expectations, however, Nakasone threw his support behind Tanaka in the election, nominally because Tanaka was in favor of normalizing relations with China.[3]

Nakasone was critical of Satō and Fukuda for their desire to maintain diplomatic relations with Taiwan. This is readily apparent in his April 17, 1972, speech to the Research Institute of Japan.

According to Nakasone, President Nixon's February visit to China had "naturally caused a piece of the San Francisco system to collapse." He also noted that while "the Soviets are following right on the heels of the Americans militarily," "America has had one of its hands bitten in the Vietnam War and been left one-handed."

Nakasone argued that "Reviewing Japan's policies, I find that there is something that we must reflect on and take steps to correct: [despite standing at a turning point in international politics], we are entirely lacking in any global policies or any ideology that would give birth to the same." "The time has come for Japan to become more proactive in its peaceful diplomacy towards the entirety of Asia." Japan should normalize relations with China, and it "should also become involved in the great global efforts aimed at the peaceful reunification of divided states [like China, Vietnam, and Korea]."

Asserting that "Japan is an ocean nation, and we are an ocean people," he also called for the "creation of an Asia-Pacific cooperative economic organization." This speech, made during the run-up to the presidential election, was a tacit criticism of the Satō government. Neither Satō nor Fukuda were in agreement with Nakasone's proposed policy toward China.[4]

The "Sankaku Daifuku Chū War"

As Satō's time as president came to an end after four terms and seven years and eight months in office, five men expressed an interest in succeeding him: Miki Takeo, Tanaka Kakuei, Ōhira Masayoshi, Fukuda Takeo, and Nakasone Yasuhiro. These five were collectively known as the "Sankaku Daifuku Chū" by the media. This phrase, created by taking one character from each of their names, is a play on words, with *sankaku* meaning "triangle" and *daifuku* being a traditional Japanese sweet that usually took the form of a round rice cake (*mochi*) with a sweetened red bean filling. Ignoring the "chū" for Nakasone for a moment, the phrase means "triangular daifuku."

I would like to take a look at one of the earliest uses of this phrase, a column that appeared in the September 17, 1971, evening edition of the *Yomiuri Shimbun*. The writer of the article regarded its usage as a form of satire:

> The phrase the "Sankaku Daifuku War" has appeared in parody of the post-Satō presidential election. This seems to be a bit of satire, likening the competition to a daifuku that, rather than being round as it should be, is malformed and triangular. Looking at it, one is completely at a loss as to where the bean paste (the core) actually is. [...]
>
> If one were to add a character for Nakasone Yasuhiro – hitherto excluded from this bit of parody – the phrase would become the "skirmish of the triangular daifuku," giving the impression of a chaotic free-for-all rather than some Battle of Sekigahara in which the fate of the realm is to be decided.

As seen from the article, Nakasone was considered a bit of an afterthought in the political competition, not a potential victor.[5]

On June 19, 1972, Nakasone attended a meeting with the other two top party leaders at party headquarters and then chaired a meeting of the General Council. When Satō appeared at the session to announce that he would be resigning, it was decided that his successor would be determined at a provisional party congress on July 5.[6]

When Nakasone began preparing to make a run for the presidency, many of his faction's Diet members told him that he should avoid the unwinnable battle. According to Satō Takayuki, Ōishi Buichi, Kōno Kenzō, Kōno Yōhei, and Tagawa Seiichi told Nakasone that they would leave the faction if he ran and the faction, in general, was "in complete disagreement over which faction to align with."

Nakasone's faction was relatively small, with only a little over forty members, meaning that defeat was certain. And if members started defecting to other factions, the very survival of the faction would be threatened. With no choice but to abandon his candidacy, Nakasone voted for Tanaka with the hope that his faction's votes would prove decisive. His actions here would help lay the groundwork for the future Nakasone government.[7]

The "Kakufuku War"

With Nakasone out of the running, only Miki, Tanaka, Ōhira, and Fukuda remained. The election was held at Hibiya Public Hall on July 5, 1972. As General Council chairman, Nakasone was on stage watching as the ballots were counted.

110   *"Neoliberalism" and the Oil Crisis*

Miki and Ōhira were eliminated in the first round, and Tanaka overwhelmingly defeated Fukuda in the final round, 282 votes to 190. The Nakasone faction's votes were among those 282. As Tanaka raised his right hand in his characteristic pose, the hall applauded. He thanked the crowd before shouting, "Long live the LDP!"

In marked contrast to the flush-cheeked Tanaka, Miki (who had finished last) wore a somber expression, and Ōhira closed his eyes at times. Fukuda glared at the stage, looking unwell and giving no sign of smile.[8] This marked the beginning of the "Kakufuku War" between Fukuda and Tanaka.

What were Nakasone's thoughts as he shared the stage with the victorious Tanaka? On the one hand, it was fortunate for him that Tanaka had won as, having voted for him, he could expect to be rewarded with cabinet positions for his faction. It is likely that he would have remained outside of the mainstream had Fukuda become president.

But there is no question that he was conflicted about the results. Tanaka, who had entered the Diet at the same time as him, had just become president, capping a career in which he had already served as finance minister, MITI minister, and – for a record-setting length of time – LDP secretary-general. Despite never going to college, Tanaka had just become the LDP's youngest-ever president at the age of fifty-four, the same age as Nakasone.

Nakasone, who had placed himself on the "elite" career track by attending Tokyo Imperial University and joining the home ministry, had never held a major cabinet position like that of finance, MITI, or foreign minister. He had never even been a presidential candidate, and he had certainly never been secretary-general. He had no choice but watch from the sidelines as Tanaka continued from success to success.

Appointment as MITI Minister

When the Tanaka government was formed on July 7, Nakasone was appointed MITI minister and director-general of the Science and Technology Agency. It had cost him his presidential candidacy, but he had now secured a major cabinet post. Of the other candidates, Ōhira became foreign minister, Miki was named deputy prime minister, and Fukuda did not receive any position.

Why had Nakasone voted for Tanaka rather than Fukuda? Watanabe Tsuneo of the Yomiuri Shimbun wrote that "Nakasone gave Sino-Japanese relations as his justification for supporting Tanaka. That he didn't vote for Fukuda because Fukuda opposed China and supported Taiwan. But I think that he ultimately just didn't like Fukuda's personality and got along better with Tanaka. And, in the end, politics is all about personal relations."[9]

While Watanabe thus emphasized the importance of personal factors in Nakasone's decision, there were also suspicions that he had been paid off by Tanaka. It was reported in the July 8 issue of *Shūkan Shinchō* that Nakasone had been paid 700 million yen to withdraw from the race and throw his support behind Tanaka. This information came from Nakagawa

Shunji, a Diet member belonging to the Sonoda faction, and the magazine ran a follow-up article on the topic on July 15.[10]

Nakasone filed complaints against the article's writer and the magazine's editor at the Tokyo District Public Prosecutor's Office for libel. After Nakagawa, the article's source lost his bid for reelection in the December 10 general election, he issued a formal apology to Nakasone and claimed that there was no evidence that Nakasone had been paid off. While it seems likely that the magazine article had insufficient evidence for its claims and could have been found guilty of libel, with Nakasone and Nakagawa having settled things, the local prosecutor suspended the indictment against the magazine staff.

Does that mean that money was not involved in the presidential election? Asaka Akira, one of Tanaka's secretaries, commented that "while I won't say that there wasn't any money involved, the popular stories are the result of bias [against Tanaka]." Regardless of the amount, it is difficult to believe that there was no monetary element.[11]

Meeting Zhou Enlai

Nakasone attended the Japan-South Korea Regular Cabinet Ministerial Meeting in South Korea from September 4 to 7, 1972. He then visited Australia from October 10 to 15 to participate in the Japan-Australia Ministerial Committee. Both of these trips were intended to foster mutually beneficial economic relationships, with Nakasone accompanying Foreign Minister Ōhira.[12]

In late September, Tanaka and Ōhira visited Beijing and established diplomatic relations with China. Article 7 of the Sino-Japanese joint statement included a clause reading: "Neither [Japan nor China] should seek hegemony in the Asia-Pacific region and each is opposed to efforts by any other country or group of countries to establish such hegemony." The Chinese had drafted this "anti-hegemony clause" with the Soviet Union in mind, but the Tanaka government – hoping to resolve the Northern Territories issue – did not want to damage relations with the USSR.

Nakasone had long promoted the normalization of relations with China and approved of the anti-hegemony clause as a warning to the Soviets. He boasted that "Tanaka and Ōhira may have normalized relations, but I will be the one to restore economic ties." He dispatched MITI Trade Bureau Director Komatsu Yūgorō to Beijing in November.

He visited China on January 17, 1973, and met with Premier Zhou Enlai on the following two days. This was his first visit to China in nineteen years, and Zhou told him that he had received the letter arguing for the restoration of diplomatic ties that Nakasone had sent two years earlier.

Nakasone explained that "Japan's defense policy, in accordance with our constitution, is to only maintain the capacity to defend ourselves and resist foreign pressure. We will not possess nuclear weapons, conscript soldiers, or engage in war outside of our territory."

112   *"Neoliberalism" and the Oil Crisis*

When Zhou expressed his understanding of the Japanese position by saying that "Japan needs the American nuclear umbrella, given that the Soviet Union possesses nuclear weapons," Nakasone clarified how he saw the relationship between the two countries: "My view is somewhat different from that of the premier. Japan is an independent state. The security treaty, the stationing of American troops, the provision of bases to the United States ... these are all things that we have independently decided were in the national interest of Japan."

Nakasone spent much of his time in Beijing discussing defense issues as well as trade, and he shared Zhou's belief that "the Soviet Union is the most dangerous country." He also met with Liao Chengzhi, president of the Sino-Japanese Friendship Association, and they agreed to host a Chinese exhibition in Osaka in the following year. While Nakasone's visit to China served as the first step toward official Sino-Japanese trade, the hostility toward the USSR that he and the Chinese shared was somewhat divergent from the policies of the Tanaka government.[13]

Nakasone returned to Japan on January 21 and met with Thai Prime Minister Thanom and Commerce Minister Prasit. The Thais wanted to correct their trade imbalance with Japan, and Nakasone said that "in light of our long and special relationship with Thailand, we are prepared to offer entirely untied projects and loans." A Thai-Japanese joint statement was released on the 25th.[14]

Nakasone wrote a series of articles on his impressions of China, which ran in the *Jōmō Shimbun* from February 6 to 10; these were later collected into a pamphlet, "Record of My Visit to China." He wrote to Zhou that "it is his nature to be extremely warm towards those he trusts. He is a truly Chinese statesman." Zhou also reportedly told his wife that "Nakasone has the resourcefulness of a prime minister."[15]

Visiting the Middle East

Trade frictions with the US remained, with the media devoting significant coverage to the "US-Japan trade war." In October 1972, Nakasone placed restrictions on the export of cars and other products to the US as an emergency measure. When the US then devalued the dollar in February 1973, Nakasone was forced to find ways of reducing the impact of the "dollar shock" on small and mid-sized businesses.

With things with the US seeming to have settled down, Nakasone took a nine-day-long trip to the Middle East in May. Nakasone wanted to secure ways of purchasing oil without having to go through the major US and European oil companies, and the trip was intended to lay the groundwork for Japan to gain additional access to resources. This was referred to as the "Hinomaru crude oil" concept.

His first visit was to Iran, where he met with Finance Minister Amouzegar and Minister of Economic Affairs Ansary. The US was exploring the idea of having the developed nations form a league of oil-consuming countries during this period, and Iran was paying close attention to Japan's response to the initiative.

When Amouzegar asked, "Will Japan be joining the league of oil-consuming countries that America is calling for?" Nakasone responded negatively, saying, "We haven't heard anything from the United States about such an idea, and we haven't looked into it. But Japan would be opposed to such a league if it would invite a confrontation with the oil-producing nations or provoke them."

According to Nakasone, "unlike other the developed nations, Japan's hands are clean when it comes to nations possessing resources. We have no political ambitions towards them." Amouzegar smiled and seemed satisfied. His statements here not only gave the Iranians a favorable impression of him but also spread to the countries he would be visiting afterward.

A country's stance on the Palestinian question was important in establishing friendly relations with the Arab states. When asked about Palestine in Kuwait, he answered that "Japan agrees with UN Resolution 242 and is opposed to territorial acquisition by force. We feel that the right of self-determination of the Palestinian people is self-evident." UN Resolution 242, passed on November 22, 1967, called for the withdrawal of the Israeli military from the occupied territories.

He met with King Faisal and Petroleum Minister Yamani in Saudi Arabia and also visited the United Arab Emirates and Bahrain before returning home. His trips were made six months before the Oil Crisis struck Japan, during a period when it was rare for serving cabinet ministers to visit the Middle East.[16]

"Resource Security" and "Neoliberalism" – The Era of the Welfare State

On July 25, 1973, the Agency for Natural Resources and Energy was established as an external bureau of MITI with jurisdiction over securing energy and managing the electrical industry. The leading figure behind the agency's creation was former MITI administrative vice-minister Morozumi Yoshihiko, but Nakasone also gave the idea his support.[17]

Nakasone called a special meeting of MITI and the new agency's leadership on the day of its founding to give an unusually long opening address:

> Security has hitherto been considered in a military sense, but it is now necessary for it to expand to include resource security. Indeed, in circumstances like those of Japan, resource security could be said to be a more urgent concern. Moving forward, resource security will need to assume a role that surpasses and extends the existing framework for military security. It must be considered when determining foreign policy, particularly commercial and trade policy.

114   *"Neoliberalism" and the Oil Crisis*

Nakasone was arguing that, with resource nationalism on the rise, it was necessary for Japan to be aware of "resource security" when pursuing trade policy.

He continued: "Location policy needs to go beyond the boundaries of the Japanese Archipelago and be considered with a more global perspective. One of the unaddressed issues with the argument for remodeling the Japanese Archipelago is that it is not done with a global area in mind, at least not explicitly." This reference to one of Tanaka's signature policies – his "plan for remodeling the Japanese Archipelago" – shows that a year into the position of MITI minister, Nakasone was increasingly confident in the role and willing to extend criticism even to the prime minister's ideas.

What kind of policies did Nakasone view as necessary for responding to a global era? In the latter half of his speech, he argued for a "neoliberalism" that would serve as a turning point toward Japan becoming a welfare state:

> We are entering a time of transition from a growing state to a welfare state, and I believe it permissible for some portion of our liberties to be temporarily limited if it means protecting our liberty and welfare as a whole. I feel that we have entered an era in which we must permit greater restrictions and limitations than we have in the past where necessary to protect the greatest amount of liberty and welfare. If I were to give this principle a name, I would call it "neoliberalism." [...]
>
> I believe that we have come to regard interventions and restrictions as obviously permitted when they are based on modern ideas. We see this in land, material shortage, electrical power, and oil issues, as well as restrictions on PCB and mercury. MITI has traditionally been extremely cautious on this point. While that caution must continue moving forward, it cannot be permitted to hesitate needlessly, either. There can be no hesitation when it comes to protecting liberty and welfare in the modern sense.
>
> But it is important that such intervention be accompanied by participation; without it, the effort will come to naught in the modern sense. In the past, controlled economies have been a time of bureaucratic control without any participation. But under neoliberalism, there will be both [government] intervention and participation by those effected.

Nakasone's "neoliberalism" had two characteristics. First, it was not laissez-faire; the welfare state would intervene in companies in areas such as oil. Second, it attempted to expand the base of government by promoting participation by affected industries, workers, and consumers via advisory councils and the like.

An opportunity for such "neoliberal" intervention would arrive unexpectedly soon with the Oil Crisis.[18]

The Oil Crisis

When the first reports of the Yom Kippur War between Israel and the Arab states arrived in Japan on October 6, 1973, Tanaka and Ōhira were in Europe. The Organization of Arab Petroleum Exporting Countries decided in the wake of the war that it would be reducing the amount of oil provided to countries not designated as "friendly." Neither the United States nor Japan received this designation.

As Nakasone tasked the Agency for Natural Resources and Energy with finding ways to secure oil, MITI was flooded with complaints from Japanese consumers about shortages of toilet paper and other goods. He informed the oil and electrical companies of planned new regulations and set up the Joint Committee on Emergency Oil Measures to determine ways to improve the situation.

On November 16, the cabinet approved the Outline of Emergency Oil Measures, and Nakasone informed major businesses that used large amounts of energy, like steel, aluminum, automobile, and cement producers, that they would have to reduce their energy consumption by 10% effective November 20.

US Secretary of State Henry Kissinger had arrived in Japan on November 14 on his way home from the Middle East. When Nakasone visited him at Hotel Okura the next day, Kissinger reported on the situation, explaining that while efforts toward peace were being made, "no deadline can be placed on the negotiations."

Nakasone "implied that Japan would be acting on its own," emphasizing that "the reduction in oil exports to Japan and the rapid increase in prices could have a serious impact on next year's House of Councillors election. It would only take a swing of thirteen seats for the opposition to gain control, and if that happens, it will have serious consequences for the US-Japan security treaty and Japanese defense policy."

In other words, Nakasone would be shifting Japanese policy so as to adopt a more pro-Arab stance.

He had Mizuno Sōhei, president of the Arabian Oil Company, approach Saudi King Faisal about increasing oil exports to Japan, nominally because "the production of fertilizer for developing countries like Indonesia and India would have to be halted due to oil shortages." After returning to Japan, Mizuno reported that the king had told him that, should Japan publicly adopt pro-Arab policies, he believed that it would be designated a "friendly" country and be provided with more oil.

Nakasone recommended that Tanaka do so, and on November 22, a set of remarks by Chief Cabinet Secretary Nikaidō Susumu were released in which he expressed sympathy for the Arab position. Foreign Minister Ōhira viewed relations with the United States as being of great importance and was opposed to this action, but Nakasone persuaded him that it was necessary.

116 *"Neoliberalism" and the Oil Crisis*

Tanaka also dispatched Deputy Prime Minister Miki to the Middle East as a special envoy. The Arab leaders regarded Nikaidō's remarks positively and decided not to apply an additional 5% reduction in oil exports to Japan. Nakasone submitted two emergency pieces of legislation to the Diet to help address the Oil Crisis (the Emergency Measures to Stabilize the Public's Livelihood Act and the Act to Standardize the Supply and Demand of Petroleum), which were passed on December 22.[19]

Returning to the Middle East

Nakasone's next step was to travel abroad personally. From January 7 to 18, 1974, he visited Iran, Britain, Bulgaria, and Iraq. He had prepared a $1 billion economic assistance package for Iran with which to negotiate for additional oil.

When his plane arrived above the Iranian capital of Tehran, it was forced back by a blizzard. After spending the night in Karachi, Pakistan, he finally arrived in Tehran the next day, where a tight schedule awaited him.

It was immediately apparent that Iran would be adopting a high-pressure approach in the negotiations. His counterpart was Economic Minister Ansary, who he had met on his previous visit. Nakasone proposed a government loan to fund the construction of an oil refinery, but Ansary responded coolly and hinted that Iran would prefer to deal with Europe instead. When, at the final stage of the negotiations, Ansary demanded another billion dollars in aid, Nakasone told him that it would be "utterly impossible" and broke off the talks.

Having failed to reach a compromise with Iran, Nakasone headed for London, which was dark due to electricity rationing. He discussed inviting Japanese businesses to help develop the North Sea oil field with Minister for Industrial Development Chataway and then paid a goodwill visit to Bulgaria before heading for Iraq.

There were good omens in Iraq. Unlike Iran, Iraq was very interested in having Japan provide assistance for government projects such as the construction of cement and chemical fertilizer facilities. There were great expectations for the development of Iraqi oil deposits, and Nakasone was able to reach an agreement with Minister for Public Works Jazwari under which Japan would provide $1 billion in loans for various projects, and Iraq would provide Japan with 90 million tons of crude oil.

The working level officials at MITI and the foreign ministry had arranged $500 million of aid for the negotiations with Iraq. When the Iraqis hesitated at that figure, Nakasone told them to "leave it to me" and immediately agreed to $1 billion. The negotiations with Iran falling through meant that he had much greater leeway. He also spoke with then-vice-chairman of the Revolutionary Command Council, Saddam Hussein, during his visit.[20]

Japan's Future

Prices peaked in mid-February. On March 16, Nakasone had the Head-quarters for Emergency Measures to Stabilize the Public's Livelihood, and the cabinet raised the price of oil to 8,946 yen per kiloliter. Several other countries had already raised the price to roughly 10,000 yen per kiloliter several months earlier, but Nakasone had wanted to hold off until prices had settled down.

Nakasone compared this decision to "a major piece of surgery, like drilling a hole into the most fundamental level of Japan's economic structure." The increase in the price of oil had only a relatively small impact, with prices only increasing by 0.7% in March.

In April, electrical companies requested permission to raise their prices. On May 21, he authorized the nine electrical companies to raise their prices by an average of 56.82%. The cost for industrial usage was increased by 76.95%, limiting the increase for households to 28.59%. Regulations legally restricting oil and electricity usage were lifted, but administrative guidance continued. Nakasone also rescinded government intervention in the prices of individual goods like kerosene from June to September.

While Japan had managed to overcome the Oil Crisis, it remained highly reliant on foreign sources of energy, and its future was unclear. In his book *A Voyage Without a Map: MITI and the Oil Crisis,* Nakasone compared the Japanese economy to an invalid: "Having been forced to undergo major plastic surgery by both domestic and foreign forces, the sick person that is the Japanese economy lies exhausted upon their sickbed, frightened of inflation and recession, and anxious about their balance of payments."

The Oil Crisis was over, but the domestic and international situations remained fluid, and Nakasone was unable to be optimistic about the future.[21]

To make matters worse, the LDP was defeated in the July 7 House of Councillors election, losing six seats. Tanaka's popularity was fading, and he had come under criticism for his involvement of businesses in his politicking.

At the Shinsei Dōshikai's Seventh Youth Political Training Meeting on September 12, Nakasone argued that the "clouds above the hill" (a reference to a Shiba Ryōtarō novel of the same name) had disappeared:

> In the quarter century since the war – no, in the hundred years since the Meiji period began – the Japanese have always raced forward, never looking to the side, their eyes locked on the "clouds above the hill."
>
> Now, having reached one summit, rather than looking to the future, the Japanese feel a kind of disappointment, emptiness, and anxiety. The pollution and price problems of the past few years have caused them to forget the greatness of all they have achieved thus far and stirred up remorse for what they've lost.

118 *"Neoliberalism" and the Oil Crisis*

In the speech, Nakasone argued that the LDP needed to transform into an "open political party" in order to respond to a rapidly changing era and that the government needed to change from being an "LDP government" to a "government of the people."[22]

As secretary-general in the Miki government that followed Tanaka, Nakasone would be able to devote himself to managing the party.

Notes

1 Liberal Democratic Party, "Tōsoku" (January 21, 1971), 11.
2 Nakasone Yasuhiro, *Rīdā no Jōken.* (Tokyo: Fusō-sha, 1997), 64. Nakasone was also alarmed at the increase in the number of non-voters in Diet elections. In Asukata Ichio, Nakasone Yasuhiro, "Sengo Minshushugi o Kangaeru Zadankai," *Asahi Shimbun* (February 25, 1972), Nakasone said that "The political parties are operating out of inertia. If they fail to correct this, they will be abandoned by the public. Their lack of interest is a harbinger of this. Satō's support levels may be down, but the Socialist Party's haven't increased in response. Apathy, however, has."
3 Yamada Eizō, *Seiden Satō Eisaku* (Tokyo: Shinchō-sha, 1988), 2:391. Fukuda Takeo, *Kaiko 90 Nen* (Tokyo: Iwanami Shoten, 1995), 195–206. Satō Eisaku, *Satō Eisaku Nikki,* ed. Itō Takashi (Tokyo: Asahi Shimbun, 1997), 4:366, 368.
4 Nakasone Yasuhiro, "Nihon Seiji no Rekishiteki Chōsen – Yūgen no Chikyū ni Mugen no Jinshū ga Ariuru ka?" (April 17, 1972), 2, 9, 15, 23–24, Collection of the author. Nakasone Yasuhiro, *Seiji to Jinsei – Nakasone Yasuhiro Kaikoroku* (Tokyo: Kōdansha, 1992), 279–88. Nakasone Yasuhiro, Itō Takashi, Satō Seiburō, *Tenchi Ujō – Gojū Nen no Sengo Seiji o Kataru* (Tokyo: Bungei Shunjū, 1996), 261–69. Satō 4:421, 5:68–69, 79, 99. Nakasone's "Nihon Seiji no Rekishiteki Chōsen" is a renaming of Nakasone Yasuhiro, "Tenkanki no Seiji" (Naigai Jōsei Chōsakai, 1972). In Ishibashi Masashi, Nakasone Yasuhiro, "'Jimin-Shakai' Dairenritsu no Susume," *Bungei Shunjū* (February 1970), 100–101, Nakasone argued that "So as not to cause friction with the Chinese Communists, Japan will turn its eyes to the seas and become a Pacific welfare state. [...] In cooperation with America, Japan will create something like a US-Japan Pacific pact to contribute to the culture and welfare of the Pacific sphere, including Australia and Canada, calmly providing funds and seeking competitive coexistence." According to Tagawa Seiichi, *Nicchū Kōryū to Jimintō Ryōshū-tachi* (Tokyo: Yomiuri Shimbun, 1983), 50–51, 63–65, 68, 72, when Sino-Japanese Friendship Association Vice President Wang Guoquan visited Japan in August 1971, Nakasone attempted to have Satō make contact with him but was unsuccessful. On the normalization of diplomatic relations between Japan and China, see also: Hattori Ryūji, *China-Japan Rapprochement and the United States: In the Wake of Nixon's Visit to Beijing,* trans. Graham B. Leonard (London: Routledge, 2022).
5 *Yomiuri Shimbun,* September 17, 1971 evening.
6 *Asahi Shimbun,* June 19, 1972 evening edition.
7 Satō Takayuki, *Kensatsu Osorubeshi – Seiji to Kane to Minshushugi ni tsuite* (Tokyo: Nesuko, 1987), 23–32. Satō Takayuki, *Ware, Kaku Tatakaeri – Iki Jigoku 13 Nen kara no Seikan* (Tokyo: Tokyū Ējenshī, 1989), 162–167. Satō Eisaku 5:141–42, 169.
8 *Asahi Shimbun,* July 5, 1972 evening.
9 Watanabe Tsuneo, *Ten'un Tenshoku: Sengo Seiji no Rimenshi, Hansei, Kyojingun o Akasu* (Tokyo: Kōbunsha, 1999), 147–50. Niigata Nippō Jigyō-sha, *Aikyō*

"Neoliberalism" and the Oil Crisis 119

Mugen Ozawa Tatsuo to Sono Jidai (Niigata: Niigata Nippō, 2001), 97–98. Watanabe Tsuneo, *Watanabe Tsuneo Kaikoroku*, ed. Mikuriya Takashi, Itō Takashi, and Iio Jun (Tokyo: Chūō Bunko, 2007), 309–13.

10 "Iyoiyo Ōzume 'Sōsaisen' Kane to Kensei no Mōja no Ōmisemono," *Shūkan Shinchō* (July 8, 1972), 32–35. "'Nakasone-ha Kuroi Uwasa no Kiji' Taizai kara Keisai made no Shinsō," *Shūkan Shinchō* (July 15, 1972), 128–33. National Graduate Institute for Policy Studies COE Oral Policy Research Project, *Matsuno Raizō Ōraru Hisutorī* (Tokyo: GRIPS, 2003), 1:239.

11 *Asahi Shimbun,* July 4 evening, July 11–12, 18, September 19, December 21, 1972, January 8, 1973 evening. *Shūkan Shinchō* (July 8, 1972), 32–35. *Shūkan Shinchō* (July 15, 1972), 128–33. Asaka Akira, *Tanaka Kakuei – Saigo no Hissho ga Kataru Jō to Chiei no Seijika*, ed. Fukunaga Fumio, et al (Tokyo: Daiichi Hōki, 2015), 98. Page 138 of Tachibana Takashi's *Seiji to Jōnen – Kenryoku, Kane, Onna* (Tokyo: Bunshun Bunko, 2005), holds that "setting aside the question of whether the figure of 700 million yen is accurate or not, it is inconceivable that Nakasone received no money at all."

12 Ministry of Foreign Affairs Eurasian Affairs Bureau Oceania Section, "Dai Ikkai Nichigō Kakuryō Iinkai (Gaiyō Hōkoku)" (October 28, 1972), Nichigō Kakuryō Iinkai (Dai Ikkai) 2010-4289, MOFA. Nakasone Yasuhiro, *Nakasone Yasuhiro ga Kataru Sengo Nihon Gaikō* (Tokyo: Shinchōsha, 2012), 230–31. Takahashi Kazuhiro, "'Keizai Taikoku' Nihon no Keizai Gaikō Senryaku – Ajia Taiheiyō Keizaiken no Keisei to Nihon, 1968–73 Nen" in Hatano Sumio, ed., *Reisen Hen'yō-ki no Nihon Gaikō – "Hiyowana Taikoku" no Kiki to Mosaku* (Tokyo: Minerva Shobō, 2013), 126–27. Hattori Ryūji, *Ōhira Masayoshi Rinen to Gaikō* (Tokyo: Iwanami Shoten, 2014), 117.

13 Ministry of Foreign Affairs Asian Affairs Bureau China Section, "Nicchū Kankei Shuyō Jikō (Kokkō Seijōka Ikō Shōwa 48-nen 6-gatsu made)" (July 10, 1973), Nicchū Kokkō Seijōka (Jūyō Shiryō) 2011-720, MOFA. Ministry of Foreign Affairs Asian Affairs Bureau China Section, "Gaikō Mondai in Kan suru Chūgoku Shunō no Hatsugen (Jikō-betsu 72.10-73.5)," Nicchū Kokkō Seijōka (Jūyō Shiryō) 2011-720, MOFA. Nakasone, *Tenchi Ujō*, 276–84. CPC Central Committee Party Literature Research Center, ed. *Zhou Enlai Nianpu* (Beijing: Central Party Literature Press, 1997), 2:574. Nakasone Yasuhiro, *Jiseiroku – Rekishi Hōtei no Hikoku to shite* (Tokyo: Shinchōsha, 2004), 131–32. Nakasone, *Nakasone Yasuhiro ga Kataru*, 227–30, 231–34, 253. Japanese Modern Historical Manuscripts Association, "Yamashita Hideaki Ōraru Hisutorī (Zoku)" (Tokyo: Japanese Modern Historical Manuscripts Association, 2007), 19–20, 39. Qiu Lizhen, *Nihon no Taichū Keizai Gaikō to Inayama Yoshihiro – Nicchū Chōki Bōeki Torikime o Megutte* (Sapporo: Hokkaido University, 2010), 111–12. Wang Taiping, *"Nicchū Kokkō Kaifuku" Nikki – Gaikōbu no "Tokuhain" ga Mita Nihon*, trans. Fukuoka Aiko (Tokyo: Bensey Publishing, 2012), 274, 289, 313, 319–20, 435–48, 452–54, 466, 492, 501, 628–30. Hattori Ryūji, "2011-nen 12-gatsu 22-nichi Kōkai Fairu 'Nicchū Kokkō Seijōka' Hoka," *Gaikō Shiryōkan-Hō* No. 26 (2012), 102. Wang Xueping, ed. *Sengo Nicchū Kankei to Ryō Shōshi – Chūgoku no Chinichi-ha to Tainichi Seisaku* (Tokyo: Keio University, 2013), 166, 168, 172–76, 181, 250, 324. Ōsawa Takeshi, "Bunkaku-ki Chūgoku no Tainichi Seisaku Kikō o Yomu – 'Ō Taihei Nikki' no Shiryō-teki Kachi," *Tōhō* No. 388 (2013), 24–28. Nakashima Hiroshi, "Ō Taihei/Fukuoka Aiko-yaku, 'Nicchū Kokkō Kaifuku' Nikki – Gaikōbu no "Tokuhain" ga Mita Nihon," *Chūgoku Kenkyū Geppō* 67:4 (2013), 48–50. I made freedom of information requests to METI and the foreign ministry for records of Nakasone's visit to China, but both said that none exist.

120   *"Neoliberalism" and the Oil Crisis*

14 Ambassador to Thailand Fujisaki Masato to Foreign Minister Ōhira (January 24, 1973), Nichi-Tai Bōeki Gōdō Iinkkai (Dai Gokai), 2010-4155, MOFA. Takahashi 134-35.
15 Nakasone Yasuhiro, "Chūgoku o Tazunete," Parts 1 to 5, *Jōmō Shimbun* (February 6 to 10, 1973. Nakasone Yasuhiro, "Chūgoku Hōmon no Ki" (March 1, 1973), 18. Mainichi Shimbun Seijibu, *Anpo* (Tokyo: Kadokawa Bunko, 1987), 236–38. Xiao Xiangqian, *Eien no Rinkoku to shite,* trans. Takeuchi Minoru (Tokyo: Saimaru Shuppankai, 1997), 167–68.
16 *Asahi Shimbun,* April 30, 1973. Nakasone Yasuhiro, *Kaizu no Nai Kōkai – Sekiyu Kiki to Tsūsanshō* (Tokyo: Nihon Keizai Shimbun, 1975), 1–30. Ishikawa Yoshitaka, *Oiru Gaikō Nikki – Dai Ichiji Sekiyu Kiki no Genchi Hōkoku* (Tokyo: Asahi Shimbun, 1983). 125, 155, 196. Tsūshō Sangyō-shō Tsūshō Sangyō Seisaku-shi Hensan Iinkai, ed. *Tsūshō Sangyō Seisaku-shi, Dai Jūnikan – Dai IV Ki Tayōka Jidai (1)* (Tokyo: Tsūshō Sangyō Chōsakai, 1993), 19, 148, 156, 204. Nakasone, *Tenchi Ujō,* 273. He Liqun, "Dai Ichiji Sekiyu Kiki Zengo no Nakasone Yasuhiro – 'Shigen Gaikō' o Megutte," *Kokusai Kōkyo Seisaku Kenkyū* 15:2 (2011), 83–99.
17 Yanagita Kunio, *Ookami ga Yatte kita Hi* (Tokyo: Bunshun Bunko, 1982), 17. Nakasone, *Nakasone Yasuhiro ga Kataru,* 239.
18 Nakasone, *Kazu no Nai Kōkai,* 35–45. Nakasone, *Tenchi Ujō,* 270–71.
19 For examples of prior research on this, see: Yanagita 25-297; Nakanishi Hiroshi, "Sōgō Anzen Hoshō-ron no Bunmyaku – Kenryoku Seiji to Sogo Izon no Kōsaku," *Nenpō Seijigaku* (199), 103; Ikegami Mana, "Dai Ichiji Seikyu Kiki ni Okeru Nihon no Gaikō – Sekiyu Kakuho to Nichibei Kankei," *Hōgaku Seijigaku Ronkyū* No. 79 (2008), 165–96; Ikegami Mana, "Nihon no Shin Chūtō Seisaku Keisei Katei no Kōsatsu – Dai Ichiji Sekiyu Kiki to Kisshinjā Kōsō o Chūshin ni," *Hōgaku Seijigaku Ronkyū* No. 87 (2010), 1–30; Satō Susumu, "1970 Nendai Ajia ni Okeru Gurōbaru-ka no Hakyū to Nihon – 'Daizu Shokku' to 'Sekiyu Shokku' e no Taiō," *Kokusai Seikei* No. 14 (2008), 23–26; Takayasu Kensuke, *Shushō no Kenryoku – Nichiei Hikaku kara miru Seikentō to no Dainamizumu* (Tokyo: Sōbunsha, 2009), 154–174; Shiratori Jun'ichirō, "Kokusai Enerugī Kikan no Sōritsu to Nihon Gaikō – Dai Ichiji Sekiyu Kiki ni Okeru Senshinkoku Chōwa no Mosaku," *Kokusai Seiji* No. 160 (2010), 17–33; Shiratori Jun'ichirō, "Enerugī Anzen Hoshō Seisaku no Taidō – Sekiyu Shijō no Kōzō Hendō to 'Taigai Sekiyu Seisaku' no Keisei, 1967–1973," *Kokusai Anzen Hoshō* 38:4 (2011), 106–23; Shiratori Jun'ichirō, "Dai Ichiji Sekiyu Kiki ni Okeru Nihon Gaikō Saikō – Shōhikoku-kan Kyōchō Sankaku to Chūtō Seisaku 'Meikaku-ka'," *Hōgaku Seijigaku Ronkyū* No. 89 (2011), 59–93. Notes on this section are collected in endnote 21.
20 See the following endnote.
21 Ambassador to the US Yasukawa Takeshi to Ōhira (November 1, 1973), Chūtō Mondai/Dai Yoji Chūtō Sensō, 2013-1278, MOFA. Memorandum of Conversation between Kissinger and Nakasone (November 15, 1973), Digital National Security Archive, (http://nsarchive.chadwyck.com; accessed on January 28, 2012). "Kanbō Chōkan Danwa ni Sai shite no Hōdō Kankeisha to no Gimon Gito," Chūtō Mondai/Dai Yoji Chūtō Sensō (Nikaidō Kanbō Chōkan Danwa), 2013-1977, MOFA. Ambassador to Saudi Arabia Takasugi Kanji to Ōhira (November 24–25, 1973), Chūtō Mondai/Dai Yoji Chūtō Sensō (Nikaidō Kanbō Chōkan Danwa), 2013-1280, MOFA. Ambassador Kitahara Hideo, Permanent Mission of Japan to the International Organizations in Geneva, to Ōhira (November 25, 1973), Saudi Arabia Sekiyu Jōsei, 2012-1416, MOFA. Takasugi to Ōhira (December 27, 1973), Saudi Arabia Sekiyu Jōsei, 2012-1417, MOFA. Ministry of Foreign Affairs, Near and Middle Eastern and African Bureau, "Miki Tokushi Chūkintō Hakkakoku Hōmon" (January 1974), Miki,

"Neoliberalism" and the Oil Crisis 121

Kosaka Tokushi Chūtō Shokoku Hōmon, 2013-1907, MOFA. *Asahi Shimbun,* January 17 evening, January 18, 1974. Nakasone, *Kaizu no Nai Kōkai,* 154–58, 173, 180-92. Nakasone, *Seiji to Jinsei,* 289–92. Nakasone, *Rīdā no Jōken,* 129. Nakasone, *Jiseiroku,* 102–04. Nakasone, *Nakasone Yasuhiro ga Kataru,* 234–44. Koino Shigeru, *Kasumigaseki 30 Nen – Gekidō no Tsūsan Gyōsei* (Tokyo: Jihyōsha, 1981), 138–43. Ishikawa, *Oiru Gaikō Nikki,* 227. Tsūshō Sangyō-shō Tsūshō Sangyō Seisaku-shi Hensan Iinkai, ed., *Tsūshō Sangyō Seisaku-shi, Dai Jūsankan – Dai IV Ki Tayōka Jidai (2)* (Tokyo: Tsūshō Sangyō Chōsakai, 1993), 43–45, 52, 74, 184–85. Nakasone, *Tenchi Ujō,* 273–75. Tamura Hideji, *Arabu Gaikō 55 Nen* (Tokyo: Keisō Shobo, 1983), 2:234. Niigata Nippō Jōdōbu, *Saishō Tanaka Kakuei no Shinjitsu* (Tokyo: Kōdansha, 1994), 95–97. NHK Shuzai-han, *NHK Supesharu Sengo 50 Nen Sono Toki Nihon wa Daigokan Sekiyu Shokku Gen'ei ni obieta 69 Kakan Kokutetsu Rōshi Funsō Suto-ken Dakkan Suto no Shōgeki* (Tokyo: Nihon Hōsō Shuppan Kyōkai, 1996), 48, 98, 118–21, 129, 146. National Graduate Institute for Policy Studies COE Oral Policy Research Project, *Miyazaki Hiromichi Ōraru Hisutorī* (Tokyo: GRIPS, 2004), 154–59. National Graduate Institute for Policy Studies COE Oral Policy Research Project, *Yamashita Hideaki Ōraru Hisutorī* (Tokyo: GRIPS, 2005), 254, 258. Ōhira Masayoshi, *Ōhira Masayoshi Zenchosaku-shū* (Tokyo: Kōdansha, 2012), 7:76. Orita Masaki, *Gaikō Shōgenroku Wangan Sensō, Futenma Mondai, Iraku Sensō,* ed. Hattori Ryūji and Shiratori Jun'ichirō (Tokyo: Iwanami Shoten, 2013), 33–35.

22 Nakasone Yasuhiro, "Shin Jidai ni Kotaeru Seiji" (September 1974), author's collection, 7–10.

References

Asaka Akira. *Tanaka Kakuei – Saigo no Hissho ga Kataru Jō to Chiei no Seijika.* Edited by Fukunaga Fumio, Hattori Ryūji, Amamiya Shōichi, and Wakatsuki Hidekazu. Tokyo: Daiichi Hōki, 2015.

CPC Central Committee Party Literature Research Center, ed. *Zhou Enlai Nianpu,* Vol. 2. Beijing: Central Party Literature Press, 1997.

Fukuda Takeo. *Kaiko 90 Nen.* Tokyo: Iwanami Shoten, 1995.

Hatano Sumio, ed. *Reisen Hen'yō-ki no Nihon Gaikō – "Hiyowana Taikoku" no Kiki to Mosaku.* Tokyo: Minerva Shobō, 2013.

Hattori Ryūji. "2011-nen 12-gatsu 22-nichi Kōkai Fairu 'Nicchū Kokkō Seijōka' Hoka." *Gaikō Shiryōkan-Hō,* No. 26 (2012).

Hattori Ryūji. *Ōhira Masayoshi Rinen to Gaikō.* Tokyo: Iwanami Shoten, 2014.

He Liqun. "Dai Ichiji Sekiyu Kiki Zengo no Nakasone Yasuhiro – 'Shigen Gaikō' o Megutte." *Kokusai Kōkyo Seisaku Kenkyū* 15:2 (2011), 83–99.

Ishikawa Yoshitaka. *Oiru Gaikō Nikki – Dai Ichiji Sekiyu Kiki no Genchi Hōkoku.* Tokyo: Asahi Shimbun, 1983.

"Iyoiyo Ōzume 'Sōsaisen' Kane to Kensei no Mōja no Ōmisemono." *Shūkan Shinchō* (July 8, 1972).

Koino Shigeru. *Kasumigaseki 30 Nen – Gekidō no Tsūsan Gyōsei.* Tokyo: Jihyōsha, 1981.

Mainichi Shimbun Seijibu. *Anpo.* Tokyo: Kadokawa Bunko, 1987.

Nakashima Hiroshi. "Ō Taihei/Fukuoka Aiko-yaku, 'Nicchū Kokkō Kaifuku' Nikki – Gaikōbu no 'Tokuhain' ga Mita Nihon." *Chūgoku Kenkyū Geppō* 67:4 (2013), 48–50.

"'Nakasone-ha Kuroi Uwasa no Kiji' Taizai kara Keisai made no Shinsō." *Shūkan Shinchō* (July 15, 1972).

122 *"Neoliberalism" and the Oil Crisis*

Nakasone Yasuhiro. "Chūgoku o Tazunete," Parts 1 to 5. *Jōmō Shimbun*, February 6 to 10, 1973.

Nakasone Yasuhiro. *Jiseiroku – Rekishi Hōtei no Hikoku to shite*. Tokyo: Shinchōsha, 2004.

Nakasone Yasuhiro. *Kaizu no Nai Kōkai – Sekiyu Kiki to Tsūsanshō*. Tokyo: Nihon Keizai Shimbun, 1975.

Nakasone Yasuhiro. *Nakasone Yasuhiro ga Kataru Sengo Nihon Gaikō*. Edited by Nakashima Takuma, Hattori Ryūji, Noboru Amiko, Wakatsuki Hidekazu, Michishita Narushige, Kusunoki Ayako, Segawa Takao. Tokyo: Shinchōsha, 2012.

Nakasone Yasuhiro. *Rīdā no Jōken*. Tokyo: Fusō-sha, 1997.

Nakasone Yasuhiro. *Seiji to Jinsei – Nakasone Yasuhiro Kaikoroku*. Tokyo: Kōdansha, 1992.

Nakasone Yasuhiro, Itō Takashi, Satō Seiburō. *Tenchi Ujō – Gojū Nen no Sengo Seiji o Kataru*. Tokyo: Bungei Shunjū, 1996.

National Graduate Institute for Policy Studies COE Oral Policy Research Project. *Matsuno Raizō Ōraru Hisutorī*. Tokyo: GRIPS, 2003.

National Graduate Institute for Policy Studies COE Oral Policy Research Project. *Miyazaki Hiromichi Ōraru Hisutorī*. Tokyo: GRIPS, 2004.

National Graduate Institute for Policy Studies COE Oral Policy Research Project. *Yamashita Hideaki Ōraru Hisutorī*. Tokyo: GRIPS, 2005.

National Graduate Institute for Policy Studies COE Oral Policy Research Project. *Yamashita Hideaki Ōraru Hisutorī (Zoku)*. Tokyo: GRIPS, 2007.

NHK Shuzai-han. *NHK Supesharu Sengo 50 Nen Sono Toki Nihon wa Dai Gokan Sekiyu Shokku Gen'ei ni obieta 69 Kakan Kokutetsu Rōshi Funsō Suto-ken Dakkan Suto no Shōgeki*. Tokyo: Nihon Hōsō Shuppan Kyōkai, 1996.

Niigata Nippō Hōdōbu. *Saishō Tanaka Kakuei no Shinjitsu*. Tokyo: Kōdansha, 1994.

Niigata Nippō Jigyō-sha. *Aikyō Mugen Ozawa Tatsuo to Sono Jidai*. Niigata: Niigata Nippō, 2001.

Ōhira Masayoshi. *Ōhira Masayoshi Zenchosaku-shū*. Tokyo: Kōdansha, 2012.

Orita Masaki. *Gaikō Shōgenroku Wangan Sensō, Futenma Mondai, Iraku Sensō*. Edited by Hattori Ryūji and Shiratori Jun'ichirō. Tokyo: Iwanami Shoten, 2013.

Ōsawa Takeshi "Bunkaku-ki Chūgoku no Tainichi Seisaku Kikō o Yomu – 'Ō Taihei Nikki' no Shiryō-teki Kachi." *Tōhō*, No. 388 (2013).

Qiu Lizhen. *Nihon no Taichū Keizai Gaikō to Inayama Yoshihiro – Nicchū Chōki Bōeki Torikime o Megutte*. Sapporo: Hokkaido University, 2010.

Satō Eisaku. *Satō Eisaku Nikki*. Edited by Itō Takashi. Tokyo: Asahi Shimbun, 1997.

Satō Takayuki. *Kensatsu Osorubeshi – Seiji to Kane to Minshushugi ni tsuite*. Tokyo: Nesuko, 1987.

Satō Takayuki. *Ware, Kaku Tatakaeri – Iki Jigoku 13 Nen kara no Seikan*. Tokyo: Tokyū Ējenshī, 1989.

Tamura Hideji. *Arabu Gaikō 55 Nen*. Tokyo: Keisō Shobo, 1983.

Tsūshō Sangyō-shō Tsūshō Sangyō Seisaku-shi Hensan Iinkai, ed. *Tsūshō Sangyō Seisaku-shi, Dai Jūnikan – Dai IV Ki Tayōka Jidai*. Tokyo: Tsūshō Sangyō Chōsakai, 1993.

Wang Taiping. *"Nicchū Kokkō Kaifuku" Nikki – Gaikōbu no "Tokuhain" ga Mita Nihon*. Translated by Fukuoka Aiko. Tokyo: Bensey Publishing, 2012.

Wang Xueping, ed. *Sengo Nicchū Kankei to Ryō Shōshi – Chūgoku no Chinichi-ha to Tainichi Seisaku*. Tokyo: Keio University, 2013.

Watanabe Tsuneo. *Ten'un Tenshoku: Sengo Seiji no Rimenshi, Hansei, Kyojingun o Akasu*. Tokyo: Kōbunsha, 1999.

Watanabe Tsuneo. *Watanabe Tsuneo Kaikoroku*. Edited by Mikuriya Takashi, Itō Takashi, and Iio Jun. Tokyo: Chūō Bunko, 2007.

Xiao Xiangqian. *Eien no Rinkoku to shite*. Translated by Takeuchi Minoru. Tokyo: Saimaru Shuppankai, 1997.

Yamada Eizō. *Seiden Satō Eisaku*. Tokyo: Shinchō-sha, 1988.

Yanagita Kunio. *Ookami ga Yatte kita Hi*. Tokyo: Bunshun Bunko, 1982.

8 The "Sankaku Daifuku Chū" Era

LDP Secretary-General, General Council Chairman, and Director-General of the Administrative Management Agency

The "Shiina Decision"

On November 10, 1974, near the end of the Tanaka government, Nakasone met with Secretary of State Kissinger at the State Guesthouse in Tokyo and discussed a wide variety of issues with him, including energy, the situation in the Middle East, and Sino-Soviet relations. Kissinger had come to Japan with President Ford, and, unlike their meeting during the Oil Crisis, there was little sense of urgency to the discussion.[1]

Prime Minister Tanaka had come under increasingly heavy criticism for his use of money politics and announced his resignation on November 26. The public widely expected his successor to be one of the other four members of the "Sankaku Daifuku Chū."

Tanaka led the largest faction in the party and was allied with Ōhira, meaning that it was very likely that Ōhira would win any presidential election. Ōhira thus favored that approach for choosing a successor. Miki, Fukuda, and Nakasone naturally rejected this and wanted an agreement to be reached through discussion.

The relationship between Ōhira and Fukuda was shaped by the "Kakufuku War"; Ōhira's alliance with Tanaka made Fukuda dislike him. Fukuda was also a proponent of stable growth and had been critical of the Ikeda government's income-doubling plan. According to his memoirs, he had interpreted Ikeda's adoption of a "low visibility" approach as a tacit criticism of Kishi and had felt that it "dragged the hard-working Kishi's name through the mud. I cannot deny that there was an emotional element to my response to this outrageous behavior."

And as Ōhira was a close confidante of Ikeda's and had served as both chief cabinet secretary and foreign minister under him, he was likely angered by Fukuda's criticism of him.

Nakasone found himself in the same position of Miki and Fukuda; he had no hope of winning against the Tanaka-backed Ōhira. But Ōhira's advantage among the party's Diet members wasn't the only reason to avoid a presidential election. There were also concerns that such an election could lead to the party splitting.[2]

DOI: 10.4324/9781003351931-9

Miki, Ōhira, Fukuda, and Nakasone thus met and agreed to leave the decision to Vice President Shiina Etsusaburō. The decision to entrust Shiina with this responsibility also reflected a desire to regain the public's trust in light of the large amount of money that had been involved in the previous presidential election.

On December 1, Shiina named Miki, who was well known for his integrity, as president in what became known as the "Shiina Decision" (Shiina Saitei).[3] Shiina likely chose "Clean Miki" to avoid the splitting of the party that could have potentially resulted from choosing either Ōhira or Fukuda.

In the run-up to the Shiina Decision, Shiina had also shown interest in becoming president himself. This idea was the brainchild of Tanaka, who, toward the end of his government, had focused on Shiina succeeding him rather than Ōhira. Tanaka expected to return to the premiership and had envisioned a temporary Shiina government serving in the meantime. Shiina had agreed to this.

This idea did not gain wide acceptance outside of the Tanaka faction, however, and led Ōhira to complain to a reporter that "the sumo referee has decided to put on a belt and come out to compete himself."[4]

LDP Secretary-General

In any case, Nakasone had no chance of becoming president. He would later say of Shiina's choice that "Tanaka had been brought down by his use of money, so it was naturally judged to be in the LDP's interest for whoever followed him to be completely [free of those concerns]. The party has always operated on the pendulum theory, swinging between right and left, clean and corrupt. In that sense, I think it was logical that Miki got the nod."

Shiina's decision was considered surprising, given that Miki had come in last in the presidential election held two years earlier. Miki himself later described it as having been like "a bolt from the blue."

But according to Nakasone, Miki had actually been tipped off about the decision in advance and was already hard at work on his choices for the cabinet and the main party posts when the announcement was made. As evidence of this, he immediately summoned Nakasone to ask him to serve as secretary-general.

From Nakasone's perspective, this was an ideal position on the path to becoming prime minister, and he readily accepted. He conjectured that Miki chose him for the post because "I was young, and 'Clean Miki' may have wanted to give his government a youthful image."

The secretary-general wielded massive power over party positions and which candidates were officially recognized by the party. Succeeding in the position was a critical test for becoming president. Nakasone was fifty-six at the time, meaning that he was nine years behind Tanaka, who had been appointed to the post at the age of forty-seven.

126 *The "Sankaku Daifuku Chū" Era*

Ōhira remained finance minister, and Fukuda became both deputy prime minister and director-general of the EPA. Tanaka may have resigned, but he considered this only a temporary setback and the era of the "Sankaku Daifuku Chū" would continue. Shiina remained vice president.

The course of events from the announcement of the Shiina Decision to Nakasone's appointment as secretary-general is suggestive of his faction's position within the party's factional politics. Put bluntly, things had developed advantageously for him.

First, Nakasone had been able to distance himself from the discord that existed between the other major faction leaders. His electoral contests with Fukuda in Gunma 3rd may have been referred to as the "Jōshū War," but he held no deep-seated resentment against any of the other four. He stood in marked contrast with Ōhira in this regard, who had sided with Tanaka against Fukuda in the "Kakufuku War."

Second, Tanaka had not yielded control of his faction to anyone else, meaning that – despite being the largest faction in the party – the Tanaka faction would not be putting forward any candidates for party president. Additionally, Nakasone had backed Tanaka during his successful bid for the presidency rather than running against him. Tanaka owed him a debt.

Third, while Miki, Fukuda, and Ōhira were all in their sixties, Nakasone was only fifty-six. It would take some time for their factions to assume new leadership after they served as president, and Nakasone would be in a position where he could take advantage of that changing of the guard.

Nakasone held his first press conference as secretary-general on December 9 after the Miki government was formed. He said that "the birth of the Miki government conforms to the currents of history; the LDP can be said to have chosen the path of what could be called reform conservatism." He also invoked the slogan "a clean party."

Nakasone and Miki shared a sense of comradery from their time working together to bring down the Yoshida government as members of the Reform and Democratic parties. They were also in agreement that the party needed to rid itself of the kind of money politics that Tanaka had practiced.

But the two men also differed when it came to fundamental government policies. According to Nakasone, who had always been seen as a hawk, "Miki belonged to the left wing of conservatism; he was quite a bit to the left of the moderates." This difference would become clear in the ways they approached the JNR general strike and the Lockheed scandal.[5]

A "Japanese-Style Welfare State"

Nakasone's first job as secretary-general was putting the party's finances in order and paying off its loans. The party had accumulated twelve billion yen in loans (partly due to the July 7, 1974 House of Councillors election, which had become known for its corporate involvement). The Miki government was in the middle of reforming the Political Funds Control Law and having difficulty raising money

The "Sankaku Daifuku Chū" Era   127

Nakasone went to see Hanamura Nihachirō, head of Keidanren's Executive Bureau, with LDP Financial Bureau Director Hosoda Kichizō to find some way of paying off the party's loans. Inevitably, Hanamura found himself going around to various banks and businesses soliciting contributions to the LDP.

Hanamura served as a contact point for corporate donations to the LDP, which is why he went to plead for money in Nakasone's place. One of his nicknames was "director of the business community's political department."

With his assistance, the LDP was able to cut its loans in half. Hanamura said that Nakasone and Hosoda were "impudent about the matter, commenting to me that 'we should have told you that we owed even more.'"[6]

The loans were a practical concern, but what policies was Nakasone devoting his energies to during this period? The Shinsei Dōshikai held its Eighth Youth Political Training Session at the National Olympic Memorial Youth Center in Yoyogi on September 11, 1975. Nakasone's speech at the event – "A Course for the Construction of a Japanese-style Welfare State" – was intended to provide a vision of what a post-high-speed growth Japan could look like:

> The policy of stable growth that we should be looking for is one aimed at constructing a Japanese-style welfare state that seeks to bring about "progressive security" and "social justice." It is on the basis of the great principles of progress and justice that we will achieve long-term. strong welfare. Bringing this about will require a thoroughly examined, comprehensive framework, preparations for that framework's implementation, and a timetable based on a long-term financial outlook.

This was the "neoliberalism" that Nakasone had advocated for during his time at MITI, developed in a direction that emphasized the importance of welfare. Nakasone wanted to make this construction of a "Japanese-style welfare state" a positive legacy of stable growth.[7]

Nakasone was not the only one who viewed welfare as important, of course, and his efforts were in line with what Miki put forward in his "life cycle plan" (shōgai sekkei keikaku). The Miki government's signature policy, this was a comprehensive welfare policy covering education, employment, housing, medical care, and care for the elderly. This was an era in which both the government and the opposition were united in the belief that welfare policies were necessary.[8]

The JNR General Strike

Demands by the National Railway Workers' Union (Kokurō) to be granted the right to strike were another long-standing issue that came to a head at this time when, on November 26, 1975, it decided to strike.

This strike lasted eight days, the longest railway stoppage in Japanese history. Public employees had been prohibited from striking by the Ashida government in 1948 in Cabinet Order No. 201.

128　*The "Sankaku Daifuku Chū" Era*

According to NHK reporting, Miki and Labor Minister Hasegawa Takashi were inclined to grant the union a conditional right to strike. Nakasone and Shiina, however, were opposed. Nakasone met with Miki on November 23 during the run-up to the strike, and the two men reached an agreement that any Kokurō strike would be severely punished. Miki had felt that granting of a conditional right to strike was inevitable and wanted to act to prevent the union from striking, but Nakasone flatly rejected this.

Once the strike began, Nakasone was determined to "not yield a single inch" to the strikers. On December 1, the LDP General Council adopted the stance that legal order must absolutely be maintained. Nakasone felt that the strike was "actually an incredible opportunity to set Kokurō straight with popular support." He believed that, with the expansion of private railways and automobile ownership, the strike was doomed to fail.

The weeklong strike earned public enmity, and it was canceled on December 3, its eighth day. Nakasone regarded the strike as having been thoroughly illegal, and this, along with JNR's increasing amount of debt, convinced him that comprehensive reform remained an important task. His actions here foreshadowed the efforts he would make as prime minister to break up and privatize JNR.[9]

Yanba Dam

While Nakasone's response to the strike had been made from a national perspective, he showed a different side when it came to dam construction. There were plans to construct Yanba Dam at Naganohara in western Gunma. While Infrastructure Minister Maehara Seiji would famously announce the cancellation of the dam in 2009 during the Democratic Hatano Yukio government, the preparatory work for the dam was already completed and construction ready to start in 1970.

During the Miki government, it was Kanemaru Shin, director-general of the National Land Agency and a member of the Tanaka faction, who pushed for construction on the dam to proceed. Tokyo, highly reliant on underground water sources for industrial water, was experiencing a water shortage at the time, which was causing a sea-level zone to expand around Kōtō Ward due to subsidence.

Yanba Dam would eliminate the water shortage in Tokyo and prevent any further subsidence. But Kanemaru reports that Nakasone warned him against bringing up the matter during cabinet meetings. Naganohara, the planned location for the dam, was in Nakasone's district, and the local population was opposed to the dam.

Kanemaru went to the secretary-general's office and demanded to know whether Nakasone was "secretary-general of Gunma or of Japan?" He bitterly noted that "Tokyo doesn't have enough water. And isn't it the responsibility of government to take steps to resolve shortages? There are other gentlemen from Gunma responsible enough to support the dam."

The "Sankaku Daifuku Chū" Era   129

This was a reference to Fukuda, who, despite also representing Gunma 3rd, took a broader perspective and backed the dam. After Kanemaru left his office, Nakasone reportedly telephoned National Land Agency Deputy Director-General Hashiguchi Osamu and pressured him on the issue.

When Kanemaru learned of Nakasone's actions, he ordered Hashiguchi to "not change a single word" of the plans for the dam. "I felt that the idea of [Nakasone] ever becoming prime minister was absolutely outrageous." This incident would lead to Kanemaru publicly declaring that he "detested" Nakasone.[10]

Nakasone gives a different account of the dispute, however. According to him:

> The thing is, both Tanaka and Kanemaru belonged to the construction *zoku*. This was common knowledge at the time. They had even worked out twenty-year plans allocating where, when, and how many dams were going to be built in Japan. [...] I had no personal interests in the matter. Not in either the Ministry of Construction nor the Science and Technology Agency. Which is to say, I was not a zoku Diet member.

It is likely true that Nakasone wanted to rise above the special interests of the zoku Diet members (legislators closely connected to a particular policy area). But Kanemaru's account still seems the more convincing.[11]

The Lockheed Scandal

One of the major blows to the Miki government was the Lockheed scandal, a corruption scandal of unprecedented magnitude in which American aerospace manufacturer Lockheed was believed to have bribed powerful Japanese politicians to secure purchase orders for its aircraft. The most notable of these was then-Prime Minister Tanaka, but others like Hashimoto Tomisaburō and Satō Takayuki were also involved.

Hashimoto had been LDP secretary-general under Tanaka and Satō head of the PRC's Transportation Division. Hashimoto was a member of the Tanaka faction, but Satō belonged to the Nakasone faction.

After the scandal was uncovered on February 4, 1976, Miki held a press conference in which he vowed to undertake "a thorough investigation of the matter for the sake of ensuring sound democratic governance" and stated that it would be treated as of the highest priority. Nakasone found Miki's reaction excessive and advised him that "it would be better not to go overboard. Don't go crazy and lose any fingernails clawing away at it. The stability of your government is at stake and being too heartless towards the Tanaka faction could damage party solidarity."

Nakasone contacted the US embassy on February 6 regarding the scandal and received information from American reporters (via the company Nichimen) a few days later stating that Tanaka and Finance Minister Ōhira

130   *The "Sankaku Daifuku Chū" Era*

were involved in the scandal. Ōhira would ultimately be cleared of any involvement, but this was not initially clear.

According to American records, Nakasone contacted the US embassy on February 18 and 19 to request that they help cover up the scandal under the rationale that "were the LDP to suffer a crushing electoral defeat, it could mean the destruction of the US-Japan security framework." While Miki worked to investigate the scandal, Nakasone was acting in the opposite direction.

On February 23, both houses of the Diet unanimously passed resolutions requesting that the American government provide the Diet with its materials related to the Lockheed scandal. The following day, Miki wrote a letter to President Ford requesting his cooperation in making the identities of those involved public. Nakasone was not informed of the letter in advance.

An aspect of the scandal that caused problems for Nakasone was Lockheed's use of Kodama Yoshio in its Japanese activities. Kodama was a political fixer close enough to Nakasone that his secretary, Tachikawa Tsuneo, had lived in Nakasone's home as a student. Kodama had originally been a confidante of Kōno Ichirō (having been introduced to him by Miki Bukichi), and Nakasone had first met him in that context in 1955 or 1956. As mentioned earlier, when Kōno called Nakasone to the Imperial Hotel to discuss his intention to form a new political party, Kodama had been one of those in the room.

While Kodama did not testify before the Diet, pleading sickness, he was indicted for his involvement. Nakasone came under attack in the General Council from Diet Member Tamaki Kazuo of the Fukuda faction and others on the grounds that his relationship with Kodama meant that he must have taken the money. Nakasone also became a target for media suspicion.

On June 13, six Diet members – including Kōno Yōhei, Nishioka Takeo, and Tagawa Seiichi – declared that they were "breaking away from corruption" and left the LDP to form the New Liberal Club. It was none other than Kōno who, as the new party's representative, delivered their resignations to Nakasone.

Nakasone attempted to persuade Kōno to stay, saying that "While it may be beneficial in the short-term to follow an immediate trend, that same act, when viewed from the perspective of a lengthy political career, will serve not as a medal but rather as a wound. As someone who has been doing this longer, I ask you to seriously reconsider this." He was unable to prevent them from leaving, however.

Kōno criticized the party in the magazine *Chūō Kōron* following his departure, saying that "There is almost no discussion [in the LDP] of what should be done in the future, or opinions offered on the direction we should take. What the party is not lacking in, however, are arguments over policy that are focused on party and factional interests above all else and completely divorced from the livelihoods of the public. Nothing but problems that make you distrust politics." Kōno would later return to the LDP during

The "Sankaku Daifuku Chū" Era   131

the Nakasone government, although he would join Miyazawa Kiichi's
Kōchikai rather than rejoin the Nakasone faction.[12]

Resigning as Secretary-General

Tanaka was arrested on July 27. According to Nakasone, he was shocked to
receive a phone call from Justice Minister Inaba Osamu early that morning
letting him know that it was going to happen. As Inaba was a member of his
faction, it is plausible that he would have given Nakasone advance notice.

Upon his arrest, Tanaka immediately submitted his resignation from the
party to Nakasone through the Tokyo chief public prosecutor. Nakasone
then reported to the General Council that Tanaka had left the party. Tanaka
also resigned from the Nanokakai, the Tanaka faction. Both of these acts
were merely pro forma, however.

After Tanaka was released on bail on August 17, the Tanaka, Fukuda,
Ōhira, and Shiina factions rebelled against Miki, forming the Council for
Establishing Party Unity (Kyotō Taisei Kakuritsu Kyōgikai; Kyotōkyō) on
the 19th. The council's goal was popularly known as "bringing down Miki"
(*Miki-oroshi*). The LDP was now split between the mainstream Miki and
Nakasone factions on one side and Kyotōkyō on the other. It found itself
facing its most serious crisis since its formation twenty-one years earlier.

As secretary-general, it was Nakasone's job to support Miki, and he publicly advocated for the thorough investigation of the Lockheed scandal the
public were demanding. This was only in public, however. The party breaking up would make becoming prime minister more difficult, and he had no
intention of committing political suicide with Miki.

According to Diet Member Okuno Seisuke, who knew Nakasone from
their time at the home ministry, Nakasone told him around this time that
"People may comment that I put myself out in the limelight and strike poses,
but I've gotten pretty good at it." Okuno, who did not belong to any faction,
remarked that that kind of attitude "was probably necessary if you wanted
to gain power despite only having a small faction."

Nakasone was already in a difficult position, caught between Miki,
Kyotōkyō, and the public, but things became even more worse after it became
public that he was secretly conducting negotiations with the Democratic
Socialist Party, causing him to lose face.

While engaged in the private discussions aimed at securing passage of
the budget, he recorded a message about the talks for his Gunma office's
telephone service (a recorded message system accessed by telephone). In the
recording, he said, "Following lengthy talks with the Democratic Socialist
Party, we have formed a pact that will allow the budget to be passed on
April 10."

When *Akahata*, the Communist Party's newspaper, learned of the recording, it published sections of it. The article had major repercussions as the LDP
had publicly said that it intended to reach a decision on the budget through

132 The "Sankaku Daifuku Chū" Era

five-party talks. Nakasone's intention had been to boast of his accomplishments to his constituents, but the fact that he would record himself saying that he had formed a "pact" with a particular opposition party was enough to make many wonders if he was qualified to be secretary-general.

Nakasone sent the Democratic Socialist Party a letter of apology, but that was insufficient to resolve the matter, and Speaker of the House of Representatives Maeo Shigesaburō summoned Nakasone to his office. Nakasone bowed his head and apologized for the "difficulty that my rash actions have caused you, Mr. Speaker, and the parties," but Maeo replied that he "should be apologizing to the public for that telephone message."

Ōhira was even harsher in his assessment, writing in a notebook that "Developments in the Lockheed [scandal] hasten Miki's fall from power and weaken the Tanaka faction. The Nakasone faction will not recover."

The incident provided Nakasone with a good opportunity to resign as secretary-general, and he put forward a compromise under which "I will support the Miki government until the end of the [Diet] term, and you will permit me to resign." This would hold Kyotōkyō in check, but it would also prevent Miki from calling a general election as he had planned. On September 15, Nakasone resigned as secretary-general, nominally to take responsibility for the disorder he had caused. He had served in the position for twenty-one months.[13]

Formation of the Fukuda Government

It was on September 26, 1976, more than ten days after his resignation, that Nakasone was able to calmly speak about the Lockheed scandal and the divisions within the LDP. On that day, he gave a speech at the LDP Youth Division General Rally at Hibiya Public Hall in which he apologized for the party's infighting, saying that he bore "complete responsibility as secretary-general." He also argued for political reforms and for a presidential election open to all party members.

While Nakasone acknowledged in his speech that factions had had a negative influence on money and personnel decisions within the party, he did not reject them altogether:

> Gather ten goldfish together, and they'll split into a group of three and a group of seven. That's even more true of people. The LDP will suffer if we lose the kind of vitality as policymakers [that factions produce]. If we go too far [in suppressing factions], we will become totalitarian like the Communist Party, where everyone avoids displeasing [General Secretary] Miyamoto Kenji.[14]

The LDP suffered a major defeat in the December 5 general election that was triggered by the expiration of the House of Representatives' term.

The "Sankaku Daifuku Chū" Era 133

The party failed to secure a majority for the first time in its history and only barely managed to maintain its majority by admitting twelve unaffiliated conservative Diet members to the party.

Miki was replaced by Fukuda as prime minister on December 24. Ōhira, who had also been a candidate for the position, became secretary-general. The most pressing issue for the new prime minister – who prided himself on his economic skill – was economic reconstruction and grappling with rapidly increasing prices.

Fukuda's rise to prime minister seems to have been the result of an agreement between him and Ōhira. Under this agreement – commonly known as the "Daifuku pact" – Ōhira would support Fukuda's bid for the presidency, and, in exchange, Fukuda would only serve a two-year term rather than the usual three. He would then step down and yield to Ōhira. Nakasone, who had been in the mainstream during the Miki government, did not even run in the election. It was subsequently agreed at a party congress to reduce the president's term to two years.[15]

When asked about the Daifuku pact years later, Nakasone said, "I thought it obvious, given how aggressive Kyotōkyō was, that they would be able to bring about a Fukuda government if Fukuda and Ōhira were able to reach an agreement. But I did not expect any such government to be long-lived, given it would involve dragging down 'Clean Miki' after he had done popular things."[16]

"Neoliberalism" and Political Participation

With conservative and progressive forces equally matched in the Diet and hints of future trouble within the party, what expectations did Nakasone have for the future? In a February 16, 1977 speech to the American Club, he continued to argue for "neoliberalism" and spoke of expanding public political participation:

> Under neoliberalism, politicians decide which direction to move forward. Since business leaders and bureaucrats are obviously better than they are at business, the politicians should make skillful use of that while they take on the role of working with the public and being responsible to them. In this way, participation is carried out through a union of the public and the private sectors.

While politicians worked with the public and determined the broad policy direction, details of the economy would be left to business leaders and bureaucrats. Faced with the difficult situation of near parity between the government and opposition, Nakasone sought to restore the LDP's connections to the public and pushed for public participation in politics to an even greater extent than he had before.

134   *The "Sankaku Daifuku Chū" Era*

He also said that

> politics has very much lost its direct connections to the public, that sense of personally feeling the pulse of the public and making decisions. The political parties are becoming mouthpieces for government agencies, branch offices for them. [...] If we don't breathe new life into them, create something fresh like the Freedom and People's Rights Movement of the Meiji era, the public will abandon the political parties.

The speech reflected the danger that Nakasone felt toward the contemporary situation. He argued that the LDP should be interacting with the public rather than the bureaucracy and needed to earnestly consider increasing means of direct popular participation, such as by introducing national referendums.[17]

Testifying before the House of Representatives

The Lockheed scandal remained a personal danger to Nakasone. He appeared as a witness before the House of Representatives' Special Investigatory Committee on the Lockheed Issue on April 13, the first serving member of the Diet to be so called.

Most of the questioning concerned Nakasone's relationship with Kodama. And when questioned by Yokomichi Takahiro of the Socialist Party, he admitted that he had been questioned by the Tokyo Public Prosecutors Office twice.

Even so, Nakasone flatly denied any involvement in the scandal, saying that "neither my hands nor my spirit have been stained by this incident. I have not betrayed the public." The public prosecutors would also decide not to indict him in relation to the case.

Nakasone's ability to make it through the Lockheed scandal largely unscathed marks a point of divergence in his political career from Tanaka, who would spend the rest of his life embroiled in a legal battle over the scandal. Even so, Tanaka would continue to wield enormous political power, leading the media to refer to him as the "shadow shogun." And Nakasone's relationship to Tanaka would remain key to his pursuit of the LDP presidency.

Tanaka's transformation into the "shadow shogun" marks the beginning of a second phase for the "Sankaku Daifuku Chū," and Nakasone would continue searching for a foundation for factional politics.[18]

Two Foreign Tours

Prime Minister Fukuda visited Malaysia, Burma, Indonesia, Singapore, Thailand, and the Philippines from August 6 to 18, 1977.

In a speech in Manila on the 18th, Fukuda said that Japan would not become a military power but would instead build a "relationship of mutual confidence

The "Sankaku Daifuku Chū" Era 135

and trust based on 'heart-to-heart' understanding" with Southeast Asia and contribute to the region's peace and prosperity. Unusual for Japanese foreign policy, this "Fukuda Doctrine" was the advocation of an ideal, and it was well-received in many of the countries involved.

Two weeks later, Nakasone – who had been busy with party business and the Lockheed scandal – visited Southeast Asia, seemingly following Fukuda's footsteps. Now without any position in the government, Nakasone traveled from September 4 to 13, meeting with Singaporean Prime Minister Lee Kuan Yew, Malaysian Prime Minister Hussein, Indonesian President Suharto, and Philippines President Marcos.

Of all these meetings, it was the words of Philippines Foreign Minister Romulo that had the greatest impression on him. He told Nakasone that "The Fukuda Doctrine is a mistake. The word 'doctrine' is one generally used by a superior towards a subordinate." Asked what term would have been preferable, Romulo answered "pledge."

Japan was successfully advancing into Southeast Asia economically during this period, but the impression that Nakasone received was that "while you may think that pushing forward economically is enough to win you respect, that is not true."

After gathering his thoughts on this topic, he released a pamphlet – *The International Situation and Japan's Role* – which was published by his faction in November. Nakasone used Romulo's comment to try to dampen some of the enthusiasm toward the generally well-received Fukuda Doctrine, thereby tacitly showing some antagonism toward Fukuda.

Nakasone would himself make use of Romulo's lesson and avoid putting forward a doctrine when he visited Southeast Asia as prime minister. He adopted a humble attitude that was easily accepted by local leaders, and this also seems to have informed the passive approach with which he addressed the peace problem in Cambodia, which was still undergoing civil war.

After touring Southeast Asia, Nakasone visited the US from September 18 to October 5, meeting with National Security Advisor Brzezinski, former President Ford, and former Secretary of State Kissinger.

Particularly noteworthy was his meeting with former Ambassador to Japan Johnson. Johnson had served as the chief US delegate at the SALT (Strategic Arms Limitation Talks) negotiations prior to his retirement, and he handed Nakasone some of the documents from them.

The documents revealed the actual state of the US-Soviet negotiations, and Nakasone's found that he could not look away from them:

> I realized that the US and USSR were carrying out the highest-stakes game in the history of human civilization. As I read them, I became solemn, and we went to get a drink at a bar. I was profoundly struck by the sense that the US and USSR exist in a world that we don't know, engaged in psychological warfare and a sweat-inducing struggle for existence backed by the most incredible, cutting-edge weapons of our civilization.[19]

136　The "Sankaku Daifuku Chū" Era

While Nakasone had been busy with domestic politics, Japan had increased its presence in Southeast Asia with the well-received Fukuda Doctrine and international tensions had eased, as symbolized the SALT talks. As he engaged in his first foreign travels in quite a while, Nakasone renewed his analysis of the international situation and engaged in his specialty, foreign policy.

A "Copernican Change in Political Principles" – Returning to the General Council

Shortly after returning from the US, Nakasone sounded out Fukuda about being appointed to a position in the party leadership. He soon received a phone call at a teahouse in his district from Fukuda asking him to become General Council chairman.

He was surprised that Fukuda had contacted him at the teahouse but accepted the position. He interpreted Fukuda's motives as an attempt to "incorporate me into his camp in preparation for his reelection attempt."

Nakasone thus became General Council chairman for the second time on November 28, 1977. As discussed earlier, his first appointment to the position had come about as part of Satō's maneuvers to have him support Fukuda as his successor; he had now been appointed by Fukuda for a similar reason. According to Nakasone, the General Council was "with the exception of the General Assembly of Diet Members, normally the highest deliberative body for the management of party business related to policy and personnel."

Where did he focus his attention as chairman? I would like to use his pamphlet, *I Can Hear the Sound of the Sea*, derived from a lecture he gave at Meiji Jingū Kaikan Hall, to provide some hints.

In his lecture, Nakasone lamented "repeated challenges to the basis of the Japanese state's existence." This was a reference to the ongoing struggle over Narita Airport, the Japanese Red Army's Dhaka hijacking, and the violation of Japanese territorial waters by Chinese fishing boats near the Senkaku Islands.

And yet, despite these challenges, the leadership of the LDP, out of consideration of the opposition parties and others, had been "unable to maintain purity," resulting in "only the General Council serving as the backbone of the LDP." Nakasone argued that a "Copernican change in political principles" was thus needed:

> At this point, I believe that Japanese politics must make a change. It must abandon its traditional standard of the economy, which it pursues out of inertia, to face a world overflowing with greater and wider energy. A "Copernican" change in political principles is demanded. A restoration of governability. A release from that aspect of politics known as the economy (which is, of course, one of its most important)

The "Sankaku Daifuku Chū" Era   137

and the promotion of politics' original functions aimed at the development of comprehensive, total ethnic unity and progress.

As he called for restoring the government's ability to govern, Nakasone argued that there had been an overemphasis on the economy "from Yoshida to the Kishi, Ikeda, Tanaka, and Fukuda governments." He brought up education, science, welfare, security, diplomacy, local governments, and the constitution as important areas as important non-economic areas to focus on. The vision put forward in his lectures can be regarded as the "antithesis" of the contemporary government helmed by "Economic Fukuda."

Nakasone's description of the General Council as the "backbone of the LDP" was undoubtedly an exaggeration. It was the party's policy divisions – which were dominated by *zoku* Diet members – that made policy decisions in actual practice. These decisions, after they passed through the PRC, would typically be accepted by the General Council untouched. While the General Council would sometimes erupt in discontent, it was widely known, as described by one finance ministry official, that the General Council existed to provide "a place to let off steam."[20]

"Weathervane"

Despite being unhappy with the Fukuda government's overemphasis on the economy, that was a domestic policy matter, and there is no sign that Nakasone had any major conflicts with Fukuda over foreign policy. The aforementioned Fukuda Doctrine and the Sino-Japanese peace treaty were the major issues on Fukuda's foreign policy agenda, and Nakasone was also in favor of the treaty.

On April 12, 1978, during the peace treaty negotiations, Chinese fishing boats violated Japanese territorial waters near the Senkakus. The Chinese explained that this had been accidental.

Nakasone spoke at the Hokkaido Junior Chamber International Congress in Sapporo on April 22. Referencing the violation, he said that "it's all fine and good that the Chinese have reportedly said that it was an accident," but "the Senkaku Islands are not the only problem. There are also issues in Japan-Korea relations and in the Middle East."

He went on to say,

> I believe that what Japan needs most right now is a 'weathervane.' People often refer to me as the weathervane of the political world [as a criticism], but it seems to me that nothing is more necessary. The body of a weathervane may move freely, but its legs are fixed in place. That's why it's able to indicate the direction of the wind. And you cannot sail a ship without knowing which way the wind's blowing. [...] What's important is having a firm grasp on the other party's situation and keeping an eye on the direction of the wind as you skillfully steer the ship.[21]

138   *The "Sankaku Daifuku Chū" Era*

Nakasone prepared the LDP for the signing of the Sino-Japanese peace treaty in August and spoke to Vice-Premier Deng Xiaoping when he came to Japan in October.[22]

Unease with Fukuda

By the early autumn of 1978, eighteen months into the Fukuda government, the question of whether Fukuda would continue as prime minister had become the central point of interest of the political world. Secretary-General Ōhira continued to believe that, in accordance with the Daifuku pact, Fukuda would step down after two years and yield the presidency to him.

Talks between Fukuda and Ōhira broke down, however, and the political situation began to focus on the first LDP preliminary presidential election that would be held in November. This preliminary election was open to party members and allies and was held prior to the main election in which Diet members voted.

Ōhira called Nakasone to Hotel Okura on October 13. When he arrived, he found the normally calm Ōhira in a bloodthirsty mood.

Ōhira told Nakasone that Fukuda had reneged on his promise to yield power and furiously stated that he had "never met anyone who would act in such a faithless manner." Now facing an election, he wanted to prevent a Nakasone-Fukuda alliance, and Nakasone interpreted Ōhira's comments as Ōhira asking him to run as a candidate.

Nakasone himself had become increasingly uneasy about Fukuda and his tendency to concern himself with only economic policy. As mentioned earlier, Fukuda had returned Nakasone to the position of General Council chairman in the expectation that he would support his reelection. But it had been nearly twelve years since the formation of the Nakasone faction, and, having now served in a number of important posts, Nakasone felt no compunctions about running as a presidential candidate for the first time.[23]

On October 20, Nakasone published his book *Theory for a New Conservatism* through Kōdansha. He had spent the first half of the Fukuda government, during which he had had no position, traveling around the country, and the book was based on conversations he had had during those travels, such as with dairy farmers in Fukushima and fishermen in Hokkaido. The book –clearly published with the presidential election in mind – covered topics like "personalist education," "building humanist cities," "comprehensive security," and "dreams of a Pacific culture."[24]

Nakasone's First Presidential Candidacy

He also released a pamphlet, *Members of the Liberal Democratic Party, Rise Up in Accordance with the Spirit and Platform of the Party's Founding!* While the election was seen as a contest between Ōhira and Fukuda, it was also Nakasone's first time running, and he needed to put up a good fight with an

The "Sankaku Daifuku Chū" Era 139

eye on the next election. MITI Minister Kōmoto Toshio of the Miki faction was also a candidate.

What made Nakasone different from the other candidates? Fukuda, Ōhira, Nakasone, and Kōmoto held a joint press conference on November 4. In their statements, Fukuda emphasized "Japan's place in the world," and Ōhira called for "flexible yet firm governance." Nakasone argued forcefully for "energetic government," and Kōmoto said that he would make "resolving our economic problems my greatest priority."

There were two comments by Nakasone that made him stand out. First, he said that it was "obvious that legislation for dealing with [military] emergencies should be enacted," and second, he said that he wanted to "quickly step into the ring and spend five to eight years consulting with the people" on constitutional revision.

While Fukuda's position on emergency legislation came close to Nakasone's, all of the candidates other than Nakasone were opposed to constitutional revision. During this period, Nakasone was an advocate for what he called "constitutional correction" (*kenpō shūsei*).

1.5 million party members and allies cast votes in the party's first preliminary election, with the two most successful candidates advancing to the main election carried out by Diet members. The general belief was that Fukuda would come in first and Ōhira second.

Nakasone came in a distant third in the November 27 preliminary election behind Ōhira and Fukuda:

Ōhira Masayoshi	550,891
Fukuda Takeo	472,503
Nakasone Yasuhiro	290,957
Kōmoto Toshio	88,091

Ōhira's success in the election was due to the support of his long-time ally Tanaka. No one was more surprised by these results than Fukuda, who – believing that he would come in first – had argued that everyone who came in second or lower should bow out of the main election.

With Fukuda thus having no choice but to drop out, Ōhira was chosen as president. Fukuda had fallen into his own trap. While Tanaka had not been a candidate, the election still very much served as a proxy battle in the "Kakufuku War."[25]

Ōhira's Appraisal of Nakasone

With the formation of the Ōhira government on December 7, 1978, Nakasone was now the sole member of the Sankaku Daifuku Chū not to have become prime minister. He must have felt as if his time was coming close.

Nakasone informed the Ōhira camp following the election that he "would [accept] secretary-general or, if that doesn't work, finance minister," but

140 *The "Sankaku Daifuku Chū" Era*

he once again found himself without any position. While Ōhira had finally found himself in the position of prime minister and had personally encouraged Nakasone to run, he did not actually regard him very highly. As discussed earlier, the two had differed in how they had wanted to respond to the Oil Crisis.

During the presidential election, Ōhira had answered questions from the magazine *Ekonomisuto*. One of these had asked his opinion of Nakasone's claim that "legislation covering emergency situations is needed."

He answered that "I believe that Nakasone is offering a thought-provoking opinion, saying, as a politician, 'this is what I think.' But that's all it is, and any actual action would have to be taken by the government or the party. So, if his statement spurs the government into preparing legislation and submitting it to the Diet, then I think it's fine that he made it an issue."

While this answer was circumlocutious in Ōhira's usual style, it was a rejection of Nakasone's argument. And when a *Shūkan Asahi* reporter asked for his appraisal of Nakasone, Ōhira only said that he "is a bit like a poet. He's an ideas man."

Ōhira had advocated for a "final settlement of the postwar" (*sengo no sōkessan*) during his campaign, and – at first glance – this phrase would seem to resemble the "final settlement of postwar politics" (*sengo seiji no sōkessan*) slogan that Nakasone would later adopt. However, according to Morita Hajime, Prime Minister Ōhira's chief secretary, Ōhira's slogan "contained absolutely no sense of nostalgia for the prewar period. That was where it differed from Nakasone's."

Morita also recalled that (excluding Tanaka) "there was a clear hierarchy in Ōhira's mind. Fukuda was the most trustworthy, followed by Miki. Nakasone came last. This was clear in his mind. He repeated it many times."

While Ōhira had disparaged Fukuda during his meeting with Nakasone at Hotel Okura, he still placed him two levels above Nakasone. Again, according to Morita, "he was critical of Nakasone for being too concerned about what others thought and for being indecisive." Ōhira "felt that he had no integrity."

Even so, Morita believed that, had Ōhira been alive for Nakasone's government, he would have felt that "Nakasone did a better job than [he] had expected."[26]

The Forty-Day Conflict

By the beginning of the Ōhira government, the accumulation of bonds had placed the government's finances in a dangerous situation. Ōhira felt responsible as he had authorized the issuance of Japan's first deficit bonds as finance minister under Miki. He sought to introduce a general consumption tax to help rectify the situation but with the government and opposition nearly evenly matched in the Diet, a general election was inevitable.

On September 7, 1979, The Socialist and Democratic Socialist parties and the Kōmeitō submitted a motion of no confidence against him in the

The "Sankaku Daifuku Chū" Era   141

House of Representatives. Ōhira immediately dissolved the body and called an election without even waiting for Socialist Chairman Tagaya Shinnen to explain why the motion had been submitted.

The LDP were unable to improve their position in the Diet in the October 7 election (they lost a seat), however, and Fukuda and Miki began pressuring Ōhira to take responsibility and resign. According to a memo written by Ōhira, Nakasone also approached him to suggest "that I take responsibility in a manner easily understood by the public" and proposed that remedial measures be decided upon by the powerful members of the party. It seems likely that Nakasone believed that his time had come.

The confrontation between Ōhira and the LDP factions opposing him became known as the "Forty-Day Conflict."

On November 6, a strange situation developed in the House of Representatives where, while the mainstream Ōhira and Tanaka factions voted for Ōhira as prime minister, the counter-mainstream Fukuda, Miki, and Nakasone factions voted for Fukuda. Ōhira just barely managed to hang on, the gap between the two candidates a mere seventeen votes.

Here, Nakasone chose to stand with former LDP president Fukuda in the "Kakufuku War." Under normal practice, having voted for someone other than their party's president for prime minister in the Diet, it would have been expected for Fukuda and Nakasone to leave the party. There can be no doubt that Ōhira's already low opinion of Nakasone would have fallen even further.

Even so, when the second Ōhira government was formed on November 9, he sounded out Nakasone about becoming finance minister in the name of party reconciliation. According to Kurihara Yūkō of the Ōhira faction, however, Nakasone refused the offer. With the government weak and highly likely to be short-lived, Nakasone already had his sights set on a post-Ōhira political landscape.[27]

The "Unexpected Dissolution"

On April 25, 1980, Nakasone published *Cities in Communion: Proposals for Entering the 21st Century* through Sankei Publishing. This book was a sequel to *Theory for a New Conservatism*, and in it, he described his concern that growing selfishness would destroy the communities that had flourished in rural villages and downtown urban areas. Contemplating the redevelopment of Tokyo and regional cities, he proposed the creation of "cities in communion" and the use of "humanitarian urban planning."

From April 27 to May 9, Nakasone visited China with leaders of his faction like Hara Kenzaburō and Etō Takami. They met with Secretary General of the Central Secretariat Hu Yaobang, the man seen as the likely successor to Deng Xiaoping. This meeting would later be useful for Nakasone when he became prime minister.

On May 16, the Socialist Party submitted a motion of no confidence. After lengthy vacillating, Nakasone ultimately entered the Diet chamber

142 The "Sankaku Daifuku Chū" Era

at the very last moment and voted against the motion alongside the Tanaka and Ōhira factions. This time, Nakasone stood against Fukuda.

However, since the Fukuda and Miki factions had absented themselves from the vote, the motion passed and Ōhira dissolved the body. As even the opposition parties had expected it to fail, this became known as the "unexpected dissolution" (*hapuningu kaisan*). It had only been seven months since the last general election.

Looking back on his decision to vote against the motion, Nakasone explained that "Since the motion of no confidence had been submitted by the Socialist Party, we all had to act to protect the government. I mean, that's just the normal operation of constitutional government, right?" But that is likely not the only reason for his vote. He had, after all, only returned to the chamber at the last minute, and he had voted for Fukuda to become prime minister during the Forty-Day Conflict.

Gotōda Masaharu, a leader of the Tanaka faction, believed that Nakasone owed the support that he would later receive from the Tanaka faction, the support that allowed him to become prime minister, to his decision to enter the chamber here:

> I believe that the Nakasone faction's entrance into the Diet chamber was one of the reasons that Nakasone Yasuhiro was later able to become prime minister. Had he left at that time, he would never have been able to be prime minister. It would have been an indelible blot on his career. [...] He absolutely would not have received the support of the Tanaka faction if he had not entered at that time. And he would have thus been unable to become prime minister.

Nakasone had once again switched sides in the Kakufuku War and was again leaning toward Tanaka. Abe Shintarō chose the opposite course. A member of the Fukuda faction, Abe was PRC chairman and exited the chamber just as Nakasone was entering.

Ōhira's dissolution led to elections being held for both houses of the Diet on the same day for the first time, but he himself passed away during the electoral campaign. The LDP won an overwhelming victory, partly due to mourning over Ōhira.[28]

Director-General of the Administrative Management Agency under Suzuki

Nakasone's intention had been to try to become prime minister should the Ōhira government fall. It would have been only natural for him to follow now that all of the "Sankaku Daifuku" had held the position. But Ōhira chose to dissolve the Diet rather than resign, and, while he may have died, the LDP was victorious in the ensuing election. And it would likely not have been as successful without the sympathy vote caused by his sudden death.

The "Sankaku Daifuku Chū" Era   143

Ōhira's sudden death led to an unexpected political situation: Suzuki Zenkō, a member of the Ōhira faction, became prime minister with the support of the Tanaka faction. While Nakasone had been attempting to reach the political summit from early on in his career, Suzuki had not. His becoming prime minister was the result of happenstance, and Nakasone was not pleased by the development.

But even if Suzuki found himself the beneficiary of unexpected good fortune, the reason that he became prime minister rather than Nakasone was because he had powerful backers. Important members of the Tanaka faction, like Nikaidō Susumu and Kanemaru Shin, stood between Nakasone and the premiership. Nikaidō, in particular, was close to Suzuki and would serve as General Council chairman and then secretary-general during the Suzuki government.

The Suzuki government was launched on July 17, 1980, with Nakasone reluctantly participating as director-general of the Administrative Management Agency (AMA). He had hoped to be finance minister, having never held the position, and was not pleased when Watanabe Michio, a member of his faction, was chosen instead.

According to Nakasone,

> As Uno Sōsuke, a member of my faction (and future prime minister), had been serving as AMA director-general, some suggested that offering the position was an insult. Because it meant a faction leader was taking over for one of their subordinates. But administrative and fiscal reform was the most important issue facing the nation, and so I decided to take a shot at it.

Nakasone was chided by former prime minister Kishi at this time. While Kishi had retired from the Diet, he remained a top LDP advisor. He told Nakasone, "Don't think about becoming prime minister. Just act on the task you have in front of you now, administrative reform. That will be the foundation for the revival of Japanese politics."

While Nakasone was encouraged by Kishi's words, that was not Kishi's actual intent. It was not Nakasone, but rather Fukuda, who he hoped would become prime minister.

In an interview, he said that "I don't think there's anyone other than Fukuda who can actually get [fiscal reconstruction] done. Someone like Nakasone, who is in the position now, [...] doesn't have the ability needed. But Fukuda has already been prime minister, so I guess it would be difficult [for him to regain the position]."[29]

The Second Provisional Commission on Administrative Reform and "Financial Reconstruction without Raising Taxes"

Nakasone immediately adjusted his focus and began to tackle the task of administrative and fiscal reform. The Second Provisional Commission on Administrative Reform (Rinchō) was established as an advisory body

144   *The "Sankaku Daifuku Chū" Era*

within the Prime Minister's Office to push these reforms forward with former Keidanren president Dokō Toshio as its chairman. Known for his ability to quickly change gears and for his "optimism," it is fair to say that Dokō shared some of Nakasone's character.

Rinchō was created in March 1981 and would release its final findings two years later during the Nakasone government. It was the successor to a commission that had been created during the Ikeda government two decades earlier; that commission had recommended strengthening the cabinet's ability to regulate the government.

In addition to Chairman Dokō, Rinchō had eight members: Enjōji Jirō (advisor, Nihon Keizai Shimbun), Miyazaki Hibiki (president, Asahi Kasei), Sejima Ryūzō (senior advisor, Itochu Corporation), Tanimura Hiroshi (chairman, Tokyo Stock Exchange), Maruyama Yasuo (deputy chairman, Sōhyō), Kanasugi Hidenobu (deputy chairman, Dōmei), Tsuji Seimei (professor emeritus, University of Tokyo), and Hayashi Keizō (executive president, Japanese Red Cross Society). Sejima was a notable inclusion. He had had the unusual career of attending the Imperial Japanese Army Academy, serving on the staff of the Kwantung Army, and being interned in Siberia before joining Itochu.

Nakasone felt that Dokō and Seijima became the focal points of Rinchō, and he would rely upon Sejima for diplomatic efforts after becoming prime minister. Nakasone and Miyazaki were also old acquaintances through the Kōkikai, one of his support organizations. Tanimura was a former administrative vice-minister of finance, and both Sōhyō and Dōmei were present to represent labor and provide balance.

Nakasone had long advocated for a "neoliberalism" that promoted increased participation by the public and relevant industries in the creation of policy, and those ideas were finally able to take shape with Rinchō. The inclusion of Dokō, Sejima, and Miyazaki – three representatives of the business world – led to the Socialists and Communists criticizing Rinchō as being "led by the business community."

The prominent role played by the business community was intentional on Nakasone's part, and he acknowledged that he "considered it important to make use of the business community in resolving matters rather than having to rely on the strength of the party." He had long interacted with the business world through the Kōkikai and elsewhere, and he made use of those personal connections for Rinchō.

Rinchō would swell into a massive organization consisting of nearly two hundred people – advisors, specialists, researchers, etc. – in addition to the nine members mentioned above. As the number of consultants grew, former bureaucrats would account for more than 40% of them.

Nakasone and Rinchō encouraged private-sector activity under the slogan "fiscal reconstruction without a tax increase." The amount of outstanding public debt increased each year, and they promoted reducing spending on public works and subsidies and loosening regulations. Nakasone went

The "Sankaku Daifuku Chū" Era   145

so far as to say in a cabinet meeting that "any bureau directors that oppose administrative reform should be demoted."[30]

Private-Sector Activity

What kind of society did Nakasone envision coming about as a result of Rinchō? A glimpse can be seen from the August 27 speech he gave to the Sanyo Conference on Current Events at Okayama International Hotel.

According to Nakasone, the purpose of administrative reform was restoring private-sector vitality and thereby "building a Japanese-style welfare society." Under Japanese-style welfare, the reasons for living – such as contributing to society – would be supported by companies and regions.

He also warned against bloat and pointed out the inefficiency of government agencies, noting that "on average, private railways have less than half the number of railway station employees that JNR does."

While the West had raised taxes to overcome the lack of funds caused by the Oil Crisis, Japan had made it through by issuing government bonds. While it had been able to maintain the economy, it now carried a massive 82 trillion-yen bond debt, and Nakasone argued that it was indispensable for Japan to "reduce expenditures, staffing, and budgets through administrative reform without raising taxes."

It was, for this reason, Nakasone explained, that he had "established the Second Provisional Commission on Administrative Reform to provide a place where representatives of the entire population could discuss these matters. Ninety-seven notable business and labor leaders (including Dokō-san), journalists, academics, representatives of regional organizations, and former government officials were invited."

Both the government and opposition parties had been invoking the idea of Japanese-style welfare since the 1970s, but this was the first time that Rinchō and its mission of administrative and fiscal reform had been included in the concept. Rinchō's success or failure would now determine Nakasone's political future.

Fortunately for him, unlike its predecessor during the Ikeda government, the second commission enjoyed great public interest and favorable media coverage. And when Dokō was shown eating dried sardines on television, his sense of the common man increased Rinchō's support. Rinchō served as a predecessor to the private advisory bodies that Nakasone would later make heavy use of in his attempt to be a "presidential prime minister."

As the 1982 budget was put together under the principle that there would be no increases over the previous year, any ministry that wanted to take on a new program had to eliminate an existing expense. Rinchō would carry on its activities into the beginning of the Nakasone government, and he would carry out its findings by privatizing Japan's three largest public corporations. The position of prime minister was finally coming within reach of Nakasone.[31]

146   The "Sankaku Daifuku Chū" Era

Notes

1 Discussion between Nakasone and Kissinger (November 20, 1974), Fōdo Beikoku Daitōryō Hōnichi, 2014-3044, MOFA.
2 Fukuda Takeo, *Kaiko 90 Nen* (Tokyo: Iwanami Shoten, 1995), 144–57. Baba Shūichirō, *Ran wa Yūzan in Ari – Moto Jimintō Fukusōsai Nikaidō Susumu Kikigaki* (Fukuoka: Nishi Nihon Shimbun, 1998), 247.
3 Chiba Saburō, *Sōzō ni Ikite – Waga Shōgai no Memo* (Tokyo: Karuchā Shuppansha, 1977), 422.
4 Hori Shigeru, *Sengo Seiji no Oboegaki* (Tokyo: Mainichi Shimbun, 1975), 154–58. Shiina Etsusaburō Tsuitōroku Kankōkai, ed., *Kiroku Shiina Etsusaburō* (Tokyo: Shiina Etsusaburō Tsuitōroku Kankōkai, 1982), 2:248–95. Baba 148–49. Morita Hajime, *Kokoro no Ittō – Kaisō no Ōhira Masayoshi – Sono Hito to Gaikō*, ed. Hattori Ryūji, Nobori Amiko, and Nakajima Takuma (Tokyo: Daiichi Hōki, 2010), 18, 135–36.
5 *Asahi Shimbun,* December 10, 1974. Uchida Kenzō, *Habatsu* (Tokyo: Kōdansha Gendai Shinsho, 1983), 99. Nakasone Yasuhiro, Itō Takashi, Satō Seiburō, *Tenchi Ujō – Gojū Nen no Sengo Seiji o Kataru* (Tokyo: Bungei Shunjū, 1996), 292–96. Tominomori Eiji, *Sengo Hoshutō-shi* (Tokyo: Iwanami Gendai Bunko, 2006), 294. Nakasone Yasuhiro, *Nakasone Yasuhiro ga Kataru Sengo Nihon Gaikō* (Tokyo: Shinchōsha, 2012), 253–56.
6 Diary of Hosoda Kichizō (December 12, 1974, January 3, 11, February 14, 28, March 11, 17–18, April 15, May 10, June 12, 16, 1975, January 8, 12, 19, 1976), "Hosoda Kichizō Kankei Bunsho" 11, 12, 13, Modern Japanese Political History Materials Room, NDL. Miyawaki Michio, *Hosoda Kichizō – Zenjinzō* (Tokyo: Gyōsei Mondai Kenkyūjo Shuppankyoku, 1984), 204–05. Hanamura Nihachirō, *Seizaikai Paipuyaku Hanseiki – Keidanren Gaishi* (Tokyo: Tokyo Shimbun, 1990), 212–14, 242. Nakasone, *Tenchi Ujō,* 303. Japanese Modern Historical Manuscripts Association, *Hosoda Kichizō Ōraru Hisutorī* (Tokyo: Japanese Modern Historical Manuscripts Association, 2006), 2:19–21.
7 Nakasone Yasuhiro, "Sengo Bunmei Jidai no Sōzō" (September 1975), author's collection, 17–18.
8 *Yomiuri Shimbun* (August 13, 1975). Miki Takeo Shuppan Kinenkai, ed., *Gikai Seiji to tomo ni – Miki Takeo Enzetsu, Hatsugen-shū* (Tokyo: Miki Takeo Shuppan Kinenkai, 1984), 1:57.
9 NHK Shuzai-han. *NHK Supesharu Sengo 50 Nen Sono Toki Nihon wa Dai Gokan Sekiyu Shokku Gen'ei ni obieta 69 Kakan Kokutetsu Rōshi Funsō Sutoken Dakkan Suto no Shōgeki* (Tokyo: Nihon Hōsō Shuppan Kyōkai, 1996), 310–76. Nakasone, *Tenchi Ujō,* 298–309. Kasai Yoshiyuki, *Mikan no "Kokutetsu Kaikaku"* (Tokyo: Tōyō Keizai Shinpō, 2001), 64, 292. Kasai Yoshiyuki, *Kokutetsu Kaikaku no Shinjitsu – "Kyūtei Kakumei" to "Keimō Undō"* (Tokyo: Chūō Kōron Shinsha, 2007), 64. National Graduate Institute for Policy Studies COE Oral Policy Research Project, *Matsuno Raizō Ōraru Hisutorī* (Tokyo: GRIPS, 2003), 2:12–13.
10 Kanemaru Shin, *Tachiwaza Newaza* (Tokyo: Nihon Keizai Shimbun, 1988), 135–36.
11 Nakasone, *Tenchi Ujō,* 289.
12 See the following endnote.
13 Kodama Yoshio, *Kodama Yoshio Chosaku Senshū – Fūun* (Tokyo: Nihon Oyobi Nihonjin-sha, 1972), 2:430–32, 3:260, 331–32, 375–76, 378, 386, 427. Kodama Yoshio, *Namagausa Taikōbō* (Tokyo: Kōsaidō Shuppan, 1975), 200. Kodama Yoshio, *Ware, Kaku Tatakaeri* (Tokyo: Kōsaidō Shuppan, 1975), 252–54, 284, 292. Hayashi Fusao, "Kodama Yoshio Shōron – Kaisetsu ni Kaete," in Kodama Yoshio, *Gokuchū Gokugai* (Tokyo: Kōsaidō Shuppan,

The "Sankaku Daifuku Chū" Era 147

1974), 337, 342. James D. Hodgson to Henry A. Kissinger (February 20, 1976), Presidential Country Files for East Asia and the Pacific, Box 8, Gerald R. Ford Presidential Library. Diary of Hosoda Kichizō (February 24; April 1, 5, 14–15; June 1, 8, 17–18; July 10, 27, 29; August 2, 5, 30; September 15, 1976), "Hosoda Kichizō Kankei Bunsho," 13, NDL. *Akahata,* April 13, 1976. *Asahi Shimbun,* April 15 evening, April 16, September 11 evening, September 12, 20, 1976, February 12, 2010. *Yomiuri Shimbun,* July 27, 1976 evening. "Nakasone Kanjichō Shūshūan (September 11, 1976), author's collection. Kyotōkyō, 'Naze Wareware wa Miki Sōsai no Taijin o Motometa ka' (September 1976), author's collection. Kyotōkyō, Kyotōkyō Sōkai ni okeru Fukuda Takeo Aisatsu" (October 21, 1976), author's collection. Kyotōkyō, "Seimeian" (October 29, 1976), author's collection. A.C. Kotchian, *Rokkīdo Urikomi Sakusen – Tōkyō no 70 Nichikan,* trans. Murakami Yoshio (Tokyo: Asahi Shimbun, 1976), 152, 210–12, 220, 242, 347–50. Kōno Yōhei, "Hoshu o Sasaeru tame ni Saru," *Chūō Kōron* (August 1976), 194–95. Mainichi Shimbun-sha Seiji-bu, ed., *Kuromaku Kodama Yoshio* (Tokyo: Yell Shuppan, 1976), 78–81, 97–98, 130. Maeo Shigesaburō, *Seijika no Hōjōki* (Tokyo: Risō-sha, 1981), 66–67. Miki Takeo Shuppan Kinenkai, 1:430–44. Nakasone, *Tenchi Ujō,* 296–98, 309–14. Okuno Seisuke, *Ha ni Tayorazu, Gi o Wasurezu – Okuno Seisuke Kaikoroku* (Tokyo: PHP Kenkyūjo, 2002), 238. Nakasone Yasuhiro, *Sengo Seiji* (Tokyo: Yomiuri Shimbun, 2005), 39–41. Nakasone, *Nakasone Yasuhiro ga Kataru,* 261–65. Niigata Nippo Hōdōbu, *Saishō Tanaka Kakuei no Shinjitsu* (Tokyo: Kōdansha, 1994), 97. Hata Tsutomu, *Shōsetsu – Tanaka Gakkō* (Tokyo: Kōbunsha, 1996), 23. Tominomori 305–08. Hirano Sadao, *Rokkīdo Jiken – "Homurareta Shinjitsu"* (Tokyo: Kōdansha, 2006), 56, 64, 107, 120–26, 129, 167, 170, 172–73, 176–81, 184, 187, 196–201, 206, 221–22, 224–26, 239–43. Okuyama Toshihiro, "Himitsu Kaijo Rokkīdo Jiken," *Sekai* (January 2011), 114–24. Ōhira Masayoshi, *Ōhira Masayoshi Zenchosaku-shū* (Tokyo: Kōdansha, 2012), 7:123. Wakatsuki Hidekazu, *Taikoku Nihon no Seiji Shidō 1972–1989* (Tokyo: Yoshikawa Kōbunkan, 2012), 63. Arima Tetsuo, *Kodama Yoshio – Kyokai no Shōwa-shi* (Tokyo: Bunshun Shinsho, 2013), 242–43, 246, 263–68, 274, 283–366. Katō Tetsurō, ed., *Beikoku Kokuritsu Kōbunshokan Kimitsu Kaijo Shiryō CIA Nihonjin Fairu* (Tokyo: Gendai Shiryō Shuppan, 2014), 1:xxvii, 4:266–68, 317.

14 Nakasone Yasuhiro, "Seinen Shokun ni Kataru – Kyō to Ashita no Nihon ni tsuite" (October 1976), author's collection, 1, 9–10, 15–18.

15 Jiyū Minshutō, ed., *Jiyū Minshutō Tōshi* (Tokyo: Jiyū Minshutō, 1987), 730–31.

16 Nakasone, *Tenchi Ujō,* 314–15.

17 Nakasone Yasuhiro, "Atarashii Sekai Keiyaku to Nihon – Gendai no Shikaku kara" (March 1977), author's collection, 22, 28–29.

18 *Mainichi Shimbun,* April 13, 1977 evening. Horikoshi Sakuji, *Sengo Seiji 13 no Shōgen – Seiji Kisha Shuzai Memo kara* (Tokyo: Asahi Shimbun, 1989), 162–66. Tachibana Takashi, *Rokkīdo Saiban to sono Jidai* (Tokyo: Asahi Bunko, 1994), 1:174–76.

19 Nakasone Yasuhiro, *Kokusai Jōsei to Nihon no Yakuwari* (Tokyo: Seisaku Kagaku Kenkyūjo, 1977), 3–4, 11–20. Nakasone, *Nakasone Yasuhiro ga Kataru,* 332–37.

20 Nakasone Yasuhiro, *Uminari ga Kikoeru* (Tokyo: Seisaku Kagaku Kenkyūjo, 1978), 4–9. Nihon Keizai Shimbun, ed., *Jimintō Seichōkai* (Tokyo: Nihon Keizai Shimbun, 1983), 61. Satō Seizaburō, Matsuzaki Tetsuhisa, *Jimintō Seiken* (Tokyo: Chūō Kōron-sha, 1986), 99. Nakasone, *Tenchi Ujō,* 317–18.

21 Nakasone Yasuhiro, "Hato no Kanata ni – Bōfūken no Nihon" (April 1978), author's collection, 5, 9–11.

148   The "Sankaku Daifuku Chū" Era

22   Furusawa Ken'ichi, *Shōwa Hishi Nicchū Heiwa Yūkō Jōyaku* (Tokyo: Kōdansha, 1988), 144–46, 173, 217. Miyake Wasuke, *Gaikō ni Shōri wa Nai – Daremo Shiranai Nihon Gaikōri no Ura* (Tokyo: Fusō-sha, 1990), 159. Kurihara Yūkō, *Shōgen, Honne no Seiji – Sengo Seiji no Butaiura* (Tokyo: Nagai Shuppan, 2007), 53. Nakasone, *Nakasone Yasuhiro ga Kataru*, 266–70.

23   Nakasone, *Tenchi Ujō*, 319–20. Nakasone Yasuhiro, "Seiji ni Kandō to Risō o Torimodosō," in Kibe Yoshiaki, *Jinsei Meguriai* (Tokyo: Hōyū Shuppansha, 1978), 55. Ōhira 7:423.

24   Nakasone Yasuhiro, *Atarashii Hoshu no Riron* (Tokyo: Kōdansha, 1978). Nakasone Yasuhiro, *Jiseiroku – Rekishi Hōtei no Hikoku to shite* (Tokyo: Shinchōsha, 2004), 154. Nakasone, *Sengo Seiji*, 45. Nakasone Yasuhiro, *Hoshu no Yuigon* (Tokyo: Kadokawa one Tēma 21, 2010), 120–22. Nakasone, *Nakasone Yasuhiro ga Kataru*, 272–76. Nakasone, *Tenchi Ujō*, 315–17.

25   See the following endnote.

26   Seisaku Kagaku Kenkyūjo, ed., "Jimintōin Shokun Rittō no Seishin/Kōryō de Tachiagarō" (October 20, 1978), author's collection. *Asahi Shimbun*, November 5, 1978. Jiyū Minshutō 792. Nakasone, *Tenchi Ujō*, 324–25. Fukunaga Fumio, *Ōhira Masayoshi* (Tokyo: Chūkō Shinsho, 2008), 8–9, 164, 236. Morita 92–94, 127–28, 172, 181–82, 196, 231–32. Ōhira 6:562–63, 573, 7:8, 11–12, 19.

27   See the following endnote.

28   Nakasone Yasuhiro, *Kokoro no Fureau Toshi – 21 Seiki e no Teigen* (Tokyo: Sankei Shuppan, 1980). Nakasone, *Nakasone Yasuhiro ga Kataru*, 276–84. Kurihara Yūkō, *Ōhira Moto-Sōri to Watashi* (Tokyo: Kōsaidō Shuppan, 1990), 168. Nakasone, *Tenchi Ujō*, 325–31. Okushima Sadao, *Jimintō Kanjichōshitsu no 30 Nen* (Tokyo: Chūkō Bunko, 2009), 108–22. Gotōda Masaharu, *Jō to Ri – Kamisori Gotōda Kaikoroku*, ed. Mikuriya Takashi (Tokyo: Kōdansha Plus Alpha Bunko, 2006), 2:28–29. Gifu Shimbun, ed., *Shisei Ikkan – Mutō Kabun Hanseiki* (Gifu: Gifu Shimbun, 2008), 125–27. Ōhira 7:209–10.

29   See the following endnote.

30   Hosoda Kichizō, *Kokuyū Tetsudō o Kataru* (Tokyo: Rikuun Keizai Shimbun, 1981), 204. Uji Toshihiko, *Suzuki Seiken – 863 Nichi* (Tokyo: Gyōsei Mondai Kenkyujo, 1983), 95–103, 289–97. Kanbara Masaru, *Tenkanki no Seiji Katei – Rinchō no Kiseki to sono Kinō* (Tokyo: Sōgō Rōdō Kenkyūjo, 1986), 39–45. Hanamura 187–90. Nakasone, *Seiji to Jinsei*, 300–06. Nakasone, *Sengo Seiji*, 42–44. Nakasone, *Nakasone Yasuhiro ga Kataru*, 493–94. Ibayashi Tsugio, *Zaikai Sōri Sokkin Roku – Dokyō Toshio, Inayama Yoshihiro to no 7 Nenkan* (Tokyo: Shinchō-sha, 1993), 111–12, 170–75, 180, 183, 185. Watanabe Tsuneo, *Ten'un Tenshoku: Sengo Seiji no Rimenshi, Hansei, Kyojingun o Akasu* (Tokyo: Kōbunsha, 1999), 152–55. Kimura Mitsugu, *Sōri no Hinkaku – Kantei Hishokan ga Mita Rekidai Saishō no Sugao* (Tokyo: Tokuma Shoten, 2006), 178–80. Watanabe Tsuneo, *Watanabe Tsuneo Kaikoroku*, ed. Mikuriya Takashi, Itō Takashi, and Iio Jun (Tokyo: Chūō Bunko, 2007), 364–67, 371–72. Hara Yoshihisa, ed., *Kishi Nobusuke Shōgenroku* (Tokyo: Chūō Bunko, 2014), 116–17, 472, 476. According to Abe Takashi, head of the Sankei Keizai Shimbun's political desk, Nakasone met with him and Sankei Shimbun Vice President Kobayashi Yoshiharu (the older brother of Nakasone's wife Tsutako). Abe says that, while Nakasone was dissatisfied with being the minister in charge of administrative reform in the Suzuki government, when Abe argued that administrative reform was the most important item on the government's agenda and a good opportunity for Nakasone to join up with the business community's mainstream, Nakasone wrote this down in a notebook. Interview with Abe (June 9, 2012).

The *"Sankaku Daifuku Chū" Era* 149

31 Nakasone Yasuhiro, "Gyōsei Kaikau, Sono Shisō to Hōkō" (October 1981), author's collection, 1, 4, 7–11, 15, 21–22, 31. This is based on the speech he gave at Okayama International Hotel on August 27, 1981. See also: Nakasone Yasuhiro, "Gyōsei Kaikaku no Rinen to Kōdō," *Gekkan Jiyū Minshu* (September 1981), 56–67.

References

Arima Tetsuo. *Kodama Yoshio – Kyokai no Shōwa-shi*. Tokyo: Bunshun Shinsho, 2013.

Baba Shūichirō. *Ran wa Yūzan in Ari – Moto Jimintō Fukusōsai Nikaidō Susumu Kikigaki*. Fukuoka: Nishi Nihon Shimbun, 1998.

Chiba Saburō. *Sōzō ni Ikite – Waga Shōgai no Memo*. Tokyo: Karuchā Shuppansha, 1977.

Fukuda Takeo. *Kaiko 90 Nen*. Tokyo: Iwanami Shoten, 1995.

Fukunaga Fumio. *Ōhira Masayoshi*. Tokyo: Chūkō Shinsho, 2008.

Furusawa Ken'ichi. *Shōwa Hishi Nicchū Heiwa Yūkō Jōyaku*. Tokyo: Kōdansha, 1988.

Gifu Shimbun, ed. *Shisei Ikkan – Mutō Kabun Hanseiki*. Gifu: Gifu Shimbun, 2008.

Gotōda Masaharu. *Jō to Ri – Kamisori Gotōda Kaikoroku*. Edited by Mikuriya Takashi. Tokyo: Kōdansha Plus Alpha Bunko, 2006.

Hanamura Nihachirō. *Seizaikai Paipuyaku Hanseiki – Keidanren Gaishi*. Tokyo: Tokyo Shimbun, 1990.

Hara Yoshihisa, ed. *Kishi Nobusuke Shōgenroku*. Tokyo: Chūō Bunko, 2014.

Hata Tsutomu. *Shōsetsu – Tanaka Gakkō*. Tokyo: Kōbunsha, 1996.

Hayashi Fusao. "Kodama Yoshio Shōron – Kaisetsu ni Kaete." Kodama Yoshio, ed. *Gokuchū Gokugai* (Tokyo: Kōsaidō Shuppan, 1974).

Hirano Sadao. *Rokkīdo Jiken – "Homurareta Shinjitsu."* Tokyo: Kōdansha, 2006.

Hori Shigeru. *Sengo Seiji no Oboegaki*. Tokyo: Mainichi Shimbun, 1975.

Horikoshi Sakuji. *Sengo Seiji 13 no Shōgen – Seiji Kisha Shuzai Memo kara*. Tokyo: Asahi Shimbun, 1989.

Hosoda, Kichizō. *Kokuyū Tetsudō o Kataru*. Tokyo: Rikuun Keizai Shimbun, 1981.

Ibayashi Tsugio. *Zaikai Sōri Sokkin Roku – Dokyō Toshio, Inayama Yoshihiro to no 7 Nenkan*. Tokyo: Shinchō-sha, 1993.

Japanese Modern Historical Manuscripts Association. *Hosoda Kichizō Ōraru Hisutorī*. Tokyo: Japanese Modern Historical Manuscripts Association, 2006.

Jiyū Minshutō, ed., *Jiyū Minshutō Tōshi*. Tokyo: Jiyū Minshutō, 1987.

Kanbara Masaru. *Tenkanki no Seiji Katei – Rinchō no Kiseki to sono Kinō*. Tokyo: Sōgō Rōdō Kenkyūjo, 1986.

Kanemaru Shin. *Tachiwaza Newaza*. Tokyo: Nihon Keizai Shimbun, 1988.

Kasai Yoshiyuki. *Kokutetsu Kaikaku no Shinjitsu – "Kyūtei Kakumei" to "Keimō Undō."* Tokyo: Chūō Kōron Shinsha, 2007.

Kasai Yoshiyuki. *Mikan no "Kokutetsu Kaikaku."* Tokyo: Tōyō Keizai Shinpō, 2001.

Katō Tetsurō, ed. *Beikoku Kokuritsu Kōbunshokan Kimitsu Kaijo Shiryō CIA Nihonjin Fairu*. Tokyo: Gendai Shiryō Shuppan, 2014.

Kibe Yoshiaki. *Jinsei Meguriai*. Tokyo: Hōyū Shuppansha, 1978.

Kimura Mitsugu. *Sōri no Hinkaku – Kantei Hishokan ga Mita Rekidai Saishō no Sugao*. Tokyo: Tokuma Shoten, 2006.

Kodama Yoshio. Kodama Yoshio Chosaku Senshū – Fūun. Tokyo: Nihon Oyobi Nihonjin-sha, 1972.

150　The "Sankaku Daifuku Chū" Era

Kodama Yoshio. *Namagausa Taikōbō*. Tokyo: Kōsaidō Shuppan, 1975.
Kodama Yoshio. *Ware, Kaku Tatakaeri*. Tokyo: Kōsaidō Shuppan, 1975.
Kōno Yōhei. "Hoshu o Sasaeru tame ni Saru." *Chūō Kōron* (August 1976).
Kotchian A.C. *Rokkīdo Urikomi Sakusen – Tōkyō no 70 Nichikan*. Translated by Murakami Yoshio. Tokyo: Asahi Shimbun, 1976.
Kurihara Yūkō. *Ōhira Moto-Sōri to Watashi*. Tokyo: Kōsaidō Shuppan, 1990.
Kurihara Yūkō. *Shōgen, Honne no Seiji – Sengo Seiji no Butaiura*. Tokyo: Nagai Shuppan, 2007.
Maeo Shigesaburō. *Seijika no Hōjōki*. Tokyo: Risō-sha, 1981.
Mainichi Shimbun-sha Seiji-bu, ed. *Kuromaku Kodama Yoshio*. Tokyo: Yell Shuppan, 1976.
Miki Takeo Shuppan Kinenkai, ed. *Gikai Seiji to tomo ni – Miki Takeo – Enzetsu, Hatsugen-shū*. Tokyo: Miki Takeo Shuppan Kinenkai, 1984.
Miyake Wasuke. *Gaikō ni Shōri wa nai – Daremo Shiranai Nihon Gaikōri no Ura*. Tokyo: Fusō-sha, 1990.
Miyawaki Michio. *Hosoda Kichizō – Zenjinzō*. Tokyo: Gyōsei Mondai Kenkyūjo Shuppankyoku, 1984.
Morita Hajime. *Kokoro no Ittō – Kaisō no Ōhira Masayoshi – Sono Hito to Gaikō*. Edited by Hattori Ryūji, Nobori Amiko, and Nakajima Takuma. Tokyo: Daiichi Hōki, 2010.
Nakasone Yasuhiro. *Atarashii Hoshu no Riron*. Tokyo: Kōdansha, 1978.
Nakasone Yasuhiro. *Hoshu no Yuigon*. Tokyo: Kadokawa one Tēma 21, 2010.
Nakasone Yasuhiro. *Jiseiroku – Rekishi Hōtei no Hikoku to shite*. Tokyo: Shinchōsha, 2004.
Nakasone Yasuhiro. *Kokoro no Fureau Toshi – 21 Seiki e no Teigen*. Tokyo: Sankei Shuppan, 1980.
Nakasone Yasuhiro. *Kokusai Jōsei to Nihon no Yakuwari*. Tokyo: Seisaku Kagaku Kenkyūjo, 1977.
Nakasone Yasuhiro. *Nakasone Yasuhiro ga Kataru Sengo Nihon Gaikō*. Edited by Nakashima Takuma, Hattori Ryūji, Noboru Amiko, Wakatsuki Hidekazu, Michishita Narushige, Kusunoki Ayako, Segawa Takao. Tokyo: Shinchōsha, 2012.
Nakasone Yasuhiro. *Sengo Seiji*. Tokyo: Yomiuri Shimbun, 2005.
Nakasone Yasuhiro. *Uminari ga Kikoeru*. Tokyo: Seisaku Kagaku Kenkyūjo, 1978.
Nakasone Yasuhiro, Itō Takashi, Satō Seiburō. *Tenchi Ujō – Gojū Nen no Sengo Seiji o Kataru*. Tokyo: Bungei Shunjū, 1996.
National Graduate Institute for Policy Studies COE Oral Policy Research Project. *Matsuno Raizō Ōraru Hisutorī*. Tokyo: GRIPS, 2003.
NHK Shuzai-han. *NHK Supesharu Sengo 50 Nen Sono Toki Nihon wa Dai Gokan Sekiyu Shokku Gen'ei ni obieta 69 Kakan Kokutetsu Rōshi Funsō Suto-ken Dakkan Suto no Shōgeki*. Tokyo: Nihon Hōsō Shuppan Kyōkai, 1996.
Nihon Keizai Shimbun, ed. *Jimintō Seichōkai*. Tokyo: Nihon Keizai Shimbun, 1983.
Niigata Nippō Hōdōbu. *Saishō Tanaka Kakuei no Shinjitsu*. Tokyo: Kōdansha, 1994.
Ōhira Masayoshi. *Ōhira Masayoshi Zenchosaku-shū*. Tokyo: Kōdansha, 2012.
Okuno Seisuke. *Ha ni Tayorazu, Gi o Wasurezu – Okuno Seisuke Kaikoroku*. Tokyo: PHP Kenkyūjo, 2002.
Okushima Sadao. *Jimintō Kanjichōshitsu no 30 Nen*. Tokyo: Chūkō Bunko, 2005.
Okuyama Toshihiro. "Himitsu Kaijo Rokkīdo Jiken." *Sekai* (January 2011).

The *"Sankaku Daifuku Chū" Era*   151

Satō Seizaburō and Matsuzaki Tetsuhisa. *Jimintō Seiken*. Tokyo: Chūō Kōron-sha, 1986.

Shiina Etsusaburō Tsuitōroku Kankōkai, ed. *Kiroku Shiina Etsusaburō*. Tokyo: Shiina Etsusaburō Tsuitōroku Kankōkai, 1982.

Tachibana Takashi. *Rokkīdo Saiban to sono Jidai*. Tokyo: Asahi Bunko, 1994.

Tominomori Eiji. *Sengo Hoshutō-shi*. Tokyo: Iwanami Gendai Bunko, 2006.

Uchida Kenzō. *Habatsu*. Tokyo: Kōdansha Gendai Shinsho, 1983.

Uji Toshihiko. *Suzuki Seiken – 863 Nichi*. Tokyo: Gyōsei Mondai Kenkyujo. 1983.

Wakatsuki Hidekazu. *Taikoku Nihon no Seiji Shidō 1972–1989*. Tokyo: Yoshikawa Kōbunkan, 2012.

Watanabe Tsuneo. *Ten'un Tenshoku: Sengo Seiji no Rimenshi, Hansei, Kyojingun o Akasu*. Tokyo: Kōbunsha, 1999.

Watanabe Tsuneo. *Watanabe Tsuneo Kaikoroku*. Edited by Mikuriya Takashi, Itō Takashi, and Iio Jun. Tokyo: Chūō Bunko, 2007.

9   1,806 Days as Prime Minister

Seeking to Be a "Presidential Prime Minister"

I. Tanaka Kakuei's Shadow and the Results of Proactive Diplomacy: Nakasone's First Term

The Meanderings of the Suzuki Government

As Nakasone pursued administrative and fiscal reforms as director-general of the Administrative Management Agency, the Suzuki government was lost. Suzuki was an old hand at domestic politics, as would be expected from someone who had served as chairman of the Liberal Democratic Party's (LDP's) General Council ten times. But he was unskilled at foreign policy, causing a scandal following the May 1981 US-Japan summit by telling the press that the US-Japan alliance had no military connotations. Foreign Minister Itō Masayoshi ultimately took responsibility for the gaffe and resigned.

Then, in the summer of 1982, it became widely reported that the Ministry of Education had sought to have history textbooks replace the term "invaded" (*shinryaku*) with "advanced into" (*shinshutsu*) when describing Japan's military action in Asia. This heightened tensions with South Korea and China at a time when the Suzuki government was already experiencing difficulties with South Korea over Japanese economic cooperation. South Korea had strongly sought increased support by linking the matter to Japan's national security and been rebuffed by Foreign Minister Sonoda Sunao. The decline in Japan's foreign relations under his leadership led Suzuki to come under fire from significant LDP figures including Fukuda Takeo and Kishi Nobusuke.[1]

Nakasone's Ideals and His Vision for His Administration

On the evening of September 25, shortly after he learned that Suzuki would not be running in the November LDP presidential election, Nakasone paid a call to Tanaka Kakuei's home in Mejiro. He had been told that Tanaka did not trust him, and he wanted to alleviate his concerns. Tanaka assured him that it was all a "complete misunderstanding."

DOI: 10.4324/9781003351931-10

1,806 Days as Prime Minister 153

Before the start of the October 5 cabinet meeting, Suzuki approached Nakasone and said, "Please succeed me. There's no one else." Nakasone responded that he would "move ahead with that in mind." Tanaka called him on the 8th and told him that he had his "total support during this change of government."

Nakasone may have had the support of Tanaka and Suzuki, but that did not mean that he could rest easy. He needed to approach the leaders of the Tanaka faction next. While Suzuki may have successfully stolen the premiership away from them in the last election, they were still highly influential, and Nakasone's faction was only the fourth largest in the party. The Tanaka faction remained the largest faction and Kanemaru Shin, one of its most prominent members, had openly declared his dislike of Nakasone during their conflict over Yanba Dam.

Nakasone sought to overcome this by appointing Gotōda Masaharu, one of the faction's leaders and one of his seniors at the home ministry, as his chief cabinet secretary. Gotōda had previously served as commissioner general of the National Police Agency and was chairman of the LDP's committee on electoral systems at the time. He was also someone with whom Nakasone had held monthly dinners to discuss administrative reform.

Nakasone met with Gotōda to sound him out on the idea, saying that "There's going to be a realignment of the political landscape in the near future. I've seen the signs. And when that happens, I'd like you to join me at the prime minister's office and give me your support [...] When I put together a government, administrative reform is going to be the most pressing order of business. I want you there to help keep the bureaucrats in check."

While Gotōda's abilities were naturally a major reason behind Nakasone's invitation, the factional considerations behind the choice cannot be ignored. Standard practice was for the chief cabinet secretary to belong to the same faction as the prime minister; giving such an important position to a member of the Tanaka faction would draw media criticism, but he was prepared to accept that.

Gotōda ultimately accepted Nakasone's offer, although he initially avoided giving an answer. He later explained that while he would have been willing to accept any other position, "I felt that [the chief cabinet secretary] should come from the same faction as the prime minister, as they could be considered the 'head clerk' of the government."

In preparation for forming a government, Nakasone ruminated over his political ideals and wrote "Notes on the New Government's Policies" on October 10. In this document, he wrote that "The ultimate purpose of government is to serve culture and respect liberty; there can be no abuse of authority towards religion or learning. My basic creed is personalism and humanism. In the East, this is the path of great learning. In the West, it is epitomized by Kant's famous reference to the 'starry heavens.'"

The problem facing Nakasone was how he was going to apply those ideals in actual practice. Looking over the more than thirty volumes of notes

154　*1,806 Days as Prime Minister*

accumulated by Nakasone, he seems to have identified three primary tasks for his new government: resolutely carrying out administrative and fiscal reform; repairing relations with South Korea and the US; and undertaking reform of education and the labor movement. In making situational assessments, appealing to the public, and coordinating with Tanaka, he would make full use of the "Nakasone Machine," individuals like Sejima Ryūzō of Rinchō, Asari Keita of the Shiki Theater Company, Miura Kineji of the Asahi Shimbun, Watanabe Tsuneo of the Yomiuri Shimbun, and Ujiie Seiichirō of Nippon TV.[2]

Dissatisfaction in the Tanaka Faction

Tanaka's decision to back Nakasone led to dissent within his faction. As mentioned earlier, Gotōda believed that the chief cabinet secretary should belong to the same faction as the prime minister, and Kanemaru was known for his dislike of Nakasone. Before backing Nakasone, the two men decided to go see Tanaka to ascertain his true intentions.

When Gotōda and Kanemaru visited Tanaka's home on the evening of October 21, they found him in high spirits, drinking Old Parr and eating roasted matsutake mushrooms with soy sauce. Gotōda pressed him as to why he "would want to carry around such a shabby *mikoshi*?" (an idiom meaning to flatter someone and raise them to a figurehead position).

Tanaka responded that he was "picking it up precisely *because* it's so shabby." When Kanemaru asked him to explain further, Tanaka said, "I mean, if a mikoshi is shabby, you can just toss it aside at any time, right?" causing Kanemaru to burst into laughter.

Beyond this explanation, Tanaka also felt a sense of obligation toward Nakasone for his assistance in the creation of the Tanaka government, and that was something that he could not allow his followers to get in the way of. Kanemaru and the others resistant to Nakasone decided to back Tanaka's play on the basis that "part of politics is doing what your boss says."

Later, after Gotōda became chief cabinet secretary, Kanemaru once teased him by asking him, "How does it feel to be carrying such a shabby mikoshi?" Gotōda got an embarrassed look on his face, scratched the back of his head, and asked Kanemaru to give him a break. It is worth noting that all of this is according to an account given by Kanemaru; Gotōda attributed the "shabby mikoshi" comparison to Kanemaru rather than himself.

In any case, the issue of how he was going to keep the Tanaka faction on his side would be a major issue for Nakasone as he governed.[3]

"Twelve Hours Stuck Together in a Room"

The presidential campaign began on October 16, and Nakasone, Kōmoto Toshio, Abe Shintarō, and Nakagawa Ichirō declared their candidacies. Normal procedure would be to hold a preliminary election in which Diet members and party supporters could cast their votes. But Suzuki wanted to avoid that, believing that it would result in a lengthy political vacuum and delay the implementation of stimulus measures and reforms.

He thus called a meeting with Secretary-General Nikaidō Susumu and Fukuda Takeo at LDP headquarters at 5 p.m. on October 22. This meeting would later be described as "the twelve hours stuck together in a room" (*misshitsu no jūni jikan*).

Fukuda was present as a representative of the party's Supreme Advisory Council, a group made up of those LDP Diet members who had previously served as prime minister, deputy prime minister, or a speaker of one of the Diet's chambers. The council had been introduced at a party congress while Ōhira was president. While Ōhira had never actually summoned the council himself, Suzuki did so frequently – as befitted an advocate for the "politics of harmony."

The meeting stretched late into the night, but Suzuki, Nikaidō, and Fukuda were unable to reach an agreement. Suzuki wanted votes cast at a special party congress rather than a preliminary election. He had Nakasone in mind as his successor. Fukuda feared that Suzuki's proposal could split the party, however, and refused to back it; Nikaidō was inclined to support Fukuda.

With time running out (a preliminary election would be called as normal in the absence of any agreement), an unexpected figure burst into the presidential office where the discussions were being held: Tamura Hajime, chairman of the party's Diet Affairs Committee. Pounding the table, he insisted that "We must avoid a preliminary election! Can't you work this out somehow? Perhaps by making Nakasone prime minister but Fukuda president?"

Tamura was also chairman of the party's Presidential Election Management Committee, but he had never held any of the highest party positions and had absolutely no grounds for injecting himself into the discussion. Both Tamura and Nikaidō belonged to the Tanaka faction, but even Nikaidō was taken aback by Tamura's actions. He did not believe that Tanaka was behind them.

In an odd turn of events, however, Tamura's idea of separating the positions of president and prime minister appealed to Suzuki and Nikaidō. With the talks seemingly otherwise deadlocked, they went to work convincing Fukuda to back the proposal. Fukuda was hesitant but ultimately accepted the idea under the provision that it would only be a temporary measure until the party congress scheduled for January. By this point, it was 1 a.m. on October 23.

With an agreement in hand, Suzuki and the others presented the proposal to Nakasone. He avoided giving a clear response and briefly exited the room. He then called Tanaka, who told him that he "absolutely must not accept that deal."

According to Nikaidō, Tanaka chewed Nakasone out over the idea: "You absolutely cannot accept any separation of the premiership and the presidency. Turn them down flat. And then start getting ready for the preliminary

156   *1,806 Days as Prime Minister*

election." Fukuda was Tanaka's mortal enemy, and he could not stomach an arrangement under which Fukuda became party president.

Previously, when it had been time to choose Tanaka's successor, Nakasone had joined with Miki and Fukuda to reject Ōhira's proposal that the party's Diet members vote on the matter, resulting in the "Shiina Decision." Ōhira had wanted an open election because he had believed that Tanaka's backing meant that he would win. Nakasone, knowing that he had no chance in such an election, had sought an alternative. This time, the backing of the Tanaka faction was behind *him*, and there was no need to accept a negotiated resolution. At 5 a.m., Suzuki and the others abandoned their attempts to reach a consensus and decided to hold a preliminary election.

Had Nakasone accepted the proposal, he would have found himself caught between Tanaka and now-President Fukuda, something that would have hamstrung his government. It is difficult to believe that such a government could have lasted the five years that Nakasone's actual government did.

While Nakasone had opposed the plan, it was actually Tanaka's enmity toward Fukuda that played the greatest role in killing it. Tanaka was particularly angered by Fukuda's role in the Forty-Day Conflict, which he saw as having shortened his ally Ōhira's life. Tanaka felt that Fukuda had behaved extremely recklessly, and while Ōhira's sudden death occurred more than two years after the conflict, the two events were inextricably linked in his mind. And this long-established grudge killed the plan to make Fukuda party president.[4]

The Birth of the "Cabinet of the Capable"

When the preliminary election was held on November 24, Nakasone won an overwhelming victory with the backing of the Tanaka faction, securing an outright majority and precluding any need for further voting. The vote totals were:

Nakasone Yasuhiro	559,673 votes
Kōmoto Toshio	265,078 votes
Abe Shintarō	80,443 votes
Nakagawa Ichirō	66,041 votes

It goes without saying that it was the support he had received from the Tanaka and Suzuki factions that had enabled Nakasone to win so decisively. The others withdrew their candidacies and Nakasone was named party president at a special congress held the following day. At the age of sixty-four, he had now fulfilled his long-held ambition and become prime minister. He spent the evening at his office at the AMA working out plans for his cabinet.

Nikaidō was appalled when Nakasone revealed the lineup of his new government. Of the twenty positions in the cabinet, six would be going to the Tanaka faction (see Table 9.1). The most prominent of these would be Gotōda as chief cabinet secretary and Takeshita Noboru as finance minister,

1,806 Days as Prime Minister 157

Table 9.1 Factional Breakdown of Nakasone's Cabinets

	1st Gov't	2nd Gov't	2nd Gov't, 2nd Cabinet	2nd Gov't, 3rd Cabinet	3rd Gov't
Tanaka	6 (1)	6 (1)	6 (1)	6 (1)	8 (2)
Suzuki	4 (1)	4 (1)	4 (1)	4 (1)	3
Abe	3	4 (1)	4 (1)	4 (1)	3
Nakasone	2 (1)	3	3	3	4 (1)
Kōmoto	2	2	2	2	1
Neutral/Independent	3 (1)	0	0	0	1
New Liberal Club	0	1	1	1	0

Source: *Asahi Shimbun*, July 23, 1986.
Note: Numbers in parentheses indicate the number of members of the House of Councillors.

but he was also appointing figures like Katō Mutsuki (who was suspected of having been involved in the Lockheed scandal) as director-general of the National Land Agency. And while Hatano Akira, Nakasone's choice for justice minister, was unaffiliated with any faction, he was known to be close to Tanaka. With the verdict in the Lockheed case still pending, this was a controversial choice. There was no question that Nakasone's personnel choices would cause a media backlash.

The press was shocked when the cabinet was made public, with some newspaper reporters calling it a "third Tanaka government" (it also gained the popular appellation of the "Tanakasone government"). Nakasone was not surprised by the media's coverage, although he was annoyed by it.

Nakasone later compared his contemporary mindset to that of a "pitcher who'd gotten into a jam" and explained that his intention had been to create a "cabinet of the capable" (*shigoto-shi naikaku*):

> My intention had been to create a "cabinet of the capable," and [the lineup] was entirely the result of that. From the moment the Nakasone administration took sail, it was a voyage through rough seas. "A pitcher who'd gotten into a jam, bases loaded, no outs." That was me. The only way I was going to get out of that critical situation was by putting together the best cabinet I could by tapping the people who had the right skills for the job and whom I had faith in. [...]
>
> The Tanaka faction was large and had a large number of people who were able to get things done. Its lineup was like a ready-made list of names for putting together a cabinet. That's all. Of course, that meant that the power of the Nakasone faction was reduced. Normally, it wouldn't have been odd for me to have four members of my faction in the cabinet, but I only appointed two.

Nakasone may have truly intended to form a "cabinet of the capable," but it is difficult to see the idea that the cabinet just happened to include so many

158 *1,806 Days as Prime Minister*

members of the Tanaka faction as anything other than a post hoc justification. With the verdict in the Lockheed case pending and his new position dependent on Tanaka's support, there was no way that he would have been able to appoint a justice minister opposed to Tanaka.

In addition to giving a number of positions to the Tanaka faction, he also made the wise decision to give the key posts of finance and foreign minister to Takeshita and Abe. The two men were rivals who had gone into politics at the same time, and their inclusion contributed to the stability and energy of his new administration. As for the three major party posts, he kept on Secretary-General Nikaidō and PRC Chairman Tanaka Rokusuke and appointed Hosoda Kichizō as chairman of the General Council.

Nakasone moved into the prime minister's residence on December 19, becoming the first prime minister to live there since Satō Eisaku a decade earlier. Shortly afterward, his daughter Mieko asked him what it was that he most hoped to accomplish as prime minister. Nakasone answered that he wanted to make Japan into a country that would defend itself.[5]

Nakasone's First Policy Speech

The Nakasone government famously adopted "the final settlement of postwar politics" (*sengo seiji no sōkessan*) as its slogan. That was not initially the case, however; when Nakasone delivered his first policy speech as prime minister on December 3, 1982, he instead called for making Japan into "a vigorous nation of culture and welfare."

More specifically, he called for fiscal reform, reform of Japanese National Railways (JNR), "the realization of an active, stable society in which everyone can live comfortably," and strengthening the "relationship of trust between Japan and the United States." He also asserted that Japan had a "proactive role" to play in the world:

> Every year, the global expectations that our nation play a more proactive role in the world grow stronger. Japan's national strength now accounts for a tenth of the global economy, and no progress can be made towards peace on Earth and human prosperity without contributions from us.[6]

Nakasone was proud of the great heights that Japan's international status had reached.

A "Presidential Prime Minister" and "Directive Politics"

Distinctive to Nakasone was his perception of himself as a "presidential prime minister" close to an American president. He later said:

> The status of the Japanese prime minister under the current constitution could be said to lay somewhere between that of the American

president and the British prime minister. And, of the two, they're closer to the former. The change in the status of the Emperor from sovereign to symbol means that the authority of the prime minister has increased compared to what it was under the prewar constitution.

Speaking purely in terms of the theoretical institution, the authority of the prime minister had certainly increased from what it was before the war. In actual practice, however, both the media and the public had become wary of strong leadership and there had been many short-lived governments since the 1970s.

Nakasone was Japan's seventeenth prime minister of the postwar period. By comparison, Britain had only nine prime ministers (Atlee to Thatcher) and America only eight presidents (Truman to Reagan). Nakasone's view of the Japanese prime minister as being closer to the American president than somewhere in between the two positions was a fairly unique perspective.

But what did Nakasone mean when he spoke of a "presidential prime minister"? He explained that such a prime minister engaged in what he referred to as "directive politics":

> As prime minister, I created the "five cabinet offices" under Chief Cabinet Secretary Gotōda.[7] But I didn't really think they had all that much significance.
>
> A prime minister who surrounds himself with windchimes merely hinders himself. Such groups are just going to end up dominated by officials from various ministries. The more important thing is how you conduct yourself as prime minister. I found it far more effective to summon the administrative vice-ministers of the relevant ministries and give them instructions directly.
>
> Because I considered myself to be a presidential prime minister, I implemented directive politics.

Beyond his approach of directly exercising control over vice-ministers, another aspect of Nakasone's "presidential" leadership was his extensive use of private advisory councils (see Table 9.2), which he attempted to use to promote policymaking under the auspices of the prime minister's office (rather than the bureaucracy).

To give an example of Nakasone's use of these groups, when he wanted to surpass the 1% of GNP cap on defense spending, he had Kyoto University professor Kōsaka Masataka, head of the Research Committee on Peace Issues, issue a report in support that he (and Takeshita) then used to suppress internal party opposition from figures like Fukuda and Suzuki.

Nakasone's use of these groups was not without controversy, however. The top-down nature of his approach to governing led to criticism that he was side-stepping and undermining the deliberations of the Diet and LDP.

Nakasone's approach could be considered another example of brain trust politics, something that the Satō and Ōhira governments had also engaged in.

160   *1,806 Days as Prime Minister*

Table 9.2 Nakasone's Private Advisory Councils (1983–1987)

Founding	Name	Chair
1/1983	Committee to Examine the Standards and Certification System	
6/1983	Panel on Culture and Education	Ibuka Masaru
8/1983	Research Committee on Peace Issues	Kōsaka Masataka
2/1984	Advanced Information-Oriented Society Panel	Yamashita Isamu
6/1984	Council for Promoting Projects Related to Women's Issues	Takahashi Nobuko
8/1984	Panel on the Issue of Cabinet Members Visiting Yasukuni Shrine	Hayashi Keizō
9/1984	Research Committee on Economic Policy	Makino Noboru
9/1984	Panel on Crisis Management Issues	Yazawa Ichirō
12/1984	Advisory Council on Foreign Economic Issues	Ōkita Saburō
5/1985	Exploratory Committee on Subsidies	Ishi Hiromitsu
10/1985	Council on Price Stabilization Policies	Tsuchiya Kiyoshi
10/1985	Research Committee on Adjusting the Structure of the Economy for International Harmony	Maekawa Haruo
9/1986	Panel on Promoting Use of Private-Sector Vitality	Saitō Eishirō
10/1987	Panel on the Promotion of Sports	Saitō Eishirō

Source: Nakasone Peace Institute, ed. *Nakasone Naikaku-shi Shiryō-hen*. Tokyo: Nakasone Peace Institute, 1995.

But while the advisors to those earlier governments had generally looked at mid and long-term tasks and policy ideas, Nakasone also received advice on more immediate political aspects of governing, such as whether he should visit Yasukuni Shrine and how to conduct elections.

Nakasone drew on some former members of Ōhira's brain trust, like University of Tokyo professor Satō Seisaburō, Gakushuin University professor Kōyama Ken'ichi, and University of Tokyo professor Kumon Shunpei for his private advisory councils. Kumon and Satō had also belonged to Rinchō. Kōyama played a central role in the Provisional Council on Education that Nakasone established to promote traditional culture. He was also a member of the 21st Century Sino-Japanese Friendship Committee and would serve as a go-between for Nakasone and Chinese Communist Party General Secretary Hu Yaobang.

Nakasone and the Media

The atmosphere at the prime minister's office completely changed with Nakasone's arrival. He kept very long hours, and this tension spread to the staff. He kept paper next to his bed so that if he had an epiphany in the middle of the night, he could immediately write it down.

As Nakasone's hold on the party was weak, he took great pains when dealing with the media. Usual practice at the time was for prime ministerial press conferences to be conducted seated, but Asari Keita advised him that

1,806 Days as Prime Minister   161

it would look better if he stood. He thus proposed this change after he took office, noting that "Everyone does this standing in the West. You never see them sit and talk."

The prime minister's office press club was opposed, however, and press conferences continued to be conducted seated. Again, according to Nakasone, "My guess is that the younger reporters were concerned that they'd get criticized by older reporters if they just went along with my proposal." It would only be with the government of Hosokawa Morihiro a decade later that prime ministers would begin standing at press conferences.

Movements in media coverage were analyzed not only by his brain trust but by the "Nakasone Machine" as well. Asari, in particular, watched television until late at night and provided Nakasone with advice such as "You look better when being photographed from this angle," or "Coming under fire from prior prime ministers helps your approval rating, so let them come after you."

Nakasone placed great importance on television and summoned NHK President Shima Keiji to the prime minister's office every couple of months. Upon his arrival, Nakasone would greet him with a thick stack of papers, a summary of NHK's news coverage (likely put together by the Cabinet Research Office).

Nakasone had underlined areas in the summary where he was displeased with NHK's reporting and grilled Shima on them, saying, "Mr. Shima, your recent news programs certainly seem to have had some problems, haven't they? They seem to have a tendency to overemphasize things disadvantageous to the government."

While Nakasone was helpless when it came to newspapers or private broadcasters, NHK was a public broadcaster, and he, therefore, felt justified in stamping out what he saw as bias. Shima later referred to these meetings in a book as undergoing "the Nakasone check."

According to Shima, "I would listen respectfully but never acted on anything he said. So, I don't feel that the meetings had any actual influence on our work. But in any case, no serving prime minister before or since Nakasone has gone to such lengths."

Nakasone was particularly fond of the *Yomiuri Shimbun* and would make comments while reading the paper's editorials along the lines of "The Yomiuri's tenor is wonderful. Watanabe does a pretty good job.[8] So good, in fact, that I wish I could make the leaders of all the other newspapers read these. NHK would also do well to consult them."

Nakasone was very conscious of media trends and was generally successful in maintaining a high approval rating. This interest extended to coverage of himself in foreign newspapers as well, something that he received help on from Takushoku University professor Okumura Fusao. Okumura sent him clippings from foreign papers like the *People's Daily, Le Monde,* and the *New York Times,* and Nakasone would review these on the weekend.

While he also received information on foreign affairs from the foreign ministry, Nakasone placed greater importance on the information provided

162   *1,806 Days as Prime Minister*

by Okumura, saying, "The foreign ministry's reports were indirect; by the time they reached me, they'd passed through so many hands that they were dirty. [...] But [foreign] newspaper articles give you the sense of actually being there."[9]

"The Final Settlement of Postwar Politics"

As mentioned earlier, "the final settlement of postwar politics" – the Nakasone government's famous catchphrase – was conspicuously absent at the time of the government's formation. But what did this phrase mean? Nakasone would later list three areas that he felt were encapsulated by the slogan: "the rectification of Yoshida politics," "the implementation of administrative and fiscal reforms," and "striving to make international contributions."

While the last two are largely self-explanatory, the first – "the rectification of Yoshida politics" – likely requires further explanation. According to Nakasone, Yoshida had been a "believer in a false one-nation pacifism" and "one of reasons for my dispute with Yoshida was his basic policies on defense and constitutional issues." He felt that Yoshida's approach to national security had been too perfunctory and that he had overemphasized the economy. "We lost the drive to defend our nation through our own efforts because of the idea that everything would be fine as long as we relied on the United States."

While it is true that Nakasone had opposed Yoshida ever since his time in the conservative opposition in the 1950s, all of his comments along these lines were made after he left office, and they undeniably give the impression of having been come up with after the fact. When Nakasone first began using the expression "the final settlement of postwar politics" at the beginning of his government, it was in a very different context.

Nakasone began using the phrase following the opening of the LDP Election Strategy Headquarters' offices in December 1982. 1983 was going to be a very electorally significant year: unified local elections were planned for April and a House of Councillors election for June – and there was always the possibility that the House of Representatives would be dissolved and a general election called as well. Nakasone emphasized that "Next year, the thirty-seventh year of the postwar period, will be the year of its final settlement."

A January 10, 1983 *Nihon Keizai Shimbun* column clearly shows the actual truth behind the slogan by placing it in the context of the Lockheed trial and the forthcoming elections:

> The closing arguments and verdict in the Lockheed case against Tanaka Kakuei. The unified local and House of Councillors election. And, of course, the inevitable dissolution of the House of Representatives and ensuing general election. All of these events hint at wild fluctuations to come in the political landscape. The government and LDP both see the

coming year – a true season for politics – as a crossroads for Japanese politics. Prime Minister Nakasone has repeatedly stated that "1983 will be the year of the final settlement of postwar politics."

In other words, when Nakasone initially conceived the idea of "the final settlement of postwar politics," it was in the context of his immediate goal of overcoming the 1983 elections rather than in service to any grand vision like "rectifying Yoshida politics."

Because the media and public were highly critical of the money politics that Tanaka represented, it was plausible that the LDP might suffer a major defeat in the coming elections, potentially even losing control of the government. Rather than being coined due to ideals or a higher goal on the part of Nakasone, the "final settlement of postwar politics" can be viewed as an exaggerated phrase chosen with the impending Lockheed verdict in mind.

Such exaggerated phrasing was not something discovered by Nakasone only after he became prime minister, after all. As director-general of the Defense Agency, he had chosen to rename the Fourth Defense Program the "New Defense Program" to draw more attention to it, and he had called for the three non-nuclear principles as transportation minister despite being well aware that they were inconsistent with reality. Nakasone had a tendency to prefer grandiose phrasing that went further than would perhaps have been justified by the actual state of things.[10]

Setting Aside Constitutional Revision

On January 24, 1983, two weeks after the aforementioned *Nihon Keizai Shimbun* column, Nakasone attended his first regular session of the Diet as prime minister. While he did give a policy speech, you would not find any calls for "the final settlement of postwar politics" in it.

Looking for something along the lines of that phrase, you *would* find a reference to "a great turning point in Japan's postwar history," but in quite a different context:

> I keenly feel that Japan is standing at a great turning point in its postwar history. I feel that we need to earnestly examine our history – both prewar and postwar – and come to conclusions about what should be carried on for future generations, what should be changed, and what direction we should adopt moving forward. And we should take those conclusions and adopt new guidelines for progressing anew.

Of the aforementioned three elements of the "final settlement," the only one to be clearly referenced in the speech was administrative and fiscal reform. There was no definite reference to the others, and one would be particularly hard-pressed to find something connected to "rectifying Yoshida politics." Instead, Nakasone again called for making "Japan into a vigorous

164   *1,806 Days as Prime Minister*

nation of culture and welfare," the slogan that he had used in his first policy speech a month earlier. There was nothing particularly novel about this slogan; development of the welfare state had been a frequent topic of political conversation since at least the Miki government.

It was at the August 27 LDP Karuizawa Seminar that Nakasone invoked the "final settlement" in a public setting for the first time. This was, however, once again in the context of winning a general election, as he emphasized that "it is important that we bring up problems in areas like the economy, foreign policy, welfare, and education and deliberately call for the public to make decisions on them." When that general election did come – in December – the LDP suffered a major defeat.

Later, after Nakasone formed his second government and entered the latter stage of his time in office, the phrase "the final settlement of postwar politics" became a staple invoked whenever he made major speeches to the Diet. It seems to have become a fixture as his control of the government became firm.

There is another point that should be kept in mind. While it is generally believed that Nakasone intended to carry out constitutional revision as part of his effort to "rectify Yoshida politics," his actions in office actually moved in the opposite direction.

When pressed on the matter by Socialist Diet Member Iwatare Sukio at the February 19, 1983 meeting of the House of Representatives Budget Committee, Nakasone clearly stated, "I will not take up constitutional revision as part of my political agenda while in office."

Similarly, when he debated Socialist Chairman Ishibashi Masahi on September 19, he spoke of the "esteem" he had for the constitution and shut down any discussion of constitutional revision.

From a purely practical perspective, Nakasone was in no position to take on constitutional revision, which would have required the approval of two-thirds of both houses of the Diet. The LDP only held 56.2% of the seats in the House of Representatives, and the Socialists – advocates of "unarmed neutrality" – held 20.94%. And in the House of Councillors, the LDP had only 54.6% of seats.[11]

Nakasone acknowledged his lack of action on constitutional revision in his memoirs: "Faced with the important task of administrative reform while in office, I stated that I would not 'take up constitutional revision as part of my political agenda.' [...] I truly regret avoiding the issue politically." He even set aside the less-ambitious "constitutional correction" that he had promoted in 1978. But, looking at the contemporary situation objectively, postponing constitutional revision was no doubt inevitable, given the difficulty of reaching a consensus on the issue even within the LDP.[12]

Miki's Request, Ōhira's Legacy

What did other LDP politicians make of Nakasone's call for "the final settlement of postwar politics"? Miki Takeo is notable among the party's major

1,806 Days as Prime Minister   165

figures for taking the slogan, putting his own interpretation on it, and then using it to make a request of Nakasone.

Miki referenced the slogan at a January 26, 1983 press conference held following the prosecution's closing statement in the Tanaka trial, saying, "Prime Minister Nakasone emphasized upon taking office that now is the time for the final settlement of postwar conservative politics. And it is the entrenchment of political ethics that will serve as the foundation for that settlement. There is no need to say more."

Miki wanted the final settlement to include the entrenchment of political ethics and leaving the money politics of Tanaka behind, a point he also emphasized in an interview with Kyodo News:

> Having to stand trial for almost eight years has been hard on Tanaka, but this case also caused serious damage to Japanese politics. We must seize this opportunity and turn this disaster into a lesson. It must serve as a new starting point for political reform. We cannot allow it to just pass us by. This is the kind of moral problem that lies as the foundation of the "final settlement of postwar politics" that Nakasone has been talking about.

With the elections coinciding with the verdict of the Lockheed case, there was no avoiding having the kind of money politics associated with Tanaka becoming a point of political contention. But Nakasone's cabinet included numerous members of the Tanaka faction. It would be difficult for him to escape Tanaka's influence, at least until the lower court decision was issued.[13]

Comparing Nakasone's final settlement to Ōhira's "final settlement of the postwar" throws its nature into relief. Ōhira put forth this concept more than seven years before becoming prime minister and put work into expanding the idea after taking office, establishing nine study groups on topics such as the garden city concept and comprehensive security.

In comparison, Nakasone first spoke of his final settlement as part of an electoral strategy immediately after taking office. And while he worked to make good use of the policy research groups and brain trusts that could be considered part of Ōhira's legacy, it is hard to believe that there was ever a thoughtfulness behind his slogan comparable to that of Ōhira.

How did the two men compare in the realm of foreign policy? One of Ōhira's study groups was devoted to exploring the Pacific Rim cooperation concept, an endeavor that ultimately resulted in the establishment of Asia-Pacific Economic Cooperation (APEC) following his death. While Nakasone had previously advocated for a Pacific economic and cultural sphere and would go on to endorse "Pacific cooperation" with countries like Australia (a topic that will be discussed later on in this chapter), his efforts in this direction had strong Cold War connotations. I feel that Nakasone did not produce any foreign policy ideas while in office with the originality of Ōhira's Pacific Rim cooperation concept.

166   *1,806 Days as Prime Minister*

Of course, this comparison between Ōhira and Nakasone has focused on ideas, and they are only one aspect of politics. Ultimately, actual achievements are more important than grand ideas, and Nakasone would far exceed Ōhira in terms of his accomplishments in both domestic and foreign policy. That is the topic I would like to turn to next.[14]

Telephone Meetings

One of the major characteristics of Nakasone's time in government was his strategic foreign policy and the way that it conformed to the realities of the Cold War. It was in the realm of foreign policy that Nakasone was most able to explicitly play the role of a "presidential prime minister." Japan's relations with the United States and South Korea had deteriorated under the Suzuki government, and he made repairing those relationships a priority as he took office.

On November 27, 1982, the day after he became prime minister, Nakasone spoke with South Korean President Chun Doo-Hwan, American President Ronald Reagan, and the leaders of the ASEAN states by telephone.

When Nakasone told Chun that he hoped for "a new friendly relationship between Japan and South Korea" and said he would "sincerely make efforts in that direction," Chun replied, "I will also work to make that happen. We should discuss things with each other often." South Korea desperately wanted economic assistance from Japan and saw the birth of the Nakasone government as a good opportunity for improving relations.

After Reagan called to offer his congratulations, Nakasone told him that he was "looking forward to meeting with you at the earliest opportunity. I would like us to work together and make the already friendly relationship between Japan and the United States even closer."

While serving as MITI minister during the first Oil Crisis, Nakasone had adopted a stance that was clearly more favorable to the Arab states than the US. But now that he was prime minister, he was reverting to his original position of regarding the US as the cornerstone of Japanese foreign policy. This shift in his diplomatic focus was brought about by changes in the international environment, namely the beginning of the New Cold War between the US and USSR following the two oil crises and the Soviet invasion of Afghanistan.

Shortly after taking office, Nakasone explained to a journalist that while he had "gotten into a huge fight [with the Americans] during the oil crisis, especially with Kissinger, [...] the situation has changed. I'm going to move to strengthen the human bonds of trust between Japan and the United States and make the US-Japan security framework the cornerstone of our relationship. I think that's the most important thing."

Looking beyond US-Japan relations, whenever Nakasone had found himself without a cabinet position (a not uncommon occurrence), he had taken advantage of the situation and traveled overseas, visiting places like America, China, and Southeast Asia in the hopes of finding the direction that Japan needed to go in. The time had now come for him to make full use of the knowledge gained in those visits.[15]

A Sudden Visit to South Korea

A visit to the United States had been organized for January 1983. For most prime ministers, preparing for a US-Japan summit would have demanded their full attention. Even so, Nakasone decided that he wanted to visit South Korea before his departure for America.

New Japanese prime ministers generally try to avoid any risk early on and initially concentrate on domestic policy. It would not have occurred to Suzuki or any of Nakasone's other predecessors to pack a visit to Korea into the brief window of time before his summit with Reagan. But Nakasone was different, and the multilayered nature of his foreign policy stands out from those who had come before him; with the revival of Cold War tensions, he sought to deepen Japan's relations with not only the US but with other countries like South Korea and China as well. His sudden trip to South Korea would serve as the first step in that effort.

With his trip to America fast approaching, only limited dates were available for a Korean visit. And Korea's complicated feelings toward Japan meant that the idea carried a fair amount of risk. While Satō Eisaku had attended Park Chung-hee's presidential inaugurations in 1967 and 1971, these visits had merely amounted to Satō paying his respects to Park.[16] There had never been a formal visit to South Korea by a Japanese prime minister, and the South Korean president had never visited Japan. Nakasone was taking a substantial gamble.

Tapping Sejima Ryūzō

Nakasone's use of Sejima Ryūzō as a go-between with South Korea is well-known. Sejima was a corporate advisor to the Itochu Corporation and had served on Rinchō. He was also acquainted with President Chun and Kwon Ik-hyun, secretary-general of the ruling Democratic Justice Party and a confidante of Chun's. Chun and Kwon had been classmates together at the Korea Military Academy, and they got along well with Sejima, a graduate of the Imperial Japanese Army Academy. Sejima described Kwon as a "dear friend" in his memoirs.

Sejima had also visited Korea two or three times during the Suzuki government, but relations between Japan and South Korea became strained after the latter demanded $6 billion in economic aid on the grounds that South Korea was contributing to Japan's security. Foreign Minister Sonoda Sunao angered the Koreans by responding that "it is not for the recipient to criticize what they receive."

Unlike Sonoda, Nakasone recognized that "under the postwar settlement with South Korea, Japan assumed responsibility for providing economic assistance for South Korea's development in the place of reparations."

168 *1,806 Days as Prime Minister*

On November 30, 1982, three days after becoming prime minister, Nakasone summoned Sejima to his home, telling him that he needed to see him that evening "no matter what." While the two had met periodically in the past, this was the first time they would do so at night or that Nakasone had had Sejima come to his home.

Nakasone was aware that he was standing at a crossroads, and he met Sejima wearing a *hakama* and a *haori* coat featuring his family crest in black. After the two men enjoyed a light dinner on the house's second floor, he got to the heart of the matter:

> Sejima, I have spent a great deal of time considering what I would do if I became prime minister, and how I should go about doing it. My belief is that I should first resolve the diplomatic issues facing our nation, particularly those demanding urgent attention, before moving on to important domestic policy matters. And the diplomatic issues demanding urgent attention at the moment are getting our relations with South Korea back on track and improving things with America. We've already made arrangements for a visit [to the US] in January, but I'd like to normalize things with South Korea before that if at all possible. I humbly ask for your assistance on this matter.

Nakasone had thus decided to prioritize foreign over domestic policy, and he wanted to visit South Korea, meet with President Chun Doo-hwan directly, and get the relationship between Japan and South Korea on a solid footing before his planned trip to the US.

Sejima was surprised by Nakasone's request, but "taking the various circumstances facing our country into account, I felt that the prime minister's reasoning was correct and that what he put forward was a true diplomatic strategy."

When Sejima told him that "normalizing relations between our countries will require reaching a compromise on the economic assistance issue that has caused so many problems over the past two years," Nakasone responded, "You can exercise a certain degree of flexibility when it comes to concessions."

Nakasone dispatched Sejima to Korea shortly afterward. He did not conceal his use of Sejima as an envoy from the foreign ministry, however. He gathered Gotōda, Abe, Takeshita, Parliamentary Vice-Minister of Foreign Affairs Sunobe Ryōzō, and Asian Affairs Bureau Director Kiuchi Akitane at the prime minister's office on December 1, discussed the matter with them, and obtained their agreement to having Sejima arrange economic assistance to South Korea.

Sejima held an inconspicuous meeting with Kwon in the VIP room at Busan Airport on December 8. Kwon relayed Chun's desire for "as much economic assistance as possible, provided that it causes no problems for Prime Minister Nakasone, who has of course only just taken office."

Sejima reported on the meeting to Nakasone and also made contact with International Finance Bureau Director Ōba Tomomitsu of the finance ministry. Nakasone had directed the finance ministry to provide economic assistance on a large scale. Sejima then met with Kwon again at the Osaka Plaza Hotel on December 23 and presented a letter from Nakasone to Chun in Seoul on the 30th.

Nakasone's use of Sejima was successful, and he was able to put together a $4 billion economic assistance package prior to his visit to South Korea. He later recalled: "I trusted Sejima Ryūzō's ability to build a consensus and negotiate. When dealing with a difficult negotiating partner like South Korea, I felt that it appropriate to tap someone who had experience negotiating with non-Japanese."[17]

Meeting Chun Doo-Hwan

January 11, 1983 marked the first visit by a Japanese prime minister to South Korea. It was also Nakasone's first trip abroad as prime minister.

Nakasone wrote in his diary: "At Gimpo Airport, the Hinomaru was raised and Kimigayo played by Koreans for the first time in thirty-seven years, for the first time since the end of the war. It had a profound impression on me. The Koreans generally seemed to have confused expressions on their faces, the result of their anti-Japanese educations."

At the summit, Nakasone said, "Just as Japan and South Korea are the closest to each other geographically, so must they have the friendliest of relations. Today I visit South Korea, taking advantage of the resolution of the economic assistance issue through the heroic decision-making of His Excellency the President. Through this visit, I hope to make the already friendly relationship between our countries even stronger."

Chun responded, "It has been thirty-seven years since South Korea became independent, and this is the first time I have seen the Hinomaru and the Taegukgi fly alongside one another in harmony here in the capital of Seoul. It is something to be celebrated, and it could not have come to pass without the heroic decision-making of His Excellency Prime Minister Nakasone."

At a banquet held that evening, Chun described Nakasone's visit as "monumental in every sense." Nakasone said that "it is a fact that there has been unfortunate history between us, and that is something we must solemnly deal with. [...] I truly hope that, moving forward, we will both be neighbors worthy of the other's trust."

Nakasone made frequent use of Korean in his speech. The Korean dignitaries were surprised when he began speaking in Korean, and many were moved to tears.

Following the banquet, Nakasone and Chun talked late into the night in a room at the Blue House. According to Prime Minister's Secretary Hasegawa Kazutoshi, Chun said, "Mr. Nakasone, I've fallen for you." in Japanese. Nakasone returned to Japan on January 12.[18]

170 *1,806 Days as Prime Minister*

The "Ron-Yasu" Relationship and the "Unsinkable Aircraft Carrier"

With the visit to South Korea safely over, improving relations with the United States was the next task facing Nakasone. He believed that "the fate of my government rests on this opening stretch" and, prior to making his American visit, he directed Gotōda to increase the defense budget and relax restrictions on sharing weapon technology to bring Japan closer to US desires in these areas. He also had a former ambassador to the UN Katō Toshikazu lay the groundwork for his visit.

Nakasone landed in Washington on January 17. It was his first meeting with Reagan, and the two men found that they were on the same wavelength when it came to the reduction of American and Soviet mid-range nuclear forces. Nakasone confirmed with Reagan that Japan and the US "shared the same destiny."

He told Reagan, "I'm going to be the catcher at this summit, and I want you to be the pitcher. Just remember that sometimes the pitcher has to listen to what the catcher has to say." Reagan agreed, saying, "The pitcher throws the ball based on the signs they get from the catcher. I want you to give me lots of signs."

When Reagan said, "I'd like you to call me Ron from now on. What's your first name?" Nakasone answered "Yasu." This was the beginning of the "Ron-Yasu" relationship.

Nakasone wrote in his memoirs that "Diplomacy is hand-made. Especially in modern times, it is the bonds of trust and leadership forged between leaders through that hands-on approach that move the world."

This was not a spontaneous development, however; it had been arranged ahead of time by working level officials on both sides. Rather than Nakasone, it had been Envoy to the US Kunihiro Michihiko who had conceived of the idea and, once Nakasone's secretary Hasegawa had obtained his approval, he had worked with Special Assistant to President Gaston Sigur to lay the groundwork for the exchange.

Another aspect of Nakasone's first US summit that drew a lot of attention was his description of Japan as "an unsinkable aircraft carrier." His use of the phrase caused a media uproar at home; in the US, it was seen as a sign of Nakasone's resolve and reduced the distrust of Japan that had developed during the Suzuki government.

Most accounts say that Nakasone used the phrase during a breakfast hosted by the Washington Post. This is a misunderstanding, however, as Nakasone never actually used those words. Rather, they were a non-literal translation supplied by Muramatsu Masumi, his civilian interpreter.

What Nakasone actually said at breakfast was that he wanted to make Japan into "a giant ship with massive walls" to prevent Soviet aircraft from violating Japanese airspace. Because of the positive American reaction to "unsinkable aircraft carrier," however, he decided not to correct Muramatsu.

Foreign Ministry Economic Affairs Bureau Director Murata Ryōhei, who attended the breakfast, recalled that he "thought it was an excellent translation and felt no discomfort hearing it." Even so, the foreign ministry dismissed Muramatsu as the controversy over the phrase grew.

Nakasone also told the *Washington Post* that "Becoming able to bottle up the submarines and surface vessels of the Soviet Pacific fleet in the Sea of Japan by closing off the three straits [the Sōya, Tsugaru, and Tsushima Straits] is a clear objective of my government."[19]

Apprehensions about Nakasone's Diplomatic Efforts

There were also those who were critical of Nakasone's flamboyant diplomatic efforts, and they were not limited to the media. That the opposition parties condemned Nakasone's "unsinkable aircraft carrier" statement goes without saying. His greatest critic within the LDP was Suzuki Zenkō, and this opposition would lead Suzuki to back Nikaidō as a replacement for Nakasone (as will be discussed).

How did foreign policy specialists feel about Nakasone's efforts? One typical assessment came from Tokyo Institute of Technology professor Nagai Yōnosuke, a well-known scholar of international politics. Nagai was concerned about Nakasone's foreign policy for two reasons.

First, he felt that Nakasone was opening the door to military cooperation with the US and that the purpose of the proposed "three-strait blockade" and the means through which it would be carried out needed close examination. Second, he noted that "Nakasone took his first steps as a politician rebelling against the Yoshida doctrine's policy of cooperation with the United States" and described Nakasone as a "closet Gaullist" (someone who wanted to pursue an independent diplomatic course).

He dubbed Nakasone a "military realist" and portrayed his objectives as being at odds with the "political realism" of himself and the Yoshida doctrine. He also argued that the "Yoshida doctrine is eternal." Nakasone caused concern among proponents of the Yoshida doctrine like Nagai. and contrary to his intentions, arguments in favor of the doctrine spread.[20]

Nakasone was an ardent fan of the 19th-century naval reformer Katsu Kaishū, and he responded to the widespread criticism by quoting him: "They are free to criticize as they like; I am acting in accordance with my beliefs."[21]

Visiting Southeast Asia

On the heels of his trips to Korea and the US, Nakasone visited Southeast Asia next, stopping in Indonesia, Thailand, Singapore, the Philippines, Malaysia, and Brunei from April 30 to May 10, 1983. A G7 summit was scheduled for late May, and one of the purposes of his trip was conferring with these countries' leaders in preparation for the summit. He made arrangements through the foreign ministry's Asian Affairs Bureau to try

172 *1,806 Days as Prime Minister*

to avoid the anti-Japanese demonstrations that had accompanied Tanaka's visits in January 1974.

In an overview of the visits Nakasone wrote in his diary, the importance of making "personal friendships" and gaining local understanding of Japan's defense policies is clear:

1 Established personal friendships with each country's leaders.
2 Obtained official understanding of and support for Japan's defense policies.
3 Proposed the Japan-ASEAN Ministerial Meeting on Science and Technology and obtained agreement.
4 First visit by a prime minister to Brunei since its independence. Obtained promise to visit Japan next year.
5 Malaysia promised to attend Expo '85. Important information about North Korea in Malaysia.
6 Philippines President Marcos expressed understanding of Japan's defense policies. Welcomed Japan's new style of leader and said he wanted to collaborate with us.

According to his later recollections, Nakasone explained to his hosts that Japan sought "autonomous defense, but without nuclear weapons. Our policies are centered on defense of the Japanese archipelago out to a range of 1,000 nautical miles, reaching to the north of the Philippine Strait, and we have no interest in anything south of Taiwan."[22]

The Williamsburg Summit

Nakasone departed for the United States again on May 26. He met with Reagan at the White House the following day, and the two leaders discussed US-Soviet relations and other topics before celebrating his sixty-fifth birthday.

The ninth G7 summit was held from May 28 to 30. The chief point of contention at the summit was whether or not the US should deploy Pershing II missiles in response to the Soviet deployment of SS-20 medium-range nuclear missiles.

When Reagan asked Nakasone to make a comprehensive keynote address at the beginning of the summit, Nakasone laid out the following five principles:

1 The summit's themes should be disarmament and economic recovery.
2 For reasons of deterrence and maintaining equilibrium, the fundamental position taken on US and Soviet intermediate-range nuclear forces was the global "Zero Option" [total elimination].
3 Should the Soviets fail to agree to withdraw their SS-20 missiles, the West should implement its existing plans.

1,806 Days as Prime Minister   173

4 The Soviets should not be pushed into a corner, however, and negotiations should proceed with a great deal of patience.
5 Regarding the economy, there should be greater levels of policy coordination, and exchange rates should be stabilized to provide for continued growth.

Nakasone's address was followed by extensive discussion by the national leaders. One point of contention was the draft joint statement's referring to global security as "indivisible." Given the limited amount of time in which the leaders were able to meet, the wording of the statement had been put together and polished at the working level prior to the summit.

French President Mitterrand was strongly opposed to the use of "indivisible." France possessed an independent nuclear force and did not belong to NATO's military command, and he felt that the summit should devote its energies to economic matters. West German Chancellor Kohl also aligned himself with Mitterrand for domestic political reasons.

While British Prime Minister Thatcher insisted that "the Soviet Union can only be resisted through force," Canadian Prime Minister Trudeau was hesitant about having the joint statement address the intermediate-range nuclear forces issue.

The venue took on a cool air, and the summit seemed on the verge of breaking down. Any other Japanese prime minister would likely have avoided saying anything under these conditions, but Nakasone spoke up:

The only one who benefits from a break down of this meeting is the Soviets. We need to show the strength of our solidarity, that we won't take a single step backwards. If the Soviet Union doesn't withdraw its SS-20s, then the Pershing II missiles should be deployed by December as planned.

I will be fiercely attacked upon my return to Japan. [People will demand to know] when Japan joined NATO. [I will be accused of] doing an about face and committing Japan to collective self-defense. But I want to be clear. Right now, issues of security are indivisible on a global scale, or between the East and the West. Japan has traditionally kept quiet during this type of debate. But for the sake of peace, I'm going to move beyond Japan's traditional boundaries and risk a political crisis.

Reagan immediately followed up by proposing that they "just give putting together the wording for the statement a try" and directed Secretary of State Schultz to do so based on the discussions thus far. Reagan and Nakasone were working as a team.

It was thus incorporated into the summit's statement on political matters that Pershing IIs would be deployed if the negotiations with the Soviets over reducing intermediate-range nuclear forces failed to reach an agreement. It was a historic statement that would serve as the prelude to the collapse of the USSR.

174 *1,806 Days as Prime Minister*

Nakasone's statements at the summit were not known in detail by the public at the time. Instead, the primary topic focused on by Japanese media was Nakasone's appearance in the middle of the summit's commemorative photograph, standing next to Reagan. There was also an episode at the summit where, during a coffee break, Nakasone discussed the Bible with Mitterrand.[23]

The 1983 House of Councillors Election

Despite some of Nakasone's more proactive statements (epitomized by the "unsinkable aircraft carrier") drawing some criticism domestically, in general, things were going smoothly for him in terms of domestic policy, foreign policy, and the running of his government.

The LDP maintained a stable majority following the June 26, 1983 House of Councillors election; Socialist Party Chairman Asukata Ichio took responsibility for his party's defeat and stepped down.

In the leadup to the election, Tanaka Kakuei had sought to have Nakasone dissolve the House of Representatives to allow for a joint election of both houses, but Nakasone had refused to dissolve the Diet without a good reason.

Tanaka had wanted both elections over with before the release of the verdict in his trial that autumn, but Nakasone felt that a prime minister "cannot dissolve the Diet before he has a few more accomplishments under his belt. Besides, I said this would be a cabinet of the capable, so see what they can do."[24]

Secretary-General Nikaidō (who belonged to the Tanaka faction) also supported the call for a double election, and Nakasone's failure to confide in him on the matter led to a rift in their relationship.

According to Nikaidō, when he visited Nakasone at the prime minister's office on April 26 to request the dissolution of the House of Representatives, he learned that Nakasone had been determined for quite a while to avoid a double election. "While there is no question that the power to dissolve the Diet rests with the prime minister, it is the secretary-general who actually takes the lead in elections. For Nakasone to have not revealed even a hint of his intentions to me, the secretary-general … I was dumbfounded and forced to wonder whether he truly had so little trust in me."[25]

The Downing of Korean Air Flight 007

Early on the morning of September 1, 1983, the shocking news that a Korean Air flight from New York to Seoul had been shot down by a Soviet Sukhoi Su-15 fighter reached the prime minister's office. All 269 passengers and crew were dead, including 28 Japanese.

The SDF had intercepted communications between the Soviet fighter and ground control during the incident and, according to recently declassified diplomatic records, Nakasone directed Foreign Minister Abe to transmit the following information to the American and South Korean governments only a few hours later:

> According to analysis of our radar information, an aircraft believed to be flight KE-007 from New York to Seoul via Anchorage disappeared at 3:29 a.m. on the 1st above the seas west of Moneron Island (46°30'N 141°30'E). There is thought to be a high likelihood that it was shot down.

He also called South Korean President Chun on the evening of September 2 and told him, "I would like to offer our assistance and maintain close contact with you during the investigation and resolution of this incident. You will have our full and sincere assistance in responding to any Korean requests."

Chun thanked him, saying, "I apologize for having to do this by phone, but I would like to express my gratitude for the active cooperation provided by the Japanese government, and especially you, Mr. Prime Minister." When Nakasone told him, "I plan to work together with the nations of the world to address this matter in every venue, including the United Nations," Chun thanked him in Japanese.

Nakasone decided to make the intercepted Soviet communications public, and Japan submitted them to the UN Security Council on September 6 alongside the United States. The Soviet Union acknowledged the factual nature of the communications, and the US Senate passed a resolution thanking Japan for its assistance.

Revealing that Japan had intercepted the communications was not without cost. It was clear that the revelation would result in the Soviets making changes to their communication methods, making future interceptions by the SDF significantly more difficult.

Despite this downside, Nakasone had believed that it was "an amazing opportunity to strike a blow against the Soviet Union in front of the entire world. I felt that, in this case, there was no damage done by providing the communications logs and more or less revealing Japan's ability to intercept communications."

Making the communications public not only made it clear where Japan stood vis a vis the USSR, but it also strengthened Japan's cooperative relationships with the US and South Korea. In the policy speech he gave to the 100th Diet on September 10, Nakasone called for Japan to be an "international state" and "play a proactive role globally."[26]

Tanaka Kakuei and the Lockheed Verdict

Despite most things going well for Nakasone, the impending lower court verdict in the Lockheed case cast a shadow over his government's future. On October 12, 1983, the Tokyo District Court sentenced Tanaka Kakuei to four years in prison and fined him 500 million yen.

176 *1,806 Days as Prime Minister*

Tanaka immediately filed an appeal and, after posting 300-million-yen bail, announced that he would not be resigning from the Diet. That the sentence included jail time did not come as a surprise to Nakasone, who stated that the situation was "sad but cannot be helped. Moving forward, I must carry out my administration with responsibility and foster an atmosphere of completely free ideas."

The immediate political situation – particularly the influence the verdict would have on the next general election – was a problem that could not be escaped, however. It had been three years and three months since the last general election, meaning that holding another election in the near future was unavoidable. But while the verdict hurt the LDP going into that election, it also had the potential to be an excellent opportunity for reducing Tanaka's influence.

Nakasone met with Tanaka at Hotel Okura on October 28 and told him, "Taking into consideration popular opinion and the mood within the party, I feel that the best thing to do here is to trust in your wisdom and rely upon you to decide what your best course is moving forward. I know there are various issues concerning your future, but I will responsibly look over you." This was a roundabout way of asking Tanaka to resign from the Diet.

Tanaka responded, "If you feel that way, well … I guess it can't be helped," but avoided making any explicit statement about his future course of action.

When the criticism of the Fukuda and Miki factions passed through Tanaka's mind and his eyes became watery, Nakasone cried as well. Nakasone and Tanaka had both entered the Diet at the same time, and both had been reelected fourteen times, serving together for thirty-six years. They were both faction leaders and men who knew the difficulties of being prime ministers. There were times when they shared an understanding that surpassed any factional considerations.

Nakasone pushed Tanaka to make a public statement, saying, "you should let the public know what your state of mind is," and Tanaka released a conversation that same day in which he spoke of "prudence and self-discipline." He still showed no sign of resigning, however. Despite this, eleven months into Nakasone's government, it appeared that the power relationship between the two men had switched places.[27]

The Rejected Letter

Despite these developments, the Tanaka faction remained the largest faction in the party, and Tanaka – far from resigning – tenaciously sought to expand his power. Nakasone was no doubt impatient. Tanaka's resolve to remain in the Diet held firm. If nothing changed, the coming election could only be a difficult one, and, depending on the results, his government might prove to be a short-lived one.

But if Tanaka took responsibility now, it would somewhat improve the electoral prospects and make a second Nakasone government more likely.

1,806 Days as Prime Minister 177

After debating with himself over what to do, Nakasone secretly wrote a letter to Tanaka on November 3 in which he pushed him to resign:

> The more the trust and loyalty between you and I are confronted by dangers to the party in the Diet and elsewhere, the more I am determined to adhere, firmly and deeply, to the lifelong blood pledge between us.
>
> [...]
>
> Could I ask you to take off your badge for a month to save the nation, save the party, and save this government? I know it is an unreasonable request, but I must ask you to do this to save us from this dangerous situation and bring about an overwhelming victory.
>
> [...]
>
> The political situation will change completely if this plan is carried out. Those now on the offensive – both within and without of the party – will be put on the defensive. Miki and Fukuda will be sent reeling, and I have no doubt that the election will be prove an overwhelming victory.

In this fourteen-page-long letter, Nakasone proposed that Tanaka resign from the Diet and then be absolved by the electoral results. He assured Tanaka that he would almost certainly be reelected and return to the Diet after an absence of just a month.

Nakasone entrusted the letter to one of his most trusted staff members, Chief Secretary Kamiwada Yoshihiko, and had him pass it to Satō Akiko, Tanaka's secretary.

He did not have to wait long for the reply from Tanaka's office: another letter, this time ten pages long. It was not sent by Tanaka himself, however, but rather by Satō. And it was a rejection of the proposal:

> It would be a waste of time to give this letter to Tanaka; I fear that it would raise his blood pressure and destroy the bonds of trust that you and he share. [...]
>
> One who has held the office of prime minister cannot resign from the Diet for so much as a minute or second. To remove his badge for a month and then immediately be elected would be a cheap trick meant to deceive the public.

Satō was saying that Tanaka would not resign from the Diet and that she would not show Nakasone's letter to Tanaka so as not to damage the relationship between them. Satō's penmanship was beautiful, but there was no avoiding the fact that it was a rejection of Nakasone's proposal, which she had deemed a "waste of time."

Satō was known as the "Queen of the Etsuzankai" (Tanaka's political organization) and was Tanaka's lover as well as his secretary. No one

178   *1,806 Days as Prime Minister*

involved in politics was unaware of her status. And she had deemed a recommendation to resign put forward by the serving prime minister a "deception." The letter into which Nakasone had poured so much effort had been dismissed by a woman close enough to Tanaka that she had born his child.

Of course, the contents of Satō's reply – that Tanaka would not resign and that she would not even show him the letter – were likely within the realm of Nakasone's expectations. When handing the letter to Kamiwada, he had told him: "I leave it to [Satō's] discretion whether or not to show the letter to [Tanaka]." He had not even sealed the envelope so that Satō could read it more easily.[28]

The Great Defeat of the Lockheed Election

With Tanaka refusing to resign, Nakasone had no choice but to try to use his own accomplishments to regain the public's trust. Knowing that he would have to dissolve the Diet and call an election soon, he attempted to use foreign policy efforts, his specialty, to increase his popularity.

He met with West German Chancellor Kohl on November 1, 1983 during the latter's visit to Japan, hosted Reagan at the Hinode Sansō in western Tokyo on the 11th, and welcomed Chinese Communist Party General Secretary Hu Yaobang on the 24th. He discussed the intermediate-range missile issue and the Middle East with Kohl, free trade and US military airfields with Reagan, and established "peaceful friendship, equal reciprocity, long-term stability, and mutual trust" as the four principles of Sino-Japanese friendship with Hu.[29]

Nakasone followed up this series of meetings – which could perhaps be deemed "speed diplomacy" – by dissolving the Diet on November 28. With the shadow of the Lockheed verdict looming overhead, he was, of course, not optimistic about the results. As for Tanaka himself, the man whose guilty verdict had caused all this, he believed that he enjoyed a great deal of sympathy from the people of Niigata.

Meanwhile, Gotōda, Nikaidō, and Kanemaru supported Nakasone's dissolution of the Diet, albeit for a negative reason. The Diet had been hopelessly stalled since the release of the Lockheed verdict, and there seemed to be no way to get it back under control without carrying out an election.

They felt that the government would be unable to hold meetings of the Budget Committee come January or get anything done for the remainder of the House of Representatives' term, which would expire in June. Not calling an election would be dooming them to a slow death. Gotōda believed that, while the party would certainly lose seats if an election was called now, it would still fair better than it would if elections were put off until the end of the term.

When Nakasone asked Gotōda, "How many seats do you think we'll lose?" Gotōda answered, "about twenty." Should Gotōda's prediction hold true, the LDP would be able to hold on to its majority and Nakasone might be able to retain his position.

1,806 Days as Prime Minister 179

Nakasone agreed to the dissolution because Nikaidō and Kanemaru managed to reach a deal with the opposition parties under which they would allow the passage of important bills related to administrative reform in exchange for an early election. As these bills included those for the creation of the Management and Coordination Agency and the revision of the prime minister's office, it was a trade that made the early dissolution advantageous to the government.

One noteworthy remark made by Nakasone during the electoral campaign was his statement at a press conference in Aomori that "the Shimokita Peninsula should become one of several bases for nuclear power in Japan."

The Federation of Electric Power Companies had been privately seeking to put a nuclear fuel cycle facility in Aomori, and Nakasone's statement showed that this had been approved.

It had been Nakasone who, thirty years earlier, had first submitted a budget request for nuclear power, and he remained a proponent. The Shimokita Peninsula would go on to become an important part of Japan's energy policy.

The LDP suffered a greater than expected defeat in the December 18 general election. It failed to secure a majority in the House of Representatives, winning only 250 seats (a loss of 36). Despite the Lockheed verdict being the cause of this defeat, Tanaka himself won an overwhelming victory in his own race, receiving a record 220,000 votes, and the Tanaka faction held firm at 63 members (a loss of only 2).[30]

Forming a Coalition with the New Liberal Club

Despite being prime minister, Nakasone came in second in Gunma's 3rd district to Fukuda. After barely managing to cobble together a majority by adopting nine independent candidates, he released a statement stating as LDP president that, he would "completely eliminate Tanaka's political influence" from the party. This statement was the result of continued pressure from members of the Supreme Advisory Council, such as Fukuda and Miki, who felt that the "heavy responsibility" borne by Tanaka meant that he should resign from the Diet.

Tanaka had left the party during the Miki government, making this an extremely unusual case of a party president releasing a statement concerning the political influence of an outside politician. The statement itself had been drafted by Nakasone with some changes made by Nikaidō.

According to Nikaidō, Nakasone's original draft had not mentioned Tanaka directly, saying only that he would "completely eliminate the political influence of those outside the party." Fukuda had been dissatisfied with this, however, and had pressed Nakasone to go farther: "Your wording is weak. You should explicitly mention Tanaka." It was ultimately Nikaidō (not Nakasone) who agreed to this and amended the statement to include Tanaka's name.

180   *1,806 Days as Prime Minister*

Nikaidō was a politician so enamored by Tanaka that he had once publicly stated that "my chief interest is Tanaka Kakuei." But his actions here would have a lasting impact and damage Tanaka's trust in him. The election brought about a split in the Tanaka faction. Nikaidō took responsibility for the party's defeat, and after it was decided that Nakasone would continue to serve as president, he resigned as secretary-general.

As Nakasone had thoroughly expected that the party would suffer a major defeat, he had already made preparations beforehand for a coalition with the New Liberal Club. His former secretary Yoda Minoru was now a Diet member for that party, and he was able to secure a coalition agreement in advance from New Liberal Club Secretary-General Yamaguchi Toshio through him.

Nakasone launched his second government on December 27, with Tagawa Seiichi of the New Liberal Club (and a former member of the Nakasone faction) joining the cabinet as minister of home affairs. This was the first coalition government ever formed by the LDP, and Nakasone knew that no more failures of this kind would be permitted. He was facing a critical point in his career.[31]

II. "Pacific Cooperation" and Privatization: Nakasone's Second Term

Forming Nakasone's Second Cabinet

Having managed to overcome his major electoral defeat through a coalition with the New Liberal Club, Nakasone now changed his chief cabinet secretary in an effort to show that he was working to eliminate Tanaka Kakuei's influence over his government. He tapped Fujinami Takao, a member of his own faction, to replace Gotōda.

Even so, Gotōda remained within the cabinet, having moved laterally into the position of director-general of the AMA. The two men approached the position of chief cabinet secretary very differently. While Gotōda had never hesitated to speak his mind, Fujinami was a close confidante of Nakasone's, loyal to him and restrained in his criticism.[32]

For the top three LDP positions, Nakasone chose Tanaka Rokusuke for secretary-general, Kanemaru Shin for chairman of the General Council, and Fujio Masayuki for chairman of the PRC. The position of vice president initially went vacant, but he appointed Nikaidō Susumu, "head clerk" of the Tanaka faction, to the post on April 11, 1984.

According to Nikaidō, among the party's major figures, Suzuki Zenkō was the most dissatisfied with Nakasone's choices for the party positions. He had wanted Miyazawa Kiichi, his successor and acting head of the Kōchikai, to receive one of them. Not only had Nakasone failed to accede to his wish, his choice for secretary-general – Tanaka Rokusuke – was a member of Suzuki's own faction who had clashed with Miyazawa in the past. Nakasone had appointed Tanaka without consulting with Suzuki, making his actions appear to Suzuki like an attempt to challenge his faction's solidarity.

Suzuki strongly believed that, had he not chosen to yield and open a path for Nakasone, he would have been able to serve another term as prime minister. Despite this, Nakasone repeatedly emphasized in his press conferences and while traveling abroad that "Japan had been on the verge of international isolation when I became prime minister." It was difficult for the usually mild-mannered Suzuki to have a criticism of his foreign policy spread so widely.

Nakasone's presidential term would expire in the fall, and his grudge toward Nakasone led Suzuki to begin looking for a way to prevent his reelection. He ultimately settled on backing the candidacy of a member of the Tanaka faction and a key source of support for Nakasone: Nikaidō.

Nakasone was not kindly disposed toward Nikaidō due to his frustrations over the elections that had been held while he was secretary-general. Meanwhile, Nikaidō was close to Suzuki despite their different factional allegiances, and he had reportedly become bothered by Nakasone's "vanity and faithlessness." But before discussing their maneuvers for a Nikaidō presidency, I would first like to follow Nakasone's management of his administration and his diplomatic efforts toward Asia.[33]

Nakasone's Domestic and Foreign Policy Agenda

How did Nakasone view the operation of his administration now that he had settled on the lineup of his second government? His January 26, 1984 speech at the 43rd LDP Party Congress at Hibiya Public Hall does a good job of showing what his mental state was like. In the speech, he called out the money politics that Tanaka had epitomized, stating that he must "conscientiously address" the "political ethics issue."

He also listed administrative, fiscal, and educational reform as issues on his domestic agenda and once again called for the "final settlement of postwar politics," saying that "with our great economic power, the time has come for us to make progress in becoming a nation of politics and culture."

He repeated his call for expanded Japanese involvement in international affairs, saying that Japan should "occupy an honorable place in international society and bear a suitable amount of responsibility – that is the proper international role for Japan."[34]

While the most significant task that the second Nakasone government would tackle would be the breaking up and privatization of JNR, Nakasone continued to have his eye on spectacular foreign policy accomplishments.

Nakasone's Policy toward Asia – His "Honeymoon" with Hu Yaobang

When Hu Yaobang had visited Japan in November 1983, he had requested that Nakasone make a reciprocal visit to China. Nakasone thus chose to make China the destination of the first foreign trip of his second government.

182 *1,806 Days as Prime Minister*

From March 23 to 25, he met with Hu, Premier Zhao Ziyang, and Chairman of the Central Advisory Commission Deng Xiaoping, and discussed increasing yen loans to China and the future outlook for Sino-Soviet relations.

Nakasone made a noteworthy statement over the course of these discussions regarding the first of these topics. On the 24th, Nakasone told Hu that "while you have expressed your gratitude for our economic assistance to China, I'm afraid I can't accept it, as it is only natural that we provide it. It is an expression of remorse for the great trouble we caused you during the war." Given that there was no formal relationship between the yen loans and the Chinese renunciation of compensation for the war, it was bold of Nakasone to speak of them as an "expression of remorse."

Hu invited Nakasone, his wife, his son Hirofumi, and his son's wife to his home in Zhongnanhai for dinner. There he served two of Nakasone's favorite foods (*tamagoyaki* and *kuri kinton*). They were joined by Li Zhao (Hu's wife), Hu's son Hu Liu, and his grandson. Nakasone and Hu thus were able to deepen their understanding of one another in the company of family.

It was unusual, then and now, for a Chinese leader to host a foreign guest and their family at their personal residence in Zhongnanhai. But Nakasone and his family had welcomed Hu to the prime minister's residence a year earlier, so Hu was returning the gesture. The act also effectively served the purpose of showing those in China and abroad that the two men enjoyed a close relationship.

Nakasone wrote in his diary at the time: "Conclusion to the China visit. Confirmation that there will be no more war between China and Japan. Sino-Japanese cooperation will be a force for peace and stability in Asia and the world."

That fall, Hu invited 3,000 young Japanese to visit China, and 1984 was referred to by some as the best year in the several millennia-long history of Sino-Japanese relations. While China was not yet the giant that it has gone on to become, there have not been many leaders in the history of Japanese foreign relations who have been able to maintain collaborative relationships with both China and the United States.

Nakasone continued his diplomatic efforts aimed at Asia. A month later, he visited South Asia and discussed Japanese economic assistance and nuclear disarmament with Pakistani President Zia and Indian Prime Minister Gandhi. He visited an Afghani refugee camp in Pakistan and addressed the Indian legislature on the "spiritual exchange" that had existed between Japan and India since ancient times.

He met with President of the Coalition Government of Democratic Kampuchea Sihanouk in Tokyo on May 31 and discussed the ongoing civil war in Cambodia. At the London G7 summit held from June 7 to 9, he successfully had "Each of us rejects the use of force as a means of settling disputes" incorporated into Article 6 of the summit's "Declaration on Democratic Values" – a passage that drew from the language of Article 9 of the Japanese constitution.[35]

1,806 Days as Prime Minister 183

Relations with Korea remained positive, and Chun Doo-hwa became the first South Korean president to visit Japan on June 9. When he called on Nakasone later that day, he explained that "I decided to come to Japan because of my determination that we must sow the seeds of a new chapter in our history, with an eye on what our nations will be like a thousand years from now."

Nakasone responded, "I have heard that you had to overcome opposition from various groups within Korea in order to make this visit. In addition to expressing my heartfelt gratitude and respect for that brave decision, I would also like to answer your call. May we lay a foundation for Japan and South Korea that lasts a thousand years."

As part of that "foundation," Nakasone and Chun frankly discussed South Korea's military balance with the North and its relations with China and the United States. When they met again on September 7, Nakasone explained that "My diplomacy is hands-on and stresses the bonds between people's hearts. We speak of diplomacy occurring between nations, but friendship between their political leaders is important." Things were going smoothly for Nakasone on the diplomatic front.[36]

Nakasone's Reelection as President and the Threat of a Nikaidō Candidacy

Nakasone received a new term as president at a general meeting of the party's Diet members on October 31, 1984. As he was the only candidate, there was no need to hold an election. He was the fourth president whose bid for reelection was uncontested; he shared the distinction with Kishi Nobusuke, Ikeda Hayato, and Satō Eisaku. While Ikeda and Satō were deceased, Kishi was still alive. He had resigned from the Diet but still had high hopes that Nakasone would pursue constitutional revision.[37]

Shortly before the meeting, the party had been rocked by an insurgent effort to have Vice President Nikaidō replace Nakasone as president. Fukuda and Miki were favorably inclined toward the idea, and Suzuki brought the plan to Tanaka. Tanaka's policy was to not allow anyone from his faction run for the presidency, however, and he chose to hold to that position and maintain a cooperative relationship with Nakasone.

As mentioned earlier, Suzuki had become increasingly critical of Nakasone. Years later, he would say that "We had put together an economic assistance package for South Korea amounting to $4 billion. An agreement was about to be formally signed when my government resigned [in November 1982]. [...] All that was left on the issue of economic assistance to Korea was the actual signing of the agreement. It had been my government that had sown the seeds, but when it came time for the harvest festival, it was Nakasone who got to reap the fruits to great acclaim."

Suzuki's jealousy of Nakasone can be seen in his tone. But Nakasone was able to get the drop on him here. He pursued two efforts to stymie Nikaidō's candidacy.

184　*1,806 Days as Prime Minister*

First, having learned in advance of the effort to back Nikaidō for the presidency, he had had Chief Cabinet Secretary Fujinami contact Suzuki and tell him that he would be appointing Miyazawa as General Council chairman. Suzuki had long wanted Miyazawa to receive one of the party's top three positions and learning that it would soon come to pass dulled his ardor for the Nikaidō plan.

Second, Nakasone made an ally of General Council Chairman Kanemaru and used this relationship to make himself the sole candidate for the presidency. Kanemaru went to see Nikaidō and listened as he listed his issues with Nakasone, including his management of the party. When he had finished, Kanemaru sternly rebuked him, saying, "I understand how you feel. But you can't turn back the hands on a clock."

Kanemaru's view was that an era of new leadership was coming, one in the hands of men like Takeshita, Abe, and Miyazawa. Nikaidō had been born in 1909 and was nine years older than Nakasone. Kanemaru and Nikaidō both belonged to the Tanaka faction, but he was opposed to Nikaidō's candidacy. From Nakasone's perspective, this meant that he had managed to drive a wedge into the Tanaka faction.

As Kanemaru went to work cementing Nakasone's sole candidacy, some among the party's powerful figures asked him, "What are you going to do should Nakasone prove bad for the country and the people?" He defiantly responded that "I'm prepared for us to die on each other's swords should he go too far." Nakasone invited him to the prime minister's residence afterward and thanked him, telling him that "I'd always thought you were a frightening man, and now I owe my life to that fact."

On October 31, Nakasone oversaw the meeting where he secured a new presidential term (standing in for Secretary-General Tanaka Rokusuke, who was ill). He chose Kanemaru as the new secretary-general, named Miyazawa General Council chairman as expected, and had Fujinami remain PRC chairman. As for Nikaidō, the man at the center of all the drama, he still had half a year remaining in his term as vice president, and he remained in that position for the time being. As the vice presidency was a position that could easily go vacant without causing any problems, however, he would lose the position following the July 1986 joint election.[38]

The Fall of Tanaka Kakuei

Tanaka may have received more than 220,000 votes in the December 1983 election, but he was losing the ability to maintain control over his faction – something evident from the discord within the faction over the Nikaidō candidacy. His refusal to allow anyone in his faction run as a presidential candidate was fostering dissatisfaction, especially as Finance Minister Takeshita was an obvious future party leader.

Nakasone had fallen behind Tanaka in the competition for party leadership years earlier, but Tanaka's decline meant that it was becoming easier for him to maintain control of the party. The time was fast approaching for a generational change in the leadership of each faction, and Nakasone was not confronted by strong rivals the way that Tanaka had had to compete with Fukuda.

Going into 1985, the cracks in the Tanaka faction were becoming apparent. First, Takeshita held the first meeting of the Sōseikai on February 7. This was nominally a policy research group, but it was actually intended as a vehicle through which Takeshita, Kanemaru, Hashimoto Ryūtarō, Ozawa Ichirō, and Kajiyama Seiroku could carry out a change in the Tanaka faction's leadership. Nakasone wrote the following on February 9: "Launch of Takeshita's Sōseikai. Tanaka faction in chaos. History moves steadily forward."

To make matters worse for Tanaka, he suffered a cerebral infarction (a type of stroke) on February 27, hospitalizing him. When Nakasone met with the political editors of the major newspapers the following day, he said, "As you all know, Kaku suffered a cerebral infarction yesterday and has been hospitalized. [...] I hope that his condition proves to not be serious and that he recovers quickly."

Despite his grave words, Nakasone was extremely pleased by this turn of events, and this was obvious from his face. The political editor for the *Nihon Keizai Shimbun* later recalled, "I have never seen Nakasone in as good of a mood as he was on that day."

While Tanaka was discharged from the hospital on April 28, he began a lengthy recovery at home, and his daughter Makiko closed his office in Hiranuma. With Tanaka's political career coming to an end, Nakasone now felt that he had a "free hand." He had always had to take Tanaka into consideration previously and was elated at the new sense of freedom.

The period from Tanaka's downfall to the end of the Nakasone government in November 1987 marks the final phase of the "Sanaka Daifuku Chū" era. Tanaka's control as the "shadow shogun" had come to an end, but the new leaders in the party – Takeshita, Abe, and Miyazawa – were not yet ready to stand up to Nakasone. It was an extremely advantageous political situation for him.

Nakasone, who had been listed last in Sankaku Daifuku Chū and had been beaten by them all to the premiership – and even by Suzuki, a man who never expected to become prime minister – now had total control of Japanese politics in both name and reality.

Tanaka had been critical of Nakasone's moves to privatize JNR. With him now gone, Nakasone sped up his efforts to that end. While Nakasone may have only been the leader of a weak faction, he was now going to try to surpass the accomplishments of all of the Sankaku Daifuku prime ministers.[39]

The Road to the Plaza Accord

Nakasone was now approaching the zenith of his life. Before examining the breakup and privatization of JNR, I would first like to look at foreign policy.

186 *1,806 Days as Prime Minister*

The first half of 1985 again saw Nakasone engaging in a remarkable amount of travel overseas. On New Year's Day, he participated in a ceremony at the Imperial Palace and then left for Los Angeles that night for a US-Japan summit. While Nakasone did a remarkable amount of travel, it was unusual for him to do so in the first three days of the year.

The summit meeting in Los Angeles was sparked by growing criticism in the US (particularly from Congress) related to the country's now more than $30 billion trade deficit with Japan.

Reagan wanted the Japanese markets for telecommunications, electronics, lumber, pharmaceuticals, and medical equipment to be opened up, and Nakasone promised to take steps in that direction.

Another long-standing issue the leaders needed to discuss was national security. Reagan had launched his Strategic Defense Initiative (SDI; also known as "Star Wars") – a defense system intended to intercept nuclear ballistic nuclear missiles at four stages: at launch, during their boost phase, in space, and during terminal entry.

While Reagan insisted that "the ultimate goal of the program is the elimination of nuclear weapons," Nakasone was hesitant. "I completely understand [the rationale behind] America's SDI research. But because we're not necessarily familiar with all of its details, I would ask that you provide us with information and confer with us at each major stage of the program moving forward. I would also ask that you exercise adequate caution, particularly prior to its deployment."

Nakasone informed Reagan that he had secured a 6.9% increase in the defense budget and a 10.0% increase in ODA spending and that he was considering eliminating the 1% of GNP cap on defense spending.

After he returned home, Nakasone got to work finding a way to ease the trade frictions. He announced a series of economic policies aimed at foreign trade on April 9 that included lowered tariffs and a plan to expand imports. He also appeared on television to "ask all of the Japanese people" to "please buy foreign goods." This direct appeal via television had been his idea. But while Nakasone had done what he could to honor his promise to Reagan, the US Semiconductor Industry Association filed a complaint with the US Trade Representative in June alleging that Japan was engaged in unfair trade practices.

A more drastic response was needed to ease the economic frictions. The finance ministers of five developed nations (including Takeshita) met at the Plaza Hotel in New York and agreed on September 22 to take actions to correct the high value of the dollar. At its core, the Plaza Accord was an agreement that each nation would intervene in their exchange rates with the goal of reducing America's trade deficit.

Nakasone had told Takeshita in late July that "I suspect it's too late for us to clinically try actions one by one to [correct US-Japan trade frictions]. A more drastic and fundamental structural correction has become necessary, I think." Two of Nakasone's economic advisors – Hosomi Takashi (a former finance ministry financier and president of the Overseas Economic Cooperation Fund) and Nakagawa Yukitsugu (president of the Nomura Research Institute and a former director of the Bank of Japan) – had told him that a stronger yen was desirable for resolving the economic frictions.

Japan underwent a serious recession in the wake of the Plaza Accord as the value of the yen increased from 240 yen to the dollar to 140 yen.

According to Nakasone, "I received some criticism after the signing of the Plaza Accord, and there are those who argue that that act served as the origin of the bubble economy and the lengthy recession that followed. But the Plaza Accord was unavoidable given the contemporary conditions. The response to the recession that followed was too half-hearted, however. It especially needed to be stronger once we got into the 1990s."

In other words, Nakasone later argued against the idea that the Plaza Accord served as the origin of the bubble economy. Does that mean that the Nakasone government's economic policies and the bubble were entirely unrelated?

Examining the course of events a little more closely, there was actually another agreement reached between the Plaza Accord and the beginning of the bubble: the Louvre Accord. On February 22, 1987, near the end of Nakasone's time in office, seven countries agreed to intervene in their exchange rates once again, this time to prevent further weakening of the dollar. Finance Minister Miyazawa represented Japan at this meeting.

The dollar continued to fall despite the Louvre Accord, however, and Nakasone released a six-trillion-yen plan on May 29 intended to expand domestic demand. Even Nakasone's advisor Nakagawa would later admit that this stimulus measure had been excessive, noting that it was "a trillion yen too much." This action was taken just as Japanese industry was overcoming the recession that had been triggered by the rise in the yen. It also ran counter to Nakasone's efforts to reduce the budget deficit and boosted the trends that led to the bubble economy.[40]

"Pacific Cooperation" and Australia

I would like to return to January 1985. After his meeting with Reagan in Los Angeles, Nakasone spent a day resting in Hawaii, returning home on January 5. He left for the South Pacific a week later, visiting Fiji, Papua New Guinea, Australia, and New Zealand from January 13 to 20.

Nakasone was the first Japanese prime minister to visit Fiji. Prime Minister Mara welcomed him, noting that "We have natural resources, but Japan has people, technology, knowhow, and experience. I would thus like to strengthen the cooperative relationship between our countries." Nakasone responded, "Our nation has no peace and stability unless the same exists in the Pacific. I thus greatly desire to further promote our cooperation with the nations of the Pacific."

As can be seen from his meeting with Papua New Guinean Prime Minister Somare, when Nakasone spoke of "Pacific cooperation," he meant using

188   *1,806 Days as Prime Minister*

economic, cultural, and technological exchange to strengthen Japan's relations with the "nations of the Pacific" (including ASEAN).

Nakasone discussed SDI and nuclear disarmament with Australian Prime Minister Hawke and New Zealand Prime Minister Lange.

Nakasone viewed Australia as the key to "Pacific cooperation" and frequently invoked security during his meetings there, such as saying at one point that "Global security needs to be considered from a global perspective. We cannot sacrifice any one region. The security of the free world is indivisible."

Hawke echoed this sentiment, noting that "Japan and Australia share the view that the number of nuclear weapons held by other nations must not increase as the number of possessed by the superpowers is reduced,"

In general, Nakasone's "Pacific cooperation" was intended to foster the solidarity of the free world and prevent Asia from being disregarded as the US and USSR took steps toward nuclear disarmament. In that sense, it can be considered to have been part of Nakasone's Cold War strategy.[41]

Meeting Gorbachev

From the Soviet perspective, it was the arrival of Gorbachev that marked the beginning of a new phase of the Cold War. General Secretary of the Communist Party Chernenko died on March 10, 1985, and was succeeded by Gorbachev. Nakasone visited the USSR from March 12 to 15 for Chernenko's funeral and met with Gorbachev on the 14th. This was the first Japan-Soviet summit to be held since Tanaka's meeting with Brezhnev in 1973 eleven years earlier.

Nakasone told Gorbachev that "our fundamental position is that we would like to resolve the Northern Territories issue and rapidly conclude a peace treaty, thereby establishing a stable foundation for the long-term relationship between our nations."

Gorbachev was not responsive to this approach, however, saying, "Prime Minister, you have touched on the so-called 'territorial issue,' but you surely know our position on this matter. I have nothing new to say on the topic."

Despite this unpromising exchange, Gorbachev did boost Nakasone somewhat at the end of the meeting by telling him as they shook hands that "I would like to talk with you again."

Nakasone later wrote that "In my time as a politician, I've known three people who were able to send people off with a good feeling in this way. The first was Hatoyama Ichirō, the second was Reagan, and the third was Gorbachev. I think being able to do this is an important factor in becoming a global politician."[42]

The Bonn Summit

A month and a half after his visit to the USSR, Nakasone attended the G7 summit in Bonn. Just before the beginning of the summit, he met privately with Chancellor Kohl and discussed the Japanese economy, the situation on the Korean Peninsula, Sino-Japanese relations, and "Pacific cooperation."

When Nakasone argued that "if the Geneva negotiations [between the US and USSR] are to be successful, the West cannot become split over the SDI issue," Kohl agreed.

In a private meeting with Reagan, the men were united in their opposition to the US Congress' protectionism and reaffirmed their belief that "the security of the free world is indivisible" with regard to SDI.

Two statements were released following the end of the summit: an economic statement on expanding employment and achieving growth without inflation and a political statement in which the members confirmed, on the fortieth anniversary of the end of the Second World War, their shared belief in freedom and democracy.

During the summit, Nakasone put forward Japan's four conditions for continued SDI research: that SDI would not be used to achieve nuclear superiority and total deterrence would continue to be maintained; that stockpiles of offensive nuclear weaponry would continue to be reduced; that SDI would operate under the restrictions of the Anti-Ballistic Missile Treaty; and that America's allies and the Soviets would be consulted on the production and deployment of SDI. He reconfirmed his acceptance of SDI based on these conditions.

Britain's Thatcher proved to be a cause of worry at the summit. She had been prime minister for six years at this point, and Nakasone wrote in his diary that "Thatcher has no vigor. When we were together, she complained about the contract for the bridge over the Bosporus. The British Empire has truly fallen far." This was a reference to a Japanese company securing the contract for building a bridge in Turkey.[43]

While Nakasone had visited many countries around the world since becoming prime minister, he had oddly enough only visited Western Europe to attend the G7 summits in London and Bonn. He now visited France, Italy, the Vatican, and Belgium from July 12 to 21, discussing SDI, Gorbachev's diplomatic efforts, and economic frictions with their leaders.

French President Mitterrand remained opposed to SDI, but Nakasone rebutted this by asserting that "it is undeniable that SDI was one of the things that brought the Soviets to the negotiating table in Geneva." He viewed SDI as a "political bargaining chip." This was his third visit to Europe in 1985 and came on the heels of the Bonn summit and his March visit to the USSR.[44]

Making an Official Visit to Yasukuni Shrine

Nakasone had expressed a strong desire to carry out an official visit to Yasukuni Shrine as prime minister as part of the "final settlement of post-war politics."

190 *1,806 Days as Prime Minister*

He wrote a haiku in 1975 to mark the thirtieth anniversary of the end of the war:

Anniversary of the end of the war	*shūsenki*
the cicadas of the archipelago	*rettō no semi*
cry incessantly	*naki yamazu*

In later years, he explained that the reason he had pushed for an official visit was that "My brother died in the war. Many of my comrades and subordinates died. I believed that I had to make an official visit as prime minister at least once and pay my respects to their noble spirits. Previous prime ministers had not said that their visits were official. They lacked this kind of awareness."

The reason that past prime ministers had refrained from saying that they were making official visits was because doing so could be considered a violation of the constitution's separation of church and state. The Cabinet Legislation Bureau's interpretation was that it might be unconstitutional for government ministers to perform such visits.

Nakasone had visited Yasukuni nine times between April 1983 and April 1985, including for the shrine's spring and autumn festivals and to mark the anniversary of the end of the war. He had avoided making any clear statement as to whether these were private or official visits, however, and he had paid for his offerings with his own money. Even so, he had clearly had the mindset of a public official during the visits and had signed his name as "Nakasone Yasuhiro, Prime Minister" in the shrine's registry.

As with his revision of the 1% of GNP limit on defense spending, Nakasone made use of a private advisory council for this issue. He had established the "Panel on the Issue of Cabinet Members Visiting Yasukuni Shrine" in August 1984 as a private advisory group of Chief Cabinet Secretary Fujinami. The group included constitutional scholars and was headed by Hayashi Keizō, the president of the Japanese Red Cross.

The group's findings, which were released on August 9, 1985, were that such a visit could be constitutional provided that steps were taken to reduce its religious nature. Being a private advisory group, the council was not subject to the Diet in the way that an official group would have been.

Also motivating Nakasone's official visit was increasing pressure from three groups within the LDP: Sakurauchi Yoshio's Diet Members' Council on Bereaved Families, Tamura Hajime's Diet Members' Council on the Souls of the War Dead, and Okuno Seisuke's Let's All Worship at Yasukuni Shrine Diet Members Association.

Nakasone visited Yasukuni on August 15, 1985, the fortieth anniversary of the end of the war. Proper religious etiquette during such a visit would be to bow twice, clap twice, and then bow again. To reduce the religious nature of the visit, he only bowed once. He made no religious offering but instead provided 30,000 yen from public funds for a flower offering. Afterward, he proudly told the assembled reporters that he had made "an official visit as prime minister." When asked about the inevitable criticism that would come from China and other countries, he said that he would "work hard to convince them of my sincerity."[45]

Nakasone had not taken the potential effect of the visit on relations with China lightly. Immediately before making the visit, he had dispatched Noda Takeshi, a member of his faction and the director of the Japan-China Society, to China in an attempt to stem the criticism. He had also approached the shrine through Sakurauchi and others about having the A-Class war criminals enshrined separately but was unable to convince them.

Anti-Japanese demonstrations in China increased following his visit, and it also endangered the position of the pro-Japan Hu Yaobang. In July 1986, he sounded out Hu through former Keidanren president Inayama Yoshihori about the possibility of the Chinese government accepting one official visit to Yasukuni a year, but the Chinese rejected this. The visit was also strongly criticized in South Korea.

Nakasone found that he had no choice but to refrain from making further visits. Years later, he described his mental state at the time as follows: "I had never had any intention of insisting upon repeat visits. [...] While I would of course have continued to visit if there hadn't been any international opposition from countries like China, my belief was that the spirits of the war dead would not be pleased if I damaged our relations with Asia by insisting on the visits."[46]

The consequences of Nakasone's decision to refrain from further visits can be viewed in two ways. First, by ending the visits, he secured his relationships with Hu and Chun. Second, by prioritizing foreign relations over the visits, he caused the Yasukuni question to be associated with international politics rather than merely a constitutional issue.

Relevant to the first point, Hu fell from power in January 1987, and Chun's term as president would be ending in February 1988. Nakasone would never be able to again establish relationships of trust with Chinese and Korean leaders comparable to those he had had with Hu and Chun.

And it is important in considering the second point to note the Yasukuni issue remains with us today. Regardless of Nakasone's intentions, it is undeniable that his focus on making an official visit to the shrine has had a negative legacy.

Of the two consequences, it is the second that continues to be of great relevance today.

Addressing the United Nations

With leaders from many nations gathering in New York for the fortieth anniversary of the founding of the United Nations in October, Nakasone chose America as the setting for repairing relations with South Korea and China. He met with South Korean Prime Minister Lho Shin-yong on October 22. Lho requested the transfer of technology from Japan, and Nakasone expressed a willingness to expand imports from South Korea.

192   *1,806 Days as Prime Minister*

The next day, Nakasone met with Chinese Premier Zhao Ziyang and told him, "I will not waver from promoting Sino-Japanese cooperation with a steadfast spirit." Zhao replied that "Sino-Japanese relations are continuing to make progress in areas including politics, economics, and culture, and this accomplishment cannot be divorced from your efforts."

He also met with leaders like Reagan and Indian Prime Minister Gandhi, but the Yasukuni issue did not surface at any of those meetings.

He began his address to the UN General Assembly that day with the words "Having suffered the scourge of war and the atomic bomb, the Japanese people will never again permit the revival of militarism on their soil. These basic tenets of Japanese policy are at one with the lofty Purposes and Principles set forth in the Charter of the United Nations."

He next listed three points as showing that Japan had made "the United Nations a central pillar of its foreign policy": "our efforts to promote world peace and disarmament, especially to banish nuclear weapons from this earth"; "its efforts to promote free trade and to cooperate with developing countries"; and "its cooperation with peoples throughout the world in the development of culture and civilization."

He then began speaking of philosophy from a Japanese perspective:

I composed this haiku one evening:

Afar and above the dark and endless sky,
the Milky way runs
toward the place I come from

We Japanese generally believe that the great natural universe is our home, and that all living things should co-exist in harmony with the natural universe. We believe that all living things – humans, animals, trees, grasses – are essentially brothers and sisters.

I doubt that this philosophy is unique to the Japanese. I believe that better understanding of it could contribute much to the creation of universal values for our international community.

He closed his address by expressing the hope that the time would come when it could be said, "the Earth is one, and that mankind everywhere is co-existing in harmony and working for the well-being of all life on this verdant globe."

This was not the first time that a Japanese prime minister had addressed the UN; Satō Eisaku and Suzuki Zenkō had done so before. But it was rare for a prime minister to speak philosophically, and the response he received from the audience greatly exceeded those of his predecessors. While the draft of the speech had been prepared by the foreign ministry, the latter half, in which he recited a haiku and spoke of philosophy, had been entirely his own work. It was a notable speech and one delivered on a global stage.

1,806 Days as Prime Minister 193

While Nakasone had stumbled with the Yasukuni issue, he had shown himself able to recover (something indispensable to any leader who hoped to helm a long-lived government) and had done so through diplomatic efforts. It was an achievement typical of his approach to politics.[47]

Laying the Foundation for the Tokyo Summit

Nakasone reshuffled his cabinet on December 28, 1985, and brought Gotōda back as chief cabinet secretary. While Nakasone never revealed to Gotōda the rationale for his reappointment, the breakup and privatization of JNR was a long-standing part of Nakasone's domestic agenda. Gotōda believed that Nakasone thought that he would be able to carry out his administrative reforms and keep the cabinet in line.[48]

Nakasone had much on his mind going into 1986. A G7 summit was scheduled to be held in Tokyo in May. If he prioritized the privatization of JNR, it was also likely that he would dissolve the Diet and call a general election. His term as LDP president would also expire in October. While securing a third term was generally out of the question, if he managed to secure a major electoral victory, it was possible that he might be able to stay on. Nakasone wrote in his diary on New Year's Day that "This will be a year of great ups and downs. People say that it will be a quiet, calm year, but both the world and Japan are in an era of upheaval."[49]

His first foreign trip of the year was to Canada. He arrived on January 12 and visited Toronto, Ottawa, and Vancouver. During his meeting with Canadian Prime Minister Mulroney, Mulroney spoke of unemployment in Canada and strengthening free trade. He also said that he wanted to put international terrorism on the agenda of the upcoming G7 summit. At the time, it was believed that support from Libya was behind a series of terrorist attacks occurring across the globe.

For his part, Nakasone touched on military disarmament, the north-south problem, "Pacific cooperation," and the expansion of Japan-Canadian economic relations. He also said that he wanted to create closer relations within the "northern Pacific triangle" (an area that included the United States).

Speaking before the Canadian House of Commons, Nakasone praised Canada's role in the world, saying, "I note with keen interest Canada's unique role in the international arena. [...] Canada has not just reacted passively to superpower politics, but, taking full advantage of its self-defined role as a 'middle power,' is contributing actively to the building of peace as an international mediator, or as a quiet but effective negotiator." It was rare for a Japanese prime minister to visit Canada, and Nakasone's motive in doing so was, in part, to lay the foundation for the G7 summit in Tokyo.[50]

Reagan's Letter

Nakasone returned to Japan on January 16, and he welcomed Soviet Foreign Minister Shevardnadze to the prime minister's residence two days

194   *1,806 Days as Prime Minister*

later. He had written a letter to Gorbachev advocating for the revitalization of the Soviet-Japanese dialogue, and Shevardnadze handed Nakasone the reply. In his letter, Gorbachev wrote that he welcomed a diverse range of exchanges with Japan and that he was negotiating with Reagan on nuclear disarmament.

After reading the letter, Nakasone firmly noted that "Asia cannot be sacrificed in any reduction of nuclear and conventional weapons. I strongly hope that reductions in Asia are undertaken in a manner proportional to those carried out in Europe."[51]

Nakasone received a letter from Reagan on February 6 that addressed the INF negotiations and included the proposal that he would be making to the Soviets. Reagan proposed that if the USSR withdrew all SS-20s from west of the Urals and reduced its SS-20 deployments in Asia by half, the US would withdraw its nuclear missiles from West Germany.

Reagan's proposal would leave SS-20 missiles deployed in Asia and inspired a rare case of resentment toward him by Nakasone, who felt that "Japan is being regarded as an acceptable sacrifice."

Holding to his position that "it is unjust for the [SS-20s] to be removed from Europe but not Asia, and I will not stand for it," he had the foreign ministry put forward a substitute proposal to Reagan. Under this proposal, the USSR would gather all of its SS-20s at Barnaul in the center of the country. The US gave Japan's proposal serious consideration after receiving it.[52]

The Camp David Talks

Nakasone visited Washington on April 12, heading to Camp David by helicopter for his eighth meeting with Reagan on the 13th and 14th.

Nakasone sought to convince Reagan to abandon his INF proposal by insisting that "having INFs [intermediate-range nuclear forces] remain in Asia will lead those who want their removal to argue for using FBSs [forward-based systems] as bargaining chips. It has the potential to greatly hamstring the credibility of the US-Japan security framework, so I cannot accept it."

That Nakasone was willing to argue with an American president over nuclear strategy – a very unusual act for a Japanese prime minister – speaks to the closeness of the Ron-Yasu relationship.

The other major topic at the summit was resolving the trade frictions between the countries. Reagan stressed that Japan needed to increase its imports of American goods, saying that "According to the Maekawa Report, you will be setting national targets. We understand this to mean that Japan will become a major importer of goods. This is vital."

Reagan was referring to a report issued by the Research Committee on Adjusting the Structure of the Economy for International Harmony, a private advisory group headed by former Bank of Japan president Maekawa Haruo. It had concluded that Japan should reduce its current account balance surplus and urgently undertake structural adjustment of its economy.

The Nakasone government was in the process of acting on the group's findings, and he told Reagan that he "recognized restoring the balance of trade as a national goal."[53]

The report called for stimulating domestic demand by enacting a policy of low interest rates and eliminating regulations on large-scale retail stores and land. Some economists argue that Nakasone's attempts to stimulate domestic demand through private-sector activity and the relaxation of regulations contributed to the development of the later bubble economy.[54]

The Tokyo Summit

The G7 Tokyo summit was held from May 4 to 6, 1986 at the State Guest Houses in Akasaka. International terrorism was a major focus of discussion at the summit. The US had bombed Libya a month earlier for its support of terrorist organizations.

After coordinating the views of the participants, Nakasone released a "statement on international terrorism" that designated Libya a sponsor of international terrorism. The summit's economic statement spoke of structural adjustment and coordinating economic policies. A statement on the April accident at the Chernobyl nuclear plant was also adopted.[55]

Reflecting on Nakasone's preparations for the summit, Yanagiya Kensuke (administrative vice-minister of foreign affairs at the time) recalled that "We held a 'prime ministerial briefing' or study session pretty much every day, sometimes for more than four hours. The study sessions had pretty much wrapped up by May 2. The prime minister was extremely passionate about studying. He read a lot and peppered us with questions. My impression was that he was able to grasp things quickly. And he was outstanding when it came time to actually serve as head of the summit."

Nakasone testified to the Diet at this time that there was no reason to be concerned about Japanese nuclear power plants due to differences in construction from Chernobyl. In December 1987, Reagan and Gorbachev reached a historic agreement to withdraw all ground-based intermediate-range missiles, including those in Asia.[56]

The Privatization of NTT

Nakasone made his primary domestic policy objectives the privatization of Nippon Telegraph and Telephone Public Corporation (NTT), Japan Tobacco and Salt Public Corporation, and JNR, and he pursued this based on Rinchō's findings. I would like to go back four years, to 1983, and follow the course this took.

NTT had occasionally been profitable, and Yamagishi Akira, chairman of Zendentsū (the Japan Telecommunications Workers' Union) opposed privatization. Nakasone knew Shintō Hisashi, the president of NTT, from meetings of business leaders he had attended, and he had great esteem for his creativity and drive.

196 *1,806 Days as Prime Minister*

Shintō was able to convince Yamagishi to accept privatization by suggesting that they leave the issue of the breakup of the corporation for the time being. Nakasone also had Deputy Chief Cabinet Secretary Watanabe Hideo try to persuade Yamagishi.

There was also resistance to the privatization from members of the LDP's postal *zoku* – Diet members who belonged to the LDP's Communications Policy Division (the party's counterpart to the Ministry of Posts and Telecommunications) and exerted influence over areas that fell within that ministry's remit. The zoku included figures like Kanemaru, Yamashita Toku, and Katō Tsunetarō. Nakasone personally worked to convince Yamashita and Katō to accept privatization, and he had Sejima Ryūzō persuade Kanemaru, who was effectively the zoku's leader.

Kanemaru, who was now serving as secretary-general, expressed understanding for Nakasone's position and began backing him on the issue. He had once been known for his opposition to Nakasone, but that was no longer the case. He would later write that "a minor daimyo of the Sengoku period had no choice but to shift with the tides in order to protect himself. But it seems to me that once they had finally been enthroned in Edo Castle, they felt secure and were able to exercise their true ability. I think this idea is related to how Nakasone was able to raise his approval ratings after he became prime minister."

On May 10, 1984, Nakasone introduced a bill to the Diet reforming NTT. Following some amendments, it passed the House of Councillors on December 14 and the House of Representatives on December 20. After it became certain that the privatization of NTT was going to go through, Tanaka Kakuei (who had not yet suffered his stroke at this point) and the postal zoku threw strong support behind making then-NTT Vice President Kitahara Yasusada the first president of the new NTT. Kitahara was a very talented technician known for his management skills.

Nakasone used Nakayama Sohei, a senior advisor to the Industrial Bank of Japan, to convince Tanaka to instead back Shintō for the position. The now private Nippon Telegraph and Telephone Corporation was formed on April 1, 1985, with Shintō remaining president. Japan Tobacco and Salt Public Corporation was also privatized on the same day, becoming Japan Tobacco. This meant that the import of foreign tobacco had now been liberalized.[57]

The Breakup and Privatization of JNR

The breakup and privatization of JNR was an extremely difficult affair. At the time, JNR held 22 trillion yen of loans, the interest on which was increasing at a rate of 3.8 billion yen a day.

On June 10, 1983, Nakasone formed the Committee for Overseeing the Reconstruction of JNR (an advisory council) on the basis of the findings of Rinchō's Fourth Section, which was in charge of administrative rationalization.

Nakasone chose President of Sumitomo Electric Kamei Masao to serve as the committee's chairman. Kamei was head of Rinchō's Third Section (which was in charge of regional rationalization) and Nakasone had great respect for his ability.

At the same time, Nakasone also ordered JNR President Nisugi Iwao to undertake reforms meant to smooth the way for privatization. Tanaka Kakuei had been largely responsible for the choice of Nisugi as JNR president. Meanwhile, JNR's union and Vice President Nawata Kunitake were opposed to any radical reforms.

The restructuring plan put forward by JNR on January 10, 1985 was intended to facilitate privatization but also maintained the existing arrangement of having a single company responsible for the entire country. The plan was poorly received by the Committee for Overseeing the Reconstruction of JNR, who were in favor of breaking the company up, and Nakasone also interpreted the lack of any division of the company as the leadership merely following the letter of his instructions rather than the spirit.

Because of the massive size of JNR, failing to break it up into constituent parts responsible for themselves would drastically reduce the effectiveness of any privatization.

Nakasone first put pressure on Nisugi to do "what he had promised" and then ultimately dismissed him in late June. He also forced Nawata and other directors to resign. He chose former vice-minister of transportation Sugiura Takaya, a proponent of breaking up the company, to be the new president. Nakasone later described this personnel change as the "decisive moment" in the privatization of JNR.

The LDP's transportation zoku also resisted breaking the company up. For members of the zoku like Katō Mutusuki (a member of the Fukuda faction), JNR's vested interests and its union's block votes were important. Katō had strong ties to Nawata, and while he accepted privatization, he was against breaking up JNR.

The zoku were not unified on this point, however. While Mitsuzuka Hiroshi, chairman of the LDP's Subcommittee on the Reconstruction of JNR, was – like Katō – a member of the transportation zoku and the Fukuda faction, he also favored breaking the company up. He believed that that was the only way to do away with its employees' mindset that the Japanese government could be expected to take care of them.

Nakasone was able to use former MITI Minister Okonogi Hikosaburō to bring Katō and his other zoku opponents in line. He also reached out to the Japan Railway Workers' Union, which was aligned with the Democratic Socialists (as opposed to the National Railway Workers' Union associated with the Socialist Party).

By dismissing President Nisugi (who was close to Tanaka) and placating the zoku, Nakasone had established a set of personnel connections tailored to reforming JNR. Furthermore, he appointed Mitsuzuka as transportation

198　*1,806 Days as Prime Minister*

minister after his cabinet reshuffle on December 28, thereby putting him in charge of the privatization.

The cabinet approved the Railway Business Act and the Act for Enforcement of the Japanese National Railways Reform Act on March 14, 1986 and submitted them to the Diet. Under the framework established by these bills, JNR would be broken up into six private companies.

Nakasone supported dividing Honshu between three companies, feeling that the original plan of having only two would result in companies that were too powerful. Placing a company in charge of the Tōkai region between them would eliminate any collusion between the companies in charge of the east and west and help ensure the companies remained proactive.

As will be discussed in the following section, Nakasone made the July 6 double elections into a referendum on the privatization of JNR and won an overwhelming majority of 304 seats. Hashimoto Ryūtarō was appointed transportation minister in the third Nakasone government.

Nakasone's rationale for replacing Mitsuzuka with Hashimoto was that Hashimoto was very familiar with administrative reform from his time as chairman of the LDP's Research Commission on Public Finance and Administration and was thus an appropriate choice for overseeing the final stages of privatization.

After the Diet passed the privatization bills on November 28, Nakasone happily wrote in his diary that "Hill 203 has finally fallen. [...] This is the result of the 304 seats." His government had successfully overcome a massive hurdle. "Hill 203" was a reference to a pivotal event during the Siege of Port Arthur in the Russo-Japanese War.

The JR of today was born on April 1, 1987. Nakasone later described the significance of this moment as follows: "The breaking up and privatization of JNR increased the rate at which Kokurō fell apart, weakened Sōhyō, and furthered the decline of the Socialist Party. It played a great role in bringing about the end of the 1955 System."[58]

The privatization of Japan's three large public corporations can be considered the greatest reform undertaken by Nakasone during his lengthy administration. It laid out a vision of Japan's future – a vision that looked at things from a national perspective rather than that of the interests of the zoku Diet members.

III. The Weight of 304 Seats: Nakasone's Third Term

The "Playing Dead" Dissolution

On June 2, 1986, the House of Representatives was dissolved in an extraordinary session of the Diet, paving the way for a joint election of both houses to be held on July 6. This came to be known as the "playing dead" dissolution (*shinda-furi kaisan*).

A bill had been passed on May 22 correcting malapportionment in the House of Representatives, ensuring that the largest electoral district had a population that was less than three times that of the smallest district. This meant that eight prefectures would gain a seat and seven would lose one. A House of Councillors election was scheduled for July, but because the malapportionment bill included a thirty-day notification period before the seat changes went into effect, coordinating things so that a general election could be held on the same day was considered difficult.

Nakasone himself had initially stated that he would not call an extraordinary session of the Diet to dissolve it. A reporter assigned to him asked him about it shortly before it happened:

R: You haven't changed your mind about dissolving the Diet?
N: No.
R: You once said that it was okay to lie about that.
N: No, someone else said that. That was the chief cabinet secretary.
R: So, you're not lying when you say you're not going to dissolve it.
N: Right.
R: Are you lying about lying?
N: Like they said in *Hagoromo*, "Suspicion is for the human realm."

Hagoromo is a famous Noh play concerning the feather cloak of a *tennyo* (a heavenly maiden). In the play, the maiden tells a fisherman who has found her cloak that "Suspicion is for the human realm. There is no falsehood in heaven." Nakasone was thus saying that he was telling the truth.[59]

Contrary to his words, however, Nakasone would do just that ten days after the passage of the reapportionment bill under the pretext that a new Diet should be elected now that the unconstitutional difference in the value of votes had been corrected. His actual goal was to catch the opposition parties off guard, however.

304 Seats

On May 11, Nakasone had written in his diary that he was "pretending to be asleep. Playing dead":

Asari Keita and Satō Seizaburō came. They said that I should dissolve the Diet after the bill passes and get out of the unconstitutional situation immediately. I already felt that way and have been making arrangements with Kanemaru and Fujinami to hold a joint election on July 6. But I have to make it seem for the time being that I'm discouraged because such an early dissolution is impossible due to the thirty-day notification period. I'm pretending to be asleep. Playing dead.

Nakasone had had the head of the Ministry of Home Affairs' electoral department investigate the matter and learned that he would be legally allowed to

200 *1,806 Days as Prime Minister*

hold a joint election if he called an extraordinary session of the Diet to dissolve it after the regular session had ended. Chief Cabinet Secretary Gotōda, Secretary-General Kanemaru, and Diet Affairs Committee Chairman Fujinami were the only other people aware of his plans.

The LDP won a great victory in the election, taking 304 seats in the House of Representatives, a gain of 54. They also gained 11 seats in the House of Councillors. The Socialist Party lost 25 seats in the House of Representatives, reducing its size to 86. Chairman Ishibashi Masashi and the rest of the party's leadership resigned. The Democratic Socialists won 26 seats (a loss of 11), and the New Liberal Club won 6 (a loss of 2).

Nakasone attributed the LDP's victory to the privatization of JNR and the success of the Tokyo summit. However, despite this great success, Nakasone once again found himself coming in second to Fukuda in Gunma's 3rd district, just as he had in 1983.[60]

His eldest son Hirofumi was elected to the House of Councillors in the election. Hirofumi was forty years old and had accumulated a fair amount of experience, such as spending three years as a secretary to the party president. He had accurately judged it a good time to run as a candidate.

Gunma held two seats in the House of Councillors, and the other went to Fukuda Hiroichi, Fukuda Takeo's younger brother and the then-parliamentary vice-minister of agriculture, forestry, and fisheries. Hirofumi came in first, leaving Hiroichi (who was running for reelection for the first time) in second.

According to the July 7 evening edition of the *Asahi Shimbun*, Kanemaru said that, in light of the landslide victory, "it would be beautiful if a consensus emerged on extending [Nakasone's] term [as president]." The chances of Nakasone continuing on as prime minister had increased significantly, and his term as president (normally two years) would be extended by a year at the general meeting of the LDP's Diet members on September 1.

The Outcome of the "1986 System"

The third Nakasone government was formed on July 22, 1986. One notable personnel change made at this time was the appointment of Miyazawa as finance minister. This was his first entry into the cabinet since serving as chief cabinet secretary during the Suzuki government.

As with Takeshita (now secretary-general) and Abe (General Council chairman), Miyazawa was seen as one of the party's new leaders and a likely candidate to follow Nakasone as president. Nakasone intended to have the three compete against one another. Miyazawa was also acting chairman of the Kōchikai, a status that would become formal after his appointment as finance minister.

Rounding out the three major party leadership positions was Itō Masayoshi (a member of the Miyazawa faction) as PRC chairman. Vice President Nikaidō, who had opposed the dissolution of the House of Representatives as an "unjustified" act, received no position. No one was chosen to succeed him as vice president.

According to Nikaidō, Nakasone had asked him to serve as speaker of the House of Representatives or foreign minister, but he had refused these, saying, "I'm determined to watch over the Tanaka faction while Tanaka is not well. I have no intention of serving in any position other than that of vice president." He said he was "absolutely shocked" when Nakasone then told him that he wouldn't be appointing a vice president.[61]

On August 12, Kōno Yōhei, the head of the New Liberal Club, visited Nakasone at the prime minister's office. With the party having been reduced to only six seats in the House of Representatives and a single seat in the House of Councillors, Nakasone had reached out to Kōno (a former member of the Nakasone faction) through Inaba Osamu, Sakurauchi Yoshio, and Asari Keita to suggest that its members return to the LDP. Kōno's visit was for the purpose of giving his answer.

When Kōno formally asked to be allowed to return to the LDP, saying that he wished to "dissolve the New Liberal Club as a party, merge with the conservatives, and help play a role in national governance," Nakasone welcomed the offer and said he would "accept all members of the New Liberal Club, whether they're serving in the Diet or not."[62]

The New Liberal Club thus dissolved after ten years of existence. Tagawa Seiichi was the only Diet member from the party to choose not to join the LDP. Of the other six, four (including Yamaguchi Toshio) joined the Nakasone faction. Kōno chose to join the Miyazawa faction, however.

The speech that Nakasone delivered at the LDP's Karuizawa Seminar on August 30 gives a good idea of his contemporary view of things. In the speech, he described the LDP's landslide victory in the joint election as the "beginning of a 1986 System" and argued that the public had given their approval for the "final settlement of postwar politics." The reporters covering the event came away with the impression that he was bursting with confidence.

Nakasone would later expand on what he meant by a "1986 System" by explaining that the public had given their approval for his policies like the breakup and privatization of JNR and the Tokyo summit, and that the LDP had "extended its wing to the left and robbed the Socialist Party of the foundation it needed for its survival."[63]

The Fujio and "Intelligence Level" Statements

Subtle changes can be seen in the way that Nakasone managed his third government. Up until this point, while the Nakasone government had struggled with domestic policy, things had generally been smooth when it came to foreign policy. During his third government, the LDP enjoyed a stable majority of more than 300 seats, but his relations with foreign countries would be undermined first by a statement by Education Minister Fujio Masayuki and then by his own statement concerning ethnic minorities in the United States.

In the October issue of *Bungei Shunjū* (which went on sale on September 10), Fujio stated that the Korean people were partially responsible for

202   *1,806 Days as Prime Minister*

Japan's annexation of Korea. Nakasone obtained a copy of the article while the issue was still undergoing proofing, and Fujio was dismissed from his post on September 8, shortly before it went on sale. Even so, the "Fujio Statement" became a sensation.

When he traveled to Seoul for the opening ceremony of the Asian Games on September 20, Nakasone apologized to Chun Doo-hwan, saying, "I regret that a certain member of my cabinet made an inappropriate remark. As prime minister, I take his statement seriously and have dismissed him."[64]

His other diplomatic wound was self-inflicted. While giving a lecture at the LDP's national training session on September 22, Nakasone remarked that "there are a fair number of blacks, Puerto Ricans, Mexicans, and the like in America and, on the average, their [level of intelligence] is still extremely low."

While Nakasone defended himself by saying that "That was taken out of context. I think that if you read the entire lecture, you would see that it was not racist and did not disparage other countries," the staff at the Japanese embassy in Washington was forced to visit the White House and Congress to explain it.[65]

Despite the missteps toward Korea and the United States, Sino-Japanese relations were going well. Nakasone visited China on November 8 and met with Hu Yaobang (he would not be dismissed from his position until January). Hu said that he was "satisfied with the state of relations between our countries," and Nakasone replied that "our nations differ in terms of their histories and systems, but we can make great contributions to the peace and stability of Asia and the world if we cooperate." The Fujio Statement and Nakasone's visit to Yasukuni were not brought up during the trip.

Nakasone had been able to overcome the history issue and mend relations with South Korea and China. But he was aware that to maintain good relations with Japan's neighbors, he would need to put an end to his visits to Yasukuni. In doing so, he would create an unintended precedent for later governments.[66]

Breaking the 1% Cap on Defense Spending

A decade earlier, the Miki government had established a cap on defense spending of 1% of GNP, and this had been maintained by the following governments.

Nakasone, however, believed that this "should be gotten rid of if at all possible" as it was "illogical" to apply that kind of inflexible way of thinking to defense spending. "Limiting spending to a percentage of something else was an approach ill-suited to national defense."

On December 30, 1986, Nakasone received the approval of the Security Council (which was made up of figures like Finance Minister Miyazawa and Defense Agency Director-General Kurihara Yūkō) to break the 1% cap.

At this time, America's demands of Japan had shifted from increased defense spending to more economic aspects, however, and the Market-Oriented Sector Selective (MOSS) talks had begun at the working level.

Nakasone would later say that "I undertook the elimination of the 1% of GNP cap on defense spending out of consideration of the basic principles of national defense, not because of foreign expectations."[67]

Visiting Eastern Europe

Nakasone's 1987 diplomatic schedule was supposed to begin with a visit to Japan by Gorbachev, but this was delayed.

Russia scholar Kimura Hiroshi has suggested that, in addition to continued disagreement over the Northern Territories and developments within the Soviet Union, the delay was caused by Nakasone becoming a lame duck. It had become increasingly clear in the wake of the Fumio and "intelligence level" statements that Nakasone's term as president would not be extended for a second time. Kimura surmises that Gorbachev judged it better to wait for a new government to take power before visiting.[68]

Nakasone took advantage of the gap in his schedule created by the delay to visit Finland, East Germany, Yugoslavia, and Poland from January 10 to 17. The choice of countries set the stage for his diplomatic efforts toward the Soviets.

Nakasone had a bit of history with Finland that led him to visit it before Eastern Europe. During his first speech for the June 1983 House of Councillors electoral campaign, he had said that "Doing nothing would make us a country like Finland, begging for mercy from the Soviet Union." This had resulted in a protest from the Finnish embassy, and Nakasone retracted the statement in a letter to Finnish Prime Minister Sorsa.

When Sorsa welcomed Nakasone to Helsinki, he did not mention that unfortunate slip of the tongue and instead chose to praise him by remarking that "the wonderful results the Japanese people have achieved in the field of science and technology are the target of envy and admiration by the Finnish people." Nakasone followed this by praising Finland's policy of neutrality, lauding it as "representing the indomitable spirit of the Finnish people."

He also told Sorsa that, while he had raised defense spending to 1.004% of GNP, he respected "the spirit of fixing defense spending to 1%" and that he wanted to keep Japan's defensive capabilities "as moderate as possible."

After the two leaders discussed cultural and technological exchange between their countries, the meeting ended smoothly, with Sorsa saying that it had been "extremely interesting."

Nakasone then headed for East Germany, Yugoslavia, and Poland, becoming the first Japanese prime minister to ever visit Eastern Europe. These countries had invited him in the hopes of securing Japanese investment.

For Nakasone, the purpose of the visit was to "expand the breadth of Japanese diplomacy." He believed that "while the countries of Eastern

204   *1,806 Days as Prime Minister*

Europe belong to the Soviet sphere, their actual desire is to become economically independent. By offering economic assistance to these countries, Japan can help keep the USSR in check."

In East Germany, he held a wide-ranging discussion of international affairs and bilateral relations with Chairman of the State Council Honecker and Chairman of the Council of Ministers Stoph. The East Germans expressed an interest in economic ties and technological exchange with Japan, and Nakasone said that the Japanese government wanted to "also promote non-governmental exchange [in areas such as ammonia plants and semiconductors] by providing assistance to the civilian sector from the sidelines."

In Yugoslavia, he told President of the Federal Executive Council Mikulic that he was prepared to dispatch an economic mission to the country and that he was willing to look into opening technological cooperation as well.

Unlike the USSR, companies in Yugoslavia operated under a system of "socialist self-management" by their workers, and the country pursued a diplomatic policy of non-alignment. It thus occupied an important place strategically.

Nakasone gave a lecture on "contributing to peace and disarmament" at the University of Belgrade. Its central argument was that "scientific and technological information and developments always disseminate across borders and cause the world to change." According to Prime Minister's Secretary Fukuda Hiroshi, "The manner in which Eastern Europe would later detach itself from the Soviet Union was just as the prime minister had outlined in his lecture."

First Secretary Jaruzelski, who Nakasone met with in Poland, was close to Gorbachev. Taking cues from Gorbachev's speech in Vladivostok, he thus told Jaruzelski that "the Soviet Union has an interest in the Asia-Pacific, and I approve of them wanting to co-exist with their neighbors."

The aforementioned speech had been given by Gorbachev in Vladivostok on July 28 of the previous year. It was a comprehensive address on Asia and, in addition to discussing the Soviet withdrawal from Afghanistan and mending Sino-Soviet relations, it included mention of achieving a breakthrough in relations with Japan. Nakasone was attempting to use Jaruzelski as a "backchannel to Gorbachev" to encourage him to visit Japan.[69]

American Sanctions on Japan

After returning home, Nakasone received French Foreign Minister Raimon at the prime minister's office on March 9 and exchanged views with him on Soviet global strategy and the importation of French goods into Japan.

Trade frictions between Japan and the United States had continued to worsen, and on April 17, the Reagan administration placed sanctions on Japanese semiconductors – the first sanctions to be placed on Japan since the end of the Second World War. The measure placed a 100% retaliatory tariff on Japanese-made computers, color televisions, and electronics. The "Ron-Yasu" relationship may have been a positive one, but it was not enough to prevent the frictions between the two countries.

On April 14, Nakasone denied before the House of Representatives' Budget Committee that any "secret agreements on nuclear weapons" had been made during the 1960 revision of the US-Japan security treaty. He visited Reagan in early May. Nakasone attempted to show him that Japan was expanding its demand for foreign goods by explaining, for example, that American construction companies would take part in the building of the new Kansai International Airport, but more time would be needed for the sanctions to be lifted.

Nakasone also said regarding SDI that "I believe that Japanese participation strengthens the US-Japan security framework and Western solidarity, and that the basic concept is compatible with the position of a peaceful state. We are thus continuing to negotiate the framework for our participation in its research plan."

At the G7 summit held in Venice from June 8 to 10, Nakasone argued for solidarity on nuclear policy and joined with the other leaders in releasing a statement calling for a quick resolution to the Iran-Iraq War and guarantees of safe passage through the Persian Gulf. From the 11th to the 13th, he became the first Japanese prime minister to make an official visit to Spain.[70]

Persistence in Tax Reform

With the end of his presidential term fast approaching, Nakasone decided to make a final, zealous push at achieving tax reform. I would like to wind back the clock back a bit first before discussing developments in 1987, however.

In 1985 or 1986, Nakasone had begun examining the necessity of tax reforms like revising the ratio of direct and indirect taxation and correcting preferential tax systems like the non-tax plan for small savings (Maru-yū).

Fundamental reform of the tax system should have been the culmination of the administrative and fiscal reforms that he had championed as the "final settlement of postwar politics." This had been stymied by his own campaign promises, however. During the electoral campaign for the July 1986 joint elections, he had pledged not to introduce any large-scale indirect taxes. He had even gone so far as to demand when challenged on this point, "Does this look like the face of a liar?"

After the election, he had appointed Yamanaka Sadanori, a member of his faction, as chairman of the LDP's Research Commission on the Tax System. Despite his campaign promise, once the bills privatizing JNR were passed on November 28, Nakasone began working in earnest to find a way to introduce a new indirect tax. The government's Tax Commission had released a report supporting reducing the highest tax bracket for income and residential taxes and using the abolition of Maru-yū and the introduction of new indirect taxes to pay for this.

206 *1,806 Days as Prime Minister*

Working in line with Nakasone's desires, Yamanaka put together a plan that introduced an indirect tax and abolished Maru-yū. This was released on November 5. When the LDP's Subcommittee on Taxes pressed him on whether his plan violated the party's campaign pledge, Yamanaka lowered his head and said, "I think [the prime minister] lied. I cannot deny that this plan goes against our campaign promises."

When asked about this exchange by the press, Nakasone responded that "I have done absolutely nothing that violates my campaign promises. I had him set up the plan to provide benefits for those with home loans and educational expenses. It thus does not provide preferential treatment for the well off. I haven't lied. Yamanaka was only expressing his personal views." This view was not shared by much of the public, however, and support for his government fell.

The tax reform plan created by Nakasone and Yamanaka reduced the highest income tax bracket from 75% to 50% and lowered the current base corporate tax rate from 43.3% to 37.5%. However, it also introduced a 5% sales tax. In an attempt to parry the criticism that he was violating his campaign promise, forty categories of goods were exempted from the new tax, including food, medicine, education, and homes.

The plan naturally came under heavy attack from the opposition parties, who claimed that Nakasone had broken his promise. But there was also heavy resistance from within the LDP, including from some members of his own faction like Fukaya Takashi.[71]

Scrapping the Sales Tax

Despite the opposition, Nakasone still introduced bills for the sales tax and reforming the tax code to the House of Representatives on February 4, 1987. Special exemptions were established in the sales tax bill for small and medium-sized businesses and those with low incomes. The tax reform bill lowered income and corporate tax rates and abolished Maru-yū.

On February 10, Nakasone gave a forty-minute-long speech at the LDP National Meeting for the Promotion of Tax Reform in defense of his plan:

> The creation of new taxes is something that makes our entire body have an allergic reaction, as if blood from somewhere else was being forced into our body. The tax reforms being introduced now are intended to correct distortions in the tax code and establish a foundation that would allow Japanese business to succeed against their overseas competitors. [...]
> The historic fate of having to stand against the trends of the times is something that politicians must bear. Examples of such men include Komura Jutarō, who signed the Treaty of Portsmouth, ending the Russo-Japanese War, [...] Prime Minister Yoshida Shigeru, who reached a separate peace with the United States following the Second World

War, and Prime Minister Kishi Nobusuke who revised the US-Japan Security Treaty.

What happens to me personally is of no importance; it is the nation and the public that matter. This is the mindset with which I am approaching this issue, so please let me do this. I am staking my life on this and will take all political responsibility.

As Nakasone spoke of his "historic fate," his government's approval rating had plunged to just 24%, and disapproval had risen to 56%. He told Inaba, a member of his faction, that it was "inevitable that my popularity would go down."

As if to symbolize this new state of things, when a House of Councillors by-election was held on March 8, the Socialist candidate won easily, receiving more than twice the votes of his LDP opponent. Nakasone may have been determined to see his sales tax bill through, but the rest of the party was not. The LDP's Diet members stonewalled his efforts, and the bill was scrapped on May 27. The withdrawal of the bill caused support for his government to increase, despite it having little time remaining.

The tax reform bill passed on September 19, abolishing Maru-yū and lowering the highest income tax rate. While Nakasone's attempt at introducing a sales tax had ended in failure, it should be seen as helping smooth the way for the enactment of a consumption tax the following year. Nakasone also emphasized tax reform in selecting his successor as party president, as he believed that, due to his long time serving as finance minister, it would most likely "be Takeshita who would be able to bring the government and opposition parties together and sneak [a tax] in."[72]

Nakasone's Final Trip Overseas

Immediately after the tax reform bill was passed by the Diet on September 19, 1987, Nakasone departed from Haneda to attend a meeting of the UN General Assembly in New York. Two days later, he addressed the UN on peacekeeping and combating inequality.

That same day, Nakasone told UN Secretary-General de Cuellar that "I would like to look into carrying out appropriate financial assistance" for the UN monitoring mission that would be established following the reaching of a ceasefire in the Iran-Iraq War. He also said that he had "ordered a study on contributing about $20 million to the financial authorities" for the UN's peacekeeping force in Lebanon. When de Cuellar responded that he "didn't know how to thank him," Nakasone said that "the United Nations is a central pillar of our foreign policy."

Nakasone met with Reagan in New York, and the two men discussed expanding domestic demand, participation by US companies in the construction of Kansai International Airport, and the next-generation support fighter known as the FS-X. Nakasone sought to have the sanctions on

208 *1,806 Days as Prime Minister*

Japanese semiconductors lifted and said that he was looking into finding a way to have Japan contribute to safe passage in the Persian Gulf.

Reagan praised him, saying, "You have often played a decisive role in promoting US-Japan cooperation and Western solidarity. Mr. Prime Minister, you have changed, in a historic way, how the world sees Japan."

Nakasone also gave his thanks, saying, "I would like to thank you from the bottom of my heart for five years of friendship and cooperation. It is thanks to your friendship and guidance that our nation has gradually become able to carry out a global role."

Nakasone and Reagan had met twelve times, and the "Ron-Yasu" relationship had marked an era.

According to Fujii Hiroaki, director of the foreign ministry's North America Bureau and a frequent companion on Nakasone's trips to America, the final meeting between Nakasone and Reagan was an emotional one. He also believed that Nakasone was one of the few Japanese politicians to have had a voice in international politics.

Nakasone's last foreign trip as prime minister was to Thailand, from September 25 to 28. He attended a ceremony marking the centenary of Japanese-Thai relations and met with King Bhumibol and Prime Minister Prem. Nakasone and Prem spent several hours discussing peace in Cambodia.

Nakasone gave a lecture on Thai-Japanese relations at Chulalongkorn University entitled "Asia in a New Century – Towards an Era of Vigor and Harmony" and accepted an honorary doctorate in political science.[73]

The Secret of Diplomacy

Nakasone visited foreign countries twenty-two times while in office, a record that would stand for more than a decade until Koizumi Jun'ichirō visited fifty-one. His relationship with Reagan was particularly close. When it came to issuing joint statements, he did not do so in a "standoffish" manner; he considered it important to address the American people from the Rose Garden of the White House. While he made the US-Japan alliance the center of his foreign policy, he also made efforts toward Europe, East Asia, Southeast Asia, South Asia, and Oceania.[74]

While there were issues along the way like trade frictions and his visit to Yasukuni, and he made many problematic statements, Nakasone was the rare Japanese politician able to establish good relations not only with the leader of the US but with those of South Korea and China as well. Nakasone strengthened the US-Japan alliance while responding to pressure from the United States on the military and economic fronts. And by deepening cooperation with China and South Korea, he was able to advance Japan's strategy toward the Soviet Union advantageously under the strategic environment of the New Cold War.

Making this all the more impressive is the fact that, despite the fact that the Japanese economy soon to reach its zenith, Nakasone was the first

Japanese politician to systematically adopt a global policy. It would not be an overstatement to describe him as having reached the summit of postwar diplomacy.

If that is the case, then what did Nakasone see as being the secret to diplomacy? When Kunihiro Michiko, director of the Cabinet Office on External Affairs, asked him this, Nakasone answered that "from the moment I became prime minister, I took strategic developments into consideration as I acted."

He further argued that he had "made sure the framework with America, South Korea, and China was in place as I made efforts towards world peace and pursued diplomacy with the Soviet Union. To ensure I was on firm ground, every time there was a summit, I exchanged numerous messages with the members of ASEAN and South Korea. When it came to conducting summit diplomacy, I emphasized establishing personal bonds of trust."

The delay of his summit with Gorbachev and his inability to dispatch minesweepers to the Persian Gulf were his greatest foreign policy regrets. He had wanted to authorize such a dispatch but ultimately accepted Chief Cabinet Secretary Gotōda's arguments that a more cautious approach was needed.

On the joint US-Japan development of the FS-X, Nakasone recalled that "from the view of improving the fighter's specs, integrating American technology was a benefit."[75]

The last piece of major party business remaining for Nakasone was to designate the next president. But this went beyond merely naming a successor; it marked a turning point from the factional conflict of the "Sankaku Daifuku Chū" era to a new all-faction mainstream system. I would like to trace the course of that change in the final chapter.

Notes

1　Hara Yoshihisa, ed., *Kishi Nobusuke Shōgenroku* (Tokyo: Chūō Bunko, 2014), 468–71.

2　Gotōda Masaharu, *Seiji to wa Nanika* (Tokyo: Kōdansha, 1988), 18–22. Gotōda Masaharu, *Sasaeru Ugokasu Watashi no Rirekisho* (Tokyo: Nihon Keizai Shimbun, 1991), 108. Gotōda Masaharu, *Jō to Ri* (Tokyo: Kōdansha Plus Alpha Bunko, 2006), 2:46, 56–68. Nakasone Peace Institute, ed., *Nakasone Naikaku-shi Shiryō-hen (zoku)* (Tokyo: Nakasone Peace Institute, 1997), 18–20. Nakasone Yasuhiro, *Jiseiroku* (Tokyo: Shinchōsha, 2004), 146–57. Nakasone Yasuhiro, *Nihon no Sōri-gaku* (Tokyo: PHP Shinsho, 2004), 37–39. Nakasone Yasuhiro, *Sengo Seiji* (Tokyo: Yomiuri Shimbun, 2005), 44–45. Nakasone, *Nakasone Yasuhiro ga Kataru*, 284-85, 292–94. Nakasone Yasuhiro, *Tenchi Ujō – Gojū Nen no Sengo Seiji o Kataru* (Tokyo: Bungei Shunjū, 1996), 346–76. Watanabe Tsuneo, *Ten'un Tenshoku: Sengo Seiji no Rimenshi, Hansei, Kyojingun wo Akasu* (Tokyo: Kobunsha, 1999), 155–58. Satō Akiko, *Ketteiban Watashi no Tanaka Kakuei Nikki* (Tokyo: Shincho Bunko, 2001), 198–99. Watanabe Tsuneo, *Watanabe Tsuneo Kaikoroku*, ed. Mikuriya Takashi, et al. (Tokyo: Chūō Bunko, 2007), 377–78. According to an October 6, 2011 interview with Uji Toshihiko

210 *1,806 Days as Prime Minister*

(a reporter for the Tokyo Shimbun), Suzuki saw Miyazawa Kiichi as a future prime minister and wanted to put him forward as his successor but believed it unlikely that he would be able to gain the necessary support quickly enough. He thus turned to Nakasone in early October. See also: Uji Toshihiko, *Suzuki Seiken – 863 Nichi* (Tokyo: Gyōsei Mondai Kenkyujo, 1983), 362–80.

3 Kanemaru Shin, *Hito wa Shiro, Hito wa Ishigaki, Hito wa Hori* (Tokyo: Yell Books, 1983), 102–03, 168, 174–77. Kanemaru Shin, *Tachiwaza, Newaza* (Tokyo: Nihon Keizai Shimbun, 1988), 133–39. Gotōda, *Jō to Ri*, 2:59–60.

4 See the following endnote.

5 *Asahi Shimbun*, November 27 evening, December 20, 1982. Nakasone Tsutako, "Tsuma-tachi no 'Unmei Kyodōtai' Ron," *Bungei Shunjū* (May 1983), 143. Uji, *Suzuki Seiken* 393–96. Uji Toshihiko, "Seiji Kisha no Teiten Kansoku," *Gyōken* (1995), 316, 380. Hatano Akira, *Gyakkyō ni Katsu – "Ichinichi Shōgai" Waga Jinsei* (Tokyo: Kōdansha, 1988), 314–9. Nakasone Yasuhiro, *Seiji to Jinsei – Nakasone Yasuhiro Kaikoroku* (Tokyo: Kōdansha, 1992), 112, 306–11. Nakasone, *Jiseiroku*, 158–63. Nakasone, *Nihon no Sōri-gaku*, 40. Nakasone Yasuhiro, "Nihon o Ai suru Kōkotsukan," in "Watashi no Gotōda Masaharu" Hensan Iinkai, ed., *Watashi no Gotōda Masaharu* (Tokyo: Kōdansha, 2007), 21–22. Nakasone Yasuhiro, "Sengo Seiji no Sōkessan," *Shinchō 45* (May 2012), 52–53. Nakasone, *Nakasone Yasuhiro ga Kataru*, 23–24, 297–301. Tamura Hajime, *Seijika no Shōtai* (Tokyo: Kōdansha, 1994), 212–15. Fukuda Takeo, *Kaiko 90 Nen* (Tokyo: Iwanami Shoten, 1995), 260–64. Nakasone, *Tenchi Ujō*, 376–414, 422–23. Niigata Nippō Jōdōbu, *Saishō Tanaka Kakuei no Shinjitsu* (Tokyo: Kōdansha, 1994), 98–99. Baba Shūichirō, *Ran wa Yūzan in Ari* (Tokyo: Nishi Nihon Shimbun, 1998), 174–76. Okushima Sadao, *Jimintō Kanjichōshitsu no 30 Nen* (Tokyo: Chūkō Bunko, 2005), 138–39. Okushima Sadao, *Jimintō Kōsō-shi – Kenryōku ni Tsukareta Mōja-tachi* (Tokyo: Chūkō Bunko, 2009), 129–35. Japanese Modern Historical Manuscripts Association, *Tamura Hajime Ōraru Hisutorī*, Vol. 2 (Tokyo: Japanese Modern Historical Manuscripts Association, 2006), 12–13. Watanabe, *Kaikoroku*, 379–80, Oikawa Shōichi, *Seijika no Kyōchū – Nikugoe de Tadoru Seijishi no Genba* (Tokyo: Fujiwara Shoten, 2012), 209. Hayano Tooru, *Tanaka Kakuei* (Tokyo: Chūkō Shinsho, 2012), 356. Asaka Akira, *Tanaka Kakuei – Saigo no Hissho ga Kataru Jō to Chiei no Seijika,* ed. Fukunaga Fumio, et al. (Tokyo: Daiichi Hōki, 2015), 194.

6 Japan Public Relations Association, ed., *Nakasone Naikaku Sōri Daijin Shuyō Enzetsu-shū (Sono Ichi)*, (September 1, 1984), 6112.

7 These were the Cabinet Domestic Policy Analysis Office, the Cabinet Foreign Policy Analysis Office, the Cabinet National Security Office, the Cabinet Intelligence Research Office, and the Cabinet Public Relations Office.

8 Watanabe Tsuneo was vice president and editor-in-chief at the Yomiuri at the time.

9 Shima Keiji, *Shima Keiji Fūunroku – Hōsō to Kenryoku: 40 Nen* (Tokyo: Bungei Shunjū, 1995), 168–73. Nakasone Yasuhiro, "Naikaku Sōri Daijin no Shūren to Chakuganten o Kataru," in Masujima Toshiyuki, Kobayashi Hidetoku, eds., *Shōgen Daikaikaku wa Ika ni nasaretaka – Ishi Kettei no Chakugan* (Tokyo: Gyōsei, 2001), 8, 12–13. Gotōda Masaharu, "Watashi no Rirekisho," in Kishi Nobusuke et al., eds., *Watashi no Rirekisho – Hoshu Seiken no Ninaite* (Tokyo: Nihon Keizai Shimbun, 2007), 317. Nakasone, *Nakasone Yasuhiro ga Kataru*, 496. In a December 24, 1982 press conference, Nakasone proposed conducting the conference standing. Record of Conversation with Nakasone (December 24, 1982), author's collection.

1,806 Days as Prime Minister 211

10 See the following endnote.
11 *Nihon Keizai Shimbun,* January 10, 1983. *Asahi Shimbun,* September 20, 1983. Takemura Ken'ichi, *Nakasone Yasuhiro, Bōei/Kenpō o Kataru* (Tokyo: Iwate Shobō, 1984), 74–75, 83, 86, 155. Yomiuri Shimbun Seijibu, *Sugao no Nakasone Seiken* (Tokyo: Tokuma Shoten, 1985), 81. Nakasone Peace Institute, *Nakasone Naikaku-shi Shiryō-hen,* 82, 87–88, 284. Nakasone, *Tenchi Ujō,* 369. Nakasone, *Rīdā no Jōken,* 244–47. Nakasone, *Nihon no Sōri-gaku,* 172–76. Nakasone, *Nakasone Yasuhiro ga Kataru,* 321–23. Ishibashi Masashi, *Ishibashi Masashi Kaisōroku – "55 Nen Taisei" Uchigawa kara no Shōgen* (Tokyo: Tabata Shoten, 1999), 198–200. Japanese Modern Historical Manuscripts Association, "Matsuno Raizō Ōraru Hisutorī (Tsuiho)," *Kindai Nihonshiryō Kenkyūkai* (2008), 33.
12 Nakasone, *Seiji to Jinsei,* 216.
13 Miki Takeo Shuppan Kinenkai, ed., *Gikai Seiji to tomo ni – Miki Takeo – Enzetsu, Hatsugen-shū* (Tokyo: Miki Takeo Shuppan Kinenkai, 1984), 1:471, 473, 2:308–11.
14 On Ōhira, see also: Hattori Ryūji, *Japan and the Origins of the Asia-Pacific Order: Masayoshi Ohira's Diplomacy and Philosophy,* ed. Graham B. Leonard (Singapore: Springer, 2022).
15 Takemura 226–8. Nakasone, *Seiji to Jinsei,* 312. Nakasone, *Nakasone Yasuhiro ga Kataru,* 305–7. Victor D. Cha, *Beinichikan Hanmoku o Koeta Teikei,* trans. Funabashi Yōichi, Kurata Hideya (Tokyo: Yūhikaku, 2003), 182–83, 190–98. Shinoda Tomohito, *Kantei Gaikō – Seiji Rīdāshippu no Yukue* (Tokyo: Asahi Shimbun, 2004), 129–39. Satō Susumu, "Nihon no Chiiki Kōsō to Ajia Gaikō," in Wada Haruki, ed., *Iwanami Kōza Higashi Ajia Kingendai Tsūshi Dai Kyū Kan Keizai Hatten to Minshu Kakumei 1975–1990* (Tokyo: Iwanami Shoten, 2011), 88–90. According to Hashimoto Hiroshi, director of the foreign ministry's Information and Culture Bureau and the Asian Affairs Bureau during the Suzuki and Nakasone governments, "I believe that Prime Minister Suzuki was someone who just quietly rode his mikoshi, being carried along by his cabinet ministers and high officials. He left determining and putting together policy to his chief cabinet secretary (Miyazawa) and whoever the minister with jurisdiction was. While Prime Minister Nakasone was riding the same LDP mikoshi, he directly issued instructions to those carrying him and I believe he decided the direction he was going to go in himself." Letter from Hashimoto to the author (December 15, 2008).
16 Ministry of Foreign Affairs, ed., *Waga Gaikō no Kinkyō No. 12* (Tokyo: Ministry of Foreign Affairs, 1968), 164.
17 See the following endnote.
18 *Asahi Shimbun,* August 21, 1981, January 12, 1983. Ministry of Foreign Affairs Asian Affairs Bureau Northeast Asia Department, "Nakasone Sōri Daijin Kankoku Hōmon (Kaidan Kiroku)" (January 1983), MOFA 2013-544. Abe Shintarō, *Sōzōteki Gaikō o Mezashite* (Tokyo: Gyōsei Mondai Kenkyūjo, 1984), 126–33. Takeshita Noboru, *Shōgen Hoshu Seiken* (Tokyo: Yomiuri Shimbun, 1991), 134–35. Nakasone Peace Institute, ed., *Nakasone Naikaku-shi Shiryō-hen,* 620–21. Sejima Ryūzō, *Sejima Ryūzō Kaisōroku Ikuyamakawa* (Tokyo: Sankei Shimbun News Service, 1996), 557–68. Kyodō Tsūshin-sha Shakaibu, ed., *Chinmoku no Fairu – "Sejima Ryūzō" to wa Nan datta no ka* (Tokyo: Shinchō Bunko, 1996), 58–61. Nakasone, *Tenchi Ujō,* 389, 392–94. Gotōda, *Jō to Ri,* 2:68–70. Machida Mitsugu, *Nikkan Interijensu Sensō* (Tokyo: Bungei Shunjū, 2011), 288–94. Nakajima Toshijirō, *Gaikō Shōgenroku Nichibei Anpo Okinawa Henkan Ten'anmono Jiken,* ed. Inoue Masaya, Nakashima Takuma, and Hattori Ryūji (Tokyo: Iwanami Shoten,

212 *1,806 Days as Prime Minister*

2012), 180–82. Nakasone, *Nakasone Yasuhiro ga Kataru*, 285, 305–13. Ogura Kazuo, *Hiroku Nikkan Icchō En Shikin* (Tokyo: Kōdansha, 2013), 262–301. Hasegawa Kazutoshi, *Shushō Hishokan ga Kataru Nakasone Gaikō no Butai Ura – Bei-Chū-Kan to no Sōgo Shinrai wa ika ni Kōchiku sareta ka*, ed. Segawa Takao, et al. (Tokyo: Asahi Shimbun, 2014), 126–29. Hattori Ryūji, "Nakasone Yasuhiro Shushō Chon Dufan Daitōryō Kaidanroku – January 1983," *Chūō Daigaku Ronshū*, No. 36 (2015), 51–58. According to then-Asian Affairs Bureau Director Kiuchi Akitane, while the finance ministry had been hesitant about large-scale economic support for South Korea during the Suzuki government, the ministry changed its attitude when Prime Minister Nakasone gave them instructions. Interview with Kiuchi (June 19, 2010). For more on relations with South Korea and China, see Hattori Ryūji, *Gaikō Dokyumento Rekishi Ninshiki* (Tokyo: Iwanami Shinsho, 2015), 39–88. See also: Hattori Ryūji, *Understanding History in Asia: What Diplomatic Documents Reveal*, trans. by Tara Cannon (Tokyo: Japan Publish Industry Foundation for Culture, 2019), 48–97.

19 Ambassador to the United States Ōkawara Yoshio to Foreign Minister Abe Shintarō (January 19, 1983), MOFA 2013-545. *Asahi Shimbun,* January 19, 1983 evening. Kase Toshikazu, *Kase Toshikazu Senshū – Sensō to Heiwa Shirīzu – V. Nihon Gaikō no Kishū* (Tokyo: Yamanote Shobō, 1984), 236. Kase Toshikazu, *Kase Toshikazu Kaisōroku* (Tokyo: Yamanote Shobō, 1984), 2:181. Kase Toshikazu, *Nihon Gaikō o Shikaru* (Tokyo: TBS Buritanika, 1997), 103, 199–203. Gotōda, *Seiji to wa Nani ka*, 143–51. Gotōda, *Sasaeru Ugokasu*, 109. Cornelius K. Iida, "Tsūyaku ga Kiita Nichibei Shunō Kaidan," *Bungei Shunjū* (April 1989), 111–2. Nakasone, *Seiji to Jinsei*, 312–6. Nakasone, *Jiseiroku*, 109–5, 119, 166–9. Nakasone Yasuhiro, *Hoshu no Yuigon* (Tokyo: Kadokawa one Tēma 21, 2010), 148–52. Nakasone, *Nakasone Yasuhiro ga Kataru*, 315–21. Nakasone Peace Institute, ed., *Nakasone Naikaku-shi Shiryō-hen*, 621–23. Nakasone, *Tenchi Ujō*, 430–31, 439–42. Hasegawa Kazutoshi, "'Ron-Yasu Kankei' Tanjō no Ki," *Bungei Shunjū* (August 2004), 83–4. Hasegawa, *Shushō Hishokan ga Kataru*, 129–33. Don Oberdorfer, *Maiku Mansufīrudo* (Tokyo: Kyodō Tsūshin, 2005), 2:300. Ōkawara Yoshio, *Ōraru Hisutorī Nichibei Gaikō* (Tokyo: Japan Times, 2006), 319–20, 349–50. Japanese Modern Historical Manuscripts Association, "Shiota Akira Ōraru Hisutorī," *Kindai Nihon Shiryō Kenkyūkai* (2006), 146. Gotōda, *Jō to Ri*, 2:71–73. Yomiuri Shimbun Morioka Shikyoku, ed., *Shiina Yasuo Kaikoroku – Fuki Fuhon* (Tokyo: Tōshindō, 2006), 317. Douglas Brinkley, ed., *The Reagan Diaries* (New York: HarperCollins, 2007), 1:189–90. Japanese Modern Historical Manuscripts Association, "Kunihiro Michihiko Ōraru Hisutorī," *Seisaku Kenkyū Daigakuin Daigaku* (2008), 2:25–26. Murata Ryōhei, *Murata Ryōhei Kaisōroku – Tatakai ni Yabureshi Kuni ni Tsukaete* (Tokyo: Minerva Shobō, 2008), 1:334. *Yomiuri Shimbun* (September 19, 2009). Satō Ken, *Koshikata Yukusue – Moto Bōei Jikan no Tsurezuregusa* (Tokyo: Hakurosha, 2010), 75. Murata Kōji, *Rēgan* (Tokyo: Chūkō Shinsho, 2011), 219–21. Nakajima 184–88. Orita Masaki, Hattori Ryūji, and Shiratori Jun'ichirō, eds., *Gaikō Shōgenroku Wangan Sensō, Futenma Mondai, Iraku Sensō* (Tokyo: Iwanami Shoten, 2013), 64–66. Kunihiro Michihiko, *Waga Jinsei no Ki* (Self-published, 2015), 1:125–26. *Kaigai Seikei Jōhō* No. 584 (1983), issued by the foreign ministry's Information and Culture Bureau, compares American public opinion polling from January and March 1983 and concludes that "a substantial improvement in Americans' trust in Japan is apparent following the prime minister's visit." According to Ōkawara Yoshio (ambassador to the US from 1980 to 1985), the "Ron-Yasu" relationship was partially due to the

1,806 Days as Prime Minister 213

friendly relationship between Foreign Minister Abe and Secretary of State Schultz. Interview with Ōkawara (November 28, 2012). At the time of this book's original printing in 2015, I attributed the term "unsinkable aircraft carrier" to a liberal translation by an interpreter, but according to "Nakasone Sōri Beikoku Hōmon" [Prime Minister Nakasone's Visit to the United States] 2016-198 (DVD-R H28-1), which was released by the foreign ministry's diplomatic archives in January 2017, Nakasone said the following at a January 18, 1983 breakfast hosted by the Washington Post: "On the defense issue, the first thing we will do is strongly defend the Japanese archipelago like an unsinkable aircraft carrier and make it impossible for Soviet Backfire bombers to arrive."

20 Nagai Yōnosuke, *Gendai to Senryaku* (Tokyo: Bungei Shunjū, 1985), 22–23, 47, 69, 105, 152. Uemura Hideki, *"Sengo" to Anpo no 60-nen* (Tokyo: Nihon Keizai Hyōron-sha, 2013), 77, 217.

21 Uji Toshihiko of the Tokyo Shimbun suggested that a reason that Nakasone was attracted to Katsu was that he was an intellectual who had worked to construct the Shogunate's navy during the Bakumatsu period, but he was also a realist who then went on to become naval minister following the Meiji Restoration. Uji, "Seiji Kisha no Teiten Kansoku," 343–49. Katsu Kaishū, *Hikawa Seiwa*, ed. Etō Jun, Matsuura Rei (Tokyo: Kōdansha Gakujutsu Bunko, 2000), 152.

22 Ambassador to Indonesia Yamazaki Toshio to Foreign Minister Abe Shintarō (May 2, 1983), MOFA 2013-534. Ambasador to Thailan Ogiso Motoo to Gotōda (May 3, 1983), MOFA 2013-534. Ambassador to Singapore Fukada Hiroshi to Gotōda (May 5, 1983), MOFA 2013-534. Ambassador to the Philippines Ōkawa Yoshio to Gotōda (May 8, 1983), MOFA 2013-534. Ambassador to Malaysia Kiuchi Akitane to Gotōda (May 10, 1983), MOFA 2013-534. Kota Kinabalu Consul Kojima Toshihiro to Gotōda (May 10, 1983), MOFA 2013-534. Nakasone, *Tenchi Ujō*, 449–56. Interview with Hashimoto Hiroshi (Asian Affairs Bureau Director) (November 8, 2008). Nakasone, *Nakasone Yasuhiro ga Kataru*, 332–37. The above telegrams do not reveal what the "important information about North Korea" was.

23 Ambassador to the United States Ōkawara Yoshio to Abe (May 27, 1983). "Nakasone Sōri De Kueyaru Kokuren Jimu Sōchō Kaidan," MOFA 2014-1922. "Jonzu Hopukinsu Daigaku Kōtō Kokusai Mondai Kenkyūjo (SAIS) Sotsugyōshiki ni okeru Nakasone Sōri Enzetsu" (May 27, 1983), MOFA 2014-174. Ōkawara to Abe (May 28, 1983), MOFA 2014-174. Ambassador to the UN Kuroda Mizuo to Abe (June 1, 1983), MOFA 2014-174. Ministry of Foreign Affairs United Nations Bureau Political Department, "Nakasone Sōri Peresu De Kueyaru Kokuren Jimu Sōchō Kaidan Gaiyō (Hi Memo)" (June 1, 1983). Nakasone, *Seiji to Jinsei*, 317–18. Nakasone, *Rīdā no Jōken*, 92–93, 101. Nakasone Yasuhiro, *21 Seiki Nihon no Kokka Senryaku* (Tokyo: PHP Kenkyūjo, 2000), 104–05, 255, 260. Nakasone, *Jiseiroku*, 115–23. Nakasone, *Nihon no Sōri-gaku*, 168–71. Nakasone, *Nakasone Yasuhiro ga Kataru*, 337–43. Nakasone Yasuhiro, "Jiyū Sekai Hanei no tame ni Tatakatta Dōshi e," *Bungei Shunjū* (September 2013), 243–45. Margaret Thatcher, *Sacchā Kaikoroku*, trans. Ishizuka Masahiko (Tokyo: Nihon Keizai Shimbun, 1993), 1:374. Nakasone Peace Institute, ed., *Nakasone Naikaku-shi Shiryō-hen*, 625–31. Nakasone, *Tenchi Ujō*, 426–36. National Graduate Institute for Policy Studies COE Oral Policy Research Project, *Motono Moriyuki Ōraru Hisutorī* (Tokyo: GRIPS, 2005), 295–97. Ōkawara 319–20, 351–55. Murata 1:326. On the letters exchanged between Nakasone and Reagan around the time of the Williamsburg Summit, see "Beiso Senryaku Heiki Sakugen Kōshō (START) / Chū Kyori Kaku Senryoku Mondai" MOFA 2014-2424, 2015-229.

214 *1,806 Days as Prime Minister*

According to what Councilor at the Japanese Embassy Hōgen Kensaku later heard from Nakasone, he butted heads with Mitterrand when they left the meeting to take the commemorative photograph. He reportedly told Hōgen, "As prime minister of the country with the second-highest GNP in the world, it was out of the question for me to act subordinate to the others and stand on the fringes. I pushed forward and went to stand next to Ron." Interview with Hōgen (March 15, 2012). See also Hōgen Kensaku, *Moto Kokuren Jimu Jichō Hōgen Kensaku Kaikoroku*, eds. Katō Hiroaki, et al. (Tokyo: Yoshida Shoten, 2015), 107.

24 Niigata Nippō Jōdōbu 99–100.
25 Baba 180.
26 Abe to Ambassador to South Korea Maeda Toshikazu, Draft telegram to Ōkawara (September 1, 1983), "Kobetsu Kōkū Jōken (KAL Jiken)" MOFA 2014-2414. Draft telegram from Abe to Maeda (September 2, 1983), "Kobetsu Kōkū Jōken (KAL Jiken)" MOFA 2014-2414. Ministry of Foreign Affairs United Nations Bureau UN Policy Section, "Daikan Kōkūki Gekitsui Jiken (Anpori Kaisai o Meguru Taikyo-buri to Hyōka)" (September 19, 1983), "Kobetsu Kōkū Jōken (KAL Jiken)" MOFA 2014-2415. Nakasone, *Seiji to Jinsei*, 336–37. Nakasone, *Rīdā no Jōken*, 131–40. Nakasone, *Nakasone Yasuhiro ga Kataru*, 343–46. Nakasone, *Tenchi Ujō*, 456–61. Gotōda, *Seiji to wa Nani ka*, 76–86. Gotōda, *Jō to Ri*, 2:80–85.
27 *Asahi Shimbun*, October 13, 29, 1983. Nakasone, *Tenchi Ujō*, 471–74. Nakasone Peace Institute, ed., *Nakasone Naikaku-shi Shiryō-hen*, 634. Nakasone Peace Institute, ed., *Nakasone Naikaku-shi Shiryō-hen (Zoku)*, 30. Nakasone, *Sengo Seiji*, 51.
28 Satō Akiko 205–07. Hashimoto Gorō, *Sōri no Kiryō – Seiji Kisha ga Mita Rīdā Hiwa* (Tokyo: Chūkō Shinsho Rakure, 2012), 28–29. "Tanaka Kakuei – Nihonjin ni Mottomo Ai sareta Sōri," *Shūkan Gendai* (December 28, 2013).
29 Ministry of Foreign Affairs Eurasian Bureau 1st West Europe Section, "Kōru Doitsu Renpō Kyowakoku Shushō Hōnichi (Shōwa 58-nen 10-gatsu 31-nichi ~ 11-gatsu 4-ka) Shuyō Kaidan-ra Kiroku" (November 1983), "Kōru Seidoku Shushō Fusai Hōnichi (Kōhin)" MOFA 2014-3012. North American Bureau 1st North America Section, "Rēgan Daitōryō no Hōnichi (Hyōka)" (November 12, 1983), "Rēgan Beikoku Daitōryō Fusai Hōnichi (Kokuhin)" MOFA 2015-803. Abe to Ōkawara (November 12, 1983), MOFA 2013-546. China Section, "Nicchū Shunō Kaidan Kiroku (Sono Ichi. Teta Tēto Kaidan)" (November 24), MOFA 2010-171. China Section, "Nicchū Shunō Kaidan Kiroku (Sono Ni Zentai Kaigi)" (November 24), MOFA 2010-171. "Ko Yōhō Chūgoku Kyosantō Chūō Iinkai Sōshoki Hōnichi (Kōhin)" MOFA 2014-593. Nakasone, *Tenchi Ujō*, 465–71. Nakasone, *Sengo Seiji*, 49–51. Nakasone, *Nakasone Yasuhiro ga Kataru*, 347–51. Hattori Ryūji, "Nakasone-Ko Yōhō Kaidan Kiroku – 1983, 84, 86-Nen," *Sōgō Seisaku Kenkyū* No. 19 (2011), 161–203.
30 *Asahi Shimbun*, December 19, 1983 evening. *Yomiuri Shimbun*, December 19, 1983 evening. Nakasone, *Tenchi Ujō*, 475–76. Kabashima Ikuo, *Sengo Seiji no Kiseki* (Tokyo: Iwanami Shoten, 2004), 25–71. *Tōō Nippō* (March 19, 2006). *Tōō Nippō* (March 20, 2006). Gotōda, *Jō to Ri*, 2:92–96. Yamaoka Jun'ichirō, *Genpatsu to Kenryoku* (Tokyo: Chikuma Shinsho, 2011), 167–73. Chūnichi Shinbun Shakai-bu, ed., *Nichibei Dōmei to Genpatsu – Kakusareta Kaku no Sengo-shi* (Tokyo: Chūnichi Shimbun, 2013), 174–75.
31 Tagawa Seiichi, *Tagawa Nikki – Jimintō Ittō Shihai ga Kuzureta Gekidō no Yōkakan* (Tokyo: Goma Shobō, 1984), 18, 48–237. Nakasone, *Tenchi Ujō*, 477–88, 542–44. Baba 182–83, National Graduate Institute for Policy Studies COE Oral Policy Research Project, *Tagawa Seiichi Ōraru Hisutorī* (Tokyo:

1,806 Days as Prime Minister 215

GRIPS, 2001), 2:126–35. Nakasone, *Sengo Seiji*, 52–53. Gotōda, *Jō to Ri*, 2:97–98. Nakasone's coalition with the New Liberal Club would continue during the formation of his later cabinets as well. New Liberal Club, "Nakasone Dainiji Kaizō Naikaku no Hossoku ni Atatte" (December 28, 1985), "Shin Jiyū Kurabu Kankei Bunsho," 6–61, NDL.

32 Hoshi Hiroshi, *Kanbō Chōkan Sokkin no Seijigaku* (Tokyo: Asahi Shimbun, 2014), 58.

33 Baba 187–91.

34 Nakasone Peace Institute, *Nakasone Naikaku-shi Shiryō-hen*, 283–90.

35 Ambassador to China Katori Yoshinori to Abe (March 24, 25, 1984), MOFA 2010-172. "Nakasone-Hake Kaidanroku" (May 1, 1984), MOFA 2014-74. "Nakasone-Ganjī Kaidanroku" (May 4, 1984), MOFA 2014-74. "Nakasone-Zairu Shin Daitōryō Kaidanroku" (May 5, 1984), MOFA 2014-74. Abe to Katori (June 1, 1984), MOFA 2014-77. Ministry of Foreign Affairs, "Shunō Kaigi (6-gatsu 8-ka Gozen)," MOFA 2014-79. Ministry of Foreign Affairs, "Zentai Kaigi (6-gatsu 8-ka Gogo)," MOFA 2014-79. Ministry of Foreign Affairs, "Zentai Kaigi (6-gatsu 9-ka (Nichi) Gogo)," MOFA 2014-79. Ambassador to the UK Hirahara Tsuyoshi to Abe (June 8, 12, 1984), MOFA 2014-79. Ministry of Foreign Affairs, "Rondon Ekonomikku Samitto" (June 20), MOFA 2014-79. *Asahi Shimbun,* March 24, 1984 evening. *Yomiuri Shinbun,* March 24, 1984 evening. *Gaikō Seisho* No. 29 (1985), 402–17, 470–75. Nishiyama Takehiko, *Ōshū no Shinjidai* (Tokyo: Saimaru Shuppankai, 1992), 72. Thatcher 2:65. Hirahara Tsuyoshi, *Eikoku Taishi no Gaikō Jinsei* (Tokyo: Kawade Shobō Shinsha, 1995), 252. Nakasone, *Tenchi Ujō*, 493–501. Seo Seung-won, *Nihon no Keizai Gaikō to Chūgoku* (Tokyo: Keio University, 2004), 118–26. TBS "Jiji Hōdan" Seisaku Sutaffu, ed., *Jiji Hōdan* (Tokyo: Kōdansha, 2004), 1:12, 3:71. Shiroyama Hidemi, *Chūgoku Kyosantō "Tennō Kōsaku" Hiroku* (Tokyo: Bunjū Shinsho, 2009), 62–63. Hattori, "Nakasone-Ko Yōhō Kaidan Kiroku," 177–97. Nakasone, *Nakasone Yasuhiro ga Kataru*, 361–64, 368–70.

36 Ministry of Foreign Affairs, Asian Affairs Bureau, Northeast Asia Section, "Nikkan Shunō Kaidan (9-gatsu 6-ka oyobi 7-ka)" (September 10, 1984), MOFA 2013-543. Gotōda, *Jō to Ri*, 2:115–16. Nakasone, *Nakasone Yasuhiro ga Kataru*, 373–76, Hasegawa, *Shushō Hishokan*, 211–15.

37 Tamura Hajime (Chairman of the LDP Presidential Electoral Management Committee) to Nakasone (October 29, 1984), "Okuno Seisuke Kankei Bunsho Mokuroku" 5–21, NDL. Kishi Nobusuke, Yatsugi Kazuo, and Itō Takashi, *Kishi Nobusuke no Kaisō* (Tokyo: Bungei Shunjū, 2014), 329.

38 Tanaka Rokusuke, *Hoshu Honryū no Chokugen* (Tokyo: Chūō Kōron, 1985), 20–51. Kanemaru Shin, "Seidai Kōtai," in Yomiuri Shimbun Seiji-bu, ed., *Kenryoku no Chūsū ga Kataru Jimintō no 30-Nen* (Tokyo: Yomiuri Shimbun, 1985), 247–51. Kanemaru, *Tachiwaza Newaza*, 140–44. Gotōda, *Seiji to wa Nani ka*, 22–28. Gotōda Masaharu, *Sei to Kan* (Tokyo: Yomiuri Shimbun, 2005), 65–66. Baba 199–201. Suzuki Zenkō, *Hitoshikarazu o Ureeru. Moto Shushō Suzuki Zenkō Kaikoroku*, ed. Azumane Chimao (Iwate: Iwate Nippō, 2004), 140. Watanabe, *Watanabe Tsuneo Kaikoroku*, 395–96. Kitaoka Shin'ichi, *Jimintō – Seikentō no 38-Nen* (Tokyo: Chūō Bunko, 2008), 233, 247–49. Meanwhile, page 331 of Iwate Hōsō, ed., *Moto Sōri Suzuki Zenkō – Gekidō no Nihon Seiji o Kataru Sengo 40-Nen no Kenshō* (Iwate: Iwate Nippō, 1991) argues that "we cannot think that Suzuki was behind the scheme to back Nikkaidō. It seems more likely that it was a drama written by Nikkaidō himself."

39 *Asahi Shimbun,* July 16, 27, 1985. Nakasone, *Tenchi Ujō*, 549–50. Yamagishi Ippei, *Shōwa Kōki 10-Nin no Shushō – Nikkei no Seiji Kisha ga Mokugeki shita "Habatsu no Jidai"* (Tokyo: Nihon Keizai Shimbun, 2008), 203.

216 *1,806 Days as Prime Minister*

40 Honolulu Consul-General Nakamura Yasumi to Abe (January 4–5, 1985), MOFA 2014-59. NHK Shuzai-han, *NHK Supesharu Sengo 50-Nen Sono Toki Nihon wa Dairokkan Puraza Gōi/Ajia ga Mitsumeta "Kiseki no Ōkoku"* (Tokyo: Nihon Hōsō Shuppan Kyōkai, 1996), 21–41, 67, 71, 95–96, 102–03, 137–71. Nakasone, *Sengo Seiji*, 55–57. Gotōda, *Jō to Ri*, 2:221–23. Yamagishi 202–03. Gyōten Toyoo, *En no Kōbō – "Tsūka Mafia" no Dokuhaku* (Tokyo: Asahi Shimbun, 2013), 57, 75, 80, 89, 112, 116–17. Yonezawa Jun'ichi, *Kokusai Bōchō no Sengo-shi – 1947–2013 Genba kara no Shōgen* (Tokyo: Kinyū Zaisei Jijō Kenkyūkai, 2013), 115. Nakagawa's works include *Taikenteki Kinyū Seisaku Ron* (Tokyo: Nihon Keizai Shimbun, 1981), and *Nihon no Kaikaku – 21 Seiki e no Bijon* (Tokyo: Nihon Keizai Shimbun, 1990).

41 Ministry of Foreign Affairs, "Sōri no Taiyōshū Hōmon (Nichi-Fijī Shunō Kaidan Gaiyō)" (January 15, 1985) MOFA 2013-537. Ministry of Foreign Affairs, "Sōri no Taiyōshū Hōmon (Nichi-PNG Shunō Kaidan Gaiyō)" (January 15, 1985), MOFA 2013-537. Sydney Consul-General Tanaka Yoshitomo to Abe (January 16, 1985), MOFA 2013-537. Melbourne Consul-General Hayakawa Teruo to Abe (January 18, 1985), MOFA 2013-537. Auckland Consul-General Tomihari Chūichirō to Abe (January 20, 1985), MOFA 2013-537. Ōba Mie, *Ajia Taiheiyō Chiiki Keisei e no Michinori – Kyōkai Kokka Nichigō no Aidentiti Mosaku to Chiikishugi* (Tokyo: Minerva Shobo, 2004), 311–12. Nakasone, *Nakasone Yasuhiro ga Kataru*, 396–97. Hasegawa, *Shushō Hishokan ga Kataru*, 248–50.

42 Ambassador to the USSR Katori Yasue to Abe (March 15, 1985), MOFA 2014-192. Nakasone, *Tenchi Ujō*, 550-54. Nakasone, *Rīdā no Jōken*, 112–14. Nakasone, *Jiseiroku,* 139–43. Nakasone, *Nakasone ga Kataru*, 392–s96. Wakatsuki Hidekazu, *Taikoku Nihon no Seiji Shidō 1972–1989* (Tokyo: Yoshikawa Kōbunkan, 2012), 207–09.

43 "Nakasone-Kōru Kaidan Roku" (April 30, 1985), MOFA 2014-160. Ambassador to West Germany Miyazaki Hiromichi to Abe (May 2–3, 1985), MOFA 2014-160. Nakasone Peace Institute, ed., *Nakasone Naikaku-shi Shiryō-hen*, 645. Nakasone, *Tenchi Ujō*, 554–56. Nakasone, *Rīdā no Jōken*, 106–08. Nakasone, *Jiseiroku*, 123–24. Nakasone, *Nakasone Yasuhiro ga Kataru*, 399–403.

44 1st West Europe Section, "Sōri Hōfu (Fabiusu Shushō to no Kaidan)" (July 13, 1985, July 14, 1985), MOFA 2013-536. 1st West Europe Section, "Sōri Hōfu (Mitteran Daitōryō to no Kaidan)" (July 14, 1985), MOFA 2013-536. Ambassador to France Motono Moriyuki to Abe (July 15, 1985), MOFA 2013-536. Ambassador to Italy Nishida Seiya to Abe (July 17, 1985), MOFA 2013-536. 1st West Europe Section, "Sōri Hōi (Kurakushi Shushō to no Kaidan)" (July 17, 1985), MOFA 2013-536. Ambassador to the Vatican Nakamura Teruhiko to Abe (July 17, 1985), MOFA 2013-536. Representative of the Japanese Government to the European Union Kagami Hideo to Abe (July 20, 1985), MOFA 2013-536. Ambassador to Belgium Yamamoto Shizuhiko to Abe (July 20, 1985), MOFA 2013-536.

45 See the following endnote.

46 *Asahi Shimbun,* August 16, 1985. Nakasone Yasuhiro, *Nakasone Yasuhiro Kushū* (Tokyo: Kadokawa Shoten, 1985), 49. Nakasone Yasuhiro, "Watashi ga Yasukuni Jinja Kōushiki Sanpai o Dannen shita Riyū," *Seiron* (September 2001), 100–11. Yomiuri Shimbun Seiji-bu, ed., *Sugao no Nakasone Seiken*, 85–90. Yokoyama Hiroaki, *Nicchū no Shōheki* (Tokyo: Saimaru Shuppankai, 1994), 30–44. Nakasone, *Tenchi Ujō*, 489–93. Hashimoto Shigeru, *Seiji to Chinkon – Ningen Fujinami Takao* (Tokyo: Shinsen-sha, 2001), 175–84. *Asahi Shimbun,* August 11, 2005 evening. Gotōda, *Jō to Ri*, 2:112–14. Hata Ikuhiko, *Yasukuni Jinja no Saijin-tachi* (Tokyo: Shinchō-sha, 2010), 201, 252–54.

1,806 Days as Prime Minister 217

47 Ambassador to the UN Kuroda Mizuo to Abe (October 23, 1985, October 24, 1985, October 25, 1985), MOFA 2010-305. "Kokusai Rengō Sōsetsu 40 Shūnen Kinen Kaiki ni okeru Nakasono Naikaku Sōri Daijin Enzetsu" (October 23, 1985), MOFA 2010-305. Nakasone, *Nakasone Yasuhiro Kushū*, 189. Nakasone, *Rīdā no Jōken*, 96, 171. Nakasone Yasuhiro, *Nakasone Yasuhiro Kushū 2008* (Tokyo: Hokumei-sha, 2008), 19. Nakasone, *Nakasone Yasuhiro ga Kataru*, 422–27. Nakasone, *Tenchi Ujō*, 560–61. Nakasone Peace Institute, ed., *Nakasone Naikaku-shi Shiryō-hen (Zoku)*, 41–46. Gifu Shimbun, ed., *Shisei Ikkan – Mutō Kabun Hanseiki* (Gifu: Gifu Shimbun, 2008), 156–59. Sun Pinghua, Takeyoshi Jirō, *Nicchū Yūkō Zuisōroku – Son Heika ga Kiroku suru Nicchū Kankei* (Tokyo: Nihon Keizai Shimbun, 2012), 1:81–82, 119–20. "Address by His Excellency Mr. Yasuhiro Nakasone, Prime Minister of Japan, at the Commemorative Session of the 40th Anniversary of the United Nations (October 23, 1985),"https://www.mofa.go.jp/policy/other/bluebook/1986/1986-appendix. htm (Accessed March 15, 2022).
48 Gotōda, *Jō to Ri*, 2:151.
49 Nakasone, *Tenchi Ujō*, 564.
50 Toronto Consul-General Oka Teru to Abe (January 13, 1986), MOFA 2013-547. "Sōri no Kanada Renpō Gikai Supīchi" (January 13, 1986), MOFA 2013-547. "Address by Nakasone before the Parliament of Canada, January 13" (January 13, 1986), MOFA 2013-547. Ambassador to Canada Kikuchi Kiyoaki to Abe (January 14, 1986), MOFA 2013-547. Ministry of Foreign Affairs, North American Bureau, 1st North America Section, "Nikka Shunō Kaidan no Gaiyō" (January 14, 1986), MOFA 2013-547. Japanese Modern Historical Manuscripts Association, *Kunihiro Michihiko Ōraru Hisutorī*, 2:71. "Address by His Excellency Mr. Yasuhiro Nakasone, Prime Minister of Japan, before the Parliament of Canada (January 13, 1986)," https://www.mofa.go.jp/policy/ other/bluebook/1986/1986-appendix.htm (Accessed March 15, 2022).
51 Abe to Katori (January 18, 1986 draft), MOFA 2013-551. Sino-Japanese Joint Communique (January 19, 1986), MOFA 2013-551. Ministry of Foreign Affairs, Eurasia Bureau, Soviet Union Section, "Shevarunazze Soren Gaishō no Hōnichi no Zenpanteki Hyōka (Tsuke: Shevarunazze Gaishō Jishin ni tsuite no Kizuki no Shoten)" (January 21, 1986), MOFA 2013-551.
52 Ronald Reagan to Yasuhiro Nakasone (February 6, 1986), MOFA 2014-494. Ministry of Foreign Affairs, United Nations Bureau Disarmament Section, "Beiso Gunbi Kanri Kōshō no Genjō ni tsuite – INF Kyōtei Shōmei ni tai suru Hyōka to Kongo no Yosō sareru Ugoki," MOFA 2014-494. Iokibe Makoto, Itō Motoshige, Yakushiji Katsuyuki, eds., *Okamoto Yukio Genbashugi o Tsuranuita Gaikōkan* (Tokyo: Asahi Shimbun, 2008), 136–49, 333. Segawa Takao, "Reisen Makki no Nichibei Dōmei Kyōryoku to Kaku Gunshuku," *Kokusai Seiji* No. 163 (2011), 85–87. Nakasone, *Nakasone Yasuhiro ga Kataru*, 453–55.
53 Ambassador to the US Matsunaga Nobuo to Abe (April 14, 1986), MOFA 2013-548. Glen S. Fukushima, *Nichibei Keizai Masatsu no Seijigaku*, trans. Watanabe Satoshi (Tokyo: Asahi Shimbun, 1992), 120–21. Nakasone, *Nakasone Yasuhiro ga Kataru*, 439, 455–56. Orita 78–79.
54 Nakagawa Yukitsugu, "Makuro Keizai Seisaku," in Nakasone Peace Institute, ed., *Nakasone Naikaku-shi Rinen to Seisaku*, 646–49. NHK Shuzai-han, *NHK Supesharu Sengo 50 Nen Sono Toki Nihon wa Daigokan Sekiyū Shokku Gen'ei ni obieta 69 Kakan Kokutetsu Rōshi Funsō Suto-ken Dakkan Suto no Shōgeki* (Tokyo: Nihon Hōsō Shuppan Kyōkai, 1996), 164. Shimomura Taichi, *Tanaka Kakuei to Jimintō Seiji – Rettō Kaizō e no Michi* (Tokyo: Yūshisha, 2011), 208–09. Nakasone, *Nakasone Yasuhiro ga Kataru*, 435–37.

218   *1,806 Days as Prime Minister*

55   Nakasone, *Tenchi Ujō*, 561–63. Japanese Modern Historical Manuscripts Association, "Kunihiro Michihiko Ōraru Hisutorī," 2:72–74. Nakasone, *Nakasone Yasuhiro ga Kataru*, 439–40.

56   National Graduate Institute for Policy Studies COE Oral Policy Research Project, *Yanagiya Kensuke (Moto Gaimu Jimu Jikan) Ōraru Hisutorī* (Tokyo: GRIPS, 2004), 2:96. *Asahi Shimbun* (July 20, 2011).

57   See the following endnote.

58   Mitsuzaka Hiroshi, *Kokutetsu o Saiken suru Hōhō wa Kore shika nai* (Tokyo: Seifu Kōhō Sentā, 1984). *Asahi Shimbun,* June 22, 26, 1985, March 14, 1986 evening. Nakasone Yasuhiro, "Suisen no Kotoba" in Satō Megumi, *Tsūshin wa Jidai o Tsukuru – Kyori to Jikan o Koete* (Tokyo: Bijinesu-sha, 1985), 314. Nakasone, *Jiseiroku*, 170–85. Nakasone, *Nihon no Sōri-gaku*, 41–43. Nakasone, *Sengo Seiji*, 53–55. Nakasone, *Hoshu no Yuigon*, 138–42. Katō Mutsuki, *Zeisei Kaikaku – Katsuryoku o Motomete* (Tokyo: Tōyō Keizai Shinpō, 1986), 287–88. Yamashita Tokuo, *Kizuke Yume Rettō* (Tokyo: Ajia Shuppan-sha, 1987), 1–3, 69–74. Kanemaru, *Tachiwaza Newaza,* 150–51. Shintō Hisashi, *Naratte Oboete Mane shite Suteru* (Tokyo: NTT, 1988), 128–30. Sekiguchi Shigeru, *Mitsuzaka Hiroshi Zenjinzō* (Tokyo: Gyōken Shuppankyoku, 1992), 254–302. Nakasone Peace Institute, ed., *Nakasone Naikaku-shi Shiryō-hen*, 653–54. Yamagishi Akira, *Ware Kakutō Eri* (Tokyo: Asahi Shimbun, 1995), 158–81. Nakasone, *Tenchi Ujō*, 504–18. Kusano Atsushi, *Kokutetsu Kaitai – JR wa Gyōsei Kaikaku no Tehon to naru no ka?* (Tokyo: Kōdansha Bunko, 1997). Kasai Yoshiyuki, *Mikan no "Kokutetsu Kaikaku"* (Tokyo: Tōyō Keizai Shinpō, 2001), 229–60, 327, 343. Nisugi Iwao, *Chōsen – Kokutetsu to Konkurīto to Tomo ni 60 Nen* (Tokyo: Kōtsū Shinbun, 2003), 173–97. Japanese Modern Historical Manuscripts Association, "Hosoda Kichizō Ōraru Hisutorī" (Tokyo: Japanese Modern Historical Manuscripts Association, 2006), 2:37–38, 47–53. The LDP's Communications Policy Division had the sixth highest number of Diet members and the NTT Basic Issues Research Commission the twelfth. Satō Seizaburō, Matsuzaki Tetsuhisa, *Jimintō Seiken* (Tokyo: Chūkō Kōron-sha, 1986), 256–57. Inoguchi Takashi, Iwai Tomoaki, *"Zoku Giin" no Kenkyū* (Tokyo: Nihon Keizai Shimbun, 1987), 133. Taguchi Masaki, *Nihon no Taibei Bōeki Kōshō* (Tokyo: University of Tokyo, 1997), 83.

59   Nakasone Peace Institute, ed., *Nakasone Naikaku-shi Shushō no 1806 Nichi* (Tokyo: Nakasone Peace Institute, 1996), 942.

60   Nakasone, *Tenchi Ujō*, 564. Nakasone, *Sengo Seiji*, 58–59.

61   Baba 226–27.

62   *Nihon Keizai Shimbun,* August 13, 1986.

63   Nakasone Yasuhiro, "Shin Jidai o Kizuku Jimintō no Shimei – 1986-nen Taisei no Sutāto," *Gekkan Jiyū Minshu* (October 1986), 38–51. Hirose Michisada, *Hojokin to Seikentō* (Tokyo: Asahi Bunko, 1993), 278–79. Nakasone Peace Institute, ed., *Nakasone Naikaku-shi Shiryō-hen*, 411–27. Tagawa Seiichi, *Yareba Dekiru Yase Gaman no Michi* (Tokyo: Gyōken, 1995), 229–80. Nakasone, *Tenchi Ujō*, 548–49, 563–67.

64   Ambassador to South Korea Mikanagi Kiyona to Foreign Minister Kuranari Tadashi (September 21, 1986), MOFA 2013-542. Tōgō Kazuhiko, *Rekishi to Gaikō – Yasukuni-Ajia-Tōkyō Saiban* (Tokyo: Kōdansha Gendai Shinsho, 2008), 120. Hattori Ryūji, "Fujio Bunshō Hatsugen – Gaimushō Kiroku kara," *Chūō Daigaku Seisaku Bunka Sōgō Kenkyūjo Nenpō* No. 14 (2011), 61–80.

65   *Yomiuri Shimbun,* September 24, 1986 evening. Nakasone Peace Institute, ed., *Nakasone Naikaku-shi Shiryō-hen*, 435. Fukushima 143. National Graduate Institute for Policy Studies COE Oral Policy Research Project, *Saitō Akira*

1,806 Days as Prime Minister 219

Ōraru Hisutorī (Tokyo: GRIPS, 2005), 98. Japanese Modern Historical Manuscripts Association. "Kunihiro Michihiko Ōraru Hisutorī," 2:91. George R. Packard, *Raishawā no Shōwa-shi*, trans. Moriyama Naomi (Tokyo: Kōdansha, 2009), 334–35. Orita 80.

66 China Section, "Nakasone Sōri Hōchū no Gaiyō (Sono Ichi) (Ko Yōhō Sōshoki to no Kaidan)" (November 8, 1986), MOFA 2010-173. Hattori, "Nakasone-Ko Yōhō Kaidan Kiroku," 198.

67 Takeshita 142–44. Fukushima 290. Kurihara Yūkō, *Shōgen Honne no Seiji – Sengo Seiji no Urabutai* (Tokyo: Naigai Shuppan, 2007), 148–63. Gifu Shimbun, 153–55. Nakasone, *Nakasone Yasuhiro ga Kataru*, 418–20, 458–59.

68 Kimura Hiroshi, *Tooi Rinkoku – Roshia to Nihon* (Tokyo: Sekai Shisō-sha, 2002), 428–33.

69 *Asahi Shimbun*, January 12, 1987 evening. Ambassador to Finland Takahashi Shōtarō to Kuranari (January 13, 1987), MOFA 2013-535. Ambassador to East Germany Kimura Keizō to Kuranari (January 13, 1987), MOFA 2013-535. Ambassador to Yugoslavia Ōtsuka Hirohiko to Kuranari (January 15, 1987), MOFA 2013-535, Ambassador to Poland Matsubara Susumu to Kuranari (January 15, 1987) (January 16, 1987) (January 17, 1987), MOFA 2013-535. Anchorage Consul-General Arimatsu Seiji to Kuranari (January 17, 1987) (January 18, 1987), MOFA 2013-535. Nakasone, *Tenchi Ujō*, 569–71. Nakasone, *Rīdā no Jōken*, 68–69. Nakasone, *Nakasone Yasuhiro ga Kataru*, 459–64. Koike Masayuki, *Odoru Nihon Taishikan* (Tokyo: Kōdansha, 2000), 114–24, 138–43.

70 1st West Europe Section, "Dainijūkai Nichifutsu Gaishō Teiki Kyōgi (Kaidan Gaiyō) (Shōwa 62-nen 3-gatsu 8-ka, 9-ka)" (March 1987), MOFA 2014-498. Diet Proceedings Search System, http://kokkai.ndl.go.jp/ (accessed October 6, 2014). Matsunaga to Kuranari (April 30, 1987) (May 2, 1987), MOFA 2013-549. Ambassador to Italy Nishida Seiya to Kuranari (June 8, 1987) (June 9, 1987), MOFA 2014-178. 1st West Europe Section, "Nichidoku Shunō Kaidan Gaiyō" (June 9, 1987), MOFA 2014-178. Kuranari to Matsunaga, etc. (June 13, 1987), MOFA 2014-178. Ambassador to Spain Edamura Junrō to Kuranari (June 13, 1987) MOFA 2014-178. Acting Foreign Minister Gotōda, "Dajūsankai Shuyōkoku Shunōkaigi, Nakasone Sōri Daijin no Supein Hōmon ni tsuite" (June 16, 1987 Cabinet Meeting), MOFA 2014-178. Kuranari Tadashi, *"Ayausa" no Naka no Nihon Gaikō* (Tokyo: Shōgakkan, 1988), 164–65, 196–98, 216–20. Nakayama Masaaki, *Ashita o Kiku* (Tokyo: NTT, 1988), 229–30. Kuroda Makoto, *Nichibei Kankei no Kangaekata* (Tokyo: Yuhikaku, 1989), 11-12. Kusano Atsushi, *Amerika Gikai to Nichibei Kankei* (Tokyo: Chūō Kōron-sha, 1991), 61. Nakao Eiichi, *Sekai to tomo ni Sekai no tame ni* (Tokyo: Livre-sha, 1992), 358. Fukushima 75–77, 178. Nakasone Peace Institute, ed., *Nakasone Naikaku-shi Shiryō-hen*, 655–57. Nakasone, *Tenchi Ujō*, 581–84. Nakasone, *21 Seiki Nihon no Kokka Senryaku*, 256–57. Nakasone, *Nakasone Yasuhiro ga Kataru*, 180, 471–81, 555. Ōyane Satoshi, *Nichibeikan Handōtai Masatsu – Tsūshō Kōshō no Seiji Keizai-gaku* (Tokyo: Yūshindō Kōbun-sha, 2002), 168. Japanese Modern Historical Manuscripts Association, "Kunihiro Michihiko Ōraru Hisutorī," 2:95–96. Tamura Ryōhei, *Tamura Ryōhei Kaisōroku*, 1:378–81. Tanaka Hitoshi, *Gaikō no Chikara* (Tokyo: Nihon Keizai Shimbun, 2009), 27–28. Hatano Sumio, *Rekishi to shite no Nichibei Jōyaku – Kimitsu Gaikō Kiroku ga Akasu "Mitsuyaku" no Kyojitsu* (Tokyo: Iwanami Shoten, 2010), 182. Murakami Masakuni, *Dakara Seijika wa Kirawareru* (Tokyo: Shōgakkan, 2014), 85–86.

71 See the following endnote.

220   *1,806 Days as Prime Minister*

72 Inaba Osamu, *Kōsei Osoru Beshi* (Tokyo: Tokyo Shimbun, 1988), 164. Nakasone Yasuhiro, *Atarashii Seiki e Mukatte – Nakasone Naikaku Sōri Daijin Enzetsu-shū* (Tokyo: Nakasone Yasuhiro Jimusho, 1988), 473–92. Nakasone, *Jiseiroku*, 192–95. Nakasone, *Nihon no Sōri-gaku*, 191–95. Nakasone, *Sengo Seiji*, 58–61. Nakasone, *Seizan Jōunpo*, 209–10. Nakasone, *Tenchi Ujō*, 533–37. Nakasone Peace Institute, ed., *Nakasone Naikaku-shi Hibi no Chōsen* (Tokyo: Nakasone Peace Institute, 1996), 817–46. Nakasone Peace Institute, *Nakasone Naikaku-shi Shushō no 1806 Nichi*, 2:1274, 1400. Katō Junko, *Zeisei Kaikaku to Kanryōsei* (Tokyo: University of Tokyo, 1997), 172–206. Fukaya Takashi, *Akarui Nihon o Tsukuru* (Tokyo: Kadokawa Gakugei Shuppan, 2008), 70–72. Wakamiya Yoshibumi, *Shinbun Kisha* (Tokyo: Chikuma Purimā Shinsho, 2013), 144–45.

73 Ambassador to Thailand Kiuchi Akitane to Kuranari (September 26, 1987) (September 27, 1987), MOFA 2014-503.

74 Suzuki Kenji, *Rekidai Sōri, Sokkin no Kokuhaku – Nichibei "Kiki" no Kenshō* (Tokyo: Asahi Shimbun, 1991), 185. *Asahi Shimbun,* September 20, 2006. Nakasone made four foreign visits as prime minister in 1983, three in 1984, six in 1985, four in 1986, and five in 1987 for a total of twenty-two. Nakasone, *Nakasone Yasuhiro ga Kataru*, 619–27.

75 Nakasone Yasuhiro, *My Political Philosophy: Reshaping Japanese Politics* (Tokyo: Liberal Democratic Party, 1987), 74–75. Nakasone Yasuhiro, "Minzokushugi to Kokusaishugi no Chōwa o," *Gekkan Jiyū Minshu* (October 1987), 54–55. Nakasone, *Nakasone Yasuhiro ga Kataru,* 481–85. Gotōda, *Sasaeru Ugokasu*, 111–12, 165–66. Gotōda, *Jō to Ri*, 2:224–26. Nakasone, *Tenchi Ujō*, 589–90. Iokibe, 133–34. Japanese Modern Historical Manuscripts Association, Kunihiro Michihiko, 2:100. Murata Ryōhei, *Murata Ryōhei Kaisōroku – Sokoku no Saisei o Jisedai ni Takushite* (Tokyo: Minerva Shobō, 2008), 2:22–24, 31. Katō Hiroaki, "Reisen-ka Jieitai Kaigai Haken no Zasetsu," *Senryaku Kenkyū* No. 10 (2011), 109–28. Katō Hiroaki, "Nashonarizumu to Jieitai – 1987-nen/1991-nen no Sōkaitei Haken Mondai o Chūshin ni," *Kokusai Seiji* No. 170 (2012), 33–38.

References

Abe Shintarō. *Sōzōteki Gaikō o Mezashite.* Tokyo: Gyōsei Mondai Kenkyūjo, 1984.

Asaka Akira. *Tanaka Kakuei – Saigo no Hissho ga Kataru Jō to Chiei no Seijika.* Edited by Fukunaga Fumio, Hattori Ryūji, Amamiya Shōichi, and Wakatsuki Hidekazu. Tokyo: Daiichi Hōki, 2015.

Baba Shūichirō. *Ran wa Yūzan in Ari – Moto Jimintō Fukusōsai Nikaidō Susumu Kikigaki.* Fukuoka: Nishi Nihon Shimbun, 1998.

Brinkley Douglas, ed. *The Reagan Diaries.* New York: HarperCollins, 2007.

Cha Victor D. *Beinichikan Hanmoku o Koeta Teikei.* Translated by Funabashi Yōichi and Kurata Hideya. Tokyo: Yūhikaku, 2003.

Chūnichi Shinbun Shakai-bu, ed. *Nichibei Dōmei to Genpatsu – Kakusareta Kaku no Sengo-shi.* Tokyo: Chūnichi Shimbun, 2013.

Fukaya Takashi. *Akarui Nihon o Tsukuru.* Tokyo: Kadokawa Gakugei Shuppan, 2008.

Fukushima Glen S. *Nichibei Keizai Masatsu no Seijigaku.* Translated by Watanabe Satoshi. Tokyo: Asahi Shimbun, 1992.

Gifu Shimbun, ed. *Shisei Ikkan – Mutō Kabun Hanseiki.* Gifu: Gifu Shimbun, 2008.

1,806 Days as Prime Minister 221

Gotōda Masaharu. *Jō to Ri – Kamisori Gotōda Kaikoroku.* Edited by Mikuriya Takashi. Tokyo: Kōdansha Plus Alpha Bunko, 2006.

Gotōda Masaharu. *Sasaeru Ugokasu Watashi no Rirekisho.* Tokyo: Nihon Keizai Shimbun, 1991.

Gotōda Masaharu. *Sei to Kan.* Tokyo: Yomiuri Shimbun, 2005.

Gotōda Masaharu. *Seiji to wa Nanika.* Tokyo: Kōdansha, 1988.

Gyōten Toyoo. *En no Kōbō – "Tsūka Mafia" no Dokuhaku.* Tokyo: Asahi Shimbun, 2013.

Hara Yoshihisa, ed. *Kishi Nobusuke Shōgenroku.* Tokyo: Chūō Bunko, 2014.

Hasegawa Kazutoshi. "'Ron-Yasu Kankei' Tanjō no Ki." *Bungei Shunjū* (August 2004).

Hasegawa Kazutoshi. *Shushō Hishokan ga Kataru Nakasone Gaikō no Butai Ura – Bei-Chū-Kan to no Sōgo Shinrai wa ika ni Kōchiku sareta ka.* Edited by Segawa Takao, et. al. Tokyo: Asahi Shimbun, 2014.

Hashimoto Gorō. *Sōri no Kiryō – Seiji Kisha ga Mita Rīdā Hiwa.* Tokyo: Chūkō Shinsho Rakure, 2012.

Hashimoto Shigeru. *Seiji to Chinkon – Ningen Fujinami Takao.* Tokyo: Shinsen-sha, 2001.

Hata Ikuhiko. *Yasukuni Jinja no Saijin-tachi.* Tokyo: Shinchō-sha, 2010.

Hatano Akira. *Gyakkyō ni Katsu – "Ichinichi Shōgai" Waga Jinsei.* Tokyo: Kōdansha, 1988.

Hatano Sumio. *Rekishi to shite no Nichibei Jōyaku – Kimitsu Gaikō Kiroku ga Akasu "Mitsuyaku" no Kyojitsu.* Tokyo: Iwanami Shoten, 2010.

Hattori Ryūji. "Fujio Bunshō Hatsugen – Gaimushō Kiroku kara." *Chūō Daigaku Seisaku Bunka Sōgō Kenkyūjo Nenpō,* No. 14 (2011), 61–80.

Hattori Ryūji. "Nakasone Yasuhiro Shushō Chon Dufan Daitōryō Kaidanroku – January 1983." *Chūō Daigaku Ronshū,* No. 36 (2015).

Hattori Ryūji. "Nakasone-Ko Yōhō Kaidan Kiroku – 1983, 84, 86-Nen." *Sōgō Seisaku Kenkyū,* No. 19 (2011).

Hayano Tooru. *Tanaka Kakuei.* Tokyo: Chūkō Shinsho, 2012.

Hirahara Tsuyoshi. *Eikoku Taishi no Gaikō Jinsei.* Tokyo: Kawade Shobō Shinsha, 1995.

Hirose Michisada. *Hojokin to Seikentō.* Tokyo: Asahi Bunko, 1993.

Hōgen Kensaku. *Moto Kokuren Jimu Jichō Hōgen Kensaku Kaikoroku.* Edited by Katō Hiroaki, et. al. Tokyo: Yoshida Shoten, 2015.

Hoshi Hiroshi. *Kanbō Chōkan Sokkin no Seijigaku.* Tokyo. Asahi Shimbun, 2014.

Iida Cornelius K. "Tsūyaku ga Kiita Nichibei Shunō Kaidan." *Bungei Shunjū* (April 1989).

Inaba Osamu. *Kōsei Osoru Beshi.* Tokyo: Tokyo Shimbun, 1988.

Iokibe Makoto, Itō Motoshige, and Yakushiji Katsuyuki, eds. *Okamoto Yukio Genbashugi o Tsuranuita Gaikōkan.* Tokyo: Asahi Shimbun, 2008.

Inoguchi Takashi, and Iwai Tomoaki. *"Zoku Giin" no Kenkyū.* Tokyo: Nihon Keizai Shimbun, 1987.

Ishibashi Masashi. *Ishibashi Masashi Kaisōroku – "55 Nen Taisei" Uchigawa kara no Shōgen.* Tokyo: Tabata Shoten, 1999.

Japan Public Relations Association, ed. *Nakasone Naikaku Sōri Daijin Shuyō Enzetsu-shū (Sono Ichi)* (September 1, 1984).

Japanese Modern Historical Manuscripts Association. *Hosoda Kichizō Ōraru Hisutorī.* Tokyo: Japanese Modern Historical Manuscripts Association, 2006.

Japanese Modern Historical Manuscripts Association. *Kunihiro Michihiko Ōraru Hisutorī.* Tokyo: Seisaku Kenkyū Daigakuin Daigaku (2008).

222   1,806 Days as Prime Minister

Japanese Modern Historical Manuscripts Association. *Matsuno Raizō Ōraru Hisutorī (Tsuiho)*. Tokyo: Japanese Modern Historical Manuscripts Association, 2008.

Japanese Modern Historical Manuscripts Association. *Shiota Akira Ōraru Hisutorī*. Tokyo: Japanese Modern Historical Manuscripts Association, 2006.

Japanese Modern Historical Manuscripts Association. *Tamura Hajime Ōraru Hisutorī*, Vol. 2. Tokyo: Japanese Modern Historical Manuscripts Association, 2006.

Kabashima Ikuo. *Sengo Seiji no Kiseki*. Tokyo: Iwanami Shoten, 2004.

Kanemaru Shin. *Hito wa Shiro, Hito wa Ishigaki, Hito wa Hori*. Tokyo: Yell Books, 1983.

Kanemaru Shin. "Seidai Kōtai." Yomiuri Shimbun Seiji-bu, ed. *Kenryoku no Chūsū ga Kataru Jimintō no 30-Nen*. Tokyo: Yomiuri Shimbun, 1985.

Kanemaru Shin. *Tachiwaza Newaza*. Tokyo: Nihon Keizai Shimbun, 1988.

Kasai Yoshiyuki. *Kokutetsu Kaikaku no Shinjitsu – "Kyūtei Kakumei" to "Keimō Undō."* Tokyo: Chūō Kōron Shinsha, 2007.

Kase Toshikazu. *Kase Toshikazu Kaisōroku*. Tokyo: Yamanote Shobō, 1984.

Kase Toshikazu. *Kase Toshikazu Senshū – Sensō to Heiwa Shirīzu – V. Nihon Gaikō no Kishū*. Tokyo: Yamanote Shobō, 1984.

Kase Toshikazu. *Nihon Gaikō o Shikaru*. Tokyo: TBS Buritanika, 1997.

Katō Hiroaki. "Nashonarizumu to Jieitai – 1987-nen/1991-nen no Sōkaitei Haken Mondai o Chūshin ni." *Kokusai Seiji* No. 170 (2012), 30–45.

Katō Hiroaki. "Reisen-ka Jieitai Kaigai Haken no Zasetsu." *Senryaku Kenkyū* No. 10 (2011), 109–28.

Katō Junko. *Zeisei Kaikaku to Kanryōsei*. Tokyo: University of Tokyo, 1997.

Katō Mutsuki. *Zeisei Kaikaku – Katsuryoku o Motomete*. Tokyo: Tōyō Keizai Shinpō, 1986.

Kimura Hiroshi. *Tooi Rinkoku – Roshia to Nihon*. Tokyo: Sekai Shisō-sha, 2002.

Kishi Nobusuke, Kōno Ichirō, Fukuda Takeo, Gotōda Masaharu, Tanaka Kakuei, and Nakasone Yasuhiro. *Watashi no Rirekisho: Hoshuseiken no Ninaite*. Tokyo: Nihon Keizai Shimbun, 2007.

Kishi Nobusuke, Yatsugi Kazuo, and Itō Takashi. *Kishi Nobusuke no Kaisō*. Tokyo: Bungei Shunjū, 2014.

Kitaoka Shin'ichi. *Jimintō – Seikentō no 38-Nen*. Tokyo: Chūkō Bunko, 2008.

Koike Masayuki. *Odoru Nihon Taishikan*. Tokyo: Kōdansha, 2000.

Kuranari Tadashi. *"Ayausa" no Naka no Nihon Gaikō*. Tokyo: Shōgakkan, 1988.

Kurihara Yūkō. *Shōgen, Honne no Seiji – Sengo Seiji no Butaiura*. Tokyo: Nagai Shuppan, 2007.

Kuroda Makoto. *Nichibei Kankei no Kangaekata*. Tokyo: Yuhikaku, 1989.

Kusano Atsushi. *Amerika Gikai to Nichibei Kankei*. Tokyo: Chūō Kōron-sha, 1991.

Kusano Atsushi. *Kokutetsu Kaitai – JR wa Gyōsei Kaikaku no Tehon to naru no ka?* Tokyo: Kōdansha Bunko, 1997.

Kyodō Tsūshin-sha Shakaibu, ed. *Chinmoku no Fairu – "Sejima Ryūzō" to wa Nan datta no ka*. Tokyo: Shinchō Bunko, 1996.

Machida Mitsugu. *Nikkan Interijensu Sensō*. Tokyo: Bungei Shunjū, 2011.

Miki Takeo Shuppan Kinenkai, ed. *Gikai Seiji to tomo ni – Miki Takeo – Enzetsu, Hatsugen-shū*. Tokyo: Miki Takeo Shuppan Kinenkai, 1984.

Mitsuzaka Hiroshi. *Kokutetsu o Saiken suru Hōhō wa Kore shika nai*. Tokyo: Seifu Kōhō Sentā, 1984.

1,806 Days as Prime Minister 223

Murakami Masakuni. *Dakara Seijika wa Kirawareru*. Tokyo: Shōgakkan, 2014.

Murata Kōji. *Rēgan*. Tokyo: Chūkō Shinsho, 2011.

Murata Ryōhei. *Murata Ryōhei Kaisōroku – Sokoku no Saisei o Jisedai ni Takushite*. Tokyo: Minerva Shobō, 2008.

Murata Ryōhei. *Murata Ryōhei Kaisōroku – Tatakai ni Yabureshi Kuni ni Tsukaete*. Tokyo: Minerva Shobō, 2008.

Nagai Yōnosuke. *Gendai to Senryaku*. Tokyo: Bungei Shunjū, 1985.

Nakajima Toshijirō. *Gaikō Shōgenroku Nichibei Anpo Okinawa Henkan Ten'anmono Jiken*. Edited by Inoue Masaya, Nakashima Takuma, and Hattori Ryūji. Tokyo: Iwanami Shoten, 2012.

Nakao Eiichi. *Sekai to tomo ni Sekai no tame ni*. Tokyo: Livre-sha, 1992.

Nakasone Peace Institute, ed. *Nakasone Naikaku-shi Hibi no Chōsen*. Tokyo: Nakasone Peace Institute, 1996.

Nakasone Peace Institute, ed. *Nakasone Naikaku-shi Rinen to Seisaku*. Tokyo: Nakasone Peace Institute, 1995.

Nakasone Peace Institute, ed. *Nakasone Naikaku-shi Shiryō-hen*. Tokyo: Nakasone Peace Institute, 1995.

Nakasone Peace Institute, ed. *Nakasone Naikaku-shi Shiryō-hen (zoku)*. Tokyo: Nakasone Peace Institute, 1997.

Nakasone Peace Institute, ed. *Nakasone Naikaku-shi Shushō no 1806 Nichi*. Tokyo: Nakasone Peace Institute, 1996.

Nakasone Tsutako. "Tsuma-tachi no 'Unmei Kyodōtai' Ron." *Bungei Shunjū* (May 1983).

Nakasone Yasuhiro. *Atarashii Seiki e Mukatte – Nakasone Naikaku Sōri Daijin Enzetsu-shū*. Tokyo: Nakasone Yasuhiro Jimusho, 1988.

Nakasone Yasuhiro. *Hoshu no Yuigon*. Tokyo: Kadokawa one Tēma 21, 2010.

Nakasone Yasuhiro. *Jiseiroku – Rekishi Hōtei no Hikoku to shite*. Tokyo: Shinchōsha, 2004.

Nakasone Yasuhiro. "Jiyū Sekai Hanei no tame ni Tatakatta Dōshi e." *Bungei Shunjū* (September 2013).

Nakasone Yasuhiro. *My Political Philosophy: Reshaping Japanese Politics*. Tokyo: Liberal Democratic Party, 1987.

Nakasone Yasuhiro. "Naikaku Sōri Daijin no Shūren to Chakuganten o Kataru." Masujima Toshiyuki, Kobayashi Hidetoku, eds. *Shōgen Daikaikaku wa Ika ni nasaretaka – Ishi Kettei no Chakugan*. Tokyo: Gyōsei, 2001.

Nakasone Yasuhiro. *Nakasone Yasuhiro ga Kataru Sengo Nihon Gaikō*. Edited by Nakashima Takuma, Hattori Ryūji, Noboru Amiko, Wakatsuki Hidekazu, Michishita Narushige, Kusunoki Ayako, Segawa Takao. Tokyo: Shinchōsha, 2012.

Nakasone Yasuhiro. *Nakasone Yasuhiro Kushū*. Tokyo: Kadokawa Shoten, 1985.

Nakasone Yasuhiro. *Nakasone Yasuhiro Kushū 2008*. Tokyo: Hokumei-sha, 2008.

Nakasone Yasuhiro. *Nihon no Sōri-gaku*. Tokyo: PHP Shinsho, 2004.

Nakasone Yasuhiro. *Seiji to Jinsei – Nakasone Yasuhiro Kaikoroku*. Tokyo: Kōdansha, 1992.

Nakasone Yasuhiro. *Sengo Seiji*. Tokyo: Yomiuri Shimbun, 2005.

Nakasone Yasuhiro. "Sengo Seiji no Sōkessan." *Shinchō 45* (May 2012), 52–53.

Nakasone Yasuhiro. "Shin Jidai o Kizuku Jimintō no Shimei – 1986-nen Taisei no Sutāto." *Gekkan Jiyū Minshu* (October 1986).

224　*1,806 Days as Prime Minister*

Nakasone Yasuhiro. "Suisen no Kotoba." Satō Megumi. *Tsūshin wa Jidai o Tsukuru – Kyori to Jikan o Koete.* Tokyo: Bijinesu-sha, 1985, 3–4.
Nakasone Yasuhiro, Itō Takashi, and Satō Seiburō. *Tenchi Ujō – Gojū Nen no Sengo Seiji o Kataru.* Tokyo: Bungei Shunjū, 1996.
Nakayama Masaaki. *Ashita o Kiku.* Tokyo: NTT, 1988.
National Graduate Institute for Policy Studies COE Oral Policy Research Project. *Motono Moriyuki Ōraru Hisutorī.* Tokyo: GRIPS, 2005.
National Graduate Institute for Policy Studies COE Oral Policy Research Project. *Saitō Akira Ōraru Hisutorī.* Tokyo: GRIPS, 2005.
National Graduate Institute for Policy Studies COE Oral Policy Research Project. *Tagawa Seiichi Ōraru Hisutorī.* Tokyo: GRIPS, 2001.
National Graduate Institute for Policy Studies COE Oral Policy Research Project. *Yanagiya Kensuke (Moto Gaimu Jimu Jikan) Ōraru Hisutorī.* Tokyo: GRIPS, 2004.
NHK Shuzai-han. *NHK Supesharu Sengo 50 Nen Sono Toki Nihon wa Dai Gokan Sekiyu Shokku Gen'ei ni obieta 69 Kakan Kokutetsu Rōshi Funsō Suto-ken Dakkan Suto no Shōgeki.* Tokyo: Nihon Hōsō Shuppan Kyōkai, 1996.
NHK Shuzai-han. *NHK Supesharu Sengo 50-Nen Sono Toki Nihon wa Dai Rokkan Puraza Gōi/Ajia ga Mitsumeta "Kiseki no Ōkoku."* Tokyo: Nihon Hōsō Shuppan Kyōkai, 1996.
Niigata Nippō Hōdōbu. *Saishō Tanaka Kakuei no Shinjitsu.* Tokyo: Kōdansha, 1994.
Nishiyama Takehiko. *Ōshū no Shinjidai.* Tokyo: Saimaru Shuppankai, 1992.
Nisugi Iwao. *Chōsen – Kokutetsu to Konkurīto to Tomo ni 60 Nen.* Tokyo: Kōtsū Shinbun, 2003.
Ōba Mie. *Ajia Taiheiyō Chiiki Keisei e no Michinori – Kyōkai Kokka Nichigō no Aidentiti Mosaku to Chiikishugi.* Tokyo: Minerva Shobo, 2004.
Oberdorfer Don. *Maiku Mansufīrudo.* Tokyo: Kyodō Tsūshin, 2005.
Ogura Kazuo. *Hiroku Nikkan Icchō En Shikin.* Tokyo: Kōdansha, 2013.
Oikawa Shōichi. *Seijika no Kyōchū – Nikugoe de Tadoru Seijishi no Genba.* Tokyo: Fujiwara Shoten, 2012.
Ōkawara Yoshio. *Ōraru Hisutorī Nichibei Gaikō.* Tokyo: Japan Times, 2006.
Okushima Sadao. *Jimintō Kanjichōshitsu no 30 Nen.* Tokyo: Chūkō Bunko, 2005.
Okushima Sadao. *Jimintō Kōsō-shi – Kenryōku ni Tsukareta Mōja-tachi.* Tokyo: Chūkō Bunko, 2009.
Orita Masaki. *Gaikō Shōgenroku Wangan Sensō, Futenma Mondai, Iraku Sensō.* Edited by Hattori Ryūji and Shiratori Jun'ichirō. Tokyo: Iwanami Shoten, 2013.
Ōyane Satoshi. *Nichibeikan Handōtai Masatsu – Tsūshō Kōshō no Seiji Keizai-gaku.* Tokyo: Yūshindō Kōbun-sha, 2002.
Packard George R. *Raishawā no Shōwa-shi.* Translated by Moriyama Naomi. Tokyo: Kōdansha, 2009.
Satō Akiko. *Ketteiban Watashi no Tanaka Kakuei Nikki.* Tokyo: Shincho Bunko, 2001.
Satō Ken. *Koshikata Yukusue – Moto Bōei Jikan no Tsurezuregusa.* Tokyo: Hakurosha, 2010.
Satō Seizaburō, and Matsuzaki, Tetsuhisa. *Jimintō Seiken.* Tokyo: Chūō Kōron-sha, 1986.
Satō Susumu. "Nihon no Chiiki Kōsō to Ajia Gaikō." Wada Haruki, ed. *Iwanami Kōza Higashi Ajia Kingendai Tsūshi Dai Kyū Kan Keizai Hatten to Minshu Kakumei 1975–1990.* Tokyo: Iwanami Shoten, 2011.

1,806 Days as Prime Minister 225

Segawa Takao. "Reisen Makki no Nichibei Dōmei Kyōryoku to Kaku Gunshuku." *Kokusai Seiji*, No. 163 (2011).

Sejima Ryūzō. *Sejima Ryūzō Kaisōroku Ikuyamakawa*. Tokyo: Sankei Shimbun News Service, 1996.

Sekiguchi Shigeru. *Mitsuzaka Hiroshi Zenjinzō*. Tokyo: Gyōken Shuppankyoku, 1992.

Seo Seung-won. *Nihon no Keizai Gaikō to Chūgoku*. Tokyo: Keio University, 2004.

Shima Keiji. *Shima Keiji Fūunroku – Hōsō to Kenryoku: 40 Nen*. Tokyo: Bungei Shunjū, 1995.

Shimomura Taichi. *Tanaka Kakuei to Jimintō Seiji – Rettō Kaizō e no Michi*. Tokyo: Yūshisha, 2011.

Shinoda Tomohito. *Kantei Gaikō – Seiji Rīdāshippu no Yukue*. Tokyo: Asahi Shimbun, 2004.

Shintō Hisashi. *Naratte Oboete Mane shite Suteru*. Tokyo: NTT, 1988.

Shiroyama Hidemi. *Chūgoku Kyosantō "Tennō Kōsaku" Hiroku*. Tokyo: Bunjū Shinsho, 2009.

Sun Pinghua, and Takeyoshi Jirō. *Nicchū Yūkō Zuisōroku – Son Heika ga Kiroku suru Nicchū Kankei*. Tokyo: Nihon Keizai Shimbun, 2012.

Suzuki Kenji. *Rekidai Sōri, Sokkin no Kokuhaku – Nichibei "Kiki" no Kenshō*. Tokyo: Asahi Shimbun, 1991.

Suzuki Zenkō. *Hitoshikarazu o Ureeru. Moto Shushō Suzuki Zenkō Kaikoroku*. Edited by Azumane Chimao. Iwate: Iwate Nippō, 2004.

Tagawa Seiichi. *Tagawa Nikki – Jimintō Ittō Shihai ga Kuzureta Gekidō no Yōkakan*. Tokyo: Goma Shobō, 1984.

Tagawa Seiichi. *Yareba Dekiru Yase Gaman no Michi*. Tokyo: Gyōken, 1995.

Taguchi Masaki. *Nihon no Taibei Bōeki Kōshō*. Tokyo: University of Tokyo, 1997.

Takemura Ken'ichi. *Nakasone Yasuhiro, Bōei/Kenpō o Kataru*. Tokyo: Iwate Shobō, 1984.

Takeshita Noboru. *Shōgen Hoshu Seiken*. Tokyo: Yomiuri Shimbun, 1991.

Tamura Hajime, *Seijika no Shōtai*. Tokyo: Kōdansha, 1994.

Tanaka Hitoshi. *Gaikō no Chikara*. Tokyo: Nihon Keizai Shimbun, 2009.

"Tanaka Kakuei – Nihonjin ni Mottomo Ai sareta Sōri." *Shūkan Gendai* (December 28, 2013).

Tanaka Rokusuke. *Hoshu Honryū no Chokugen*. Tokyo: Chūō Kōron, 1985.

TBS "Jiji Hōdan" Seisaku Sutaffu, ed. *Jiji Hōdan*. Tokyo: Kōdansha, 2004.

Thatcher Margaret. *Sacchā Kaikoroku*. Translated by Ishizuka Masahiko. Tokyo: Nihon Keizai Shimbun, 1993.

Tōgō Kazuhiko. *Rekishi to Gaikō – Yasukuni-Ajia-Tōkyō Saiban*. Tokyo: Kōdansha Gendai Shinsho, 2008.

Uemura Hideki. *"Sengo" to Anpo no 60-nen*. Tokyo: Nihon Keizai Hyōron-sha, 2013.

Uji Toshihiko. "Seiji Kisha no Teiten Kansoku." *Gyōken* (1995).

Wakamiya Yoshibumi. *Shinbun Kisha*. Tokyo: Chikuma Purimā Shinsho, 2013.

Wakatsuki Hidekazu. *Taikoku Nihon no Seiji Shidō 1972–1989*. Tokyo: Yoshikawa Kōbunkan, 2012.

Watanabe Tsuneo. *Ten'un Tenshoku: Sengo Seiji no Rimenshi, Hansei, Kyojingun o Akasu*. Tokyo: Kōbunsha, 1999.

Watanabe Tsuneo. *Watanabe Tsuneo Kaikoroku*. Edited by Mikuriya Takashi, Itō Takashi, and Iio Jun. Tokyo: Chūō Bunko, 2007.

226 *1,806 Days as Prime Minister*

"Watashi no Gotōda Masaharu" Hensan Iinkai, ed. *Watashi no Gotōda Masaharu.* Tokyo: Kōdansha, 2007.

Yamagishi Akira. *Ware Kakutō Eri.* Tokyo: Asahi Shimbun, 1995.

Yamagishi Ippei. *Shōwa Kōki 10-Nin no Shushō – Nikkei no Seiji Kisha ga Mokugeki shita "Habatsu no Jidai."* Tokyo: Nihon Keizai Shimbun, 2008.

Yamaoka Jun'ichirō. *Genpatsu to Kenryoku.* Tokyo: Chikuma Shinsho, 2011.

Yamashita Tokuo. *Kizuke Yume Rettō.* Tokyo: Ajia Shuppan-sha, 1987.

Yokoyama Hiroaki. *Nicchū no Shōheki.* Tokyo: Saimaru Shuppankai, 1994.

Yomiuri Shimbun Morioka Shikyoku, ed. *Shiina Yasuo Kaikoroku – Fuki Fuhon.* Tokyo: Tōshindō, 2006.

Yomiuri Shimbun Seijibu. *Sugao no Nakasone Seiken.* Tokyo: Tokuma Shoten, 1985.

Yonezawa Jun'ichi. *Kokusai Bōchō no Sengo-shi – 1947–2013 Genba kara no Shōgen.* Tokyo: Kinyū Zaisei Jijō Kenkyūkai, 2013.

10 "Rain of Cicada Cries"

The 32 Years after Being Prime Minister

Naming President Takeshita

The candidates to succeed Nakasone had been reduced to General Council Chairman Abe, Secretary-General Takeshita, and Finance Minister Miyazawa. These three new leaders – collectively referred to as "Anchikugū" or "Anchikumiya" – did not share the same mentality of the Sankaku Daifuku Chū and were fed up with factional conflict in the party. Notably, Abe and Takeshita – the inheritors of the factions that had fought the Kakufuku War – were close enough that they called each other by friendly nicknames ("Take-chan" and "Abe-chin").

After the LDP presidential election was announced on October 8, 1987, the three men repeatedly tried to work things out between themselves but were ultimately unsuccessful. At that point, they approached Nakasone and left the decision up to him. According to Nakasone, it was Miyazawa who first suggested having him choose. "I think that he didn't want to be pitted against Abe and Takeshita."

Nakasone went with Takeshita. After naming him his successor on October 20, he told Abe and Miyazawa that he "strongly hoped that they would give Takeshita their full support." Abe served as secretary-general during the Takeshita government, and Miyazawa as deputy prime minister and finance minister. Watanabe Michio of the Nakasone faction became PRC chairman.

In making his decision, Nakasone prioritized party stability and facilitating the introduction of an indirect tax. The Takeshita faction was the largest in the party, and he believed that Takeshita would be able to maintain his good relationship with Abe.

Looking back on the tax issue, Nakasone explained that "Miyazawa wasn't the best at getting legislation enacted, and Abe was neither particularly detail-oriented nor familiar with the tax code. Takeshita was the best choice for getting an indirect tax passed as he was skilled at working things out with the opposition and had served as finance minister for quite a while."[1]

The fall of kingmaker Tanaka Kakuei and the collapse of his long-standing system of control dramatically changed how presidential successors were

DOI: 10.4324/9781003351931-11

228 *"Rain of Cicada Cries"*

chosen. Nakasone's tenure marked the final phase of the factional conflict that characterized the Sankaku Daifuku Chū era. The selection of Takeshita was the germination of the all-faction mainstream system (*sōshuryū-ha taisei*) under Takeshita, Abe, and Miyazaki.

A consensus had also been reached between the government and opposition over the building of a welfare society, and outside of certain acute areas like defense, the constitution, education, and taxation, conflict between the two sides became less intense.[2]

Regrets and Pride

Nakasone stepped down on November 6. While his government's approval rating had fallen earlier, it had recovered with the withdrawal of his sales tax bill. But while he had successfully privatized the three major public corporations and achieved major foreign policy accomplishments, he still had regrets concerning a number of tasks that remained unresolved.

In particular, education reform remained only partially addressed. A key focus of Nakasone's concerns in this area was the Fundamental Law of Education, which had been enacted alongside the constitution during the Occupation.

Nakasone felt that "The concept of the individual is front and center in all aspects [of the law]. There is no sense of community, history, or tradition. And that means that the historical, traditional, and cultural backgrounds that our people have developed are completely absent. They are not written into the law." "All aspects of education are shrouded in universal equality."

He thus established the Provisional Council on Education with former Kyoto University president Okamoto Michio as chairman to address the topic. However, the Ministry of Education had its own council – the Central Council for Education – and, supported by the education *zoku*, resisted reform. Nakasone was also concerned that attempting to revise the Fundamental Law of Education would antagonize the opposition and impede his efforts to reform JNR. His inability to enact educational reform would be, alongside the lack of progress made on constitutional revision, his greatest regret toward his time as prime minister. The Fundamental Law of Education would not be revised until 2006.[3]

One of the characteristics of Nakasone's times in office was his "presidential prime minister" methodology that made heavy use of private advisory councils.

At the time of his resignation, he said of being a "presidential prime minister" that "I believe that it was obviously the correct approach to take, in the sense that it allowed me to make reforms in a way that abandoned the self-righteousness of government, took into account the will of the people, and was open to criticism. [...] I was probably the first [prime minister] of the postwar period to experiment with something like it. I feel that, moving forward, the ruling party will be unable to be successful without making use of it."

One can feel Nakasone's pride in these words and gain a sense of his high morale leaving office. He said, "The postwar period is surely an era that saw the construction of some of the greatest monuments of Japanese history. And such an excellent era has few parallels in world history."

Nakasone's "presidential prime minister" approach also served as the origin of the modern, Kantei-led style of Japanese politics.[4]

"Rain of Cicada Cries"

Immediately after stepping down, Nakasone happily attended a party hosted by newspaper reporters in appreciation of his services. He composed a poem to describe how he was feeling and distributed it on colored slips of paper:

Kurete nao	Even as it grows dark
Inochi no kagiri	for as long as I live
Semi shigure	rain of cicada cries

He was fond of this poem as he felt that it clearly expressed his intention to remain involved in politics. He would also later use it as the title of a book compiling discussions he had with the commentator Takemura Ken'ichi.[5]

Nakasone became less intense after leaving office. Prior to becoming prime minister, he had always been busy working out policies and thinking things out while in his office. People had had to be careful to not carelessly talk to him and interrupt him. And he became even busier as prime minister. He asked those around him to speak clearly and directly; if a secretary tried to soften their words by prefacing them with "so, the truth of the matter is ..." or the like, he would cut them off and say, "Please get directly to the point. I don't need that kind of preface." But he reportedly became warmer and more relaxed after stepping down.[6]

The establishment of the International Research Center for Japanese Studies in Kyoto can be considered one legacy of Nakasone's government. This would become an international center for the study of Japan, and he had directed its creation toward the end of his government.

The International Institute for Global Peace (IIGP) was created in June 1988 with the cooperation of Prime Minister Takeshita, and Nakasone became its first chairman. The institute is located in the heart of Tokyo and conducts activities such as joint research on post-Cold War strategy.[7]

The Recruit Scandal

As Nakasone was founding the IIGP, the Japanese political world and media were heavily focused on the Recruit scandal, a bribery scandal involving the Japanese human resources company Recruit. It had been discovered that the company had provided unlisted shares in its subsidiary Recruit Cosmos to politicians and government officials, shares that were certain to increase

230 *"Rain of Cicada Cries"*

in value once Cosmos went public. And it had happened while Nakasone was prime minister.

The scandal came to light during the Takeshita government, but the opposition alleged it had been caused by "the Nakasone government's policy of loosening regulations on the private sector." Nakasone was believed to have gained 136 million yen through 26,000 shares that he had received in his secretary's name. This was the largest amount received by any individual, greatly exceeding the number of shares received by Takeshita (2,000), Abe (17,000), and Miyazawa (10,000). Recruit had carried out this scheme under its former president Ezoe Hiromasa.

Particularly because it had been working to implement a consumption tax, the Takeshita government came under heavy public criticism for having profited greatly. Its approval rating fell and failed to recover. Despite the scandal pushing Nakasone and Takeshita into a corner, the government still managed to pass the Tax Reform Act on December 24, 1988, which introduced a 3% consumption tax from April of the following year.

It was even reported on May 20, 1989 that Nakasone would resign from the Diet, but when he appeared before the Diet as a witness on May 25, he indicated that he was considering leaving that decision to the voters.

When Inaba Seiichi of the Socialist Party pressed him on his relationship with Ezoe, saying that he "is seen as having belonged to your brain trust," Nakasone answered that "I do not believe that he was part of my brain trust. He was a friend, but not a particularly close one."

Nakasone made it through by emphasizing the distance between himself and Ezoe. As the LDP had conditioned Nakasone's testimony on the prohibition of cameras, live broadcasts of the event were accompanied by a still image of him rather than a video. Viewers were likely left irritated by the unmoving image.

Ezoe remembers things somewhat differently. He said that he had participated in the Sannō Keizai Kenkyūkai and had had one-on-one meetings with Nakasone at the prime minister's residence (albeit on education reform).

According to Ezoe, the prosecution gave up on charging Nakasone and focused their efforts on Fujinami Takao, his former chief cabinet secretary, instead. Both Ezoe and Fujinami would be found guilty, with Ezoe sentenced to three years imprisonment (suspended for five) and Fujinami to three years imprisonment (suspended for four).

While Nakasone escaped resigning from the Diet, he did leave the LDP on May 31. His confidante Fujinami had been indicted at that point, and he did not want to cause any problems for Uno Sōsuke, a member of his faction. Uno was foreign minister in the Takeshita and – rarely for a powerful politician – had received no shares from Recruit. He thus rapidly came to be seen as a promising presidential candidate.

While Uno did become prime minister on June 3, his government proved short lived. He became embroiled in a scandal involving a geisha, which – together with the introduction of the consumption tax and the Recruit

"*Rain of Cicada Cries*" 231

scandal – led to an LDP defeat in the House of Councillors election held in July. It was during this election that Socialist Party Chairwoman Doi Takako famously declared that "the mountain has moved," a reference to "The Day the Mountains Move," a feminist poem by Yosano Akiko. The Kaifu government was born on August 10.

Nakasone made Sakurauchi Yoshio the head of his faction. Then, when Sakurauchi became the speaker of the House of Representatives, he named Watanabe Michio to the position. With the transition of the Nakasone faction into the Watanabe faction, all of the factions that had been headed by the Sankaku Daifuku Chū had now experienced a generational change in leadership. Nakasone seems to have pictured Yamasaki Taku, a promising mid-level member of the faction, as following Watanabe as a leader.[8]

Gorbachev and Hussein

It was through foreign policy, ever his specialty, that Nakasone continued to make his presence felt after stepping down as prime minister.

He met with Gorbachev in Moscow on July 22, 1988, and argued, in relation to the Northern Territories, that "Stalin mistakenly sent troops that are part of Hokkaido [rather than the Kuriles]. That was a mistake by Stalin."

For his part, Gorbachev did not seem to be particularly knowledgeable about the territorial dispute, initially speaking of the "three islands" (there are four) before his interpreter pointed out the mistake and he corrected himself.

He visited the USSR again on January 18, 1989 with former French president Giscard d'Estang and former Secretary of State Kissinger. He told Gorbachev that "I welcome the withdrawal of forces from Outer Mongolia. However, I also hope to see force reductions in the Far East, including Primorsky Krai." Gorbachev was reluctant, however, given that the Sino-Soviet border had not been delineated, saying that "the question of the eastern border is not a simple one."[9]

The most exciting point of Nakasone's post-prime ministerial diplomatic efforts came during the Gulf Crisis. After the Iraqi invasion of Kuwait on August 2, 1990, he met with President Hussein three times from November 4 to 6.

The US was not enthusiastic about Nakasone's proposed visit to Iraq, but he went anyway, accompanied by a delegation of LDP Diet members under Satō Takayuki of his faction. As touched on earlier, Nakasone had previously met Hussein as MITI minister and secured a loan agreement for oil. He hoped to make use of that history here.

Meeting Nakasone for the first time in sixteen years, Hussein took off his pistol and placed it far away from himself. Nakasone told him that he "must respect the UN resolution and implement it," "do everything you can to avoid an armed conflict," and "release all of your foreign hostages as quickly as possible."

232 *"Rain of Cicada Cries"*

Hussein told Nakasone that "I expect that the Iraq of today is different from the one you saw in 1974. Prior to the establishment of the current administration twenty-two years ago, Iraq was an extremely backward country. We are the ones who have built up this country, and I thus have no desire for a war that would destroy all that we have achieved."

Nakasone also said during the meeting that "You seem to slightly misunderstand Japan's position, so I would like to correct you. We are not carrying out constitutional revision. Nor is there any chance that we will do so. We would also not be able to have the SDF participate in combat under the UN Peacekeeping Operations Law. And, given the current distribution of seats in the current Diet and the state of public opinion, I suspect that that bill will not make it through the Diet."

As a result of Nakasone's discussions with Hussein, seventy-four hostages were released. He wrote a letter to US President Bush summarizing his conversations with Hussein and encouraged him to engage in direct negotiations with Iraq.[10]

Nakasone used the release of the hostages as an opportunity to return to the LDP on April 26, 1991. He visited China in May to attend the inauguration ceremony for the Chinese-Japanese Youth Center that he had helped bring about. The Miyazawa government was formed on November 5, and Nakasone met with President Yeltsin in Moscow on March 2, 1992, and told him that he "would like to see the peace treaty issue resolved within this century."[11]

The Era of Coalition Governments

The LDP failed to secure a majority in the July 1993 general election, and the Miyazawa government was replaced by the Hosokawa Morihiro government, a coalition of all the prior opposition parties with the exclusion of the communists.

At an October 12 Imperial banquet for Yeltsin, Nakasone tried to give the new prime minister inspiration, telling him, "You should look like you have no selfish motives. Good luck and boldness are things you're born with. Being a prime minister means being able to do most things if you set your mind to it. Act with determination."

He also urged Yeltsin to resolve the Northern Territories issue.[12]

The Hata Tsutomu government that followed Hosokawa was short-lived, lasting only sixty-four days, and the Murayama Tomiichi government was formed on June 30, 1994 as a coalition between the LDP, Socialists, and New Party Sakigake. Ozawa Ichirō, chairman of the Japan Renewal Party, backed former prime minister Kaifu for the position, but Kaifu was defeated by Murayama in the runoff election in the Diet.

Nakasone was sympathetic to Ozawa's support for Kaifu, absenting himself from the first round of voting and casting his vote for Kaifu in the runoff rather than for Murayama, the LDP-backed candidate. He had said at

"*Rain of Cicada Cries*" 233

a press conference that "As someone who has called for conservative centrism, I support Kaifu. Voting for the Socialist Party would not be in the national interest."

Nakasone's statement strengthened the Socialists' resolve to have Murayama lead a coalition with the LDP and Sakigake. Some Socialists who had been considering joining with Ozawa returned to the party under the rationale that they refused to "support [Kaifu] alongside Nakasone."

Nakasone showed no regret for his statement, saying, "As Murayama belongs to the Socialist Party, it should come as no surprise that Kaifu's approach is closer to mine. He was deputy chief cabinet secretary during the Miki government and one of my comrades in the movement for the direct election of the prime minister."[13]

The Turmoil of the Post-1955 System Era

Four of the Sankaku Daifuku Chū were gone. Ōhira and Miki had passed away in 1980 and 1988, and Tanaka and Fukuda would die in 1993 and 1995. Two of the LDP's new generation of leaders, Takeshita and Miyazawa, had already served as prime minister and Abe, the third, had fallen ill and died in 1991. While the Socialists, the LDP's rivals, had been able to recapture the premiership with Murayama, the LDP's decline was obvious to all.

Nakasone lamented the turmoil that the decline of the 1955 System (the party system created with the formation of the LDP and Socialist parties in 1955) had brought. This can be seen in his 1997 book, *Requirements of Leaders*:

> We have changed prime ministers four times over these past three years. First, we had the anti-LDP Hosokawa government. That had some degree of significance to it. Then, we had Takemura [Masayoshi] and Murayama jump out and form a new coalition government in opposition to Ozawa [Ichirō]. A nation cannot act on the basis of that kind of personal love and hate. Policy must be at the center. [...] Everyone has become scared of being called conservative, instead becoming self-proclaimed reformists void of any substance. [...] Right now, we are in desperate need of a politician willing to explain to the people that Japan truly lies on the border between living and dying. I am worried that, should that not happen, this nation will sink.

Nakasone believed that just as had been the case during the Meiji Restoration in the 19th century, capable personnel were indispensable if Japan were to make it through this great changing of eras:

> As of right now, we are only at the beginning of this change, and those who will come to the forefront are not yet prominent. [...] It is vital that we find those people in each field, grant them the status and authority

234 *"Rain of Cicada Cries"*

they need to be of use to the nation, and put them to work. I keenly feel and admonish myself that doing that is the great task and responsibility that faces us, [those who came before].

The Democratic Party (DPJ) was founded on September 28, 1996 by Hatoyama Yukio and others. In May of that same year, Nakasone caused a bit of a media storm by describing these efforts to form a new party as "soft-serve ice cream" at his birthday party. He would later write that "my true intention was to give them encouragement."[14]

Nakasone's Hopes for the Hashimoto Government and "Emotion"

Hashimoto Ryūtarō handily defeated Koizumi Jun'ichirō in the September 22, 1995, LDP presidential election. Nakasone had backed Hashimoto's candidacy alongside Kajiyama Seiroku. Prime Minister Murayama announced his resignation shortly afterward, and the Hashimoto government was formed in January 1996. The LDP had recovered the position of prime minister after an absence of two years and five months.

Nakasone, who had been particularly concerned by the rapid turnover of governments, had high hopes for Hashimoto, saying, "There are four national crises, four great tsunamis sweeping towards Japan right now: administrative reform, fiscal reform, national security, and education reform. Prime Minister Hashimoto is willing to take these on, even if it means that he will go down in flames. I have great admiration for his determination."[15]

In the aforementioned *Requirements of Leaders*, he said that he wanted to place the Hashimoto government on the course of a stable administration:

As I look at Japan's current situation, I reproach myself, wondering what I have spent the past fifty years doing. I cannot die as things are now. If we cannot somehow return Japan's political situation to normal and establish a suitably strong and stable government that will resolutely carry out reforms without dissolving the Diet for about four years, this nation will sink. I feel that there is no question that we will soon be facing a situation like that of the late Roman Empire. Thus, as my last act of service, I hope to summon up all my courage and place Japanese politics on a stable course. I myself have no intention of finding work outside of politics. I believe that politics is my calling and my fate.[16]

Despite these goals, Nakasone helped destabilize the Hashimoto government by recommending that Satō Takayuki be appointed to the cabinet in the September 1997 cabinet reorganization. Satō was then appointed director-general of the Management and Coordination Agency. While his sentence had been suspended, Satō had still been found guilty of accepting

"Rain of Cicada Cries" 235

bribes as part of the Lockheed scandal, and his return to the cabinet inevitably caused a backlash.

Murakami Masakuni, secretary-general for the LDP in the House of Councillors and a member of the Nakasone faction, had been uneasy about the idea, telling Nakasone, "I'm opposed. Doing this will damage your reputation."

Nakasone brushed him off, saying, "I think that your judgment is sound. But this is a matter of emotion. And it is something for Hashimoto and me to discuss."

Murakami continued to advise caution, saying that "that emotion will damage your reputation," but Nakasone refused, commenting that "I, too, have red blood running in my veins."

As had been expected, Satō became the subject of public criticism, and he stepped down as director-general after only ten days. Nakasone had hoped that Satō would be able to carry out reforms, but he said that "believing that the government itself was threatened, the prime minister bowed to public pressure and told Satō to withdraw." Murakami noted that "while the public often talks about how cold and calculating Nakasone was, he was actually quite vulnerable to emotion."

The Hashimoto government's approval rating fell from 53% to an alltime low of 35. Hashimoto suffered a defeat in the July 12, 1998 House of Councillors election and was replaced as prime minister by Obuchi Keizō.[17]

Grand Cordon of the Supreme Order of the Chrysanthemum

The remaining parts of Nakasone's life's work were constitutional revision and education reform. He held a discussion with Miyazawa on April 9, 1997, a month before the fiftieth anniversary of the postwar constitution going into force.

He argued that "we should spend the next ten years or so undertaking a thorough examination of the current constitution and creating a structure that will be able to respond to the changes and historical developments of the coming era." On education, he advocated for having the concept of the "public" (rather than the individual) permeate education and "giving teachers a sense of mission." Miyazawa was skeptical of constitutional revision.

On May 7, Nakasone received the Grand Cordon of the Supreme Order of the Chrysanthemum from the Emperor, Japan's highest state honor. Yoshida Shigeru, Satō Eisaku, and Nakasone are the only postwar prime ministers to receive the award while still alive. Fukuda, his fellow prime minister from Gunma, also received it but only posthumously.

The Prime Minister's Office gave "his five years in office, the next longest after Yoshida and Satō's more than seven years" as the reason for the award. In commenting on the decoration, Nakasone listed the reform of JNR, leading the LDP to victory in the joint election, and securing the release of the Iraqi hostages as some of the joyous moments of his career, but also

236 *"Rain of Cicada Cries"*

mentioned that he could "still vividly recall the hard times, such as when I worked hard alone on the sales tax issue, deserted by everyone."[18]

The Splitting of the Former Nakasone Faction

Watanabe Michio, who had inherited Nakasone's faction, died on September 15, 1995.

Nakao Eiichi became operating council chairman of the former Watanabe faction, and Nakasone was appointed honorary chairman. Nakao was made operating council chairman due to the faction's system of collective leadership (in which the chairman took the central role).

Some of the mid-level and younger Diet members in the faction who had wanted a generational change in leadership (like Yamasaki Taku) were dissatisfied with the choice and left the faction, forming the Kinmirai Kenkyūkai on July 16, 1998. The choice of faction chairman was left up to Nakasone and former speaker of the House of Representatives Sakurauchi, and they chose Murakami. On March 18, 1999, Nakasone and Murakami merged with Kamei Shizuka's faction to form the Murakami/Kamei faction.[19]

After splitting from the former Nakasone faction, Yamasaki became caught up in a scandal involving a former mistress and lost his seat in the 2003 general election. With the exception of Uno, who became prime minister as a safe choice in the wake of the Recruit Scandal, Nakasone's faction produced no other LDP presidents. The faction to have produced the most presidents since the beginning of this century is the Seiwakai (the former Fukuda faction) with three: Mori Yoshihiro, Koizumi Jun'ichirō, and Abe Shinzō.

Koizumi's Recommendation to Retire

The Mori Yoshihiro government, which was formed on April 5, 2000 after Prime Minister Obuchi Keizō suddenly died of a stroke twenty months after taking office, was another very unstable government. In *A National Strategy for 21st Century Japan*, Nakasone's book published that July, he laid out an argument for how Japan could overcome its lack of a national strategy and pushed for strengthening the cabinet's powers, enacting direct election of the prime minister, and creating policy-oriented graduate schools.[20]

The Koizumi government, that was formed on April 26, 2001, saw great changes in the international environment during its tenure, including the beginning of the American "War on Terror," and tensions with North Korea. Nakasone strongly backed Koizumi's support for the US in the Iraq War and described the state of the post-Iraq War world as "unipolar and pluralistic," and "an era of dispersion" while describing Japan as having been "set adrift." At the same time, he saw Koizumi's public declaration that he would "smash the LDP" as a "populist measure."[21]

"Rain of Cicada Cries"   237

Under Koizumi, a maximum age of seventy-three was put in place for the LDP's proportional representation candidates. No waiver was given to the eighty-five-year-old Nakasone. While Miyazawa (who was eighty-four) immediately accepted retirement, Nakasone vigorously protested, finding the recommendation that he retire humiliating.

On October 23, 2003, Koizumi and Nakasone met in Nakasone's office in the Sabo Kaikan building.

"I don't know what you'd like to talk about, so let's start by hearing your thoughts."

There was a television camera in the room.

Koizumi began to speak, but he did not meet Nakasone's eyes as he did so.

"Nakasone-sensei, regardless of your formal status, your words and actions are influential and draw attention both at home and abroad. I would like you to continue to be active in this fashion."

He spoke these words quickly but not fluidly and then stopped. Nakasone immediately began his rebuttal:

> I find myself utterly unable to understand your rationale. I have a duty as a politician. Constitutional revision and the Fundamental Law of Education have finally been put on the agenda and we've reached an important stage, where they're about to become a reality. I absolutely cannot stop being a politician. I have called for constitutional revision and the creation of a self-defense military since 1952, since Japan became independent. It is my life's work as a politician, what I've dedicated myself to. To not allow me to fulfill that work now, just as they are going to be completed, is unworthy of a president or prime minister. Is it not the job of presidents and prime ministers to protect the convictions of politicians?

When Koizumi remained silent, Nakasone continued:

> I ask that you keep the promise you made to me during the 1996 candidate adjustments that I would be "first on the PR list for the rest of my life." That was a commitment made by the party. By doing this, you will give the impression that there is no place for the elderly in the LDP. In conversations with reporters in Indonesia and Thailand, you said that you would respect the decisions of individual candidates [about whether to retire.]

When Nakasone asked him to "please reconsider," Koizumi looked down and said, "You can work anywhere, so ..."

"That's not the issue. It's a matter of my duty and tenacity as a politician. I want you to reconsider."

Koizumi bowed his head, stood, and left.[22]

238 *"Rain of Cicada Cries"*

Final Speech as a Diet Member

When the LDP's list of recognized candidates was released on October 27 ahead of the following month's general election, Nakasone's name was nowhere to be found. Secretary-General Abe Shinzō appeared before Nakasone in Koizumi's stead and told him that "it is unfortunate that we were unable to place you on the list, but I ask for your understanding."

Nakasone retorted, "Doesn't President Koizumi realize that morality, ethics, logic, and emotion are important to a political party? This will be a black mark on the history of the LDP." As President Hashimoto had promised him that he would always have the top spot on the party's North Kantō PR list, a promise that had been approved by the General Council, he was not merely going to acquiesce.

He considered running as an independent candidate from a single-member district, but the party's recognized candidates in what had been his former district were Chief Cabinet Secretary Fukuda Yasuo (in Gunma 4th) and Diet Member Obuchi Yūko (in Gunma 5th). Running in the 4th district would revive the old "Jōshū War" that he had had with Fukuda's father, but he had no realistic chance of winning there and losing would damage his reputation.

The leaders of his local support organization were also against him making such a run, telling him that they did not want him to run as an independent and that, now that the LDP president had decided not to recognize his candidacy, he had no choice but to obey.

Finding himself without anywhere to go, Nakasone called an emergency general meeting of his support organization on October 28 in Takasaki. His supporters understood that this meant that he would be announcing his retirement. His son Hirofumi, a member of the House of Councillors, was present, and Nakasone – known for half a century as a skilled public speaker – spoke with great difficulty:

> I must offer my heartfelt apologies to you all that we have arrived at this truly inexcusable result. [...] I have continued on in the belief that the constitutional issue, and the education issue, were to be my lifelong service to this nation. [...] There is truly nothing more unfortunate than that I will be unable to see that through.

Nakasone spoke of his belief in "lifelong service":

> I may stop being a Diet member, but I will not retire from political life. I will continue to engage in political activities both at home and abroad. [...] As I have told you before, I will engage in lifelong service. I have said that I would die active as a politician, and the time has come for me to truly carry that out.

"Rain of Cicada Cries" 239

His language then became stronger:

> I am someone who went to war. I should have died there. But because I survived, I will continue to offer my life to this nation until the very end. [...] As a witness who has seen all of the history of Japan since its defeat in war, I must create a foundation for Japan so that this nation does not err. So that our children, and our grandchildren, can live happily and without worry.

Nakasone concluded his final speech as a member of the Diet by saying that he would "offer my life to the nation." He was eighty-five years old and have been in office for fifty-six years and seven months.[23]

Nakasone's Criticism of Koizumi

Nakasone was openly angry at Koizumi's recommendation that he retire, referring to it as "political terrorism." However, he had always been a man able to quickly adjust to changing circumstances. The day he took off his Diet member's badge, he told his secretary, "Well, it's time for the second act in the play that is my life to start."[24]

He may have laid his badge aside, but he continued to maintain his offices in Hirakawachō. He became seen as the leading elder statesman of the political world, even more than he had been before, and an unending stream of guests and journalists visited his office. He also frequently appeared on television to discuss issues with other politicians like Miyazawa, Mori Yoshirō, Shiokawa Masajūrō, and Doi Takako.[25]

Nakasone maintained his membership in the LDP, and in his 2004 book *Record of Self-Examination*, he severely criticized Koizumi: "His manner of being able to instantaneously grasp a situation and immediately put forth his conclusion is prodigious. This is, however, ultimately merely a trick. No consistent ideology, philosophy, or historical view is apparent in his conclusions."[26]

He was apprehensive of Koizumi's foreign policy, particularly as it concerned Asia. In one speech, he harshly noted that "unfortunately, the Koizumi government's Asia policy should receive no points. Or even negative points."[27]

In a magazine interview, Nakasone argued that "since the formation of the Koizumi government, Japan has fallen far behind China in its East Asian policy and strategy" and that "if I were the one planning the strategy, I would expand our FTAs to various countries in East Asia and seek the creation of an economic cooperation organization that included the 'ten plus three' (the ten members of ASEAN, Japan, China, and South Korea), the US, Australia, New Zealand, and India."[28]

240 *"Rain of Cicada Cries"*

Continued Fixation on Constitutional Revision

Nakasone continued to be strongly interested in constitutional revision, and in January 2005, he joined the LDP's Committee on the Drafting of a New Constitution. He worked on his constitutional draft as head of the subcommittee on the preamble. This draft began by invoking the "unique traditions and culture" of Japan:

> The Japanese people have developed on the beautiful islands in eastern Asia washed by the waves of the Pacific and the Sea of Japan, overcoming many trials and creating and sharing unique traditions and culture, holding the Emperor as a symbol of the unity of the people, respecting harmony, and serenely recognizing diverse ideologies and life philosophies.

However, the leadership of the LDP, out of consideration of their coalition with the Kōmeitō, replaced Nakasone's preamble on the grounds that it was "excessively Japanese." While Nakasone felt that the LDP draft was "lacking in love towards and awareness of Japan," he welcomed the fact that constitutional revision seemed increasingly likely.

He had the IIGP release his personal draft for constitutional revision. While maintaining a parliamentary cabinet system, it took steps closer to a system under which the prime minister would be directly elected by having each party announce their candidate for prime minister prior to general elections. The draft made the Emperor head of state and clearly stated that a "defense force" (*bōeigun*) would be maintained. In addition to creating a constitutional court, another distinctive element of the draft was a clause reaffirming the importance of the family.[29]

As Koizumi's foreign policy had tended to focus on relations with the US, Nakasone hoped that the Abe government that followed would take a more multilateral approach and also pay attention to countries like China and South Korea. Nakasone was appointed chairman of the non-partisan Diet Members' League for the Implementation of an Independent Constitution in January 2007 and supported the passage of a bill for the national referendum required for constitutional revision. He argued that a grand coalition should be formed with the Democratic Party as a means of bringing about constitutional revision and, concerned about Sino-Japanese relations, visited China to call for the opening of "a new chapter in Sino-Japanese relations that overcomes history and seeks the development of coexistence."[30]

However, not only would the Abe government prove to be short-lived, but so would the following governments of Fukuda Yasuo and Aso Tarō. Following Prime Minister Fukuda's resignation, Nakasone bluntly told the *Yomiuri Shimbun* that "the second and third generations are lacking in boldness and fighting spirit." When Prime Minister Aso also received little popular support, he criticized him as making "rash statements and

"Rain of Cicada Cries" 241

acting in a manner that gives the impression that he has not given adequate consideration to what he is doing. The public sees him as a political lightweight."[31]

At the same time, he argued in a dialogue that the Democratic Party was "immature" for failing to reach a consensus on basic issues like constitutional revision:

> The Democratic Party abhors basic issues like the constitutional issue. When they try to address them, they can't come to a conclusion. Given that, even if we can speak of there being two major political parties in this country, we have not yet reached a place where the most important fundamental issues facing the nation can be discussed. This is one of the major flaws of Japanese politics. And I do feel that they are immature as a political party for that reason.

Nakasone believed that the turmoil of the post-1955 System era continued, and he saw the birth and meandering of the Democratic Party as worsening that.[32]

The Democratic Party in Power and the Return of the LDP

The LDP suffered a historic defeat in the August 30, 2009 general election, winning only 119 seats. Hatoyama Yukio of the Democratic Party formed a government on September 16. This was a change of government directly caused by the popular will as expressed in an election.

In a dialogue, Nakasone expressed a heightened sense of crisis, saying, "The 'realm' has changed hands, as if in a modern version of the Battle of Sekigahara. This is different from a normal change of government. The hold on political leadership that the LDP has had for roughly fifty years has been broken. This must be regarded as a historic moment, something that has only happened once in half a century. Not just the fates of the DPJ and LDP depend on these events, but the fate of all Japan."

Nakasone had emphasized with Hatoyama Ichirō and said of his grandson Yukio that "He has inherited his grandfather former prime minister Hatoyama Ichirō's personality. He is open to everyone and aspires to a softer, quieter kind of politics. There's very little sense that he gives emotional, vigorous encouragement. He comes from a science background and tries to move things forward rationally. If I had to describe him, I would call him a scholarly politician who believes in rationalism. He's markedly different from Ozawa [Ichirō]."[33]

The success of the Democratic Party made many believe that a new era had arrived where there would be a two-party system, but it did not take long for the public to become disillusioned with the DPJ.

Nakasone was particularly concerned about the downturn in US-Japan relations that had accompanied the arrival of the new government and

242 *"Rain of Cicada Cries"*

made critical comments to magazines such as "It was clumsy for a national leader to make such a mess of an issue like [the transfer of Futenma]. I have to admit that the way he handled it was terrible." "I also did not imagine that the American response would be this heavy and strong. The naivety of [Hatoyama's slogan of] 'friendship' was partly responsible for this. It was as sweet [naïve] as a creampuff."

This was a reference to Hatoyama's pledge to have USMC Air Station Futenma relocated outside of Okinawa (rather than elsewhere in Okinawa, as agreed to by the prior LDP government). He was unprepared for the degree of American resistance to changing the existing arrangements and his inability to deliver on such a prominent political promise would become a major factor in his decision to resign.

When asked whether the LDP would be able to regain power, Nakasone repeatedly answered that "they are well capable of overcoming this." He frankly told LDP President Tanigaki Sadakazu that "You can seem too well-behaved at times from the perspective of those coming from the old days. Since you're a person of good character, you should surround yourself with people who are a bit less civilized [...] and make the party boisterous."[34]

On December 24, Nakasone moved his offices from the Sabo Kaikan to the same building in Toranomon that housed the IIGP. He felt that Prime Minister Kan Naoto, who succeeded Hatoyama on June 8, 2010, was a "citizen-like conservative politician." He found him "overly serious and I do not believe he leaves himself much room to spare."

Kan met with Nakasone at Hotel New Otani on June 22 to receive advice on the summit to be held in Canada from the 25th. Nakasone advised him to find someone at the summit who he could work with: "self-righteousness won't get you anywhere at a summit. The first thing you need to do is find yourself an ally. Then, you each need to be frank with each other and do what you can to come to each other's aid during the summit."[35]

The Great East Japan Earthquake

When the Great East Japan Earthquake struck on March 11, 2011, Nakasone was in his office in Toranomon. This natural disaster was accompanied by a major accident involving nuclear energy, a field that Nakasone had long promoted.

He was greatly shocked by the event and wrote that "It is time for the Japanese people to show the world how they will fight and overcome this challenge to civilization by the forces of nature. [...] A plan for reconstruction should be put together, one with the historic awareness that it will be creating 'a new Tohoku region for the coming age' that will serve as the precursor for a new age for all of Japan."[36]

When the Kan government seemed to be slow in responding to the disaster, Nakasone severely criticized it as a "government with neither a past nor a future": "The 'citizen-ism' (*shiminshugi*) advocated for by Prime Minister Kan is a political ideology focused on the civic life all around us. It is a philosophy that neither has a past grounded in our history and cultural traditions, nor does it strive towards a future with any particular goals and ideals."[37]

How did Nakasone reflect on the nuclear energy policy that he himself had advocated for? He was frequently asked about nuclear power in interviews, and he showed signs that he was reconsidering, saying, "It has caused tremendous trouble for the residents of the area surrounding [the Fukushima plant]. It is truly extremely regrettable that the situation has become one where their lives, businesses, and even the futures of their children have been affected."[38]

He called for the collaborative development of "fundamental principles for building a new Japan," for national land planning to be reexamined, and for "a thorough revision of safety standards for nuclear energy and the promotion of alternative energy." He had high expectations for solar energy and argued that Japan could become a "solar energy state."[39]

Rebuilding the Nation

During the Noda Yoshihiko government that followed Kan, Nakasone described politicians as having become smaller in "scale" and ruminated on rebuilding Japan:

> Prime Minister Noda also has, from my perspective, little interest in history or tradition. The prime ministers of the Democratic Party have little in the way of historical views. [...]
>
> I think that part of the reason that politicians have become smaller in scale is that, with the transition of the electoral system for the House of Representatives to single-member districts, they are confined to their districts and no longer have much in the way of freedom. The old LDP factions served as training centers for politicians where senior politicians would do their best to make something of promising junior members. The new factions and the Diet members groups of the DPJ have little of that character.

This argument that the adoption of single-member districts had led to a decline in governance was not unique to Nakasone. Even former prime minister Hosokawa Morihiro (who had signed the political reform law that implemented the new electoral system) and former LDP president Kōno Yōhei agreed in an October 2011 discussion that the move had brought about a decline in politics.

What was unique to Nakasone was his argument that not only had the single-member district system and the decline in factions reduced the scale of politicians, but they had also lowered interest in the history and traditions indispensable to rebuilding the nation.

244 *"Rain of Cicada Cries"*

Under the prior multimember district system, it had been possible for Nakasone to focus on national issues like the constitution, education, foreign policy, and security, while Fukuda Takeo, in the same district, specialized in economic policy. It also could be said to have offered a wider array of choices to voters.

Under the single-member district system, Diet members were expected to be able to respond to every kind of policy, and it became more difficult for them to be repeatedly reelected. It thus became harder for them to concentrate on particular areas of specialization. While this did reduce the influence of *zoku* Diet members to Nakasone, it likely reflected a decline in politics and, by extension, a lack of national vision.[40]

Longevity and the "Final Stop"

After Nakasone turned ninety in 2008, he increasingly came to be asked about his longevity in interviews.

He answered that the secret to long life was to "be patient, drink only moderately, get enough sleep, and don't get angry." He ascribed his longevity, in particular, to his "sense of mission." He also said, "Don't think of the future. Do all you can to make the most of the present. The future is something granted by God," and that "if you're optimistic, 'a path forward will absolutely show itself.'"

His morning regimen was spending sixty to ninety minutes looking over three newspapers as he ate natto and yogurt. According to those who worked with him, he had the *Asahi Shimbun*, *Yomiuri Shimbun*, and *Sankei Shimbun* delivered to his home and read the *Nihon Keizai Shimbun* and *Mainichi Shimbun* at the office. After moving his office, he would also spend some time each day at the president's office at the IIGP in preparation for the weekly study session held on Mondays with researchers and staff. He also regularly engaged in Zen meditation, walks, and golf.

Despite greatly exceeding Yoshida Shigeru's eighty-nine and Kishi Nobusuke's ninety, Nakasone did not see any inherent meaning in a long life itself and instead viewed life as just "one step on the way to infinity":

> Looked at from the course of eternal time, life is merely an instant and living a long time has essentially no significance. The meaning in life comes not from how long you can live but from whether you are living an honest life and how you are making use of the present. If there is a secret to long life, I believe it is living in that way.
>
> If life is viewed as "one step on the way to infinity," then one cannot help but feel wonder and gratitude towards those we meet and the bonds we are able to form during the mere instant that is our life.

In one conversation, Nakasone spoke of the "final stop": "When you get to my age, life becomes like the last train of the day. Passengers got off, one at

"*Rain of Cicada Cries*" 245

a time, two at a time, until, ultimately, you're the last one left. I don't know where the train is headed or when it will reach its final stop. That's the way I've started to think about things."[41]

The only prime minister to have lived longer than Nakasone was Prince Higashikuni, who lived to be 102.

Nine Cycles of the Zodiac

On December 26, 2012, the second Abe government was formed as a coalition between the LDP and Kōmeitō. Nakasone submitted an article to the *Sankei Shimbun* in which he defended the government saying that while it was true that the Act on the Protection of Specially Designated Secrets had been "forced through," "the protection of state secrets by law has been a longstanding issue for Japan for many years."

Regarding the authorization for the use of the right of collective self-defense that Abe had advocated for, Nakasone argued that, while possible under the existing constitution, "the greatest care must be taken" in its implementation and that two requirements needed to be fulfilled when invoked: "is there both domestic and international acceptance for its use in this case?" and "are the specifics appropriate?"[42]

Nakasone turned ninety-six on May 27, 2014. The following day, 140 people – including Speaker of the House of Representatives Ibuki Bunmei and Deputy Prime Minister Aso Tarō – gathered at a Tokyo hotel for a party to "celebrate a man entering his ninth cycle of the Zodiac." Abe added a bit of levity to the party by rushing in and announcing that he was "entering my sixth cycle this year."

Nakasone cheered on his juniors by proclaiming that "the true quality of a politician is acting resolutely within the gap between ideals and reality. Wishing for the peace and prosperity of the nation, I want you all to bravely advance national politics." He then blew out the candles on a cake.[43]

Notes

1　Nakasone Yasuhiro, Itō Takashi, Satō Seiburō, *Tenchi Ujō – Gojū Nen no Sengo Seiji o Kataru* (Tokyo: Bungei Shunjū, 1996), 584–88. Nakasone Yasuhiro, *Rīdā no Jōken* (Tokyo: Fusō-sha, 1997), 81. Nakasone Yasuhiro, *Sengo Seiji* (Tokyo: Yomiuri Shimbun, 2005), 60. Nakasone Yasuhiro, *Nakasone Yasuhiro ga Kataru Sengo Nihon Gaikō* (Tokyo: Shinchōsha, 2012), 485–87. Kitaoka Shin'ichi and Tase Yasuhiro, *Shidōryoku – Jidai ga Motomeru Rīdā no Jōken* (Tokyo: Nihon Keizai Shimbun, 2003), 229–31, 248. Okushima Sadao. *Jimintō Kanjichōshitsu no 30 Nen* (Tokyo: Chūkō Bunko, 2005), 193–96. Gotōda Masaharu, *Jō to Ri – Kamisori Gotōda Kaikoroku*, ed. Mikuriya Takashi (Tokyo: Kōdansha Plus Alpha Bunko, 2006), 2:258–60.
2　Iio Jun, *Seikyoku kara Seisaku e – Nihon Seiji no Seijuku to Tenkan* (Tokyo: NTT Shuppan, 2008), 3–9.
3　Nakasone, *Tenchi Ujō*, 538–42, 600. Nakasone, *Rīdā no Jōken*, 214–31. Nakasone Yasuhiro, *Nihonjin ni Itte Okitai Koto – 21 Seiki o Ikiru Kimi-tachi e* (Tokyo: PHP Kenkyūjo, 1998), 136–37, 153–60. Nakasone Yasuhiro, *21 Seiki*

246 *"Rain of Cicada Cries"*

Nihon no Kokka Senryaku (Tokyo: PHP Kenkyūjo, 2000), 184–86, 190, 197, 209, 213, 223–24. Nakasone Yasuhiro, *Jiseiroku – Rekishi Hōtei no Hikoku to shite* (Tokyo: Shinchōsha, 2004), 195–204. Nakasone Yasuhiro, *Nihon no Sōrigaku* (Tokyo: PHP Shinsho, 2004), 67–72, 82–98, 134–40, 150–58. Nakasone Yasuhiro, *Hoshu no Yuigon* (Tokyo: Kadokawa one Tēma 21, 2010), 181–82. Nakasone Yasuhiro, "Sengo Seiji no Sōkessan," *Shinchō 45* (2012), 53. Okuno Seisuke, *Ha ni Tayorazu, Gi o Wasurezu – Okuno Seisuke Kaikoroku* (Tokyo: PHP Kenkyūjo, 2002), 294–95. Mori Yoshirō, Tahara Sōichirō, *Nihon Seiji no Ura no Ura – Shōgen Seikai 50 Nen* (Tokyo: Kōdansha, 2013), 162–67, 175–89.

4 Nakasone Yasuhiro, "Sōri Kantei o Saru ni Sai shite," *Bungei Shunjū* (December 1987), 104–06.

5 Nakasone Yasuhiro, Takemura Ken'ichi, *Inochi no Kagiri Semi Shigure* (Tokyo: Tokuma Shoten, 2003), 3. Yamagishi Ippei, *Shōwa Kōki 10-Nin no Shushō – Nikkei no Seiji Kisha ga Mokugeki shita "Habatsu no Jidai"* (Tokyo: Nihon Keizai Shimbun, 2008), 215. Nakasone Yasuhiro, *Nakasone Yasuhiro Kushū* (Tokyo: Kadokawa Shoten, 1985), 167. According to Nakasone Yasuhiro, *Nakasone Yasuhiro Kushū 2008* (Tokyo: Hokumei-sha, 2008), 43, this haiku was written in 1974 at Hinode Sansō.

6 Conversation with one of Nakasone's secretaries (January 12, 2010).

7 Nakasone Yasuhiro, et al., *Kyōdō Kenkyū "Reisen Igo"* (Tokyo: Bungei Shunjū, 1992). Nakasone Yasuhiro, "Daigakusei to Kataru – 20 Seiki no Tenken to 21 Seiki e no Tenbō," IIGP. Nakasone Yasuhiro, *Gendai, Sekai oyobi Nihon no Kadai – 21 Seiki e no Tenbō* (Tokyo: International Institute for Global Peace, 1998). Nakasone Yasuhiro and Umehara Takeshi, *Seiji to Tetsugaku – Nihonjin no Aratanaru Shimei o Motomete* (Tokyo: PHP Kenkyūjo, 1996), 67–75. Nakasone Yasuhiro, *Rīdā no Rikiryō – Nihon o Futatabi, Sonzaikan no aru Kuni ni suru tame ni* (Tokyo: PHP Kenkyūjo, 2010), 68–78. Karasawa Shunjirō, *Karasawa Shunjirō Ōraru Hisutorī Sorosoro Zenbu Hanashimashō* (Tokyo: Bungei Shunjū Kikaku Shuppan-bu, 2009), 271–72.

8 *Asahi Shimbun,* October 20, 1988, May 20 evening, May 21, 26, 1989; February 21–22, 1990. Kuroda Kyōhei, *Yamasaki Taku – Zenjinzō* (Tokyo: Gyōken Shuppankyoku, 1993), 14. Nakasone, *Tenchi Ujō*, 591–92. Gotōda 2:267. Ezoe Hiromasa, *Kaiteiban Rikurūto Jiken – Ezoe Hiromasa no Shinjitsu* (Tokyo: Chūkō Shinsho Rakure, 2010), 94, 98, 234–46, 251–54, 441–42, 473. Murayama Tomiichi, *Murayama Tomiichi Kaikoroku,* ed. Yakushiji Katsuyuki (Tokyo: Iwanami Shoten, 2012), 62–66. On the Recruit scandal and money politics, see: Mainichi Shimbun Seiji-bu, *Jimintō* (Tokyo: Kadokawa Bunko, 1989); Mainichi Shimbun Seiji-bu, *Seijika to Kane* (Tokyo: Kadokawa Bunko, 1991).

9 Ambassador Mutō Toshiaki to Foreign Minister Uno Sōsuke (July 21, 1988) (July 23, 1988), MOFA 2014-193. "Shōwa 63-Nendo Shitsumu Hōkoku Shippitsu (An) Dai Nishō Dai Jūsetsu 4 IMEMO Supīchi," MOFA 2014-193. "Sankyoku Iinkai San Shippitsusha oyobi Dō Iinkai San Chiku Iinchō to Gorubachofu Shokichō to no Kaidanroku" (January 18, 1989), MOFA 2014-200. Mutō to Uno (January 29, 1989), MOFA 2014-200. Valéry Giscard d'Estaing, Nakasone Yasuhiro, and Henry Kissinger, *Taiso Kyōdō Senryaku no Saikōchiku* (Tokyo: Trilateral Commission, 1989). Nakasone Yasuhiro, *Nihon no Futatsu no Kadai – Kokusai Kankei to Kōi Keishō* (Tokyo: Seisaku Kagaku Kenkyūjo, 1989), 1–15. Nakasone Yasuhiro, *Seiji to Jinsei – Nakasone Yasuhiro Kaikoroku* (Tokyo: Kōdansha, 1992), 319–20. Nakasone, *Rīdā no Jōken*, 104–06. Nakasone, *Nakasone Yasuhiro ga Kataru*, 509–17. Henry Kissinger and Nakasone Yasuhiro, *Sekai wa Kawaru – Kisshinjā-Nakasone Taidan*, ed. Yomiuri Shimbun (Tokyo: Yomiuri Shimbun, 1990). Nakasone, *Tenchi Ujō*, 572–80. Sun Pinghua, Takeyoshi Jirō, *Nicchū Yūkō Zuisōroku – Son Heika ga*

"Rain of Cicada Cries" 247

Kiroku suru Nicchū Kankei (Tokyo: Nihon Keizai Shimbun, 2012), 1:283–84. The records from the meeting of the Trilateral Commission in Paris do not exist (MOFA 2014-201).

10 Ambassador to Iraq Katakura Kunio to Foreign Minister Nakayama Tarō (November 5, 1990), MOFA 2014-177. Nakasone, *Tenchi Ujō*, 592–98. Michael H. Armacost, *Tomo ka Teki ka*, trans. Yomiuri Shimbun-sha Gaihō-bu (Tokyo: Yomiuri Shimbun, 1996), 150–52. Nakasone, *Rīdā no Jōken*, 178–88. Nakasone, *Nakasone Yasuhiro ga Kataru*, 519–29. Katakura Kunio, *Arabisuto Gaikōkan no Chūtō Kaisōroku – Wangan Kiki kara Iraku Sensō made* (Tokyo: Akashi Shoten, 2005), 168–75.

11 Edamura Sumio, *Teikoku Kaitai Zengo – Chū Mosukuwa Nihon Taishi no Kaisō 1990–1994* (Tokyo: Toshi Shuppan, 1997), 238–39. Xiao Xiangqian, *Eien no Rinkoku to shite*, trans. Takeuchi Minoru (Tokyo: Saimaru Shuppankai, 1997), 263–64. Kaifu Toshiki, *Seiji to Kane – Kaifu Toshiki Kaikoroku* (Tokyo: Shinchō Shinsho, 2010), 142.

12 Hosokawa Morihiro, *Naishōroku Hosokawa Morihiro Sōri Daijin Nikki* (Tokyo: Nihon Keizai Shimbun, 2010), 114. Nakasone, *Nakasone Yasuhiro ga Kataru*, 529–30.

13 *Asahi Shimbun*, June 30, 1994. Okushima 318–19. Watanabe Tsuneo, *Watanabe Tsuneo Kaikoroku*, eds. Mikuriya Takashi, Itō Takashi, and Iio Jun (Tokyo: Chūō Bunko, 2007), 443, 472–73. Iokibe Makoto, Itō Motoshige, and Yakushiji Katsuyuki, *Kan Naoto Shimin Undō kara Seiji Tōsō e* (Tokyo: Asahi Shimbun, 2008), 86. Iokibe Makoto, ed. *Nonaka Hiromu – Kenryoku no Kōbō* (Tokyo: Asahi Shimbun, 2008), 161. Nakasone, *Nakasone Yasuhiro ga Kataru*, 566. *Nihon Keizai Shimbun*, August 11, 2013.

14 Nakasone, *Rīdā no Jōken*, 33–34, 41–42, 157–61. Nakasone, *21 Seiki Nihon*, 71. Nakasone, *Hoshu no Yuigon*, 14. Fukumoto Kunio, *Omote Butai Ura Butai – Fukumoto Kunio Kaikoroku* (Tokyo: Kōdansha, 2007), 136–37.

15 Nakasone, *Rīdā no Jōken*, 8–10, 38–39, 293. Watanabe, 477–78.

16 Nakasone, *Rīdā no Jōken*, 280.

17 *Asahi Shimbun*, September 10, 21, 1997. Nakasone Yasuhiro, *Nihonjin ni Itte Okitai*, 110–12. Uozumi Akira, *Shōgen Murakami Masakuni Ware, Kuni ni Uragirareyō tomo* (Tokyo: Kōdansha, 2007), 161–63, 180–86, 214–16. Gifu Shimbun, ed., *Shisei Ikkan – Mutō Kabun Hanseiki* (Gifu: Gifu Shimbun, 2008), 246–48.

18 *Asahi Shimbun*, April 29, May 7, 1997. Nakasone Yasuhiro, *Sengo 50 Nen to Nihon no Fukkō* (privately published, 1997). Nakasone Yasuhiro and Miyazawa Kiichi, *Kenpō Kaisei Daironsō Kaiken vs. Goken* (Tokyo: Asahi Bunko, 2000), 9. Nakasone Yasuhiro, et al., *Ronsō Kyōiku to wa Nani ka* (Tokyo: Bunshun Shinsho, 2002). Nakasone Yasuhiro, Ishihara Shintarō, *Eien nare, Nihon* (Tokyo: PHP Bunko, 2003), 222–42. Hoshi Hiroshi, *Jimintō to Sengo – Seikentō no 50 Nen* (Tokyo: Kōdansha Gendai Shinsho, 2005), 132–34. Watanabe, 409–10. Kurihara Toshio, *Kunshō – Shirarezaru Sugao* (Tokyo: Iwanami Shinsho, 2011), 150, 153–54.

19 *Mainichi Shimbun*, July 17, December 1, 4, 1988; December 6, 1996; March 18, 1999 evening edition. Etō Takami, *"Shin no Akuyaku" ga Nihon o Sukuu – Popyurizumu wa Saigo ni Minshū o Kurushimeru* (Tokyo: Kōdansha, 2003), 9. Watanabe, 490. *Sankei Shimbun*, December 3, 2013.

20 Nakasone, *21 Seiki Nihon*.

21 Nakasone, *Jiseiroku*, 206–34. Nakasone Yasuhiro, "Seiji no Kihon Seisaku to Naisei," in Jiyū Minshutō, ed., *Ketsudan! Ano toki Watashi wa Kō shita – Jimintō Sōri Sōsai Kanbō Chōkan ga Kataru* (Tokyo: Chūō Kōron Jigyō Shuppan, 2006), 13–14, 20–24. Nakasone, *Nakasone Yasuhiro ga Kataru*, 543–46.

248 *"Rain of Cicada Cries"*

22 See the following endnote.
23 *Nihon Keizai Shimbun,* October 23 evening, October 28, 2003 evening. *Asahi Shimbun,* October 27, 2003. *Mainichi Shimbun,* October 28, 2003. Nakasone, *Inochi no Kagiri,* 37–48. Nakasone, *Jiseiroku,* 8–14.
24 Tanaka Shigeru, *100 Sai e! Nakasone Yasuhiro "Chōju" no Hiketsu* (Tokyo: Kōbunsha, 2014), 59–60.
25 Funabashi Yōichi, "Kokuren Kaikaku Nakasone-shi no Chūkoku," *Asahi Shimbun* (November 6, 2003). TBS, "Jiji Hōdan," in Seisaku Sutaffu, ed., *Jiji Hōdan* (Tokyo: Kōdansha, 2004), 1:7–37, 97–128, 253–85, 2:97–128, 3:67–101, 203–36. Nakasone Yasuhiro, et al., *"Shōwa 80-nen"* – *Sengo no Yomikata* (Tokyo: Bunshun Shinsho, 2005).
26 Nakasone, *Jiseiroku,* 12.
27 Nakasone Yasuhiro, "Kore kara no Nihon no Yukue," in Koizumi Jun'ichirō, et al., *Jimintō no Teiryoku* (Tokyo: Seikō Shobō, 2007), 151.
28 Nakasone Yasuhiro, "Koizumi-kun, Gaikō kara Popyurizumu o Haijo shinasai," *Chūō Kōron* (August 2005), 44.
29 Nakasone Yasuhiro, Nishibe Susumu, Matsumoto Ken'ichi, *Kenpō Kaisei Daitōron* (Tokyo: Bijinesu-sha, 2004). *Yomiuri Shimbun,* January 20, 21, 2005. Japanese Modern Historical Manuscripts Association, *Tsukamoto Saburō Ōraru Hisutorī* (Tokyo: Japanese Modern Historical Manuscripts Association, 2006), 1:108. Nakasone Yasuhiro, "Kaisetsu – Kenpō Kaisei e no Chūsūteki Sonzai," in Yasuoka Okiharu, ed., *Seiji Shudō no Jidai – Tōchi Kōzō Kaikaku ni Torikunda 30 Nen* (Tokyo: Chūō Kōron Shinsha, 2008), 337–39. Noda Yoshihiko, *Minshu no Teki – Seiken Kōtai ni Daigi ari* (Tokyo: Shinchō Shinsho, 2009), 153. *Sankei Shimbun,* April 2, 2012.
30 Nakasone Yasuhiro, "Kita Chōsen no Kaku Jikken Mondai Takokukan Gaikō no Kōki Ikase," *Asahi Shimbun,* October 14, 2006. Nakasone Yasuhiro, "Atarashii Jidai no 'Nicchūkan' Kankei," *Bōeigaku Kenkyū* No. 39 (2008), 3–11. Nakasone Yasuhiro, *Seizan Jōunpo – Nakasone Yasuhiro Taidan-shū* (Tokyo: Mainichi Shimbun, 2012), 177, 223, 269, 272.*Yomiuri Shimbun,* April 6, 8, 2007; April 24, 2008. Michigami Hisashi, *Gaikōkan ga Mita "Chūgokujin no Tainichikan"* (Tokyo: Bunshun Shinsho, 2010), 57, 88.
31 *Yomiuri Shimbun,* September 3, 2008; July 18, 2009.
32 Nakasone Yasuhiro and Matsumoto Ken'ichi, *Seiji wa Bunka ni Hōshi suru – Kore kara no Seiji to Nihon* (Tokyo: Shiatere Shinsho, 2010), 13, 16, 59.
33 Nakasone Yasuhiro and Gerald Curtis, "Nakasone Motoshushō ga Jerarudo Kātisu Kyōju ni Katatta 'Minshu Kakumei'," *Sandē Asahi* (September 20, 2009), 120–23.
34 *Yomiuri Shimbun,* September 1, December 17, 2009. *Asahi Shimbun,* September 22, 2009. Nakasone, *Hoshu no Yuigon,* 14–35. Nakasone Yasuhiro, "Gaikō no Yōtei o Hanasō," *Gaikō* No. 1 (2010), 85–97. Nakasone Yasuhiro, "Hatoyama-kun, Ozawa-kun ni Tsugu!" *Shūkan Gendai* (January 9/16, 2010), 41–44. Nakasone Yasuhiro, *Seizan Jōunpo,* 47–57, 120. Nakasone, *Rīdā no Rikiryō,* 42–43. Nakasone, *Seiji wa Bunka ni Hōshi suru,* 41.
35 *Asahi Shimbun,* December 25, 2009; June 17, 23, 2010. *Nihon Keizai Shimbun,* June 26, 2010. *Yomiuri Shimbun,* June 29, July 17, 2010. Nakasone, "Gaikō no Yōtei o Hanasō," 89. Nakasone Yasuhiro, Kiyomiya Ryū, "Seiji Shidōsha wa Jūjitsu shita Kigamae de – Nihon Saisei e no Michi," *Sekai to Nihon* No. 1181 (2011), 7–8.
36 Nakasone Yasuhiro, "'Sōshisha' shite Ikan Senban – Saiki ni wa Kokumin no Rikai Hitsuyō," *AERA* (May 15, 2011), 59. Nakasone Yasuhiro, "'Atarashii Tōhoku' Seki e Shimase," *Yomiuri Shimbun* (April 10, 2011).
37 Nakasone Yasuhiro, "Kan-shushō Taijin e Kokka naki Shiminshugi no Genkai," *Yomiuri Shimbun* (August 14, 2011).

"Rain of Cicada Cries" 249

38 *Asahi Shimbun,* April 26, 2011.
39 *Yomiuri Shimbun,* April 23, 2011. Nakasone, *Seizan Jōunpo,* 304–12.
40 *Asahi Shimbun,* October 8, 2011. *Yomiuri Shimbun,* February 1, 2012. Nakasone Yasuhiro, "'Tenkan' to wa Nan datta no ka," *Keizai Shimbun* (May 11, 2012). Nakasone Yasuhiro, "Saishō ni Gaikō Kankaku ga Nai Higeki," *Shinchō 45* (November 2012), 20–25.
41 *Asahi Shimbun,* April 26, 2011. Nakasone Yasuhiro and Shirasawa Takuji, "Ki ga Nagaku, Sake wa Bikun de, Suimin Jūbun, Haratatezu," *Bungei Shunjū* (November 2011), 260–67. Nakasone Yasuhiro and Ikegami Akira, "Doko de Machigaeta ka Nani o Aratameru beki ka," *Bungei Shunjū* (May 2012), 127–35. Tanaka 2–3, 8, 11–12, 16, 56.
42 Nakasone Yasuhiro, "Ninenme ga Hontō ni Shōnenba," *Sankei Shimbun* (December 23, 2013). Nakasone Yasuhiro, "Kaishaku Henkō e Setsumei to Settoku o," *Sankei Shimbun* (March 17, 2014). Nakasone Yasuhiro, "Kokusai Kyōchō Mushi dekinu Chūro," *Sankei Shimbun* (June 23, 2014).
43 *Sankei Shimbun,* May 29, 2014. *Nihon Keizai Shimbun,* May 29, 2014. *Mainichi Shimbun,* May 29, 2014. *Yomiuri Shimbun,* May 29, 2014. Asked about then-Prime Minister Abe's statement on the seventieth anniversary of the end of the war, Nakasone answered that "following the precedent of the Murayama and Koizumi statements, expressions of Japan's sincerity should continue to be inserted into the flow of time." Nakasone Yasuhiro, "Kokka, Sensō, Shinryaku, Yasukuni o Kataru," *Chūō Kōron* (September 2015), 110. See also: Nakasone Yasuhiro, "Daikun'i no Yuigon," *Bungei Shunjū* (September 2015), 142–58.

References

Armacost, Michael H. *Tomo ka Teki ka.* Translated by Yomiuri Shimbun-sha Gaihō-bu. Tokyo: Yomiuri Shimbun, 1996.

Edamura Sumio. *Teikoku Kaitai Zengo – Chū Mosukuwa Nihon Taishi no Kaisō 1990–1994.* Tokyo: Toshi Shuppan, 1997.

Etō Takami. *"Shin no Akuyaku" ga Nihon o Sukuu – Popyurizumu wa Saigo ni Minshū o Kurushimeru.* Tokyo: Kōdansha, 2003.

Ezoe Hiromasa. *Kaiteiban Rikurūto Jiken – Ezoe Hiromasa no Shinjitsu.* Tokyo: Chūkō Shinsho Rakure, 2010.

Fukumoto Kunio. *Omote Butai Ura Butai – Fukumoto Kunio Kaikoroku.* Tokyo: Kōdansha, 2007.

Funabashi Yōichi. "Kokuren Kaikaku Nakasone-shi no Chūkoku." *Asahi Shimbun* (November 6, 2003).

Gifu Shimbun, ed. *Shisei Ikkan – Mutō Kabun Hanseiki.* Gifu: Gifu Shimbun, 2008.

Giscard d'Estaing, Valéry, Nakasone Yasuhiro, and Henry Kissinger. *Taiso Kyōdō Senryaku no Saikōchiku.* Tokyo: Trilateral Commission, 1989.

Gotōda Masaharu. *Jō to Ri – Kamisori Gotōda Kaikoroku.* Edited by Mikuriya Takashi. Tokyo: Kōdansha Plus Alpha Bunko, 2006.

Hoshi Hiroshi. *Jimintō to Sengo – Seikentō no 50 Nen.* Tokyo: Kōdansha Gendai Shinsho, 2005.

Hosokawa Morihiro. *Naishōroku Hosokawa Morihiro Sōri Daijin Nikki.* Tokyo: Nihon Keizai Shimbun, 2010.

Iio Jun. *Seikyoku kara Seisaku e – Nihon Seiji no Seijuku to Tenkan.* Tokyo: NTT Shuppan, 2008.

250 *"Rain of Cicada Cries"*

Iokibe Makoto, ed. *Nonaka Hiromu – Kenryoku no Kōbō.* Tokyo: Asahi Shimbun, 2008.

Iokibe Makoto, Itō Motoshige, and Yakushiji Katsuyuki, eds. *Kan Naoto Shimin Undō kara Seiji Tōsō e.* Tokyo: Asahi Shimbun, 2008.

Japanese Modern Historical Manuscripts Association. *Tsukamoto Saburō Ōraru Hisutorī.* Tokyo: Japanese Modern Historical Manuscripts Association, 2006.

Kaifu Toshiki. *Seiji to Kane – Kaifu Toshiki Kaikoroku.* Tokyo: Shinchō Shinsho, 2010.

Karasawa Shunjirō. *Karasawa Shunjirō Ōraru Hisutorī Sorosoro Zenbu Hanashimashō.* Tokyo: Bungei Shunjū Kikaku Shuppan-bu, 2009.

Katakura Kunio. *Arabisuto Gaikōkan no Chūtō Kaisōroku – Wangan Kiki kara Iraku Sensō made.* Tokyo: Akashi Shoten, 2005.

Kissinger, Henry, Nakasone Yasuhiro. *Sekai wa Kawaru – Kisshinjā-Nakasone Taidan.* Edited by Yomiuri Shimbun. Tokyo: Yomiuri Shimbun, 1990.

Kitaoka Shin'ichi, Tase Yasuhiro. *Shidōryoku – Jidai ga Motomeru Rīdā no Jōken.* Tokyo: Nihon Keizai Shimbun, 2003.

Kurihara Toshio. *Kunshō – Shirarezaru Sugao.* Tokyo: Iwanami Shinsho, 2011.

Kuroda Kyōhei. *Yamasaki Taku – Zenjinzō.* Tokyo: Gyōken Shuppankyoku, 1993.

Michigami Hisashi. *Gaikōkan ga Mita "Chūgokujin no Tainichikan."* Tokyo: Bunshun Shinsho, 2010.

Mori Yoshirō, Tahara Sōichirō. *Nihon Seiji no Ura no Ura – Shōgen Seikai 50 Nen.* Tokyo: Kōdansha, 2013.

Murayama Tomiichi. *Murayama Tomiichi Kaikoroku.* Edited by Yakushiji Katsuyuki. Tokyo: Iwanami Shoten, 2012.

Nakasone Yasuhiro. *21 Seiki Nihon no Kokka Senryaku.* Tokyo: PHP Kenkyūjo, 2000.

Nakasone Yasuhiro. "Atarashii Jidai no 'Nicchūkan' Kankei." *Bōeigaku Kenkyū* No. 39 (2008).

Nakasone Yasuhiro. "'Atarashii Tōhoku' Seki e Shimase." *Yomiuri Shimbun* (April 10, 2011).

Nakasone Yasuhiro. "Gaikō no Yōtei o Hanasō." *Gaikō* No. 1 (2010).

Nakasone Yasuhiro. *Gendai, Sekai oyobi Nihon no Kadai – 21 Seiki e no Tenbō.* Tokyo: International Institute for Global Peace, 1998.

Nakasone Yasuhiro. "Hatoyama-kun, Ozawa-kun ni Tsugu!" *Shūkan Gendai* (January 9/16, 2010).

Nakasone Yasuhiro. *Hoshu no Yuigon.* Tokyo: Kadokawa one Tēma 21, 2010.

Nakasone Yasuhiro. *Jiseiroku – Rekishi Hōtei no Hikoku to shite.* Tokyo: Shinchōsha, 2004.

Nakasone Yasuhiro. "Kaisetsu – Kenpō Kaisei e no Chūsūteki Sonzai." Yasuoka Okiharu, ed., *Seiji Shudō no Jidai – Tōchi Kōzō Kaikaku ni Torikunda 30 Nen.* Tokyo: Chūō Kōron Shinsha, 2008.

Nakasone Yasuhiro. "Kaishaku Henkō e Setsumei to Settoku o." *Sankei Shimbun* (March 17, 2014).

Nakasone Yasuhiro. "Kan-shushō Taijin e Kokka naki Shiminshugi no Genkai." *Yomiuri Shimbun* (August 14, 2011).

Nakasone Yasuhiro. "Kita Chōsen no Kaku Jikken Mondai Takokukan Gaikō no Kōki Ikase." *Asahi Shimbun* (October 14, 2006).

Nakasone Yasuhiro. "Koizumi-kun, Gaikō kara Popyurizumu o Haijo shinasai." *Chūō Kōron* (August 2005).

"Rain of Cicada Cries" 251

Nakasone Yasuhiro. "Kokusai Kyōchō Mushi dekinu Chūro." *Sankei Shimbun* (June 23, 2014).

Nakasone Yasuhiro. "Kore kara no Nihon no Yukue." Koizumi Jun'ichirō, et al., eds., *Jimintō no Teiryoku.* Tokyo: Seikō Shobō, 2007.

Nakasone Yasuhiro. *Nakasone Yasuhiro ga Kataru Sengo Nihon Gaikō.* Edited by Nakashima Takuma, Hattori Ryūji, Noboru Amiko, Wakatsuki Hidekazu, Michishita Narushige, Kusunoki Ayako, and Segawa Takao. Tokyo: Shinchōsha, 2012.

Nakasone Yasuhiro. *Nakasone Yasuhiro Kushū.* Tokyo: Kadokawa Shoten, 1985.

Nakasone Yasuhiro. *Nakasone Yasuhiro Kushū 2008.* Tokyo: Hokumei-sha, 2008.

Nakasone Yasuhiro. *Nihon no Futatsu no Kadai – Kokusai Kankei to Kōi Keishō.* Tokyo: Seisaku Kagaku Kenkyūjo, 1989.

Nakasone Yasuhiro. *Nihonjin ni Itte Okitai Koto – 21 Seiki o Ikiru Kimi-tachi e.* Tokyo: PHP Kenkyūjo, 1998.

Nakasone Yasuhiro. "Ninenme ga Hontō ni Shōnenba." *Sankei Shimbun* (December 23, 2013).

Nakasone Yasuhiro. *Rīdā no Jōken.* Tokyo: Fusō-sha, 1997.

Nakasone Yasuhiro. *Rīdā no Rikiryō – Nihon o Futatabi, Sonzaikan no aru Kuni ni suru tame ni.* Tokyo: PHP Kenkyūjo, 2010.

Nakasone Yasuhiro. "Saishō ni Gaikō Kankaku ga Nai Higeki." *Shinchō 45* (November 2012), 20–25.

Nakasone Yasuhiro. "Seiji no Kihon Seisaku to Naisei." In Jiyū Minshutō, ed., *Ketsudan! Ano toki Watashi wa Kō shita – Jimintō Sōri Sōsai Kanbō Chōkan ga Kataru.* Tokyo: Chūō Kōron Jigyō Shuppan, 2006.

Nakasone Yasuhiro. *Seiji to Jinsei – Nakasone Yasuhiro Kaikoroku.* Tokyo: Kōdansha, 1992.

Nakasone Yasuhiro. *Seizan Jōunpo – Nakasone Yasuhiro Taidan-shū.* Tokyo: Mainichi Shimbun, 2012.

Nakasone Yasuhiro. *Sengo Seiji.* Tokyo: Yomiuri Shimbun, 2005.

Nakasone Yasuhiro. "Sengo Seiji no Sōkessan." *Shinchō 45* (2012), 52–53.

Nakasone Yasuhiro. "Sōri Kantei o Saru ni Sai shite." *Bungei Shunjū* (December 1987).

Nakasone Yasuhiro. "'Sōshisha' to shite Ikan Senban – Saiki ni wa Kokumin no Rikai Hitsuyō." *AERA* (May 15, 2011).

Nakasone Yasuhiro. "'Tenkan' to wa Nan datta no ka." *Keizai Shimbun* (May 11, 2012).

Nakasone Yasuhiro and Gerald Curtis. "Nakasone Motoshushō ga Jerarudo Kātisu Kyōju ni Katatta 'Minshu Kakumei.'" *Sandē Asahi* (September 20, 2009)

Nakasone Yasuhiro and Ikegami Akira. "Doko de Machigaeta ka Nani o Aratameru beki ka." *Bungei Shunjū* (May 2012).

Nakasone Yasuhiro and Ishihara Shintarō. *Eien nare, Nihon.* Tokyo: PHP Bunko, 2003.

Nakasone Yasuhiro, Itō Takashi, and Satō Seiburō. *Tenchi Ujō – Gojū Nen no Sengo Seiji o Kataru.* Tokyo: Bungei Shunjū, 1996.

Nakasone Yasuhiro and Kiyomiya Ryū. "Seiji Shidōsha wa Jūjitsu shita Kigamae de – Nihon Saisei e no Michi." *Sekai to Nihon* No. 1181 (2011).

Nakasone Yasuhiro and Matsumoto Ken'ichi. *Seiji wa Bunka ni Hōshi suru – Kore kara no Seiji to Nihon.* Tokyo: Shiatere Shinsho, 2010.

Nakasone Yasuhiro and Miyazawa Kiichi. *Kenpō Kaisei Daironsō Kaiken vs. Goken.* Tokyo: Asahi Bunko, 2000.

252 *"Rain of Cicada Cries"*

Nakasone Yasuhiro, Nishibe Susumu, Matsui Takafumi, and Matsumoto Ken'ichi. *Ronsō Kyōiku to wa Nani ka*. Tokyo: Bunshun Shinsho, 2002.

Nakasone Yasuhiro, Nishibe Susumu, Matsui Takafumi, and Matsumoto Ken'ichi. *"Shōwa 80-nen" – Sengo no Yomikata*. Tokyo: Bunshun Shinsho, 2005.

Nakasone Yasuhiro, Nishibe Susumu, and Matsumoto Ken'ichi. *Kenpō Kaisei Daitōron*. Tokyo: Bijinesu-sha, 2004.

Nakasone Yasuhiro, Satō Seizaburō, Murakami Yasusuke, and Nishibe Susumu. *Kyōdō Kenkyū "Reisen Igo."* Tokyo: Bungei Shunjū, 1992.

Nakasone Yasuhiro and Shirasawa Takuji. "Ki ga Nagaku, Sake wa Bikun de, Suimin Jūbun, Haratatezu." *Bungei Shunjū* (November 2011).

Nakasone Yasuhiro and Takemura Ken'ichi. *Inochi no Kagiri Semi Shigure*. Tokyo: Tokuma Shoten, 2003.

Nakasone Yasuhiro and Umehara Takeshi. *Seiji to Tetsugaku – Nihonjin no Aratanaru Shimei o Motomete*. Tokyo: PHP Kenkyūjo, 1996.

Noda Yoshihiko. *Minshu no Teki – Seiken Kōtai ni Daigi ari*. Tokyo: Shinchō Shinsho, 2009.

Okuno Seisuke. *Ha ni Tayorazu, Gi o Wasurezu – Okuno Seisuke Kaikoroku*. Tokyo: PHP Kenkyūjo, 2002.

Okushima Sadao. *Jimintō Kanjichōshitsu no 30 Nen*. Tokyo: Chūkō Bunko, 2005.

Sun Pinghua and Takeyoshi Jirō. *Nicchū Yūkō Zuisōroku – Son Heika ga Kiroku suru Nicchū Kankei*. Tokyo: Nihon Keizai Shimbun, 2012.

Tanaka Shigeru. *100 Sai e! Nakasone Yasuhiro "Chōju" no Hiketsu*. Tokyo: Kōbunsha, 2014.

TBS. "Jiji Hōdan" Seisaku Sutaffu, ed. *Jiji Hōdan*. Tokyo: Kōdansha, 2004.

Uozumi Akira. *Shōgen Murakami Masakuni Ware, Kuni ni Uragirareyō tomo*. Tokyo: Kōdansha, 2007.

Watanabe Tsuneo. *Watanabe Tsuneo Kaikoroku*. Edited by Mikuriya Takashi, Itō Takashi, and Iio Jun. Tokyo: Chūō Bunko, 2007.

Xiao Xiangqian. *Eien no Rinkoku to shite*. Translated by Takeuchi Minoru. Tokyo: Saimaru Shuppankai, 1997.

Yamagishi Ippei. *Shōwa Kōki 10-Nin no Shushō – Nikkei no Seiji Kisha ga Mokugeki shita "Habatsu no Jidai."* Tokyo: Nihon Keizai Shimbun, 2008.

Conclusion

Nakasone's Death and Its Impact at Home and Abroad

Nakasone passed away of old age at a Tokyo hospital on the morning of November 29, 2019, dying peacefully at the age of 101.[1]

Prime Minister Abe Shinzō said that Nakasone "took the helm during a major turning point in postwar history" and emphasized his accomplishments, including the "establishment of a strong US-Japan alliance."

He also stated at a joint news conference that Nakasone "consistently spoke of the necessity of constitutional revision" and that "I am certain that his strongly held beliefs concerning our nation's future will be passed on and span generations."[2]

Watanabe Tsuneo, director and editor-in-chief of Yomiuri Shimbun Holdings and a confidante of Nakasone's, commented that "The shock is like that of losing a parent. I've never known anyone so studious and well-read. I was also greatly impressed by his simple lifestyle. I've never respected anyone more than I did him." He recalled being "truly furious when, under Prime Minister Koizumi, they just implemented a mandatory retirement age for Diet members and forced him into retirement at the age of eighty-five." "We held a reading club every Saturday, starting from when I was just an ordinary reporter and Nakasone was a backbencher, through which we read a number of valuable works. And when we drank together at night, our discussions were about nothing but politics and books we'd read."[3]

The *New York Times* said of Nakasone's life that "he called for a stronger military and a larger global role for Japan and was one of the few Japanese leaders to win recognition on the world stage." It also argued that "more than a decade after he left office, a new generation of leaders like Junichiro Koizumi and Shinzo Abe were able to start carrying out Mr. Nakasone's vision."[4]

What kind of politician was Nakasone? I would like to recapitulate this book's major points.

DOI: 10.4324/9781003351931-12

254 *Conclusion*

The "Sankaku Daifuku Chū" Era

Nakasone, who would go on to become Japan's seventy-first prime minister, was born in Takasaki, Gunma, in 1918. After serving in the navy and home ministry, he entered politics at the age of twenty-eight during the Allied Occupation of Japan. Tanaka Kakuei and Suzuki Zenkō were also elected for the first time alongside him.

He began his political career criticizing the "bureaucratic secretive foreign policy" of Prime Minister Yoshida Shigeru and became known as a "young officer" who called for the adoption of an autonomous constitution. He was also the driving force behind early atomic energy policy.

While almost universally seen as one of the preeminent politicians of the postwar era today, he was originally outside of the mainstream of conservative politics. The leader of a small faction, he entered the cabinet as transportation minister during the government of Satō Eisaku after rapidly drawing closer to a man who he had long been critical of. Later, as director-general of the Defense Agency under the same prime minister, he called for "autonomous defense" and was seen as a far-right hawk.

Nakasone was the fifth-longest serving prime minister of the postwar period, serving for five years from 1982. But his path to the position had been a treacherous one. The 1970s to early 1980s were the "Sankaku Daifuku Chū" era of intense factional conflict within the LDP.

That his faction was not particularly large was not Nakasone's only weakness. While Fukuda Takeo – who also served in Gunma's 3rd district – staked out a place for himself as an economic expert, Nakasone's skills lay in administrative and fiscal reform (epitomized by his privatization of JNR) and foreign and defense policy. He seems to have been aware that this meant that he was less capable when it came to economic matters. One example of this is a discussion that he had with Fukuda. The discussion ran in the New Year 1966 issue of the *Jōmō Shimbun*, the two politicians' local newspaper, and the terms of the exchange – focusing on the economy and government finances – clearly placed Nakasone at a disadvantage. It seems likely that Nakasone was aware that he could not hope to compete against Fukuda when it came to these issues. If a local poll had been held asking which was the politician who best represented Gunma, Fukuda would likely have defeated Nakasone. He very much saw himself as being a representative of Japan as a whole rather than of just one particular locality.

Despite only leading a small faction and being aware that he was not gifted at economic issues, Nakasone still managed to overcome factional conflict within the LDP and secure the position of prime minister. What lay at the heart of the man? Despite having experienced the Pacific War, he seems to have been inherently optimistic. He was compared to a weathervane due to his vacillation during the "Kakufuku War," but he was able to interpret this in a way advantageous to him. That is, he argued that a weathervane was something that responded sensitively to the demands

Conclusion 255

of the wind (the times) while still remaining fixed in place. This kind of optimism resonated with his strategic thinking focused on the premiership, and Nakasone developed into one of the foremost politicians of the postwar era.

Nakasone's Political Legacy

It was in 1982 that Nakasone achieved his long-sought goal of becoming prime minister. He was sixty-four. As prime minister, it was in the fields of fiscal and administrative reform (as represented by the privatization of JNR), foreign policy, and security policy that he demonstrated his true worth as a politician. The role that Nakasone played in postwar Japan can be summarized into three points.

First, Nakasone's foreign policy represents the zenith of postwar foreign policy. He considered diplomatic and security policy to be the areas he was most proficient in, and he was able to use summits and other prominent opportunities as a means of strengthening his influence. The high-profile manner in which he stood alongside President Ronald Reagan in the center of the commemorative photograph for the 1983 G7 summit is well known. Nakasone went on twenty-two foreign trips while in office, the most by a prime minister until Koizumi Jun'ichirō. His relationship with Reagan was particularly close and referred to as the "Ron-Yasu" relationship in the media. But it should be noticed that, in addition to his efforts toward the West, he was also able to foster friendly relations with both China and South Korea. He established the four principles for Sino-Japanese relations with CCP General Secretary Hu Yaobang, and he was the first Japanese prime minister to make an official visit to South Korea. It was also during his time in office that Chun Doo-hwan became the first South Korean president to visit Japan. Nakasone's strategic philosophy allowed him to combine relations with the West with diplomatic efforts toward Asia in a multilayered manner. His discernment and ability to act were exceptional. There have been numerous prime ministers with a passion for US-Japan relations, but very few have been able to also improve relations with China and South Korea at the same time. Even though his public visit to Yasukuni Shrine damaged these relations, efforts were made not only by Nakasone but by the Koreans and Chinese as well to try to repair them. This was due in part to the relationships he had already established with their leaderships.

Second, Nakasone established the roots of the Kantei-led political style of today. The "final settlement of postwar politics" served as the byword for Nakasone politics. He would later list "the rectification of Yoshida politics," "administrative and fiscal reform," and "striving to make international contributions" as important aspects of this "final settlement." The slogan carried with it a strong sense that Japan's postwar systems must change. His devout belief in this led to the privatization of JNR, the breaking of the 1% cap on defense spending, and his official visit to Yasukuni.

256 *Conclusion*

The leading accomplishment of Nakasone politics was the privatization of the three major public corporations of JNR, NTT, and the government tobacco monopoly. Tanaka Kakuei had been critical of breaking up JNR, but with his fall Nakasone was able to accelerate his efforts to reform the company.

Becoming a "presidential prime minister" was the means through which Nakasone brought about his "final settlement." This meant forming numerous private advisory councils and making heavy use of a personal brain trust. For example, when he wanted to break through the 1% of GNP cap on defense spending, he had the Research Committee on Peace Issues issue findings calling for him to do so. Kyoto University professor Kōsaka Masataka, the head of the group, became fed up with Nakasone's pushiness.[5] His top-down usage of advisory groups while governing allowed him to avoid relying on the bureaucracy and disregard the role of the Diet.

Third, Nakasone's government brought about a transition from the "Sankaku Daifuku Chū" era, in which factional conflicts had been intense, to the "all-faction mainstream" era. It was while he was prime minister that Tanaka Kakuei suffered his stroke, weakening his control over Japanese politics, and a generation of "new leaders" like Takeshita Noboru, Abe Shintarō, and Miyazawa Kiichi rose. It was with this generational changing of the guard in mind that Nakasone chose Takeshita to succeed him as LDP president. Nakasone was one of only a few prime ministers of his era to depart from the Prime Minister's Office with a smile on his face. He was regarded as the least substantial of the Sankaku Daifuku Chū, but if one were to name an ultimate victor in the factional conflicts that raged between those five men, it would likely be him.

Long-Held Ambitions for Constitutional Revision

Even so, Nakasone was far from all powerful. I would like to raise three areas where he intended to act but ultimately failed: the sales tax, education reform, and constitutional revision.

First, the sales tax. In July 1986, he embarked on the "playing dead dissolution," nominally to correct malapportionment, but actually with the intention of catching the opposition off guard. He secured a great victory for the LDP in the ensuing election yet still failed to introduce a sales tax. That said, looking back now, we know that his acts laid the foundation for the passage of a consumption tax a year later.

Second, education reform. Nakasone's experiences as president of Takushoku University had caused him to become greatly concerned about a lack of vigor in university education and a lack of individuality on the part of students. His growing interest in education reform can also be connected to his creation of the Provisional Council on Education while he was prime minister. However, he never made any serious efforts in this area as prime minister. This is because he was concerned that attempting to amend the Fundamental Law of Education would invite the hostility of the opposition parties and delay reform of JNR. Nakasone's inability to bring about education reform due to his decision to prioritize the privatization of JNR would become a long-standing regret of his. The Fundamental Law of Education would only be revised early in the 21st century.

Third, constitutional revision. This had been Nakasone's political starting point and remained a lifelong ambition. He began his political career criticizing Yoshida Shigeru for serving as a "subcontractor" for GHQ during the Occupation, and he saw the new constitution as being the epitome of this. This led to constitutional revision – along with direct election of the prime minister and autonomous defense – becoming a pet issue of his. He believed that revising the constitution and adopted direct election of the prime minister would solidify Japan's democracy. However, members of the conservative mainstream, like Ikeda Hayato and Satō Eisaku, were skeptical of constitutional revision, and Nakasone was unable to widen the support base for his goals. And he himself did not take any steps toward constitutional revision while prime minister.

I would like to bring up an incident related to this point. I interviewed Nakasone more than thirty times. Despite already being ninety or so during these interviews, he always kept his back absolutely straight and maintained an indifferent expression on his face. There was only one time during these interviews that he became furiously angry: when I asked, "But you shelved constitutional revision as prime minister, didn't you?" He immediately rejected this assertion and declared, "I never once abandoned constitutional revision." Despite this claim, he did clearly state as prime minister that "constitutional revision will not be on the agenda of the current government."

The Anguish of "Lifelong Service"

After being forced to retire from political office in 2003, Nakasone released his constitutional draft through IIGP. While it maintained a parliamentary cabinet system, it took steps closer to the direct election of the prime minister. The Emperor was named head of state, and it made clear that Japan would maintain a "defense military." Another distinguishing characteristic of the draft was the inclusion of a clause reaffirming the importance of the family. However, this draft would never become a reality.

The last time I met him, he had a healthy complexion and told me that "the people of today don't have the spirit needed to speak of the future" and that "the secret to good health is to not worry about things." When I presented him with a copy of the original Japanese edition of this biography, he looked at the *obi* (a strip of paper wrapped around books while they're on sale), which bore a picture of him with his arms crossed, and remarked, "That's a good picture. There are no politicians today who could wear an expression like that."

258 *Conclusion*

Nakasone did not have a favorable impression of Prime Minister Abe or the candidates to succeed him as prime minister. He had been unable to find a successor in the true sense of the word. While he told me that "the secret to good health is to not worry about things," he saw himself as giving lifelong service to the country, and I believe that no other politician has agonized over things until the very last moment of their life the way that he did.

Nakasone wrote the haiku, "even as it grows dark, for as long as I live, rain of cicada cries." I find his tenacity palpable in those words. They have the spirit of a politician who saw himself as a lifelong public servant and who sought to step up for his country. He had an affection for Japan; a desire to change it, to make it even just a little better for the next generation. He was a patriot, and there are not many former prime ministers who have had such a sense of tenacity. He was a politician who served for his entire life and agonized over things until the very end.

Notes

1 Hattori Ryūji, "Tsuitō Nakasone Yasuhiro Moto-Shushō," *Chūō Kōron* (February 2020), 130–35.
2 *Nihon Keizai Shimbun,* November 30, 2019.
3 Ibid.
4 *New York Times*, November 30, 2019.
5 Hattori Ryūji, *Kōsaka Masataka – Sengo Nihon to Genjitsushugi* (Tokyo: Chūkō Shinsho, 2015), 248–58.

References

Hattori Ryūji. *Kōsaka Masataka – Sengo Nihon to Genjitsushugi.* Tokyo: Chūkō Shinsho, 2015.
Hattori Ryūji. "Tsuitō Nakasone Yasuhiro Moto-Shushō." *Chūō Kōron* (February 2020).

Timeline

1918/5/27	Born in Takasaki, Gunma
1938/4	Entered Tokyo Imperial University (Political Science Department)
1940/3	Mother Yuku died
1940/10	Passed civil service exam, accepted by home ministry
1940/12	Accepted by Naval Accounting School
1941/4	Entered home ministry
1941/4	Entered 6th supplementary student class at Naval Accounting School
1941/8	Assigned to Combined Fleet's 6th Cruiser Division
1941/11	Departed Kure aboard *Taitō Maru*
1942/3	Transferred to Magong
1943/4	Attached to Takao naval construction department
1944/11	Assigned to Ministry of the Navy Procurement Bureau (3rd Section), Yokosuka
1945/2	Married Kobayashi Tsutako
1945/2	Brother Ryōsuke died
1945/10	Returned to home ministry, assigned to Cabinet Research Office
1945/11	Son Hirofumi born
1946/1	Youth Discussion Group formed
1947/4	Elected to House of Representatives from the Democratic Party
1948/8	Began meeting with Tokutomi Sōho
1950/3	Democratic Party split into coalition and opposition factions. Joined opposition faction
1950/4	National Democratic Party formed through merger with Miki Takeo's National Cooperative Party
1950/6	Attended MRA World Congress in Switzerland, visited West Germany, France, Britain, and America
1951/2	Met Dulles, began "research on the establishment of a defense force" with former naval personnel
1952/1	Clashed with Yoshida in House of Representatives' Budget Committee
1952/2	Formation of Reform Party
1952/10	Fukuda Takeo elected from Gunma 3rd district (beginning of Jōshū War)
1953/7	Participated in Summer International Seminar at Harvard
1954/2	"Explosive Question" in the House of Representatives' Budget Committee
1954/2	Met with Ishibashi Tanzan
1954/3	Compiled 235-million-yen budget for atomic energy research
1954/6	Participated in drafting of laws creating the Defense Agency and SDF
1954/6	Visited USSR, China
1954/11	Formation of Japan Democratic Party under Hatoyama Ichirō

260   *Timeline*

1955/3	Appointed deputy secretary-general of Japan Democratic Party
1955/8	Attended UN International Conference on the Peaceful Uses of Atomic Energy in Geneva and visited France, Britain, Canada, and America
1955/11	Formation of LDP
1955/12	Basic Law on Atomic Energy passed as member's bill
1956/10	Ordered by Kōno Ichirō to meet with Hatoyama in Hawaii
1956/11	Spoke on the restoration of relations with the USSR in the Diet, speech stricken from the record
1956/12	Votes for Ishibashi as LDP president
1957/5	Appointed LDP deputy secretary-general and to Constitutional Research Committee
1957/5	Visited Burma, India, Pakistan, Iran, Iraq, Lebanon, Syria, Egypt, Austria, Yugoslavia, Hungary, Turkey, Britain, Greece, Israel, Ceylon, Singapore, Indonesia, Hong Kong, and Taiwan
1958/7	Visited Okinawa
1959/6	Received first cabinet position, director-general of the Science and Technology Agency
1960/5	Called for postponing Eisenhower visit
1960/8	Cautioned Kōno not to form new party
1961/1	Attended President Kennedy's inauguration, visited Mexico, Peru, Chile, Argentina, Uruguay, Brazil, Venezuela, and Cuba
1961/6	Research Group on a System for the Popular Election of the Prime Minister founded
1962/2	Robert Kennedy's visit to Japan
1962/11	Visited Antarctica
1963/1	Visited Hong Kong, the Philippines
1964/4	Visited South Korea, met President Park Chung-hee
1965/2	Appointed deputy chairman of the LDP Research Commission on Foreign Affairs
1965/3	Appointed chairman of the LDP Research Commission on Foreign Affairs' Afro-Asian Subcommittee
1965/4	Visited Indonesia, Malaysia, Thailand, and South Vietnam
1965/7	Kōno died
1966/3	Visited US
1966/9	Toured planned location for Ashihama Nuclear Power Plant
1966/12	Shinsei Dōshikai (Nakasone faction) formed
1967/9	Appointed president of Takushoku University
1967/10	Visited Britain, France, West Germany, and the USSR
1967/11	Appointed transportation minister in Satō government
1968/1	Called for three non-nuclear principles in cabinet meeting
1968/4	Signed land agreement for Narita Airport
1968/10	Visited Moscow, negotiated revision of the Japan-Soviet Aviation Agreement
1969/6	Attended Paris Air Show at the invitation of the French government, visited Italy and Spain
1969/6	Father Matsugorō died
1970/1	Appointed director-general of Defense Agency
1970/3	Laid out "five principles of autonomous defense" at House of Councilors' Budget Committee
1970/9	Visited US, met Defense Secretary Laird, Secretary of State Rogers
1970/10	Became first serving director-general to visit Okinawa
1970/10	*Defense of Japan* published
1970/10	Outline of New Defense Program released

1971/7	Appointed LDP General Council chairman
1972/7	Supported Tanaka Kakuei in LDP presidential election
1972/7	Appointed MITI minister and director-general of the Science and Technology Agency by Tanaka
1972/9	Attended Japan-South Korea Regular Cabinet Ministerial Meeting
1972/10	Attended Japan-Australia Ministerial Committee
1972/10	Placed restrictions on exports to the US
1973/1	Visited China, met Premier Zhou Enlai
1973/1	Visited Thailand
1973/4	Visited Iran, Kuwait, Saudi Arabia, UAE, Lebanon, and Hong Kong
1973/7	Agency for Natural Resources and Energy created
1973/10	Yom Kippur War
1973/11	Met with Secretary of State Kissinger in Tokyo
1974/1	Visited Iran, Britain, Bulgaria, Iraq
1974/5	Permitted energy companies to raise rates
1974/11	Met with Kissinger in Tokyo
1974/12	Appointed LDP secretary-general in Miki Takeo government
1975/11	Opposed JNR strike for right to strike (strike ended in December)
1976/2	Lockheed scandal uncovered, visited US embassy
1976/7	Tanaka arrested
1976/8	Tanaka, Fukuda, Ōhira, Shiina factions form Kyotōkyō against Miki
1977/9	Visited Singapore, Malaysia, Indonesia, and the Philippines
1977/9	Visited US, met with National Security Advisor Brzezinski
1977/11	Appointed LDP General Council chairman in reorganization of Fukuda Takeo's cabinet
1978/11	Came in third in LDP preliminary presidential election
1979/11	Voted for Fukuda as prime minister in the House of Representatives (Forty-Day Conflict)
1980/4	Visited China with leadership of his faction
1980/5	Voted against Socialist motion of no confidence
1980/7	Appointed director-general of the Administrative Management Agency in the Suzuki Zenkō government
1981/3	Established 2nd Provisional Commission on Administrative Reform
1982/10	Rejected proposal to separate the positions of prime minister and LDP president
1982/11	Won LDP preliminary presidential election, becomes 71st prime minister
1983/1	Visited South Korea, met with President Chun, $4 billion economic assistance package agreed on
1983/1	Visited the US, met with President Reagan. Beginning of "Ron-Yasu" relationship
1983/4	Visited Indonesia, Thailand, Singapore, the Philippines, Malaysia, and Brunei
1983/5	Attended G7 summit in Williamsburg
1983/6	Committee for Overseeing the Reconstruction of JNR formed
1983/9	Soviet communication logs related to the downing of Korean Air flight 007 submitted to UN Security Council
1983/10	Recommended Tanaka resign from the Diet (after Tanaka was sentenced to prison)
1983/11	Met with West German Chancellor Kohl, Reagan, and CCP General Secretary Hu in Tokyo
1983/12	Suffered major defeat in election. Announced that Tanaka's influence would be removed from the party and formed coalition with New Liberal Club

262 *Timeline*

1984/3	Visited China and met Hu, Premier Zhao Ziyang, and Chairman of the Central Advisory Commission Deng Xiaoping
1984/4	Visited South Asia, met Pakistani President Zia and Indian Prime Minister Gandhi
1984/5	Submitted bill for reforming NTT to the Diet (passed in December)
1984/6	Attended G7 summit in London
1984/8	Created Panel on the Issue of Cabinet Members Visiting Yasukuni Shrine under Chief Cabinet Secretary Fujinami
1984/9	Met Chun in Tokyo
1984/10	Reelected as president at general meeting of the LDP's Diet members
1985/1	Visited Fiji, Papua New Guinea, Australia, and New Zealand
1985/2	Tanaka suffered cerebral infarction
1985/3	Visited USSR for funeral of General Secretary Chernenko, met Gorbachev
1985/4	NTT, Japan Tobacco created
1985/4	Announced policies to expand imports and lower duties
1985/4	Attended G7 summit in Bonn
1985/7	Visited France, Italy, the Vatican, and Belgium
1985/8	Made official visit to Yasukuni Shrine
1985/9	Plaza Accord signed in New York
1985/10	Spoke at 40th anniversary of founding of the UN, met Zhao, Reagan, and Gorbachev
1986/1	Visited Canada, met Prime Minister Mulroney, addressed parliament
1986/1	Met with Soviet Foreign Minister Shevardnadze in Tokyo
1986/3	Bills for reforming JNR approved by the cabinet and submitted to the Diet (bill passed in November)
1986/4	Visited the US, met with Reagan
1986/5	Hosted G7 summit in Tokyo
1986/7	Won overwhelming victory in joint Diet elections
1986/8	New Liberal Club returns to the LDP
1986/9	Education Minister Fujio Masayuki dismissed
1986/9	Presidential term extended by one year at general meeting of the LDP's Diet members
1986/9	Attended opening ceremony of the Asian Games in Seoul, met Chun
1986/9	Made "intelligence level" statement at LDP's national training session
1986/11	Visited China and met Hu
1986/12	Received Security Council approval to surpass 1% of GNP cap on defense spending
1987/1	Visited Finland, East Germany, Yugoslavia, and Poland
1987/2	Submitted sales tax and tax reform bills to the Diet (sales tax bill withdrawn in May, tax reform bill passed in September)
1987/2	Louvre Accord signed in Paris
1987/3	Received French Foreign Minister Raimon at the prime minister's office
1987/4	JR created
1987/4	Reagan administration placed sanctions on Japanese semiconductors, the first sanctions on Japan since WW2
1987/4	Visited US, met with Reagan
1987/5	6-trillion-yen stimulus measure introduced
1987/6	Attended G7 summit in Venice, visited Spain
1987/9	Addressed UN General Assembly, met with Secretary General de Cuellar and Reagan
1987/10	Named Takeshita successor
1987/11	Resigned as prime minister
1988/6	Appointed president of International Institute for Global Peace

Timeline   263

1989/5	Testified before Diet on the Recruit scandal, resigned from LDP
1990/11	Met with Iraqi President Hussein during Gulf Crisis, secured release of 74 hostages
1991/4	Rejoined the LDP
1997/5	Received Grand Cordon of the Supreme Order of the Chrysanthemum
2003/10	Announced retirement from Diet after not being recognized by LDP
2005/1	Joined LDP Committee on the Drafting of a New Constitution as head of preamble subcommittee
2011/3	Great East Japan Earthquake
2019/11/29	Died

Index

Abe Shintarō 142, 154, 156, 157, 168, 175, 185, 200, 227–28, 230, 233
Abe Shinzō 236, 238, 240, 245, 253
Adenauer, Konrad 30
Allied Occupation of Japan 17–18, 19, 21, 52, 57, 228, 257
Asari Keita 72, 154, 160–61, 199, 201
Ashida Hitoshi 20, 25, 26, 27, 29, 30–31, 33, 50, 51, 52
Australia 37, 111, 118, 165, 188, 239

Canada 118, 193
Castro, Fidel 71
Chiang Kai-shek 58
China 28, 33, 37, 41, 42, 54, 75–76, 95, 108, 111–12, 141, 152, 178, 181–82, 191, 202, 208, 209, 232, 239, 240, 255
Chun Doo-Hwan 166, 167–69, 175, 183, 191, 202, 255
Cold War 61, 135–36, 166, 167, 172–73, 188
Communist Party 25, 54, 131, 132, 144
conservative merger 50–52

Democratic Party (1947) 20, 21–22, 25, 26, 27, 29, 32
Democratic Party (1996) 234, 240–42, 243
Democratic Socialist Party 131–32, 140
Deng Xiaoping 138, 182
Diet elections 19, 20–21, 25, 34–35, 51, 115, 117, 118, 132–33, 141, 142, 162–63, 164, 174, 178–79, 198–200, 201, 207, 230–31, 232, 235, 241
Dokō Toshio 144, 145
Dulles, John Foster 31, 32

Eisenhower, Dwight 62–63
electoral reform 243–44
Ezoe Hiromasa 230

Forty-Day Conflict 140–41, 156
Fujinami Takao 79, 180, 184, 190, 199, 200, 230
Fujio Masayuki 201–2
Fukuda Takeo 34–35, 74, 79, 94, 107–8, 110, 124–25, 126, 129, 141, 142, 143, 152, 155–56, 179, 183, 233, 235, 244; as prime minister 133, 134–35, 136, 138, 139; *see also* Jōshū War; Kakufuku War; Sankaku Daifuku Chū

G7 172–74, 182, 188–89, 193, 195, 205
Gorbachev, Mikhail 188, 194, 195, 203, 204, 205, 209, 231
Gotōda Masaharu 15, 142, 153, 154, 156, 168, 170, 178, 180, 193, 200, 209
Gulf War 231–32

Hashimoto Ryūtarō 185, 198, 234, 235, 238
Hatoyama Ichirō 13, 29, 50, 51, 53–54, 55, 188, 241
Hatoyama Yukio 234, 241, 242
Hirohito 32
Hu Yaobang 141, 178, 181–82, 191, 202, 255
Hussein, Saddam 116, 231–32

Ikeda Hayato 28, 32, 34, 50–51, 56, 62, 63, 69–70, 72, 73, 74, 124, 183, 257
Inaba Osamu 29, 32, 41, 52, 56, 70, 76, 77, 78, 131, 201
Ishibashi Tanzan 40–41, 51, 56, 57, 72
Ishii Mitsujirō 34, 56, 69, 70

Japan National Railways (JNR) 91, 127–28, 145, 158, 193, 196–98, 200, 201
Jōshū War 35–37, 126, 238, 254

Index 265

Kaifu Toshiki 27, 72, 231, 232–33
Kakufuku War 109–10, 124, 126, 139, 141–42, 156, 179, 254
Kan Naoto 242, 242–43
Kanemaru Shin 128–29, 143, 153, 154, 178–79, 180, 184, 185, 196, 199–200
Katsu Kaishū 29, 171, 213
Kennedy, John F. 71, 72
Kennedy, Robert F. 71
Kishi Nobusuke 35, 41, 50–51, 53, 56, 57, 57–58, 59, 62–63, 124, 143, 152, 183
Kissinger, Henry 38, 98, 115, 124, 135, 166, 231
Kitamura Tokutarō 29–30, 33, 56
Kodama Yoshio 70, 95, 130, 134
Kohl, Helmut 173, 178, 189
Koizumi Jun'ichirō 208, 234, 236–37, 239, 253
Kōmeitō 140, 240, 245
Kōno faction 56–57, 63, 67, 70, 77
Kōno Ichirō 41, 50, 51, 53, 56, 58, 59, 63, 69, 70, 73, 74, 76
Kōno Yōhei 78, 109, 130–31, 201, 243
Korean Air Flight 007 174–75
Kosaka Zentarō 29, 60–61, 107

labor disputes 20, 127–28
Laird, Melvin 98
Liberal Democratic Party (LDP) 51, 55, 76, 77, 83–84, 94–95, 96, 107, 118, 124–25, 126, 127, 130, 131, 132–33, 159, 180, 190, 201, 230, 232–33, 240, 241–42; factions 56, 69, 84, 95, 102, 131–32, 132, 134, 158, 227–28, 236, 243; formation of 51; General Council 107, 109, 128, 136; "Miki-oroshi" 131–32, 133; presidential elections of 57, 63, 69, 74, 77, 94, 107–8, 109–10, 138–39, 143, 152, 154–56, 183–84, 193, 227–28, 234; *see also* conservative merger; Forty-Day Conflict; Kōno faction; Nakasone faction; Sankaku Daifuku Chū; Seirankai; Shiina Decision; Tanaka faction
Lockheed Scandal 78, 129–31, 134, 157, 162–63, 165, 175–76

MacArthur, Douglas 28, 30–31, 53
Maeo Shigesaburō 94, 95, 132
Matsumura Kenzō 33, 34, 51, 56, 72
Miki Bukichi 41, 51, 130

Miki Takeo 27, 29, 33, 51, 94, 107, 109–10, 111, 116, 126, 141, 142, 164–65, 183, 233; as prime minister, 126, 128, 129, 130, 131–32, 133; *see also* Shiina Decision
Mitterrand, Francois 173–74, 189, 214
Miyazawa Kiichi 2, 51, 69, 180, 184, 185, 187, 200, 202, 211, 227–28, 230, 232, 233, 235, 237

Nakagawa Shunji 110–11
Nakasone faction 27, 71, 76–79, 94–95, 109, 110, 132, 138, 143, 153, 157, 231, 236
Nakasone Hirofumi 200, 238
Nakasone Matsugorō 4–5, 6, 9, 19, 21, 96
Nakasone Ryōsuke 4, 9, 16, 57, 190
Nakasone Tsutako 16, 17, 39, 88
Nakasone Yasuhiro: and Christianity, 4–5, 55; and the "final settlement of postwar politics," 140, 158, 162–63, 163, 181, 201; as director-general of the Defense Agency, 96–102; as General Council chairman, 136–37; as LDP secretary-general, 125, 126–32; as minister of transportation, 90–91, 93–94; as MITI minister, 110–18; as presidential prime minister, 159, 228, 229, 255; as president of Takushoku University, 80–81; bureaucratic career of, 9, 13, 17–19; defense policy of, 28, 37, 41, 96, 96–98, 112, 159, 170, 172, 186, 202–3; domestic policy of, 113–14, 117, 127, 141, 187, 195; foreign policy of, 118, 158, 165, 166–68, 169–71, 171–72, 175, 181, 183, 186–89, 193, 203–4, 208–9, 211, 255; grandstanding by, 34, 101–2, 131, 163; hobbies of, 72; ideological views of, 19–20, 21, 28, 97–98, 100, 108, 112, 113–14, 136–37, 137, 153, 163–64, 181, 183, 228, 233–34, 244; interest in administrative reform 143–45, 164, 181, 195–98, 205, 255; interest in education reform, 81, 181, 228, 237, 256–57; interest in nuclear energy, 17–18, 31, 37, 39–40, 59, 79–80, 89–90, 101, 179, 195, 243; interest in space, 60–62; the Nakasone Concept, 99–100, 105; neoliberalism of, 114, 133–34, 144; opposition to Yoshida and the

266 *Index*

prewar bureaucrats, 28, 35, 51–52, 254; Pacific cooperation, 108, 165, 187–88; privatization of public corporations by, 91, 195–98, 255–56; relationship with media, 160–62; rivalry with Tanaka Kakuei, 26, 27, 59, 74, 110, 134, 185; san'enshugi, 55; support for constitutional revision by, 21, 31, 52–53, 73, 97–98, 164, 235, 237, 240–41, 257; support for direct election of the prime minister by, 38, 59, 72, 236; support for rearmament by, 30–31, 31–32, 33–34; tax reform, 205–7, 227, 256; travels of, 30–31, 37–38, 41–43, 57–59, 71, 73, 74–75, 88–90, 95–96, 111–12, 116, 135–36, 166–67, 167, 169–71, 171–72, 187–89, 193, 203–4, 207–8, 220, 231–32; use of private advisory councils by, 72, 81, 159–60, 190, 228, 256; view of communism 20–21, 42, 54; views on China of 33, 58, 75–76, 78, 95, 108, 111–12, 167, 202, 209, 239; views on the United States of, 17–18, 37, 42, 43, 71, 75, 135, 158, 166, 186, 194–95; wartime experiences of 13–17; *see also* Jōshū War; Ron-Yasu relationship; Sankaku Daifuku Chū
Nakasone Yuku 4–6, 8, 9, 21
Narita Airport 93, 136
Nasser, Gamal 58
National Democratic Party 29, 31
National Police Reserve (NPR) 30
Nehru, Jawaharlal 57–58
New Liberal Club 130–31, 158, 180, 200, 201, 215
Nikaidō Susumu 115, 143, 155, 156, 157, 174, 178, 179, 179–80, 180–81, 183–84, 200–1, 215
Nippon Telegraph and Telephone (NTT) 195–96
Nixon, Richard 39, 92, 95, 96
Noda Yoshihiko 243
Northern Territories 54, 188, 231, 232
nuclear weapons 98–99, 101, 172–73, 186, 194, 205; *see also* three non-nuclear principles; Strategic Defense Initiative

Obuchi Keizō 36
Ōhira Masayoshi 34–35, 51, 93, 94, 107, 108, 109–10, 111, 115, 124–25, 126, 233; as prime minister, 133, 138, 139, 139–42, 165–66

Oil Crisis 112–13, 115–18, 140
Okinawa 58–59, 88, 90, 95, 99, 241–42
Ōno Banboku 34, 56, 59–60
Ozawa Ichirō 185, 232

Park Chung-hee 73, 167
People's Republic of China *see* China
Philippines 37, 134–35, 172
Plaza Accord 186–87

Reagan, Ronald 73, 166, 167, 172–74, 178, 186, 188, 189, 192, 194, 194–95, 205; *see also* Ron-Yasu relationship
Recruit Scandal 229–31
Reform Party 29, 31, 33, 34, 40, 50
Reischauer, Edwin 38–39, 88
Republic of China *see* Taiwan
Republic of Korea *see* South Korea
Rinchō 143–45
Ron-Yasu relationship 170–71, 194, 207–8

Sakurauchi Yoshio 25, 29, 41, 43, 56, 76, 77, 190, 201, 231
San Francisco Peace Treaty 31–32, 32, 54–55
Sankaku Daifuku Chū 108–9, 126, 134, 142, 185, 227–28, 256
Satō Akiko 177–78
Satō Eisaku 28, 34, 50, 51–52, 62, 63, 72, 167, 192; as prime minister, 74, 75–76, 77–78, 83–84, 88–89, 90, 91–92, 94–95, 98, 102, 107, 107–8, 109
Seirankai 78
Sejima Ryūzō 144, 154, 167–69
Self-Defense Forces (SDF) 41, 97, 100, 101–2, 209
Senkaku Islands 136, 137
Shidehara Kijūrō 25, 26
Shigemitsu Mamoru 29, 33, 34, 41–42, 51
Shiina Decision 125, 156
Shiina Etsusaburō 125, 126, 128
Shōwa Denkō scandal 27, 30
Socialist Party 25, 27, 51–52, 54–55, 62, 84, 140–41, 141–42, 174, 198, 201, 232–33
South Korea 37, 73, 152, 166, 167–69, 175, 183, 191, 201–2
Soviet Union (USSR) 20, 28, 41–42, 53–54, 94, 111, 170–71, 173, 174–75, 188, 193–94, 203–4, 231
Strategic Defense Initiative (SDI) 186, 188, 189, 205
Suzuki Zenkō 25, 143, 152, 153, 154–55, 159, 171, 180–81, 183–84, 192, 210, 211

Index 267

Tagawa Seiichi 33, 78, 109, 130, 180
Taiwan 15, 32, 37, 58, 75–76, 108
Takeshita Noboru 107, 156, 168, 184, 185, 200, 227–28, 229, 230
Tanaka faction 27, 125, 126, 132, 142, 143, 153, 154, 156, 157, 165, 176, 180, 183, 184–85
Tanaka Kakuei 26, 27, 57, 74, 78, 94, 107, 108, 129; as prime minister, 109–10, 111–12, 114, 116, 117, 124; following resignation as prime minister, 125, 126, 131–32, 134, 139, 152–54, 154, 155–56, 157, 162, 165, 174, 175–78, 179, 184–85, 227–28, 233
Thatcher, Margaret 173, 189
three non-nuclear principles 91–93, 98–99
Tokutomi Sōho 28–29, 42, 52

United Nations (UN) 55, 75, 97, 191–92, 207
United States (US) 42, 71, 75, 76, 88, 95, 115, 129–30, 135, 153–54, 166, 195, 208, 231–32, 236; *see also* Ron-Yasu relationship; San Francisco Peace Treaty; Strategic Defense Initiative; US-Japan security treaty; US-Japan trade frictions
Uno Sōsuke 143, 230–31
US-Japan security treaty 32, 37, 39, 54, 59, 60, 62–63, 96, 97–98, 108, 112, 115, 130, 166, 194, 205
US-Japan trade frictions 112, 186–87, 189, 194–95, 204–5, 207–8

Vietnam War 75, 94, 108

Watanabe Tsuneo 59–60, 72, 79, 81, 111, 154, 253

Yabe Teiji 8, 19, 52, 75, 80
Yasukuni Shrine 16, 160, 189–91, 202, 255
Yoshida Shigeru 20, 21, 25, 26, 27–28, 31, 32–33, 34, 40, 50, 51, 56, 162, 171, 257

Zhou Enlai 75, 111–12
zoku Diet members 129, 137, 196, 197, 198, 228, 244

Printed in the United States
by Baker & Taylor Publisher Services